The City in Arabic Literature

The City in Arabic Literature

Classical and Modern Perspectives

Edited by Nizar F. Hermes and Gretchen Head

EDINBURGH
University Press

Edinburgh University Press is one of the leading university presses in the UK. We publish academic books and journals in our selected subject areas across the humanities and social sciences, combining cutting-edge scholarship with high editorial and production values to produce academic works of lasting importance. For more information visit our website: edinburghuniversitypress.com.

Edinburgh University Press Ltd
The Tun – Holyrood Road
12 (2f) Jackson's Entry
Edinburgh EH8 8PJ

Typeset in 11/14pt Adobe Garamond by
Servis Filmsetting Ltd, Stockport, Cheshire

A CIP record for this book is available from the British Library

ISBN 978 1 4744 0652 9 (hardback)
ISBN 978 1 4744 0653 6 (webready PDF)
ISBN 978 1 4744 0654 3 (epub)

Contents

Figures

Preface

Introduction

While the spatial turn in literary and cultural studies may be a relatively recent phenomenon, an explicit concern with the space of the city has had an enduring presence in the Arabic-Islamic tradition. The trope of the *madīna* (town or city, plural: *mudun*), whether real or imaginary, ideal or corrupt, conquered or lost, earthly or celestial, is a recurrent motif throughout the premodern Arabic literary corpus. In the modern period as well, while critics have often chosen to focus on early Arab novelists' interest in the rural, the canonical texts of post-World War II/post-colonial Arabic poetry and prose reveal that the city has, time and again, served as a virtual battleground for some of the Arab world's most complex intellectual, sociocultural, and political issues. In this sense, the city is transformed into something beyond a physical structure and textual space, taking on the role instead of an auto/biographical, novelistic, and poetic arena – frequently troubled and contested – for debating the conflict between the rural and the urban, the traditional and the modern, the individual and the communal, and the Self and the Other.

From its initial conception, the aim of this volume has been to address the topic of the city in the Arabic literary tradition as a whole, its goal to explore the ways in which the city has been represented by both classical and modern authors writing in Arabic from different theosophical and ideological backgrounds. Crucial to its organizing theoretical paradigm from the beginning has been the rejection of the stark rupture that is too often seen to separate the premodern and modern Arabic literary traditions. We set out determined to view the entirety of the tradition as an evolving continuum and to create a collection relevant to scholars of both classical and modern Arabic literature. While our original vision for the volume saw it as consisting of eight chapters chronologically within the premodern period and eight chapters chronologically within the modern, it turned out that many of the contributors to this collection declined to strictly differentiate between the premodern and modern of their own accord. As a result, a significant number of the chapters gathered here move fluidly between periods, referencing, for example, the ninth-century author al-Jāḥiẓ in the same line as the contemporary Iraqi writer Muḥammad Khuḍayyir or the modern Syrian author Khalīl Ṣuwayliḥ. The result is a book that has broken down these boundaries more than we could have hoped. Although the organizational structure remains roughly chronological, starting with the Qurʾān and ending with two contemporary chapters, on Lebanese writing from 2009 to 2011 and an Egyptian graphic novel published in 2008 respectively, the continual dialogue between different periods crucial to the individual chapters of this book make it so that there is surely much of value across the spectrum, whether the reader's interest primarily resides in the classical, the post-classical, or the modern.

Like the tradition of Arabic literature itself, the definition of "literature" utilized in this volume is broad, more akin to *adab* than its far narrower English translation. Chapters address narrative discourse in a number of different forms, with historical chronicles and biographical anthologies no less important to our understanding of the place of the city within the Arabic literary heritage than the more traditional literary genres, like the *maqāma*, poetry, and more recently the novel. A number of chapters address the corpus of classical poetry that elegizes the city through nostalgic discourse, while others address that which attacks the city through invective rhetoric. Other chapters examine the praise literature composed for a particular city, a popular classical genre that we see reinvent itself in the twentieth century in the form of both poetry and prose. The volume's geographical scope includes the conventional centers of the premodern Islamic world such as Mecca, Medina, Baghdad, and Basra to its predominant modern capitals like Beirut, Cairo, and Damascus. We have been careful to write the Arab West into our interrogation of Arabic representations of the city, with chapters covering Cordoba in Andalusia, Qayrawan in Tunisia, and Marrakech in Morocco. There are nevertheless some regrettable absences. Given the vast geography of the Arabic-speaking lands, complete inclusion in a single edited collection is an impossibility. We hope to see future studies that will fill some of the gaps left here. The cities of Palestine with their specific conditions of long-term occupation, the new post-modern metropolises of the Gulf like Dubai and Doha, or the many cities of sub-Saharan Africa that possessed flourishing cultures of Arabic literary production for hundreds of years: all of these sites point to work that remains to be done. We can only hope that this volume proves useful to those who continue to pursue an understanding of the role the city plays in the Arabic literary imagination in all its great variety.

The Volume's Content

In the first chapter of this volume, "The Untranslatability of the Qurʾānic City," Mohammad Salama considers the degree to which the Qurʾānic terms *qarya* and *madīna* are translatable into the "town," "village" and "city" of our current use. Salama proposes that the linguistic significations of these two words in the Qurʾān are likely to vary, both according to the events they describe and the historical context in which they are used. While our initial inclination may be to understand the terms as neutral, he raises the question of whether one might be categorically positive and the other its negative inverse: it could be that "the *madīna* carries associations that are positive and Godly," Salama suggests, while "*[a]l-Qarya* … is a place often linked to the ungodly, the uncharitable, the dishonest, and the inhuman." At the heart of this discussion is the concept of the "untranslatable," the type of word or phrase that resists transfer from one language to another, whose meaning depends on its relationship to the larger whole of which it is a part. For the untranslatable, a term's greater linguistic context is key to discerning its meaning, and it is this with which Salama works to provide us here.

In our second chapter, "Local Historians and their Cities: the Urban Topography of al-Azdī's Mosul and al-Sahmī's Jurjan," Harry Munt addresses two of the most important genres traditionally used to tell the story of a city, the annalistic historical chronicle – a genre that would come to be defined by al-Khaṭīb al-Baghdādī's (d. 1071) *Tārīkh Baghdād* – and the biographical dictionary. Specifically, the chapter is an exploration of Abū Zakariyyā al-Azdī's (d. 946) *Tārīkh al-Mawṣil* and Ḥamza al-Sahmī's (d. 1035–6) *Maʿrifat ʿulamāʾ ahl Jurjān*, texts through which Munt highlights the constructed nature of this type of narrative representation. The depictions of al-Azdī's Mosul and al-Sahmī's Jurjan contained within these works reveal that the urban topography that interested these authors had more to do with the particular communities with which they were associated than the physical structures themselves. Physical topographies here work to reinforce the social status of certain communities, rather than simply providing descriptions of what places looked like. These narratives make clear that cities, as Munt writes, "were socially meaningful spaces," and the topographical information included in these texts was designed to convey far more than the appearance of their residences, walls, mosques, and markets.

Not all premodern authors writing in Arabic were interested in creating monumental and eulogistic histories of their cities. This is precisely what Huda Fakhreddine and Bilal Orfali argue with sophistication and humor in the third chapter of this volume, "Against Cities: On *Hijāʾ al-Mudun* in Arabic Poetry." The first part of their discussion covers several major and minor poets from the eighth century through the sixteenth who composed invective and satire targeting either their own cities or those of their patrons, sometimes earnestly and sometimes in jest. Among the insights that Fakhreddine and Orfali share with us is that the recognition of the significance of *al-maḥāsin wa-l-masāwi* (merits and faults) in medieval Arabic literary and poetic production is crucial to a discerning appreciation of *hijāʾ al-mudun.* While by all accounts hilarious and entertaining, the poems translated and analyzed here effectively speak to the richness and complexity of the corpus of this premodern Arabic sub-genre. Just as importantly, their discussion illustrates the utility of reading modern literary discourse against the classical tradition, as the chapter's second half connects the antagonism of the city found in twentieth-century Arabic poetic modernism to the earlier genre of *hijāʾ al-mudun.*

Between city-prose and city-poetry, there is predictably the *maqāma*, a genre distinctly related to the urbanization of the medieval Islamic empire. That the *maqāma* is the most urbanite hybrid of the classical Arabic genres is a well-known truism and no collection on the city in Arabic literature would be complete without its inclusion. As such, the fourth chapter of this volume, "The Literary Geography of Meaning in the Maqāmāt of al-Hamadhānī and al-Ḥarīrī," features Sarah bin Tyeer's analysis of the representation of the city/cities in the *maqāmāt* of Badīʿ al-Zamān al-Hamadhānī (d. 395/1007) and al-Ḥarīrī (d. 516/1122). By charting their physical and interpretative geography, bin Tyeer shows that the cities traversed by the antagonists of some of the most well-known *maqāmāt* of the tradition, Abūl Fatḥ al-Iskandarī and Abū Zayd al-Sarūjī, both belong to the realm of the "familiar" and become the sites of a particular type of linguistic play. Her discussion's focal point is that the cities of the *maqāmāt* are instrumental in the texts' production and dissemination of the prevailing semantic, legal, and moral discourses of the period, with their literary geography acting as a frame for both moral and legal stability.

In the fifth and sixth chapters of the volume, we move to one of the most popular genres of city-poetry in the Arabic literary heritage: *rithāʾ al-mudun* (city-elegies). In "Woe is me for Qayrawan! Ibn Sharaf's Lāmiyya, the Plight of Refugees and the Cityscape," Nizar F. Hermes explores a particularly moving premodern Maghribi city elegy, a *lāmiyya* penned in exile by Ibn Sharaf al-Qayrawānī (d. 1067) lamenting the Hilali sacking that destroyed his home city of Qayrawan, a metropolis that had been one of the Maghrib's most majestic. Hermes engages in a close reading of the *lāmiyya*, paying special attention to what he interprets as the poet's "pessimistic assessment of the doom of a fallen city and the tragic contemplation, if not condemnation, of human life." Central to Hermes' discussion of this Maghribi city elegy is the interrogation of the absence of Qayrawan's "cityscape." This, Hermes suggests, makes Ibn Sharaf's *lāmiyya* categorically different from the more well-known city-elegies from the Mashriq and al-Andalus. Notable here too is the relationship Hermes draws between the poet's expression of the wrenching pain of exile when faced with the devastation of his home city and the suffering wrought by the current wide-scale destruction of the cities of Syria, showing once again the connectivity between the classical and the modern.

Our volume's sixth chapter, "In Memory of al-Andalus: Using the Elegy to Reimagine the Literary and Literal Geography of Cordoba," by Anna Cruz, is not only a valuable contribution to the ever-growing body of work concerned with al-Andalus, it also serves as a striking counterpoint to Hermes' discussion. Here Cruz examines the elegiac/nostalgic representation of Cordoba in the *mukhammas* of the famed poet Ibn Zaydūn (d. 1071). While most often remembered for his nostalgic love poetry, less frequently addressed are the poems that Ibn Zaydūn has penned elegizing his beloved Cordoba. Like Ibn Sharaf, Ibn Zaydūn writes from the position of exile. In contrast, however, the Andalusian poet is meticulous in the attention he pays to Cordoba's cityscape and its sites of memory, both individual and communal. Cruz suggests here that, "the poet's subjective experiences create an affective map of the city, with the landscape and built environment serving a dual purpose: they act as the poet's personal memory devices to amplify and project back his emotion while also providing a phenomenology of the Cordoban caliphate during the tenth and eleventh centuries." The genre of *rithāʾ al-mudun,* Cruz asserts, allows the poet "to compensate for his loss of time, space, and identity."

With the seventh chapter, our volume turns its focus to the post-classical, a period that has only recently begun to receive the attention it deserves. Echoing some of Harry Munt's concerns, Kelly Tuttle returns to the genre of the biographical dictionary with "The Mamluk City as Overlapping Personal

Networks." Through an exploration of al-Ṣafadī's (d. 1363) *Aᶜyān al-ᶜAṣr wa-Aᶜwān al-Naṣr* (The Notables of the Age and the Supporters of Victory), Tuttle considers the intersection between an individual's personal/professional network and the Mamluk city. In her reading, the urban center is shown to be a space that is highly connected, vibrant yet unpredictable. Tuttle demonstrates how the reader "can trace the intersecting networks" as "most subjects move around the area of the Mamluk Sultanate, entering and leaving cities and positions all without leaving their networks." The consequences of this in her view are that the city depicted in al-Ṣafadī's text expands beyond its geographic boundaries, leaving us with an image of the period's urban centers as spaces that are both "vast" and "portable."

Adam Talib provocatively states, "The cities of pre-modern Arabic literature are erotic playgrounds," opening the eighth chapter of this volume, "Citystruck." Through an analysis of a wide variety of examples of urban poetry, both *faṣīḥ* (eloquent/formal) and *ᶜāmiyy* (vernacular), with occasional segues into other literary traditions, most notably Persian, Talib takes the reader on what can only be described as a *tour de force* of the city's erotic possibilities as expressed in its verse. Yet beneath this eroticism generally depicted as playful, Talib argues, the city becomes a space in which its most vulnerable communities are exposed to sexual objectification and predatory behavior. "In poetry especially," Talib writes, "all social interactions in the urban sphere were given an erotic veneer," but the city is, nevertheless, a "dangerous arena in which eloquent objectification and amusing assaults have not yet lost their sting." The hidden dangers of the city that Talib brings to light in this chapter aside, its analysis never loses sight of the humor contained within the poetic erotization of the Arab-Islamic "predatory city."

While the ninth chapter of this volume was initially intended to mark a shift in focus to the modern period, the continuing relevance of traditional genres is immediately apparent in Gretchen Head's contribution, "Between Utopia and Dystopia in Marrakech." This chapter takes the literary culture of Morocco from the first half of the twentieth century as its subject, where Ibn al-Muwaqqit serves as an example of not only the literary consequences of the country's encounter with modernity, but also of how a new method of writing the urban space becomes the source of an acute disruption in the residents' of Moroccan cities fundamental sense of orientation. Marrakech's geography is charted by both the Sufi biographical dictionary *Al-Saᶜāda al-abadīyya fī al-taᶜrīf bi-mashāhīr al-ḥaḍra al-Marrākushiyya* (Eternal Happiness in the Identification of Marrakech's Notables) published by al-Muwaqqit as a lithograph in Fez in 1918, and the satiric *al-Riḥla al-Marrākushiyya* (Travels in Marrakech), published more than a decade later by a press in Cairo. The two versions of Marrakech depicted in each of these texts bear little resemblance to one another, however. "In the former," Head contends, "al-Muwaqqit writes Marrakech in a localized model of the ideal city, or *al-madīna al-fāḍila,* while the latter edges toward dystopia, with Marrakech imagined as a paradigmatic example of the corrupt city, or *al-madīna al-fāsida.*"

From Marrakech the volume shifts to Cairo and Yasmine Ramadan's analysis of Yūsuf Idrīs' *Qiṣṣat ḥubb* (A Love Story) in our tenth chapter, "Revolutionary Cityscapes: Yūsuf Idrīs and the National Imaginary." Here Idrīs is revisited in light of recent events in Egypt as an author who wrote during an earlier transformative moment and whose work may help us think through the role of literature in times of revolution. In this chapter, the literary text is interpreted as responsible for the production of both the symbolic and material reality of the city. As a stand-in for the nation, Cairo's role in the novel is metaphorical, crafted by Idrīs as a space of extreme heterogeneity that contains within it both center and periphery, Egypt's full range of social and economic classes, migrants from the countryside as well as urbanites by birth. The city in *Qiṣṣat ḥubb* is not only mapped georgraphically, but linguistically. And here Ramadan, like Talib's earlier chapter, pays particular attention to the linguistic registers of the text, the main part of which is written in *fuṣḥā* (standard Arabic), while the dialogue is written in *ᶜāmmiyya* (colloquial Egyptian). This is crucial to the novel's constitution of the city, Ramadan argues, because, "[i]t is not one colloquial but many; the speech of the multitude of people across the social, regional, and economic spectrum that populate the enclaves of the capital."

In the volume's eleventh chapter, "Lost Cities, Vanished Worlds: Configurations of Urban Autobiographical Identity in the Arabic Literature of the 1980s," Valerie Anishchenkova takes a comparative approach, considering the intersection of personal identity and the urban environments of Alexandria, Baghdad, and Mecca in three autobiographical novels written in the 1980s. In her analysis of Idwār al-Kharrāṭ's *Turābuhā zaᶜfarān: nuṣūṣ Iskandarānīya/City of Saffron: Alexandrian Texts* (1986), ᶜĀlīyah Mamdūḥ's *Ḥabbāt al-naftālīn/Mothballs* (1986), and Ḥamza al-Būqārī's *Saqīfat al-Ṣafā/The Sheltered Quarter* (1983), Anishchenkova focuses on the profound transformations of the period and their particularly striking effects on the Arab world's cityscapes. Despite the often extreme differences in the cities about which these authors write and their varied narrative techniques, she finds "shared mechanisms of identity-making: namely, a deeply nostalgic relationship with the urban space and a highly complex network of public and private identities that inform the construction of autobiographical subjectivities." Language becomes crucial here as well, as Anishchenkova emphasizes the role of city-specific dialects and colloquialisms that come to function as a locus of nostalgia for these authors, binding the autobiographical subjects found within the texts to their "very concrete locations."

Much like Head's earlier discussion, the impossibility of drawing a clean line between the classical and modern is especially pronounced in our volume's twelfth chapter, Boutheina Khaldi's "The Sufis of Baghdad: A Topographical Index of the City." In this chapter, Khaldi considers Azīz al-Sayyid Jāsim's *Mutaṣawwifat Baghdād* (The Sufis of Baghdad, 1990), Hādī al-ᶜAlawī's *Madārāt Ṣūfiyya* (Sufi Orbits, 1997) and Umar al-Tall's *Mutaṣwwifat Baghdād fī al-Qarn al-Sādis al-Hijrī/al-Thānī ᶜAshar al-Mīlādī: Dirāsa Tārīkhiyya* (The Sufis of Baghdad in the Sixth Century AH/Twelfth Century CE: A Historical Study, 2009), three modern Iraqi texts that look back to the intersection of Sufism with Abbasid Baghdad's urban landscape. We can see here too the necessity of maintaining a broad understanding of literature as *adab*; the texts of this chapter do not fall into the poetic or novelistic categories that generally comprise our idea of twentieth-century literary discourse. There is nevertheless a sense of loss memorialized within them, and an attempt at the imaginative recuperation of the Baghdad that once was, when Sufi masters laid claim to the urban landscape maintaining social justice in the city's spaces. It is, this chapter suggests, a rhetorical turn on the part of twentieth-century Iraqi writers that must be included in our understanding of contemporary literary production. As Khaldi argues, "[t]hese studies should not be read as an anomalous historical engagement on the part of their authors, rather there is an urgency within the pages of these texts to recall old Baghdad, to save it from erasure and oblivion."

The volume's thirteenth chapter, "*Baṣrayātha*: Self-Portrait as a City" remains in Iraq, but moves from Baghdad to Basra, where William Maynard Hutchins offers us a meditation on Muḥammad Khuḍayyir's "memoir as a cityscape," *Baṣrayātha: The Story of a City.* Significantly reading Khuḍayyir's text through the author's own literary criticism, large excerpts of which are translated by Hutchins and productively put into dialogue with *Baṣrayātha* throughout his discussion, the chapter elucidates the multiplicity of influences that come together to constitute the author's vision of his home city.

Khuḍayyir is the inheritor of a prestigious tradition of Basran writers, and Hutchins suggests that we might read his work as a descendant of al-Jāḥiẓ, "Baṣra's greatest Arabic stylist," meaning as *adab,* less concerned with plot than fragmented anecdotes meant to edify, ultimately coalescing into a portrait of both the writer and the city. The text is, in Hutchins' words, "an extended prose poem that recounts and celebrates the city through its stories." Hutchins' use of Khuḍayyir's critical work as a mode of analysis makes explicit an issue that implicitly runs throughout the near entirety of this volume, namely, the reliance on critical theory written in European languages to examine Arabic source texts and the cities about which they speak. This is a tension that our next chapter takes on directly.

While the immediate subject of our fourteenth chapter, "Of Cities and Canons in an Age of Comparative Consumption," by Hanadi Al-Samman, is Khalīl Ṣuwayliḥ's Damascene novel, *Warrāq al-ḥubb* (2008; Eng. *Writing Love: A Syrian Novel*, 2012), its theoretical scope moves beyond the confines of the analysis of a single text. The way in which the authorial mapping of *Warrāq al-ḥubb* intersects with the spatial mapping of the old city of Damascus is a primary concern and often at the forefront of the chapter's discussion. Indeed, Al-Samman reads the fundamental loss at the heart of the novel as directly related to the narrator's lack of genuine access to his home city of Damascus. For Al-Samman, however, the alienation he experiences in the urban environment is connected to the erasure of the traditional Arabic literary heritage, leaving the narrator with little choice but to turn to the Western canon, whose writers "converge in his head along with key medieval Arab classical writers such as: Ibn Ḥazm, al-Jāḥiẓ, al-Ghazālī, al-Tijānī, al-Tīfāshī, and al-Nafzāwī." In the analysis that follows, we see the inequity of a literary system where contemporary authors writing in Arabic feel the suffocating weight of publishing expectations that demand their adoption of Western literary models. At the same time, the imbalance in power between Western academics and their Arab-based colleaques requires the critic to use canonical Western theoretical models lest they be consigned to the ghettos of area studies. For Al-Samman, this is something of a Gordian knot with no clear solution in sight, yet it is a critique that forces us to reflect on much of the analysis found within this very volume.

Al-Samman's chapter is not alone in pushing back against some of the literary and critical approaches to the city included in this collection. Moving from Damascus to Beirut, our fifteenth chapter, Ghenwa Hayek's "Everyday Writing in an Extraordinary City," turns to contemporary urban writing that consciously rejects the "lament and mourning for a lost Beirut grounded in the *wuqūf ʿalā al-aṭlāl* mode of classical Arabic poetry." Thinking past the much-celebrated body of modern Lebanese literature either invested in commemorating Beirut's devastated center or processing the trauma of the civil war, Hayek focuses on Sahar Mandour's 2011 novel *32* and Alexandra Chreiteh's 2009 novel *Dāyman Coca-Cola* to investigate a new mode of writing interested in the daily lives of Beirut's middle-class youth. These texts are part of a trend, Hayek asserts, that deliberately breaks from the country's literary past, using parody "to deconstruct some of the most dominant cultural modes of representing Beirut and Lebanon." Additionally, and reminiscent of the volume's previous chapter, global patterns of representational consumption are called into question, whether it be the image of Beirut as a site of excessive glamour, or its opposite, the common Western portrayal of the city as a "gritty warzone." These authors, Hayek argues, insist upon their right to an urban existence that is neither of these things, but is instead simply ordinary.

In our final chapter, we return to Cairo, the only city within this volume to be the exclusive subject of two discrete chapters, a reflection of its position as the dominant urban capital of the Arab world for much of the twentieth century. There is no repetition in content, however; Chip Rossetti's "Translating Cairo's Hidden Lines: The City as Visual Text in Magdy El Shafee's *Metro*," presents something decidedly and refreshingly new. In discussing El Shafee's *Metro*, a graphic novel, the nature of the medium leads Rossetti to negotiate questions of narrative and visual representation simultaneously and El Shafee's visual depiction of the city's spatial organization is crucial to the chapter's interpretions. As Rossetti observes, "The city is not merely the backdrop against which the narrative plays itself out, but rather forms the two-dimensional axis that structures the relationships between characters." Similarly, *Metro*'s depiction of the chaos of Cairo's urbanity is also expressed visually through the "assault of words printed, spoken, and sung" that we see on the printed page. Yet even in this most modern of works, Rossetti sees the specter of the older tradition, drawing an analogy between the story's protagonist and the figure of the *futuwwa*, a classical embodiment of urban "chivalry, generosity, and courage," in a sense, bringing one of this volume's primary themes around full circle.

Transliteration of Foreign Terms

For the sake of consistency, Arabic terms have generally been transliterated according to the usage of *The International Journal of Middle Eastern Studies* throughout this book. We have done our best to maintain all diacritical marks for both Arabic words and individual authors' names except in those cases when the author's work is referenced in English translation, where their name is rendered as it is found in English. Well-known city names are likewise given in their common English spelling ("Beirut" for *Bayrūt*).

Acknowledgments

The creation of a book of this size and scope depends on the labor of many. We would like to extend a warm thanks to our contributors: we found the chapters with which they entrusted us to be exceptionally well-researched and sensitively written. Our appreciation for their scholarly rigor, dedication, and not least, patience, can hardly be overstated. Less visible is the labor of so many of our colleagues that significantly contributed to this volume. Each chapter was sent to two readers for double-blind peer review. We are enormously grateful to all of those who gave so generously of their time and expertise; without their help, this collection could not have been made a reality.

1

The Untranslatability of the Qurʾānic City

Mohammad Salama

Introduction

Many twentieth-century translators of the Qurʾān, including Marmaduke Pickthall (1930), Yusuf Ali (1934), and Muhamad Asad (1980) use words like "city" and "village" in translating terms like *balad* (68: 1), *qarya* and *madīna* (27: 34, 48). But to what extent are the English equivalents indeed equivalent to or commensurate with the originary and classical understandings of such terms? Etymological mutation is a process as old as language, one whose inevitable sociological transformations, as Raymond Williams reminds us in *The Country and the City*, invite us to relate texts to their social contexts. For instance, the word *madīna* appears in the Qurʾān twelve times and only with the definite article "al-," and in some cases it seems to be synonymous with *qarya* (12: 30/82 and 36: 13/20). Some may even argue that *madīna* is a very specific place that conveys the presence of a prophet or a messenger, whereas *qarya* refers to a vaster geographical space. What then are the semantic subtleties that characterize both words? What peripheral and/or central space do they imply? What do they have in common, and how do they differ from one another, and from one Qurʾānic chapter to the next, connotatively as well as denotatively? In what way(s) are they translatable into the typical "town," "village," and "city" of our current use? The point is not to pinpoint morphological anachronisms or locate the erroneous categorizations of equivalence theory in translation, but rather to investigate the complex imbrications and contextual nuances of the so-called "city" in the Qur'ān. A historically rich text like the Qur'ān continues to force us to revise our customary classifications of linguistically and socio-historically distinct words and recognize the challenges they pose to even the most advanced learners of the Islamic tradition. *Qarya* and *madīna* are only two examples of this boundless area of infinite significations. But it is precisely those challenges posed by the act of translation that make the need for translation even more compelling. We translate foreign texts precisely because we need to understand them, yet we also understand that the best of all translations must always question itself, and more so with the Qur'ān, the mother of all untranslatables.

Another goal of this chapter is to offer an Arabist reading of *qarya* and *madīna*, one that dwells on the syntactic and morphological attributions of the Qur'ān's own language and all its grammatical and tropological associations. "Arabic studies," as Michael Cooperson once put it, "has now reached a point where it can (and, I would say, must) productively historicize itself. That is, it should engage with (rather than repress) its origins and its present positionality along the various oppositions (Western vs. Islamic, classical vs. modern, etc.) invoked to define it."[1] Cooperson's astute statement sums up the *modus operandi* of this chapter, which is an attempt towards a historicization of *qarya* and *madīna* in the Qur'ān through a direct engagement with its own origins. The translatability of the so-called Qur'ānic city thus draws on specific verses from the Qur'ān and the English translations of *qarya* and *madīna* to show the contradictions and intricacies that lie in translating such terms. Pickthall's translation, *The Meaning of the Glorious Qur'ān*, is the primary example used in this chapter. I have chosen Pickthall's translation not only because it is one of the most renowned and academically honored English renditions of the meaning of the holy Qur'ān, but also because it is a remarkable and commendable work of translation in its own right. My argument will be based mainly on two close readings, one of *Sūrat al-Kahf* (The Chapter of the Cave, Q: 18) and another of *Sūrat Yūsuf* (The Chapter of Joseph, Q: 12). In addition, I have relied on the work of two oft-quoted and well-established Muslim exegetes whom many scholars reference and rely upon when examining Qur'ānic interpretation, namely, al-Ṭabarī and al-Qurṭubī. I cite them both in reference to *qarya* and *madīna* to demonstrate the complexity of the terms, and not as a point of entry into the vast realm of Qur'ānic exegesis. Reference to al-Ṭabarī and al-Qurṭubī is therefore intended to help familiarize the reader with the difficulty of translating the Qur'ānic city with all the lexicographic, historical, contextual, syntactic, and semantic connotations associated with both terms while remaining accessible to the non-specialist.

Lexicography

Arabic lexicography is a rich and voluminous field, yet attention to lexical history and shifting word usages across centuries has been sparse. Despite their thoroughness, the great Arabic dictionaries – the last of which, al-Fīruzābādī's *al-Qāmūs al-Muḥīṭ*, was composed in the fifteenth century – focused largely on the root of the word, its morphological usage as a verb, an adjective, a noun, etc., and its semantic variations and numerous meanings. They remained largely inattentive to historical semantic shifts in meaning and associations, particularly when compared to dictionaries of European languages.[2] This lacuna is obvious in the lexical mutations of certain words, like *maṭar* and *ghayth*, for instance, which as al-Jāḥiẓ rightly observes are consistently used in the Qurʾān to give opposite meanings.[3] *Ghayth* is a good rain that comes as a merciful, divine response to patience or *qunūṭ* (despair), thus saving villages and cities from drought and starvation, usually after sincere supplication and desperation. *Maṭar*, on the other hand, which also sometimes occurs as a verb, as in *amṭarnā* (We caused it to rain), is a wrathful rain that comes as divine punishment to ungodly people. However, the meanings of both *ghayth* and *maṭar* have shifted through time and the denotative associations of mercy versus wrath are not necessarily applicable in modern Arabic usage. In current parlance, *maṭar* is rarely, if ever, a punishment, and has in fact come to be used to indicate hope and bounty. Take, for example, the semantic range of the word *maṭar* in Badr Shākir al-Sayyāb's modern poem "*Unshūdat al-Maṭar*" (The Song of Rain), which he uses to invoke rain as hope, a positive salvation and rescue from poverty and drought. The word *ghayth*, on the other hand, has become synonymous with its sister noun *ghawth* in modern Arabic, almost losing its association with rain altogether, and is now mostly used to signify rescue or redemption in a primarily religious sense.

The same holds for words like *madīna* and *qarya,* two significant Qurʾānic terms charged with specific connotations and historical associations. The linguistic significations of these two words in the Qurʾān may vary according to the events they describe and the historical context in which they are used. Generally, we can distinguish two main historical frameworks for both *madīna* and *qarya* in the Qurʾān. The first is the use of both terms in events or stories of prophets in the distant past before Islam. The second is the immediate meaning the words invoke when recited to the first Muslim community, that is, their employment in a dialect contemporaneous with the Qurʾānic context of the seventh century, meaning the actual time and place in which the inhabitants of Mecca used and understood the terms. This second condition is also sensitive to semantic shifts in the uses of *madīna* and *qarya* during the twenty-three years of Qurʾānic revelation. In current Arabic usage, *madīna* refers to modern and contemporary understandings of the city. However, the *madīna*, or the "city," though coined in English in the thirteenth century, did not begin to acquire its unique, specialized English meaning as an urban area distinct from the countryside (or country) in Europe until the sixteenth century.

This distinction alone problematizes the translation of the Qurʾānic *madīna* as "city" or vice versa as both anachronistic and archaic. Meaning, when Marmaduke Pickthall translates *al-madīna* in verse 20 of Chapter 36 (*Sūrat Yāsīn* /The Chapter of Yāsīn) as follows: "And there came from the uttermost part of *the city* [italics mine] a man running. He cried: O my people! Follow those who have been sent,"[4] modern and contemporary readers might think the reference is to a man coming from the furthest point of a metropolis or highly urbanized environment, which is far from accurate. As Raymond Williams has observed, the most common usage of "city" in English refers to the rapid growth of urban communities during the Industrial Revolution.[5] Although still not completely synonymous with the Arabic, a word like "town" or "township" may have been more appropriate given that the English word "town" etymologically refers to a group of buildings/homes in an enclosure. Moreover, the city in post-Reformation Europe came to be associated with a cathedral,[6] an inference not found in the classical Arabic *madīna* overall, not to mention in the specific *madīna* to which the verse in *Sūrat Yāsīn* refers. Here the *madīna* significantly predates Christianity insofar as the verse describes the people of Lot. What complicates Pickthall's translation even further is that he renders the word *qarya* in verse 13 – the word describing where the events take place in this section of *Sūrat Yāsīn* – as "city" as well: "Coin for them a similitude: The people of *the city* [italics mine] when those sent (from Allah) came unto them."[7] This synonymous and often interchangeable treatment of *al-madīna* and *al-qarya* that appears repeatedly in Pickthall's translation creates a baffling equivalence between the two terms, one which the Arabic original intentionally avoids, and for reasons that I will elucidate below. This does not mean that Pickthall is entirely inaccurate in using the two words interchangeably, however subjective his choice might be. In this example, however, we might ask whether or not Pickthall's translation tampers with the borderlines between translation and hermeneutic interpretation.

Sūrat al-Kahf

Sūrat al-Kahf was revealed in Mecca before Prophet Muḥammad's *hijra* (migration) to Medina (Yathrib). In the current order of Qur᾿ānic recitation (*tartīb tilāwa*), it is the eighteenth chapter and contains a total of 110 verses, placed directly after *Sūrat al-Isrā᾿* (The Chapter of the Nocturnal Journey).[8] Structurally, *Sūrat al-Kahf* comprises four short narratives: the people/companions of the cave; the ungrateful man who owns two orchards; Prophet Moses's excursion with the pious man (referred to in interpretive texts as Al-Khidr); and the story of Dhū al-Qarnayn (the double-horned, Darius) and his godly heroic exploits, especially against the two tribes Gog and Magog. According to some modern exegetes, notably, Muḥammad Aḥmad Khalafallah, the unifying theme among all four stories is a rhetorical exposition of divine narrative to show Omnipotence, not merely to confirm historical happenings, but to exhort and guide humans into shunning greed and disbelief and into heeding a path of piety.[9]

Pickthall is not entirely consistent with his translation of *qarya* and *madīna* throughout the Qur᾿ān and *Sūrat al-Kahf* serves as a good example of the complications that arise as a result. In this *sūra*, the word *qarya* occurs once while *madīna* appears twice. Yet, Pickthall chooses not to treat them synonymously this time, but rather translates *qarya* as "township" and *madīna* as "city," despite the fact that many Qur᾿ānic exegetes including al-Ṭabarī and al-Qurṭubī treat the two terms as equivalents in this instance. Below are Pickthall's translations of the verses in full:

19. And in like manner We awakened them that they might question one another. A speaker from among them said: How long have ye tarried? They said: We have tarried a day or some part of a day, (Others) said: Your Lord best knoweth what ye have tarried. Now send one of you with this your silver coin unto **the city** [*madīna*], and let him see what food is purest there and bring you a supply thereof. Let him be courteous and let no man know of you.

77. So they twain journeyed on till, when they came unto the folk of a certain township [*qarya*], they asked its folk for food, but they refused to make them guests. And they found therein a wall upon the point of falling into ruin, and he repaired it. (Moses) said: If thou hadst wished, thou couldst have taken payment for it.

82. And as for the wall, it belonged to two orphan boys in **the city** [*madīna*], and there was beneath it a treasure belonging to them, and their father had been righteous, and thy Lord intended that they should come to their full strength and should bring forth their treasure as a mercy from their Lord; and I did it not upon my own command. Such is the interpretation of that wherewith thou couldst not bear.

Al-Ṭabarī does not see a distinction between the use of *qarya* and *madīna* in *Sūrat al-Kahf*, or in *Sūrat Yāsīn* for that matter. The arguments of some exegates regarding the first narrative of *Sūrat al-Kahf* – the people/companions of the cave – have other implications, however. The story tells of a group of young believers who resist the pressure from their people and/or king to worship anyone other than God. They take refuge in a cave and fall asleep for hundreds of years, yet upon waking they believe that they have only slept for a day or so. When they send one of their own back to the city (*al-madīna*) to buy food, his use of old silver coins reveals their presence. Even though they are unaware that *al-madīna* has converted to Christianity in its entirety, the employment of the term *madīna* is nevertheless a benign one and is associated with a positive context. Al-Qurṭubī makes the argument, based on Ibn ᶜAbbās's interpretation, that the people of the cave had coins with the image of their king stamped on them, although al-Qurṭubī does not dwell on the significance of this argument to a consideration of *madīna* and *qarya*. It is not far-fetched to deduce that *madīna* in this context may have a more organized structure of royal and financial governance, given the coins/money the people of the cave have in hand when they first fall asleep. In contrast, the economic affairs of the *qarya* were essentially handled by barter and ruled generally by a chief or a senior venerated member of the tribe.

The further we go back into historical time, an interpretation of the word *madīna* in the Qurᵓān as an organized structure of governance is less likely to hold. For instance, a reference to *madīna* in the time of Moses and the pluralized reference to Egypt as *madāᵓin* will necessarily connote different forms of social organization, at least structurally and architecturally, when compared to occurrences of the word *madīna* during the era of the heathen King Ducas and his flagrant persecution of Christians. Additionally, though many exegetes contend that there is a gap of some three hundred years between when the people of the cave first fall asleep and when they wake up, they continue to speak the same language and use the term *madīna* to refer to a three hundred-year-old understanding of what the term means/meant to them. In a post-Roman society combating Christianity, like that of the people of the cave, this understanding of *madīna* may make sense given that according to most Qurʾānic *tafāsīr* (exegetical texts), the persecuted group of young men were running away from an ungodly king who sought either their deaths or re-conversion as a result of their Christian faith.

Moreover, we rarely see the Arabic word *ahl* (people [of]) associated with *madīna* in the Qurʾān except for one example in *Sūrat al-Tawba* (The Chapter of Repentence, Q: 9), verse 101. In most cases, *ahl* is associated with *qarya*, denoting perhaps that unlike a *madīna*, a *qarya* does not include great numbers of people with varied backgrounds and ethnicities within its borders. *Ahl* also implies connections by blood, rendering the *qarya* more like a suburb with extended families or blood-related clans, a place with established tribal hierarchies. This understanding of *qarya* supplements the general impressions we find in the Qurʾān about the hardheaded nature of ungodly *qurā* (pl. of *qarya*). The lexicon itself is often used, especially when referring to prophets before Muḥammad and their stories, as exemplified in *Sūrat Hūd* (The Chapter of *Hūd*, Q: 11), verses 100–2. In this chapter, Pickthall translates *qurā* in verses 100 and 102 as "townships":

> **100.** That is (something) of the tidings of the townships (which were destroyed of old). We relate it unto thee (Muḥammad). Some of them are standing and some (already) reaped.
>
> **101.** We wronged them not, but they did wrong themselves; and their gods on whom they call beside Allah availed them naught when came thy Lord's command; they added to them naught save ruin.
>
> **102.** Even thus is the grasp of thy Lord when He graspeth the townships while they are doing wrong. Lo! His grasp is painful, very strong.[10]

Yet in these and other verses, for instance *Sūrat al-Isrāʾ* (17: 16, 58) and *Sūrat al-Kahf* (18: 59), *qarya* is used to refer to *qawm* (people) who disobey God and are therefore deserving of divine punishment. There is thus a strong semantic correlation between *qarya* and God's punishment in the Qurʾān, something we do not see with *madīna*. To return to *Sūrat al-Kahf*, if this understanding holds, then al-Ṭabarī's *tafsīr* on the *sūra* might miss the mark by hurriedly equating *qarya* with *madīna*. In *Sūrat al-Kahf*, *madīna* occurs twice. The first time, as noted above, in reference to the people of the cave after their reawakening and their decision to go to *al-madīna* in search of food, unaware of how long they have been asleep; their own understanding of *madīna* in this case is itself older than the date that marks their awakening.

The second time *madīna* appears in *Sūrat al-Kahf* is in the third narrative section of the *sūra* that tells the story of the Prophet Moses' excursion with an unnamed man, described as a pious servant of God and a receiver of divine mercy and knowledge (18: 65). The story of Moses predates the story of the people of the cave as well as Christianity by many centuries. Upon Moses' request to follow and learn from the unnamed pious servant, the latter begins acting in ways incomprehensible to common sense, yet with a deep divine significance unbeknownst to Moses. Significantly, Moses has been instructed not to inquire as to the cause of his actions, even though only those with special knowledge, those assigned by God to carry out His divine orders in the universe, would be able to see and understand what the servant was doing. It is in the company of the pious servant that Moses passes through a *qarya*. Both Moses and the pious servant ask *ahlahā* (the people of that *qarya*) for food, but the people of the *qarya* refuse to give them anything to eat or to take them in as guests. In the second set of verses from *Sūrat al-Kahf* cited earlier, we find the lines, "And they found therein [*fa-wajadā fīhā*] a wall upon the point of falling into ruin, and he repaired it." Based on the use of the preposition/prefix "*fa-*," which connotes immediacy and swiftness of the action to follow, it is syntactically accurate to conclude that the doer and the antecedent in *fa-wajadā fīhā* correspond respectively to both Moses and God's pious servant and the *qarya*, meaning that they both find/come upon a wall about to give in and collapse in that very *qarya*. Despite the grievous affront in the people of the *qarya*'s denial of hospitality to Moses and the pious servant, the pious servant immediately fixes the wall, successfully rehabilitating it (18: 77).

Baffled, Moses makes the comment that the pious servant should ask the people of the *qarya* for an *ajr* (repayment or compensation) for repairing the wall. With this question, Moses violates the third and final warning the pious servant had given him not to ask about his actions until he willingly explains them to him. As the pious servant parts company with Moses because of the latter's constant interruptions and impatience, he explains that everything he has done has been in order to comply with God's command. What concerns us here, however, is not the overall meaning of the verses, but the restored wall in a *qarya* whose people are clearly antagonistic and inhospitable, refusing to give food to strangers. Before dwelling on the pious servant's explanation, it is worth raising the question of upon how many doors God's pious servant and Moses may have knocked before they were turned down. The verses do not provide us with anything other than that they request food and hospitality and are turned away. This quick dismissal of the pious servant and Moses gives the impression that the *qarya* may not have been a large area of inhabitants, but was more likely a closed stretch of related families governed by a single chief. This interpretation would explain why there is little room for flexibility and no attempt to knock on other potentially hospitable doors. When the pious servant explains to Moses the real reason behind fixing the wall, he says the following: "and as for the wall, it belonged to two orphan children in the *madīna*, whose father was a pious man, and underneath the wall lies a treasure designated for both of them; so your God wanted them to grow up and grow stronger so that you could dig their treasure out."

Al-Qurṭubī not only uses the word *madīna* as an antecedent to the *qarya* mentioned above, he also uses the whole verse as evidence that a *qarya* could synonymously be called a *madīna.* Many exegetes have adopted this interpretation. What could support this morphological interchangeability between *qarya* and *madīna* is that the verse speaks of two orphan children and mentions their father in the same sentence with the past form of the verb "to be," namely "*kāna*," which, together with *yatīmayni* (two orphans) would strongly indicate that he (the father) has died, leaving his two young children behind, weak and vulnerable to a people who seem to have no compassion or mercy in their hearts. The association is far from vague: if the people of the *qarya* have the temerity to turn away the hungry and break the established laws of hospitality to strangers/guests, then they are capable of anything, including robbing two young orphaned children (at least one of them is male, grammatically speaking) of their inheritance. This adds to the probability that the orphans' father, a righteous man of God, could not trust anyone from the *qarya* with his children's inheritance and preferred to hide it under a wall, leaving it in the hands of God to look after his children and their treasure.

But this remains purely hypothetical. We do not know for certain that the people of the *qarya* and the two orphans are in fact in the same place. It is quite possible that the children and their father lived in a *madīna* far away from the *qarya*, a place with more administratively and financially organized societal conditions, and that the *qarya* is only a suburb or minimally inhabited area at the far outskirts of that *madīna*, an area safe enough to hide a treasure under a wall sure not to give in anytime soon. This supposed difference in location would make good sense if the father had been careful enough to want to hide an inheritance for his two children. The content of the treasure is unspecified, but it might have contained important and useful knowledge in manuscripts, valuable metal like silver or gold, or even coins, all of which correspond to the kind of lifestyle associated with a *madīna*. This understanding corroborates the speculation that while the father and his two children lived in the *madīna*, he may have decided to hide the treasure in a remote *qarya* instead. There it would be far from greedy eyes as opposed to under a wall in a crowded *madīna* close to people's reach. If this interpretation is plausible, then the *qarya* and the *madīna* are far from identical. In fact, the *madīna* carries associations that are positive and godly with its reference to the two orphans, the pious, though now deceased father, and God's intervention to rescue the children's treasure from premature exposure should the wall collapse. If this had occurred, their rightful inheritance would then have fallen into the hands of the Godless people of the *qarya*. *Al-Qarya,* consistent with many other associations in the Qurʾān, is a place often linked to the ungodly, the uncharitable, the dishonest, and the inhumane.

Along similar lines, we find notably positive associations attached to the word *madīna* in *Sūrat al-Qaṣaṣ*, Chapter 28, verses 15–32. In this *sūra,* Moses has fled after interfering in a fight to support a fellow man from his clan, an incident in which he accidentally kills someone from an enemy clan. Knowing of Moses' physical strength, the fellow clansman asks Moses to interfere in yet another fight. The embattled man then rebukes Moses, saying that Moses seeks to kill him just as he had killed the man before, thus cautioning him that he is on the path to tyranny on Earth. At this very moment, a *rajulun* (man) comes from the furthest point in the *madīna* (*aqṣā al-madīna*) warning Moses that the enemy tribe is mobilizing to kill him, advising him to flee immediately. Moses heeds the advice of the good man from the furthest point in the *madīna* and runs. Shortly thereafter, he meets his future wife and God assigns him the mission of saving the Israelites from the tyranny of Egypt's Pharaoh. Ironically, Moses himself had been on the path of murder and oppression, a path only interrupted and radically redirected by a good man from the *madīna*, thus changing the course of humanity forever. The structure of this event is repeated in *Sūrat Yāsīn* (Chapter 36), in the verses cited earlier, "And there came from the uttermost part of the city a man running. He cried: O my people! Follow those who have been sent." In these verses another good man (*rajulun*) from the furthest point of the *madīna* appears, replicating the syntactic structure of *Sūrat al-Qaṣaṣ* with a slight grammatical variation (Verb-Prepositional Noun Phrase-Subject-Adverb/ Verb-Subject-Prepositional Noun Phrase-Adverb) and carrying similar godly advice. In this case, the good man addresses the people of Lot and asks them to heed the word of God and follow His messengers. Here too the *madīna* would seem to be a space linked to piety.

This is not to say that al-Ṭabarī's or al-Qurṭubī's acceptance of the terms as synonymous to one another is reductive or extrapolation; it is fair, however, to argue that there are plausible interpretations that can be derived from the verses that would allow us to benefit both denotatively and connotatively from juxtaposing these words rather than terminally equating *qarya* with *madīna*. For now, suffice it to observe that neither of these two possible interpretations necessarily excludes the other, unless one of them is supported by conclusive historical evidence. Until then, the possible synonymity of *qarya* and *madīna* in this particular context remains undecidable and a matter of critical choice for translators. In either case, the rich and imbricate associations of both terms are worth recording.

Sūrat Yūsuf

Variations on *qarya* and *madīna* also occur in *Sūrat Yūsuf*, where each word appears once. *Sūrat Yūsuf*, similar to the biblical account of Joseph, tells the story of Yūsuf (Joseph) and his eleven brothers who, motivated by envy, initially seek to rid themselves of him. The *sūra* then recounts Yūsuf's rescue and life in Egypt, his piety and avoidance of sin, his imprisonment, his subsequent exoneration and release from prison, his ability to interpret dreams, and his worthiness of the king's trust and his final reunion with his family. The society of Egypt where Yūsuf presumably serves the king after his imprisonment appears to be organized in terms of economic, political, and financial government. This society has a ruler: 12: 30, 12: 51, and 12: 78 (though in this verse it is Yūsuf himself, the new "vizier" of the land,[11] but his brothers do not recognize him, at least not yet and not until he later reveals himself to them as Yūsuf). This *madīna* also has a king, 12: 43, 12: 50, 12: 51, 12: 54, 12: 72, and 12: 76; it is therefore consistent to use the term *madīna* to refer to an organized society where most of the events of Yūsuf's life take place, including a passing conversation among women about the ruler's wife and her uncontrollable infatuation with her slave-boy, Yūsuf:

> **30.** And women in the city said: The ruler's wife is asking of her slave-boy an ill-deed. Indeed he has smitten her to the heart with love. We behold her in plain aberration.[12]

The response of the ruler's wife is telling. She enjoys her power over Yūsuf and tries to seduce him. Not only this, she has also planned to showcase him to the gossiping society of women in the *madīna* so that they can appreciate his beauty:

> **1.** And when she heard of their sly talk, she sent to them and prepared for them a cushioned couch (to lie on at the feast) and gave to every one of them a knife and said (to Joseph): Come out unto them! And when they saw him they exalted him and cut their hands, exclaiming: Allāh Blameless! This is not a human being. This is no other than some gracious angel.
>
> **32.** She said: This is he on whose account ye blamed me. I asked of him an evil act, but he proved continent, but if he do not my behest he verily shall be imprisoned, and verily shall be of those brought low.

Regardless of the infelicities in Pickthall's translation (for example, "evil act" is not anywhere in the original), the *madīna* here is a governed municipality *avant la lettre*, with comfortable homes that have various doors, living rooms, kitchen utensils, but above all established values of aesthetic judgment, organized social gatherings, a legal system, and a prison for wrongdoers. Reference to *qarya* takes place in a dialogue among Yūsuf's brothers after Yūsuf has decided to keep one of them on the pretext of stealing the king's cup. A brother who decides to stay advocates that his other brothers return to their father Jacob's home to tell him that his son, this time Benjamin, was caught red-handed and that he (the father) can ask the *qarya* by which they passed as well as the caravan with which they rode if he doubts their account. Here is Pickthall's translation in full:

> **80.** So, when they despaired of (moving) him, they conferred together apart. The eldest of them said: Know ye not how your father took an undertaking from you in Allāh's name and how ye failed in the case of Joseph aforetime? Therefore I shall not go forth from the land until my father giveth leave or Allāh judgeth for me. He is the Best of Judges.
>
> **81.** Return unto your father and say: O our father! Lo! Thy son hath stolen. We testify only to that which we know; we are not guardians of the Unseen.
>
> **82.** Ask the township [*qarya*] where we were, and the caravan with which we traveled hither. Lo! We speak the truth.

83. (And when they came unto their father and had spoken thus to him) he said: Nay, but your minds have beguiled you into something. (My course is) comely patience! It may be that Allāh will bring them all unto me. Lo! He, only He, is the Knower, the Wise.

"Ask the *qarya*" in this context is metonymic for asking the people of the *qarya*. The act of asking here, however, indicates that the *qarya* visited in passing by Yūsuf's brothers was a very small community. Again, we continue to see the lexical *qarya* associated with something negative, in this case the loss of Jacob's youngest son, after the loss of Yūsuf himself earlier in the chapter. But it is a loss imbued with lying and deceit, endowing the verse with an eloquence in its expression of the dichotomy between truth and falsehood that characterizes the entire Yūsuf chapter. The brothers who lie to their father about Yūsuf, bringing home "false blood" (12: 18), are now caught in the tangle of deception that they set up from the start. They even lie directly to Yūsuf about his younger brother (not knowing that they are talking to Yūsuf himself), claiming that he is a thief just like his "brother" who "stole before" (12: 77). There is a kind of poetic justice in this example in which the brothers lie to their father who believes that they are telling the truth. The references to the *qarya*, which they use to corroborate their claim, become part of the negative connotations of their web of mendacity.

Madīna and *Qarya*: The Possibility of Interchangeability

While most of this chapter has argued for interpretations that juxtapose rather than equate the terms *qarya* with *madīna*, the question can nevertheless be approached from the opposite vantage point. The meaning in the verses might indeed tolerate an equivalence and there is sufficient evidence in the classical Arabic tradition to prove that *qarya* and *madīna* are potentially interchangeable lexemes. It is therefore not unfitting to assume that some verses could refer to the same location and use both *qarya* and *madīna* interchangeably, as some exegetes have argued, especially in a *sūra* like Yāsīn, mentioned earlier, and its reference to the unnamed man who came running from the furthest part of the *madīna* inviting the people to follow the messengers. In this very example the semantic correlations between verses 13 and 20 are suggestive of lexical interchangeability between *qarya* (36: 13) and *madīna* (36: 20):

13. And give to them the example of the people of the *qarya* when the messengers came to it;

20. And there came from the furthest point of the *madīna* a man, running. He said, "O people, follow the messengers."

Additionally, there is historical evidence that during the time of Prophet Muḥammad, *madīna* and *qarya* were used synonymously in common parlance. For example, Ibn Sallām has designated five areas in the Arabian Peninsula as *qurā*: "*wa-hunna khams: al-Madīna wa-Makka wa-l-Ṭāʾif wa-l-Yamāma wa-l-Baḥrayn* [*al-Madīna* also known as Yathrib], *Mecca, al-Ṭāʾif, al-Yamāma,* and *al-Baḥrayn*" present-day Bahrain. Lexically, *qarya* is defined as "*al-miṣr al-jāmiᶜ*,"[13] a self-sufficient and extended inhabited area. Ibn Sallām has also remarked that "*wa ashᶜaruhunna qaryatan al-madīna shuᶜarāʾuhā al-fuḥūl khamsa,*" (The most poetic of all [five *qurā*] are those of Medina, namely its five champion poets.)[14] This definition includes *al-madīna* according to al-Murtaḍā al-Zabīdī, author of *Tāj al-ᶜArūs.*[15] In the Qurʾān there are more than thirty references to *qarya,* whether in the singular, dual, or plural. In *Sūrat al-Zukhruf,* Chapter 43, verse 31, "*al-Qaryatayn*" is an explicit and direct reference to Mecca and Ṭāʾif.[16] In *Sūrat al-Anᶜām*, Chapter 6, verse 92, "*umm al-qurāā*" refers to Mecca, while "*ahl al-qurā*" or *al-qurā* could refer to Mecca, Medina, and Ṭāʾif.[17] Al-Ṭabarī's, al-Qurṭubī's, and even Pickthall's interpretations, then, that the two terms are synonymous may not be so far off the mark after all.

Conclusion

Dwelling on the translatability of the Qurʾānic "city," one soon realizes that existing semantic classifications remain insufficient and that no ultimate semantic specificity, and in this sense translatability, will ever be achieved no matter how careful one is. No act or task of translation, no English equivalent or otherwise, will completely capture the ever-evanescent significations of *qarya* and *madīna* in the Qurʾān. At stake here is a palimpsestic historicity, a history of etymology itself, that is, a history of the history of words and their transmutations across historical times (their different histories in time immemorial, from Noah to ᶜĀd, to Thamūd, to Abraham, to Moses, to Joseph, to Muḥammad, etc.) as well as narrative times (their own meaning and history in seventh-century Arabia and their change over the span of twenty-three years, the period of Qurʾānic Revelation), of which etymology is but a small branch. The discussion thus far has aimed to convey a sense of the profound and complex ambiguities associated with *qarya* and *madīna.* The words themselves, in a purely Jurjanian fashion, are inextricably linked to an overriding system of *maᶜānī* (discourse of meaning), where meaning is arrived upon discursively through a deeper structure of *naẓm* (sentence construction) and syntactic significations. Even when we are able to find different referents, contexts and designations to *madīna* and *qarya* thanks to exegetical analysis and historical references, we can still find in such different references the same connotations of *qarya* and *madīna* employed in historically earlier verses as well as in verses that address older histories. There is an undeniable lexical nostalgia at work in the invocations of *qarya* and *madīna* throughout the entire Qurʾān. This nostalgia among various *madīnas* and *qaryas* is surely more than the projection of the original signification into the present (the Prophet's time). Most fundamentally, the Qurʾān is a text, as Ibn ᶜArabī insists, whose very diction speaks to and explicates itself outside history, that is, outside the presumptuous interpretation of historical positivism which often belongs to the fleeting moment of the historical present and is often at odds with itself. In the end, the characteristic *qarya* and *madīna* remain, despite the span of twenty-three years and despite the chronological variations and historical periods, they are used to exemplify unchanging, almost immutable concepts. In other words, the Qurʾānic city proper does not exist. Or rather, it does not exist outside a theology of reward and a discourse of discipline and punishment that envelops it in a grandiose, indeed Platonic, metanarrative of good versus evil. The Qurʾānic city becomes an empty sheet or a blank referent hollowed out of all architectural signification with no specific history, no concrete or measurable content. The Qurʾānic city is thus an empty signifier for the architect, the (art) historian, and the archaeologist: it is a receding telos, or *ᶜibrā li-man yaᶜtabir* (a lesson to whoever wants to learn), whose only referent is a present continuing to vanish under the supreme power of Omnipotence itself.

The phenomenological and structural values of these two terms designating space or place, *qarya* and *madīna* – two areas of social habitation that have witnessed the congregations and migrations of humans across time – cannot be fully conceived of, or articulated rather, in terms of practical living à la Pierre Bourdieu. Think for instance of the latter's understanding of "practice" and of the relationship of the "social body" to the spatial structure and this relationship translated into an architectural morality for the practice of everyday life, including structuring homes based on public and private codes, with its own laws of hospitality, privacy, gender relations, division of labor, cooking, not to mention hunting paths, water resources, herds, farming, leisure, etc. What this means is that it is neither easy nor conceivable to translate, remediate, reproduce, reconfigure, or reimagine a city or a *madīna* using the Qurʾān. They are simply structurally inconceivable though not entirely unimaginable. In these two spaces, our experience of *qarya* and *madīna* is interrupted by the liturgical message of the Qurʾān, where the unaccommodated *arḍ* (Earth) itself is the primary architectural test of all humanity, where deeds are weighed and life is given and spent. In other words, it does not matter much if the *qarya* and *madīna* are translated as townships, villages, cities, provinces, or metropolises. All such entities are there to be subject to the Divine test; all shall receive the word of God, and their dwellers asked to make a choice between following the straight path or going astray.

Notes

1. Michael Cooperson, personal correspondence.
2. For more on this palpable yet oft-neglected lacuna in Arabic dictionaries, see Tammām Hassān's illuminating study on Arabic lexicography: *Al-Lugha al-ᶜArabiyya: Maᶜnāhā wa Mabnāhā* (1973a). See more specifically his chapter on *al-Maᶜājim* (Arabic Dictionaries) (1973a: 311–34). See also Hassān's essay on the methods of research in Arabic dictionaries in his book, *Manāhij al-Baḥth fī al-Lugha* (Methodologies in Language) (1973b: 258–73). In his essay, Hassān refers to many Arabic dictionaries as well as lexicon-based studies, including al-Suyūṭī's *al-Muzhir* and al-Juṛjānī's *Dalāʾil al-Iᶜjāz* to draw attention to the urgent need for researching etymological references in Arabic dictionaries:

   > European dictionaries such as the *Oxford Dictionary of the English Language* associate the meaning of words with specific centuries or historical periods. Current texts and studies of Arabic dictionaries lack such important etymological reference and semantic shifts. It is to be hoped that future scholarship will address this gap. (Hassān: 1973b, 269–70)

3. Al-Jāḥiẓ (1968: 26–7).
4. Pickthall (http://www.khayma.com/librarians/call2islaam/Quran/pickthall/surah36.html (all accessed on 5 January 2017)).
5. Williams (1983: 55).
6. Ibid.: 56.
7. Pickthall (http://www.khayma.com/librarians/call2islaam/Quran/pickthall/surah36.html).
8. Not all of the Cave Chapter verses are said to be Meccan. Some exegetes except verses 1–8, 28, and 107–10 as Medinan. See al-ᶜUthaymayn (2002: 7).

9. See Khalafallah (1999: 361).
10. Pickthall, http://www.khayma.com/librarians/call2islaam/Quran/pickthall/surah 11.html.
11. The word here is arḍ, referring to all of the territory over which Egypt rules.
12. Pickthall, http://www.khayma.com/librarians/call2islaam/Quran/pickthall/surah 12.html.
13. See Ibn Manẓūr, *Lisān al-ᶜArab*: http://www.baheth.info/all.jsp?term= ق ر ى.
14. The reference here is to Hassān ibn Thābit, Kaᶜb ibn Mālik, ᶜAbd Allāh ibn Ruwāha, Qays ibn al-Khutaym, and Abū Qays ibn al-Aslat. Muḥammad Ibn Sallām (al-Jumaḥī al-Baṣrī), *Ṭabaqāt fuḥūl al-shuᶜarāʾ: al-Sifr al-Awwal* (The Classifications of Champion Poets, 1974: vol. 1, 52). See also Jawād ᶜAlī, *Mufaṣṣal fī Tārīkh al-ᶜArab Qabl al-Islām* (The Detailed [Book] in the History of Pre-Islamic Arabs), chapters 137–68.
15. Al-Zabīdī (2001: vol. 39, 282–90).
16. Al-Ṭabarī (2001: vol. 20, 581–2).
17. Al-Ṭabarī (2001: vol. 9, 401–4).

Works Cited

ᶜAlī, Jawād (1993) *Mufaṣṣal fī Tārīkh al-ᶜArab Qabl al-Islām* (The Detailed [Book] in the History of Pre-Islamic Arabs), Baghdad.

Hassān, Tammām (1973a), *Al-Lugha al-ᶜArabiyya: Maᶜnāhā wa Mabnāhā*, Cairo: al-Hayʾa al-Miṣriyya al-Āmma lil-Kitāb.

—— (1973b), *Manāhij al-Baḥth fī al-Lugha* (Methodologies in Language), Casablanca: Dār al-Thaqāfa.

Ibn Manẓūr, *Lisān al-ʿArab*: http://www.baheth.info/all.jsp?term= ق ر ى (accessed on 7 January 2017)

Ibn Sallām, Muḥammad (al-Jumaḥī al-Baṣrī) (1974), *Ṭabaqāt fuḥūl al-shuᶜarā: al-Sifr al-Awwal*, Maḥmūd Muḥammad Shākir (ed.), Cairo: Dār al-Madanī.

Al-Jāḥiẓ, Abū ᶜUthmān ʿAmr ibn Baḥr (1968), *Al-Bayān wa al-Tabyīn* (The Book of Clarity and Clarification), Fawzī ᶜAṭwī (ed.), Beirut: Dār Ṣaᶜb.

Khalafallah, Muḥammad Aḥmad (1999), *al-Fann al-Qaṣaṣī fī al-Qurʾān al-Karīm* (Narrative Art in the Holy Qurʾān), Cairo: Sināʾ li-l-Nashr.

Pickthall, Marmaduke (1930), *The Meaning of the Glorious Qurʾan*, online edition http://www.khayma.com/librarians/call2islaam/Qurʾān/pickthall/surah36.html (also surah11; surah12; all accessed 5 January 2017).

Al-Ṭabarī (2001), *Tafsīr al-Ṭabarī, Jāmiᶜ al-bayān ᶜan taʾwīl al-Qurʾān* (A Comprehensive Compendium of Qurʾānic Interpretation), vol. 20, ᶜAbd Allāh bin ᶜAbd al-Muḥsin al-Turkī (ed.), Giza: Dār Hajr.

Al-ᶜUthaymaiyn, Muḥammad ibn Ṣāliḥ (2002), *Tafsīr al-Qurʾān al-Karīm: Sūra-t-al-Kahf* (Explication of the Holy Qurʾān: The Cave Chapter), Mecca: Dār ibn al-Jawzī.

Williams, Raymond (1983), *Keywords: A Vocabulary of Culture and Society*, London: Oxford University Press.

Al-Zabīdī, Murtaḍā (2001), *Tāj al-ᶜArūs min Jawāhir al-Qāmūs* (The Bride's Crown in Lexicographical Gems), vol. 39, ᶜAbd al-Majīd Qaṭāsh (ed.), Kuwait: al-Turāth al-ᶜArabī, 282–90.

2

Local Historians and their Cities: the Urban Topography of al-Azdī's Mosul and al-Sahmī's Jurjan

Harry Munt

The attempt to define the character and substantial characteristics of the "Islamic city" has been a long-cherished endeavour in twentieth- and twenty-first-century Western scholarship of the premodern Middle East. A range of studies has sought to identify key trends in the development of the urban topographies of Middle Eastern cities over the transition from Roman and Sasanian to Islamic rule and then throughout the premodern period, as well as some of the features that might be considered definitional for a Middle Eastern city in that period.[1] Quite a substantial amount of this work – albeit far from all of it – has been undertaken from an archaeological and architectural standpoint, with the literary testimonies of premodern Arabic and Persian authors being taken into account less frequently.[2] In one sense this is quite surprising, since we possess a relatively large number of extant local histories of individual cities written from the ninth century onwards. We might expect these works to be able to contribute something at least towards the debate.

This might be a reasonable expectation, but is it actually an appropriate one? We often think of many of these Arabic and Persian local historiographical works as "city" histories and their titles certainly suggest that this is the case. Nevertheless, we might question the extent to which histories of individual cities actually give us historical depictions of those cities' urban topographies. In a broader sense, the question could be posed as: are we correct to call these works, as we often do, "city histories," or are they rather histories of something else? And, following on from this, can they contribute to the debates over the perceived nature and characteristics of cities in the premodern Middle East?

By the mid-to-late eleventh century, when al-Khaṭīb al-Baghdādī (d. 1071) came to finish his enormous and what we might call "genre-defining" – at least in the sense that many later works cite it as a model for emulation – *Tārīkh Baghdād*, Arabic local historiography was already well underway as a branch of historical writing.[3] Roughly thirty works or parts of works written before his history of Baghdad are still extant today, and there are references here and there – some far more incidental than others – to more than one hundred other works that have now been lost. The geographical range of these local histories runs all the way from al-Andalus in the west to Bukhara, Samarqand and Balkh in the east. Very loosely speaking, these local histories can be divided into four different models: (1) chronographic/annalistic works; (2) prosopographical works; (3) topographical histories; and (4) local conquest narratives. These models were not, of course, mutually exclusive and features from several will often be present in works that can predominantly be categorised within one of them. The most commonly encountered example of this phenomenon is that local biographical dictionaries – including al-Khaṭīb al-Baghdādī's – will often have a so-called topographical introduction, outlining the city's foundation, key sites and, if necessary, the history of its conquest by Muslim armies as well. In many regions the prosopographical model – particularly biographical dictionaries of local *ḥadīth* scholars and jurists – was overwhelmingly the most popular form of local history-writing.

Local conquest narratives tend to deal more with broader regions than with specific cities – such as, for example, Abū Ismāᶜīl al-Azdī's perhaps late eighth- or early ninth-century *Futūḥ al-Shām*[4] – and as such will not appear much in the discussion in this chapter. On the other hand, it is perhaps obvious how extant local topographical histories, such as those of Mecca by al-Azraqī (d. *ca.* 864–5) and al-Fākihī (d. *ca.* 892–3) or the famous work on Cairo by al-Maqrīzī (d. 1442),[5] might contribute to the debates we are interested in here.[6] The focus in this chapter will be, therefore, principally on examples of works from the other two models of local history-writing: chronography and prosopography. In particular, as relatively accessible representatives of these two models of local history-writing written within a century or so of one another, we will be directing our attention towards Abū Zakariyyā al-Azdī's (d. 946) history of Mosul and Ḥamza al-Sahmī 's (d. 1035–6) history of Jurjan/Gorgan.[7] In this chapter, we will see that a study of the topographical information such authors chose to include in their works can offer an insight into something of what cities meant to premodern Arabic scholarly elites.

Al-Azdī's Mosul

Abū Zakariyyā al-Azdī was a local Mosuli scholar who composed at least two works about his hometown. The first of these – and the best known to many later premodern Muslim scholars – was a now lost prosopographical history, known as either *Ṭabaqāt Ahl al-Mawṣil* or *Ṭabaqāt Muḥaddithī Ahl al-Mawṣil*.[8] His other local history, far better known to modern historians, is an annalistically organised work – generally known simply as *Tārīkh al-Mawṣil* – a substantial portion of which, in spite of its relative lack of renown among premodern Muslim scholars, is preserved in a single manuscript now in Dublin.[9] This extant section contains the middle third of the work, which deals with the years 101 AH (= 719–20 CE) to 224 AH (= 838–9 CE), although the years 124 AH (= 741–2 CE) and 152 AH (= 769–70 CE) are missing.[10] As Chase Robinson has explained, the *Tārīkh al-Mawṣil* comprises two categories of material, local Mosuli material and "imperial" material; whereas the latter is usually of the standard *akhbār* (*isnād* and *matn*) type, the former "is heterogeneous in the extreme: lists (of *qāḍīs* and governors); documents (letters of appointment and *iqṭāᶜ*s; *waṣīyyas*); genealogical material; *rijāl* material; and, finally, narratives of local history, generally fitted with *isnāds* composed of local authorities."[11]

There is no single section of this extant manuscript in which a physical description of the city of Mosul or its twin city Nineveh, on the opposite bank of the Tigris, is given, although there may, of course, have been such a description in a lost part of the work. This can neither be confirmed nor denied confidently, but there are some indications that such a topographically descriptive section may have been included either in at least one of al-Azdī's two histories of Mosul or another work entirely. Most speculatively, we could note that the comprehensive thirteenth-century geographer Yāqūt (d. 1229) does include a brief foundation narrative for Mosul;[12] although Yāqūt cites no direct source for this passage, we know from other citations that he knew of al-Azdī's *Ṭabaqāt* at least, so it is possible that his unnamed source was Abū Zakariyyā al-Azdī.[13] Slightly more firmly, we know that Ibn al-Athīr (d. 1233) and Ibn Ḥajar (d. 1449) both cited a passage directly from al-Azdī on the early Muslim conquerors' establishment of Mosul as a garrison city (*tamṣīr*), and Ibn al-Athīr cites further information about their constructions in the city.[14] Finally, it is worth noting that al-Azdī himself mentions another work of his which may have touched on such issues, entitled *Kitāb al-Qabāʾil wa-l-Khiṭaṭ*.[15]

In what does survive of the *Tārīkh al-Mawṣil*, where al-Azdī does turn his attention to Mosul's urban topography, he was quite concerned to draw attention to certain types of buildings, principally: (1) its city wall, built in 699–700 and then razed nearly a century later in 796–7;[16] (2) the palaces of caliphs and some of their governors as well as central administrative structures in the city, such as the *dār al-imāra*;[17] (3) mosques, including the city's main congregational mosque as well as more local, tribal mosques;[18] (4) a bridge over the Tigris built before 745;[19] (5) a bathhouse, mentioned during the entry on the year 128 AH (= 745–6 CE);[20] (6) markets;[21] (7) and finally, and quite interestingly, a number of structures in the city's immediate hinterland related to agricultural estates and the processing and transportation of agricultural produce, including canals and, particularly prominently, flour mills.[22]

Much of this is the sort of topographical information that we might expect to interest a tenth-century Muslim local historian of a town in the Jazira. It is also interesting, however, to take note of what al-Azdī did not want to discuss. We hear from a number of other sources from the region, many written in Syriac, a great deal about the history of the Christian inhabitants of the region, whose community continued to thrive down past the time of al-Azdī's lifetime in the tenth century.[23] Al-Azdī, however, is very rarely interested in the history of Christian structures in Mosul, although he often alludes to their existence coincidentally. So, for example, in one place he says that, "The Banū Ḥimām in Mosul have an estate (*ḍayʿa*) known as al-Humayma, near Bashaq, next to which is the Taymuna monastery."[24] On one occasion in the work, a Christian structure features as a significant part of a story, and this is in a dispute between the Muslims and Christians over the building:

> When al-Mahdī[25] entered Mosul, the Christians came to him complaining about the destruction of the Church of Mar Tuma. According to what ʿUbayd b. Muḥammad told me, on the authority of ʿUmar, on the authority of his father, the reason for this was that the congregation [*aṣḥāb*] of the Church of Mar Tuma – which neighbours the mosque known after the Banū Asbāṭ al-Ṣayrafī, which is opposite the street [*darb*] of the Banū Ilyā al-Ṭabīb – brought within the [area of the] church other things. The Muslims of Mosul – those of them who were concerned about it – investigated the truth of the matter and so the people marched up to it and destroyed it. When al-Mahdī came to Mosul, the Christians brought their

> complaint and made a great fuss about the destruction of their church. Al-Mahdī looked into the matter; the Christians summoned those who witnessed the destruction of their church, while the Muslims summoned those who could testify to what they had incorporated within it and added to it that did not [properly] belong to it. The two parties set out with him to Balad.[26] He obliged the Christians to remove four hundred cubits from their church on account of the extension they had added to it. He also gave orders for a mosque to be built from his/its money, which is the Mosque of al-Mahdī, although it is generally known after the Banū Sābāṭ [*sic*, better Asbāṭ] because of their connection to it.[27]

In this instance, then, when a Christian structure does feature prominently in the narrative, its inclusion is used to demonstrate the efforts of the Abbasid caliph and some of the town's elites to ensure that it was not allowed to overshadow the local Muslim topography.

Throughout most of the work, Christian buildings feature only either incidentally or in demonstrations of the triumphant Islamisation of the city's topography. If al-Azdī did include a now lost foundation narrative for Mosul within one of his works, there is no evidence from the extant citations in Ibn al-Athīr's and Ibn Ḥajar's later works, or in the possible use by Yāqūt of such a narrative, that it paid any attention to the pre-Islamic Christian foundations on the site, although – again – Christian sources from the Islamic period offer a heavily Christianised foundation narrative for Mosul centered around the activities of the sixth-century holy man Ishoᶜyahb bar Qusre.[28] Al-Azdī also very rarely refers to Jewish elements in Mosul's cityscape, although we again know of a Jewish presence in the city in the Islamic period from other sources;[29] a structure known as "the fort of the Jews" (*ḥesnā ᶜebrāyē*) was known to some Syriac sources.[30]

Where al-Azdī does include topographical information, such passages tend to emphasise two things. Firstly, there are accounts of official caliphal patronage of various structures in Mosul. Such notices in many local histories serve to highlight the importance of the given city: if rulers spent their time patronising structures there, it must be a significant place. Al-Azdī here perhaps plays something of the role of the local patriot. Secondly, where topographical information is included it helps to create an image of a city and its hinterland controlled by what we might call the city's local (proto-)Sunni Muslim elites. Al-Azdī's highly selective representation of Mosul's cityscape helps to depict a city with a dominant and prosperous local landowning Sunni Muslim elite.

Al-Sahmī's Jurjan

Abū l-Qāsim Ḥamza b. Yūsuf al-Sahmī wrote a prosopographical history of his hometown of Jurjan (Pers. Gorgan) – a city in north-eastern Iran, about sixty-five miles inland from the Caspian Sea and in the modern Golestan province; the modern town is called Gonbad-e Kavus – in the early eleventh century. This work, entitled *Maᶜrifat ᶜUlamāᵓ Ahl Jurjān*, survives in a single late thirteenth-century manuscript held in the Bodleian Library in Oxford (Ms. Laud Or. 276). We know from a notice near the start of this manuscript that al-Sahmī was teaching at least part of this work in Ṣafar 419 AH (= March 1028 CE).[31] We have every indication that the work was widely known to those interested in local history-writing in the Islamic world in the centuries after al-Sahmī's death in 1035–6.[32]

As it stands, the work comprises fourteen parts, each with its own standalone introductory transmission history and colophon; it seems to be extant more or less in its entirety. Broadly speaking, the work starts with a historical and topographical introduction, which begins with a brief history of Jurjan's conquest by the early Muslim armies from the mid seventh century – from the initial raids during the caliphate of ᶜUmar b. al-Khaṭṭāb (r. 634–44) down to the final campaigns in the area of Yazīd b. al-Muhallab in 716–17 – and then surveys the eighth- and ninth-century governors of the city.[33] There then follows a more-or-less alphabetically organised biographical dictionary,[34] then a short section on those *nisba*s and place names that look similar in the Arabic script to al-Jurjānī and Jurjān,[35] then a more-or-less alphabetically organised biographical dictionary of some people from Astarabadh (about fifty miles south-west of Jurjan) not otherwise included in the work, based on Abū Saᶜd al-Idrīsī's (d. 1015) history of the inhabitants of that town,[36] and then finally some other additions to the work, the provenance of which is not altogether clear.[37]

Unlike the extant portion of al-Azdī's histories of Mosul, then, al-Sahmī's work on Jurjan does provide a brief historical and topographical introduction. This thirteen-page chapter has few sections dedicated solely to topographical information – with one section offering an important exception – but it does offer plenty of this material within its historical overview. We are told that Yazīd b. al-Muhallab, after his conquest of the region, had a city wall constructed for Jurjan and laid out the plans for approximately forty tribal mosques there, along with a mosque for himself; some of these mosques were in the center of the city (*qaṣaba*), others were in a suburb (*marbaḍ*).[38] In the section on the Umayyad governors of Jurjan, we are told of two of their building projects: al-Jahm b. Bakr al-Juᶜfī built the bridge which carried his name and Sulaymān b. Sulaym built the area known as Sulaymanabadh. We are also told that the last Umayyad governor, Nubāta b. Ḥanẓala was killed in a tavern (*ḥānūt*) by the Khurasan Gate.[39] In the section on those Abbasid caliphs who visited Jurjan in person, he mentions that the caliph al-Maᵓmūn (r. 813–33) built a *qaṣr*, perhaps here "villa," there, which was near the site of Muḥammad b. Jaᶜfar al- Ṣādiq's (d. 818–19) grave.[40] Most significantly for the topographical history of Jurjan, this section provides a complete listing of twenty-four mosques founded in the Umayyad period, together with plenty of incidental topographical information, as it locates the mosques on various streets and next to various other structures.[41]

This brief introductory section aside, as with al-Azdī's *Tārīkh al-Mawṣil* there is no concentrated focus on the city's topography throughout the bulk of al-Sahmī's history of Jurjan, but there is a certain amount of topographical information scattered throughout the prosopographical entries. Many of these entries are extremely short, comprising nothing more than a list of the given individuals' teachers and students as well as an example of a Prophetic *ḥadīth* which they had transmitted. In some entries, topographical information does appear seemingly incidentally. For example, from the entry on the famous scholar Sufyān al-Thawrī (d. 778):

> Sufyān b. Saᶜīd b. Masrūq al-Thawrī. It is said that he was born in one of the estates [*ḍiyāᶜ*] belonging to Jurjan, a village known as al-Thawriyyīn which gets its name from his tribe. Muḥammad b. Bassām al-Jurjānī recounted on the authority of al-Ḥammānī that Sufyān al-Thawrī was born in Jurjan, then moved to Kufa, and then returned to Jurjan after he had grown up/old and taught ḥadīth there. Saᶜd b. Saᶜīd al-Jurjānī, known as Saᶜdawayh, transmitted from him [and there exists] a question-and-answers work belonging to Saᶜd in which he transmitted *fiqh* and other matters from al-Thawrī.[42]

Then if we turn to the entry on Saᶜdawayh himself, we get a little more incidental topography:

> Abu Saᶜīd Saᶜd b. Saᶜīd al-Jurjānī, known as Saᶜdawayh. His mosque is next to the congregational mosque and his grave is in Sulaymanabadh. He transmitted from Sufyān al-Thawrī and Nahshal. He has a question-and-answers work based on questions he asked Sufyān in Jurjan.[43]

Some entries in the *Tārīkh Jurjān* actually offer a relatively considerable quantity of information on local street names. We are told, for example, that one Abū ᶜAmr Thābit b. ᶜAlī al-Jurjānī used to live on Ansar Street (*sikkat al-anṣār*) in the middle of the market.[44] Whereas in many cases any topographical information offered seems somewhat incidental, sometimes the provision of such data comes across as a key interest. For example, here is the opening to the entry on Abū Ṭayba ᶜĪsā b. Sulaymān al-Dārimī al-Jurjānī (d. 770):

> Abū Ṭayba ᶜĪsā b. Sulaymān al-Dārimī al-Jurjānī, an ascetic scholar. He transmitted learning from Kurz/Karaz b. Wabara, Jaᶜfar b. Muḥammad, Sulaymān, al-Aᶜmash[45] and others; his two sons Aḥmad and ᶜAbd al-Wāsiᶜ transmitted from him, as did Saᶜd b. Saᶜīd and others. His mosque is within the main part of the city [*qaṣaba*] on the street known after his son, ᶜAbd al-Wāsiᶜ b. Abī Ṭayba.[46] His residence [*dār*] was next to the mosque. He also had wealth outside [of the city] in the form of estates and properties, as well as endowments [*awqāf*] known after him until today for his children, their children and his relatives in Juzjanan, in a town called Ashburqan. These were transferred there/to him from their endowments [*awqāf*] in Jurjan and Astarabadh. His grave is near the Tayfur river at the edge of the cemetery of Sulaymanabadh.[47]

In this entry, al-Sahmī uses topographical information to affirm the important status within Jurjan's society of the family of one local religious scholar, whose descendants continued to play an important scholarly and social role in Jurjan's history.[48] Such topographical information does not appear in the majority of the prosopographical entries in the work, but where it does it reinforces the picture of a cityscape dominated by structures connected to Jurjan's religious elites.

Some modern historians have sought to reconstruct elements of the historical topography of Jurjan from notices such as these in al-Sahmī's work, as well as the catalog of Umayyad mosques offered in the introductory historical section. Albert Dietrich, for example, stated that,

> *Schließlich sei noch bemerkt, daß der Moscheenkatalog eine wichtige Grundlage zur Topographie von Gurgān bildet. Sahmīs Werk enthält noch eine Fülle weiterer topographischer Angaben, die, wenn geordnet und ausgewertet, ein getreues Abbild einer mittelgroßen frühmittelalterlichen islamischen Stadt ergeben würden.*

> After all, it should be noted that the catalog of mosques forms an important basis for the topography of Gurgān. Sahmī's work contains a wealth of further topographical details which, if collated and evaluated, would provide an accurate image of a medium-sized early medieval Islamic town.[49]

Parvaneh Pourshariati has further suggested that,

> So detailed is the information provided by al-Sahmī on the location of settlements and early mosques still existing in the author's life time, as well as other municipal information that reflect on Gurgān's early Islamic history that it would probably be possible to chart the pattern of Arab settlement in Gurgān, as well as the growth of the city by al-Sahmī's life time.[50]

It is important, however, to raise a note of caution here. Al-Sahmī presents a largely synchronic topographical depiction of Jurjan, frequently without charting the history of various streets and structures he mentions over time. Of the twenty-four Umayyad mosques mentioned in that list, for example, only five are explicitly stated to be there still in al-Sahmī's own day, although we are also told that a sixth was restored in 1008–9. A seventh is said to belong to the Shiᶜa, but we cannot be sure that al-Sahmī was referring to the period of his own lifetime here. Even when al-Sahmī seems to be talking about the topography of Jurjan in his own day, we would be advised to remain cautious. Zayde Antrim has recently demonstrated quite clearly that even when local historians seem to be offering contemporary information they sometimes let slip that they are not actually doing so. In her best example, al-Khaṭīb al-Baghdādī's topographical introduction to his *Tārīkh Baghdād* includes the following sentence, cited ultimately from Muḥammad b. Khalaf Wakīᶜ (d. 918):

> The spot now occupied by the New Prison was a fief granted to ᶜAbdallāh b. Malik, and Muḥammad b. Yaḥya b. Khālid b. Barmak made his residence there. During the reign of Muḥammad, it became part of the building which Umm Jaᶜfar erected, and which she called al-Qarār."[51]

As Jacob Lassner and Antrim both note, however, this "New Prison" was destroyed in 961–2 by the Buyid ruler Muᶜizz al-Dawla (r. 945–67), who used the rubble for his own palace at al-Shammasiyya.[52] Sarah Savant has suggested, specifically with regard to al-Sahmī's history of Jurjan, that the provision of quite detailed toponyms is often intimately linked with the process of the construction of social memory.[53] In such a process, the careful delineation of a diachronic topographical history for a city may not be a priority; neighbouring communities whose local quarters are centered around monuments built at rather different times can be seamlessly fitted together to give what is overall a rather anachronistic depiction of an urban topography.

Although al-Sahmī was writing local history of a rather different model to al-Azdī's annalistic history of Mosul, his work displays some rather similar concerns when it comes to depicting the urban topography of his town. Firstly, he shares an interest in highlighting the role of caliphs in patronising structures in the city. Secondly, he displays very little interest in either the region's pre-Islamic history, or in the history of its non-Muslim communities in the Islamic period. We know from archaeological work that there was a high level of Sasanian imperial investment in the military fortification of the Jurjan region from the fifth century.[54] The information about the non-Muslim communities of the region in the Islamic period is not quite as clear, although we can assume that there probably were some. The pre-Islamic Church of the East diocese of Jurjan, founded in the fifth century, apparently for victims of forced deportation from the Roman Empire, seems to have lasted down to the turn of the ninth–tenth centuries at least.[55] Finally, just like al-Azdī, the picture frequently gained from al-Sahmī's topographical information when it appears is that of a cityscape dominated by structures connected to property-owning (proto-)Sunni elites, more specifically in this case comprising the families of respected religious scholars.

Some Conclusions

It should by now be clear that premodern Muslim local historians such as al-Azdī and al-Sahmī were not interested in offering a mimetic topographical description of their respective cities.[56] We hardly get a chronological overview of developments in either Mosul's or Jurjan's cityscape from al-Azdī and al-Sahmī, although the annalistic format of al-Azdī's work helps ever so slightly here; nor are we getting an image of a physical city that ever existed at any one moment. Instead, and this may seem like an obvious point but it is one worth stressing, we only get depictions based on structures, streets, quarters and estates that the authors wanted us to know about. Much of what both al-Azdī and al-Sahmī appear to have wanted us to know about helped to present a picture of cities and their hinterlands dominated by property-owning and prosperous local (proto-)Sunni Muslim elites, not coincidentally a class of townsmen with which our authors heavily identified themselves.

Both al-Azdī and al-Sahmī were living at a time in which the top level of political elites in their respective regions were alternating frequently. In the Jazira around Mosul in the mid-tenth century, Abbasid authority was being gradually undermined by the increasing power of the (at least nominally) Shiᶜi Hamdanids and the renewed efforts at reconquest by the Christian Byzantines.[57] In north-eastern Iran in the late tenth and early eleventh centuries, the local Ziyarid dynasty – named after Mardawīj b. Ziyār (d. 935) – was precariously placed at first between the rival Buyid and Samanid dynasties and then on the borders of the empire of the increasingly powerful Ghaznavids.[58] In these times of rapidly changing political control, landed local elites had an extremely important role to play in the maintenance of social stability day-to-day. On quite a basic level, this meant ensuring that produce from agricultural estates ended up as food in the cities; urban unrest caused by food shortages was a problem to which eleventh-century Iran was particularly susceptible, which may explain al-Sahmī's occasional interest in Jurjan's elites' agricultural estates.[59] Chase Robinson has suggested that, "In Mosul, as elsewhere, we find that familiar confluence of property and education that produced long-lived dynasties of learning in many Islamic cities," and Richard Bulliet has demonstrated how such dynasties of learning in Iranian cities also wielded significant social authority.[60] It is in the local histories of learned elites such as Abū Zakariyyā al-Azdī and Ḥamza al-Sahmī that we can see a case being advanced – supported by carefully selected topographical information among other strategies – precisely for the significance of this social authority based on the "confluence of property and education" being invested in the correct groups. The frequent focus on (proto-)Sunni elites, their properties and structures in these histories of cities that probably had both Shiᶜi and non-Muslim landowning elites as well as religious buildings was, as in so many cases of inter-communal discourse, not simply a matter of religious polemic but carried serious social implications.[61]

It is also clear that the depictions of urban topography in these works are ones in which certain communities of inhabitants have mattered just as much as the physical structures discussed. The physical topographies on offer generally help to reinforce these social communities' status, rather than to provide simple descriptions of what the places looked like.[62] This raises a potentially bigger question: what were cities, in a meaningful sense, for Muslim scholars of the tenth and eleventh centuries? Paul Wheatley has synthesised a large amount of data concerning towns and cities across the Islamic world found in the work of the mid tenth-century traveller and geographer al-Muqaddasī (var. al-Maqdisī), concluding that it is implied in many of his descriptions that he thought congregational mosques and market places "essential attributes of the mature urban form," although he also took population size into some account.[63] This is certainly a very reasonable conclusion to draw, but it is also noteworthy that in one widely known passage al-Muqaddasī ranks urban centers into a fourfold hierarchy: at the top were the *amṣār* (sing. *miṣr*), then the *qaṣabāt* (sing. *qaṣaba*), then the *mudun* (sing. *madīna*) and finally the *qurā* (sing. *qarya*). There was no widespread agreement over the definitions of each of these four ranks of towns, but al-Muqaddasī himself, for example, defined a *miṣr* as, "Every town [*balad*] in which the highest authority [*al-sulṭān al-aᶜẓam*] resides, in which the governmental departments [*dawāwīn*, sing. *dīwān*] are gathered together, from which the provinces [*aᶜmāl*] are invested and to which the towns [*mudun*] of the region are joined."[64] This suggests that premodern Muslim scholars – just like many modern scholars – worked with some definitions of cities and towns that were functional in approach, rather than solely based around what precise physical structures they contained or how large their populations might be.

For the authors of the two local histories studied in this chapter, cities were also meaningful in ways that went far beyond their simple physical characteristics, although not quite in the same way as for al-Muqaddasī. Mosul and Jurjan were not just conglomerations of residences, walls, mosques and markets, nor were they primarily economic or administrative centers. They were socially meaningful spaces and the topographical information on offer in these histories of Mosul and Jurjan was frequently incorporated to support this understanding. This social relevance made it imperative that they were inhabited by the right sort of people and that this was reflected in the topographical depictions on offer. If, as we can only presume, they were not dominated fully by the appropriate people in reality, they certainly could be in the visions of the past expressed through local history-writing.

Notes

1. A famous and pioneering example of such a study is Sauvaget (1934). The bibliography of research since then is quite large, but interesting works with further references include Kennedy (1985 and 2006); Abu-Lughod (1987); Raymond (1994); Carver (1996); Wheatley (2001); Bennison and Gascoigne (eds) (2007); Jayyusi *et al.* (eds) (2008); Milwright (2010: 75–96); Avni (2011).
2. One important exception to this trend has been Paul Wheatley's impressively wide-ranging 2001 study, *The Places Where Men Pray Together*.

3. For some discussion (with further references) of the phenomenon of local history-writing in the premodern Middle East, see Munt (2012; for further references, see especially 29–30, n. 136).
4. Al-Azdī (2005). For some discussion, see Mourad (2000); Scheiner (2007).
5. Al-Azraqī (n. d.); al-Fākihī (1998); al-Maqrīzī (2002–4). There are a large number of studies of al-Maqrīzī's work, one of the latest of which is Rabbat (2012).
6. For a detailed study of one such work, see Munt (2015).
7. Al-Azdī, (1967); al-Sahmī (2012). For a broader study of urbanism in the regions around these two cities, see Wheatley (2001: 103–11, 165–71).
8. Al-Azdi references this work himself in his *Tārīkh al-Mawṣil* (1967: 301); for another premodern notice on the work, see al-Sakhāwī (n. d.: 283 and the translation in Rosenthal (1968: 482)). For modern discussions, see Sezgin, *Geschichte des arabischen Schrifttums* (henceforth *GAS*) (1967– : vol. I, 350); Robinson (1996: 114–20).
9. Al-Mas'ūdī (d. 956) and Ibn Ḥajar al-ᶜAsqalānī (d. 1449) were certainly aware of the work; see respectively Al-Masᶜūdī (1861–77: I, 18); and Ibn Ḥajar al-ᶜAsqalānī (1998: 180). Ibn al-Athīr (d. 1233) also used the work extensively in his monumental universal history, *al-Kāmil fī l-tārīkh*; see the discussion in Forand (1969: 103). For other modern studies which make much use of al-Azdī's history, see Kennedy (1981); Robinson (2000; and 2006).
10. The manuscript is Chester Beatty no. 3030, which was copied by Ibrāhīm b. Jamīᶜa b. ᶜAlī and dated to 16 Rabīᶜ II 654 AH (= 13 May 1256 CE); see Arberry (1955–64: I, 11). For further discussion on al-Azdī's *Tārīkh al-Mawṣil*, see *GAS* (1967– : I, 350); Robinson (2006).
11. Robinson (2006: 522).
12. Yāqūt (1866–73: IV, 683).
13. Ibid.: IV, 685.
14. Robinson (2000: 73–4).
15. Al-Azdī (1967: 96, 101).
16. For example, ibid.: 25, 289.
17. For example, ibid.: 24, 26–7, 145–6, 158.
18. For example, ibid.: 68, 91–2, 113, 147–8, 244, 248, 340–1, 364.
19. For example, ibid.: 70, 75.
20. For example, ibid.: 75.
21. For example, ibid.: 248.
22. For example, ibid.: 26–7, 96, 171–2, 197.
23. See especially Ishoᶜdnah of Basra (1896: 11–12/12 (§19), 32/28 (§50), 57/47–8 (§107), 61–2/52 (§121)); and throughout the E. A. Wallis Budge (1893)

translation/edition of Thomas of Marga, *The Book of Governors*. A fundamental study remains Fiey (1959); see also Robinson (2000: 90–108).

24. Al-Azdī (1967: 96).
25. The Abbasid caliph, reigned from 775 to 785.
26. Another town on the Tigris, a little north-west of Mosul; see al-Muqaddasī (1906: 139–40).
27. Al-Azdī (1967: 244, within the year 163 AH (= 779–80 CE).
28. Isho[c]dnah (1896: 32/28 (§50); *Chronicle of Si[c]irt*, vol. 7 (1911: 199–201).
29. See, for example, Robinson (2000: 72); and Sklare (1996: 119):

> "Ṭābā [i.e. Abū al-Khayr Ṭābā b. Salḥūn, author of an extant *Kitāb al-Manāẓir*] was a wool merchant from Mosul, where his study group met in the local synagogue on Sabbaths and holidays … The work [i.e. the *Kitāb al-Manāẓir*] was completed in the spring of 983 in Mosul. That the philosophically oriented educational activity he describes took place in Mosul is further confirmation that the area around Mosul seems to have had a tradition of philosophical activity."

30. Isho[c]dnah (1896: 32/28 (§50)); further discussion in Robinson (2000: 68–70).
31. Al-Sahmī (2012: 41).
32. See, for example, al-Ṣafadī (1931–2000: I, 48); Ibn al-Khaṭīb (1973–7: I, 90); Ibn Ḥajar al-[c]Asqalānī (1998: 180); al-Sakhāwī (n. d.: 247, 258), translated in Rosenthal (1968: 458, 465). For modern studies that pay considerable attention to this work, see Dietrich (1965); Bulliet (1994); Pourshariati (1998: 53–57); Savant (2013: 109–16).
33. Al-Sahmī (2012: 41–53).
34. Ibid.: 55–409. There are some fairly standard non-alphabetical features to this section: (1) within each letter of the alphabet, the names are not consistently provided in strict alphabetical order (the Aḥmads come first, but this is not the only example of such irregularity); (2) those known by their *kunya* come in the penultimate position, followed by women (twelve of whom are mentioned).
35. Ibid.: 409–11.
36. Ibid.: 412–40. On Abū Sa[c]d al-Idrīsī's history of Astarabadh, see also al-Sam[c]ānī (1962–82: I, 139); al-Ṣafadī (1931–2000: I, 48); al-Sakhāwī (n. d.: 247), translated in Rosenthal (1968: 458).
37. Al-Sahmī (2012: 441–55).
38. Ibid.: 45.
39. Ibid.: 50.

40. Ibid.: 53.
41. Ibid.: 51–2.
42. Ibid.: 181 (no. 338); also discussed in Savant (2013: 111).
43. Al-Sahmī (2012: 182 (no. 340)).
44. Ibid.: 146 (no. 219).
45. Since al-A[c]mash's (d. 764) first name was Sulaymān, the "*wāw*" separating these two names here may be a mistake.
46. We are told elsewhere (al-Sahmī (2012: 86 (no. 64)) that Abū al-Ḥusayn Aḥmad b. al-Ḥusayn b. [c]Alī b. Mālik al-Jurjānī used to live on [c]Abd al-Wāsi[c] Street (*sikkat [c]Abdal-Wāsi[c]*).
47. Al-Sahmī (2012: 236 (no. 492)).
48. See, for example, the entries on Abū Ṭayba's sons Aḥmad and [c]Abd al-Wāsi[c] in ibid.: 55–6 (no. 1), 201 (no. 392).
49. Dietrich (1965: 5).
50. Pourshariati (1998: 56).
51. Al-Khaṭīb al-Baghdādī (1931: 30); this translation is from Lassner (1970: 70).
52. Lassner (1970: 255, n. 35); Antrim (2012: 73).
53. Savant (2013: 111).
54. See Sauer *et al.* (2013).
55. Fiey (1993: 85–6).
56. For some other examples of this point, see Antrim (2006); Munt (2010: 159).
57. As well as the monumental study by Canard (1953), see the briefer overviews in Kennedy (2016: 229–43); Whittow (1996: 310–27).
58. There is a good, brief overview in Savant (2013: 109–10).
59. On urban unrest caused by food shortages, see Bulliet (2009: 37, 67, 86).
60. Robinson (2000: 161); Bulliet (1972).
61. Sarah Savant has interestingly suggested (2013: 113) that al-Sahmī's work deliberately downplays the differences between the various sectarian groups in Jurjan: "There is virtually no sense of conflict between the different groups. Rather, al-Sahmī's picture is one of improbable equilibrium and concord." As well as a picture of "equilibrium and concord," we might also see in this integration of many communities into one a "Sunnification" of the history of the elites of Jurjan.
62. For another expression of this idea, see Jarrar (2000: 48):

> "Prefacing some of these dictionaries with a substantial topographical description shows that in emphasizing the efflorescence of one's place, the human component has become a critical adjunct to descriptions of monumental religious architecture and ingenious town planning."

63. Wheatley (2001: 75–84, quotation from 75).
64. Al-Muqaddasī (1906: 47); for another discussion of this passage, see Wheatley (2001: 77–8).

Works Cited

Abu-Lughod, Janet (1987), "The Islamic city: historic myth, Islamic essence, and contemporary relevance," *International Journal of Middle East Studies* 19: 155–76.

Antrim, Zayde (2006), "Ibn ᶜAsākir's representations of Syria and Damascus in the introduction to the *Tārīkh Madīnat Dimashq*," *International Journal of Middle East Studies* 38: 109–29.

—— (2012), *Routes and Realms: The Power of Place in the Early Islamic World*, New York: Oxford University Press.

Arberry, A. J. (1955–64), *The Chester Beatty Library: A Handlist of the Arabic Manuscripts*, 7 vols, Dublin: Emery Walker, and Hodges, Figgis & Co.

Avni, Gideon (2011), "'From polis to madīna' revisited: urban change in Byzantine and early Islamic Palestine," *Journal of the Royal Asiatic Society*, 3rd ser., 21: 301–29.

Al-Azdī, Abū Ismāᶜīl (2005), *Futūḥ al-Shām*, ᶜIṣām Muṣṭafā ᶜUqla and Yaḥyā Aḥmad Banī Yāsīn (eds), Irbid: Muʾassasat Ḥamāda.

Al-Azdī, Abū Zakariyyā (1967), *Tārīkh al-Mawṣil*, ᶜAlī Ḥabība (ed.), Cairo: al-Majlis al-Aᶜlā li-l-Shuʾūn al-Islāmiyya.

Al-Azraqī (n. d.), *Akhbār Makka wa-mā Jāʾa fīhā min al-Āthār*, 2 vols, Rushdī Malḥas (ed.), Beirut: Dār al-Andalus.

Bennison, Amira K. and Gascoigne, A. L. (eds) (2007), *Cities in the Pre-Modern Islamic World: The Urban Impact of Religion, State and Society*, London: Routledge.

Bulliet, Richard W. (1972), *The Patricians of Nishapur: A Study in Medieval Islamic Social History*, Cambridge MA: Harvard University Press.

—— (1994), *Islam: The View from the Edge*, New York NY: Columbia University Press.

—— (2009), *Cotton, Climate, and Camels in Early Islamic Iran: A Moment in World History*, New York NY: Columbia University Press.

Canard, Marius (1953), *Histoire de la dynastie des H'amdanides de Jazîra et de Syrie*, Paris: Presses Universitaires de France.

Carver, M. O. H. (1996), "Transitions to Islam: urban rôles in the east and south Mediterranean, fifth to tenth centuries AD," in Neil Christie and S. T. Loseby (eds), *Towns in Transition: Urban Evolution in Late Antiquity and the Early Middle Ages*, Aldershot: Scholar Press, 184–212.

Chronicle of Si^c irt, ed. and trans. Addaï Scher and Robert Griveau, *Histoire nestorienne (Chronique de Séert)*, in *Patrologia Orientalis* 4 (1908: 211–313); 5 (1910: 217–344); 7 (1911: 93–203); 13 (1919: 433–639).

Dietrich, Albert (1965), "Die Moscheen von Gurgān zur Omaijadenzeit," *Der Islam* 40: 1–17.

Al-Fākihī (1998), *Akhbār Makka fī Qadīm al-Dahr wa-Ḥadīthih*, 6 vols, ^cAbd al-Malik Ibn Duhaysh (ed.), Beirut: Dār Khiḍr, and Mecca: Maktabat wa-Maṭba^cat al-Nahda wa-l-Ḥadātha.

Fiey, Jean-Maurice (1959), *Mossoul chrétienne: essai sur l'histoire, l'archéologie et l'état actuel des monuments chrétiens de la ville de Mossoul*, Beirut: Imprimerie Catholique.

—— (1993), *Pour un Oriens Christianus novus: répertoire des diocèses syriaques orientaux et occidentaux*, Beirut: Franz Steiner.

Forand, Paul (1969), "The governors of Mosul according to al-Azdī's *Tārīkh al-Mawṣil*," *Journal of the American Oriental Society* 89: 88–105.

Ibn al-Khaṭīb (1973–7), *al-Iḥāṭa fī Akhbār Gharnāṭa*, 4 vols, Muḥammad ^cAbd Allāh ^cInān (ed.), Cairo: Maktabat al-Khānjī.

Ibn Ḥajar al-^cAsqalānī (1998), *al-Mu^cjam al-Mufahras aw-Tajrīd Asānīd al-Kutub al-Mashhūra wa-l-Ajzā^ɔ al-Manthūra*, Muḥammad Shakkūr Maḥmūd al-Ḥājjī Amīr al-Mayādīnī (ed.), Beirut: Mu^ɔassasat al-Risāla.

Isho^cdnah of Basra (1896), *Livre de la chasteté*, J.-B. Chabot (ed. and trans.), Rome: École Française de Rome.

Jarrar, Sabri (2000), "al-Maqrīzī's reinvention of Egyptian historiography through architectural history," in Doris Behrens-Abouseif (ed.), *The Cairo Heritage: Essays in Honor of Laila Ali Ibrahīm*, Cairo: American University in Cairo Press, 31–53.

Jayyusi, Salma K., Renata Holod, Attilio Petruccioli and André Raymond (eds) (2008), *The City in the Islamic World*, 2 vols, Leiden: E. J. Brill.

Kennedy, Hugh (1981), "Central government and provincial élites in the early ^cAbbāsid caliphate," *Bulletin of the School of Oriental and African Studies* 44: 26–38.

—— (1985), "From *polis* to *madīna*: urban change in late antique and early Islamic Syria," *Past and Present* 106: 3–27.

—— (2006), "From shahristan to medina," *Studia Islamica* 102–3: 5–34.

—— (2016), *The Prophet and the Age of the Caliphates: The Islamic Near East from the Sixth to the Eleventh Century*, 3rd ed., Abingdon: Routledge.

Al-Khaṭīb al-Baghdādī (1931), *Tārīkh Baghdād*, 14 vols, Cairo: Maktabat al-Khānjī.

Lassner, Jacob (1970), *The Topography of Baghdad in the Early Middle Ages: Text and Studies*, Detroit MI: Wayne State University Press.

Al-Maqrīzī (2002–04), *Kitāb al-Mawāʾiẓ wa-l-Iʿtibār fī Dhikr al-Khiṭaṭ wa-l-Āthār*, 5 vols, Ayman Fuʾād Sayyid (ed.), London: Muʾassasat al-Furqān li-l-Turāth al-Islāmī.

Al-Masʿūdī (1861–77), *Murūj al-Dhahab wa-Maʿādin al-Jawhar*, trans. and ed. C. Barbier de Meynard and Pavet de Courteille, *Les prairies d'or*, 9 vols, Paris: L'Imprimerie Impériale.

Milwright, Marcus (2010), *An Introduction to Islamic Archaeology*, Edinburgh: Edinburgh University Press.

Mourad, Suleiman A. (2000), "On early Islamic historiography: Abū Ismāʿīl al-Azdī and his *Futūḥ al-Shām*," *Journal of the American Oriental Society* 120: 577–93

Munt, Harry (2010), "Ibn al-Azraq, St. Marūthā, and the foundation of Mayyāfāriqīn (Martyropolis)," in Arietta Papaconstantinou, Muriel Debié, Hugh Kennedy (eds), *Writing "True Stories": Historians and Hagiographers in the Late Antique and Medieval Near East*, Turnhout: Brepols, 149–74.

—— (2012), "Writing the history of an Arabian holy city: Ibn Zabāla and the first local history of Medina," *Arabica* 59: 1–34.

—— (2015), "Mamluk historiography outside of Egypt and Syria: ʿAlī b. ʿAbd Allāh al-Samhūdī and his histories of Medina," *Der Islam* 95: 413–41.

Al-Muqaddasī (1906), *Aḥsan al-Taqāsīm fī Maʿrifat al-Aqālīm*, 2nd ed., M. J. de Goeje (ed.), Leiden: E. J. Brill.

Pourshariati, Parvaneh (1998), "Local histories of Khurāsān and the pattern of Arab settlement," *Studia Iranica* 27: 41–81.

Rabbat, Nasser (2012), "Was al-Maqrīzī's *Khiṭaṭ* a Khaldūnian history?," *Der Islam* 89: 118–40.

Raymond, André (1994), "Islamic city, Arab city: Orientalist myths and recent reviews," *British Journal of Middle East Studies* 21: 3–18.

Robinson, Chase F. (1996), "al-Muʿāfā b. ʿImrān and the beginnings of *ṭabaqāt* literature," *Journal of the American Oriental Society* 116: 114–20.

—— (2000), *Empire and Elites after the Muslim Conquest: The Transformation of Northern Mesopotamia*, Cambridge: Cambridge University Press.

—— (2006), "A local historian's debt to al-Ṭabarī: the case of al-Azdī's *Taʾrīkh al-Mawṣil*," *Journal of the American Oriental Society* 126: 521–35.

Rosenthal, Franz (1968), *A History of Muslim Historiography*, 2nd ed., Leiden: E. J. Brill.

Al-Ṣafadī (1931–2000), *al-Wāfī bi-l-Wafayāt*, 30 vols, Sven Dedering *et al.* (eds), Leipzig, Istanbul and Beirut: various publishers.

Al-Sahmī (2012), *Tārīkh Jurjān*, 3rd ed. reprint, Muḥammad ᶜAbd al-Muᶜīd Khān (ed.), Beirut: ᶜĀlam al-Kutub.

Al-Sakhāwī (n. d.), *al-Iᶜlān bi-l-tawbīkh li-man dhamma l-taʾrīkh*, Franz Rosenthal and Ṣāliḥ Aḥmad al-ᶜAlī (eds), Beirut: Dār al-Kutub al-ᶜIlmiyya.

Al-Samᶜānī (1962–82), *Al-Ansāb*, 13 vols, Hyderabad: Dāʾirat al-Maᶜārif al-ᶜUthmāniyyah.

Sauer, Eberhard W., Omrani Rekavandi, T. J. Wilkinson and J. Nokandeh (2013), *Persia's Imperial Power in Late Antiquity: The Great Wall of Gorgān and Frontier Landscapes of Sasanian Iran*, Oxford: Oxbow Books.

Sauvaget, Jean (1934), "Le plan de Laodicée-sur-Mer," *Bulletin d'études orientales* 4: 81–114.

Savant, Sarah (2013), *The New Muslims of Post-Conquest Iran: Tradition, Memory, and Conversion*, Cambridge: Cambridge University Press.

Scheiner, Jens (2007), "Grundlegendes zu al-Azdīs *Futūḥ aš-Šām*," *Der Islam* 84: 1–16.

Sezgin, Fuat (1967–), *Geschichte des arabischen Schrifttums*, (*GAS*), 15 vols to date, Leiden: E. J. Brill.

Sklare, David E. (1996), *Samuel ben Ḥofni Gaon and His Cultural World: Texts and Studies*, Leiden: E. J. Brill.

Wallis Budge, E. A. (ed./trans.) (1893), *The Book of Governors: The Historia Monastica of Thomas Bishop of Margâ A.D. 840*, 2 vols, London: Kegan Paul, Trench, Trübner & Co.

Wheatley, Paul (2001), *The Places Where Men Pray Together: Cities in Islamic Lands, Seventh through the Tenth Centuries*, Chicago IL: University of Chicago Press.

Whittow, Mark (1996), *The Making of Orthodox Byzantium, 600–1025*, Basingstoke: Palgrave.

Yāqūt (1866–73), *Muᶜjam al-Buldān*, Ferdinand Wüstenfeld (ed.), 6 vols, Leipzig: F. A. Brockhaus.

3

Against Cities: On *Hijāʾ al-Mudun* in Arabic Poetry

Huda Fakhreddine and Bilal Orfali

CLASSICAL PERSPECTIVES

Beautifying and Uglifying the Homeland

In the premodern Muslim world, it was customary for a poet to praise his homeland. The definition of home, however, and the poet's relation to it, developed with the changing topography of organized social and political life. In a chapter titled "The Poet in the City" in his *Poetique arabe,* Jamal Eddine Bencheikh traces this development in the Arabic tradition from what he describes as a "biological" connection between the poet and his tribe to a less natural and more contrived relationship between the poet and the larger Islamic community, and after that to the select family or individuals (especially at the height of the Abbasid Empire) who claimed to be embodiments of the entire larger community. The pre-Islamic poet's relationship to his tribe was the direct source of the sociological, religious, moral and linguistic parameters of his role. These parameters were expanded and abstracted in the later period of the Islamic caliphate, becoming not necessarily more fragile, but of a more deliberate and complex politics.[1]

Regardless of the nature of the poet's homeland, its praise utilized themes of nostalgia (*ḥanīn*), alienation and/or estrangement (*ghurba*), and lament (*rithāʾ*).[2] Anthologies of *al-ḥanīn ilā l-awṭān* (yearning for the homeland) are replete with such motifs. Indeed, one finds in these anthologies chapters such as *ḥubb al-waṭan* (love of one's homeland), *al-tagharrub* (emigration), *al-safar wa-l-ightirāb* (travel and emigration), *dhikr al-ayyām al-sālifa* (remembering the past days), etc.[3] The objects of nostalgia here are the family, tribe, clan, comrades, and beloved. There is usually an emphasis on the ties that bind the poet to his homeland, his youth, the land's milk, food, drinks, soil, rain, dew, and trees. The traveler or wanderer is sad, worried, distressed, sleepless, lonely, and filled with longing. These feelings are manifestations of the poet's rootedness, loyalty, and nobility. The longing for the homeland connects to the formulaic *wuqūf ʿalā l-aṭlāl* (the conventional scene of the ruined abodes) in the pre-Islamic *qaṣīda* which continued to be popular in later times. The ruined abode, the *ṭalal*, is the lost home, the reminder of times past.

Some poets, however, did the opposite – they attacked their homelands or the cities in which they dwelled. This negative attitude to the homeland was often the flip side of praising a certain place. Praising or longing for the past place would be coupled with a shunning of the present place where the poet or littérateur is unfortunate, unhappy, and feels like an alien or a stranger. In fact praise and censure are frequently joined in Arabic literature, evident in the surviving Arabic compilations of *al-maḥāsin wa-l-masāwiʾ* (merits and faults).[4] These compilations naturally couple censure with praise. Some of the books of *al-ḥanīn ilā l-awṭān* do the same by including chapters such as *madḥ al-firāq* (praise of separation) along with *dhamm al-firāq* (censure of separation), *taḥsīn al-ghurba* (beautifying alienation) along with *taqbīḥ al-ghurba* (uglifying alienation). In these chapters where the act of leaving a place is praised, the homeland is redefined as "the place where you land."[5] This naturally challenges the idea that departure from the place of birth rids one of his family and friends. All friends, neighbors, lovers, and towns are replaceable. Lands are equal and the same and it is the seeking of livelihood, profit, money, fortune, success, riches, and abundance that is encouraged. Travel brings renewal, "*fa-ightarib tatajaddadi*", to use the words of Abū Tammām (d. 231/845),[6] while remaining in one's homeland becomes a sign of laziness. Travel is a means of escaping debasement, humiliation, hardship, oppression, and tyranny. It is freedom, a way to pursue virtue and to satisfy curiosity.[7]

Poets utilized these ready motifs for various purposes in their poems. The same idea can be looked at in opposing ways depending on the context. Beatrice Gruendler follows the historical development of the genre and illustrates some of the themes and attitudes found in anthologies of *al-ḥanīn ilā l-awṭān*. She focuses on the divided and shifting positions on geographical origin as they manifest in the shape of the home, the changing home, the choice to leave home, the idea of the universal home, freedom and ambivalence, as well as mobility and exile.[8]

The City as Patron

The notion of home as a poet's place of birth, his tribal ground, or the tribal ground of his beloved was expanded in the Umayyad period to include cities in response to the recent sociopolitical changes seen throughout the Islamic world. The poet in the high courts of the Abbasid caliphs played a double role: he was a public figure – the caliph's council, boon companion, and mouthpiece on one hand – and a private persona for whom the poet himself was solely responsible, on the other. The two were not always reconciled. A city like Baghdad was the stage upon which poets proved themselves professionally, the craft of poetry at this point becoming more clearly a profession fraught with politics, competitiveness, and rivalry. The city in this dynamic was largely equivalent to the patron, the caliph or the emir himself. Entry and exit to and from the city were basically entry and exit to and from the patron's presence and favors. A poet's relationship to the city was therefore scripted and restrained by the etiquette of the court. Poets walked a tightrope in their relationship with patrons and their cities, careful to make amends if necessary, as we see in Abū Tammām's incident with the *qāḍī* of Baghdād, Ibn Abī Du'ād. Inadvertently insulting the *qāḍī's* tribe, Abū Tammām composed two poems in order to re-enter the favor of the slighted patron and reconcile himself with the city of Baghdād.[9]

أتاني عائرُ الأنباءِ تَسْري
عقاربه بداهية نآدِ

...

بأنّي نلتُ من مضر وخبّت
إليك شكيّتي خببَ الجَوادِ

وما ربعُ القطيعةِ لي بربَعٍ
ولا نادي الأذى منّي بنادي

وأين يجورُ عن قَصْدٍ لساني
وقلبي رائحٌ برضاكَ غادي[10]

Stray news came to me creeping like scorpions
warning of great calamity,

...

> That I had marred the reputation of Muḍar and that my accusation
> galloped to you with the speed of a swift steed.
>
> I am not of those who seek rifts,
> nor do I frequent the circles of harm.
>
> How could my tongue do wrong intentionally,
> when my heart sets out, night and day, seeking your consent?[11]

A city was not a home, rather it was a stage upon which the poet either succeeded or failed. It held the potential of both protection and estrangement.

In Search of a Living

With the weakening of the Abbasid Empire, poets' connections – nearly equivalent to bondage – to the centers of caliphal power such as Baghdād began to weaken. The proliferation of courts in the fourth and fifth century of Islam and the rise of the phenomenon of the career poet are factors that made the relationship of poets to the cities they visited transitory. Exiting a city and its court was no longer as perilous or as consequential as exiting the court of the great caliphs.[12] The itinerant poet was expected to travel among different courts and did not feel compelled by loyalty or a sense of belonging that would have prevented him from lampooning the city he left. The biography of al-Mutanabbī (d. 354/965) illustrates this continuous travel in search of patronage and glory. The theme of rejection of a home occurs frequently in his poetry. In an ode sent from Egypt to his Ḥamdānid patron, Sayf al-Dawla (r. 333–56/944–67) in Aleppo, he says:

بِمَ التّعَلّلُ لا أهْلٌ وَلا وَطَنُ
وَلا نَديمٌ وَلا كأسٌ وَلا سَكَنُ

أُريدُ مِنْ زَمَني ذا أنْ يُبَلّغَني
مَا لَيسَ يبْلُغُهُ من نَفسِهِ الزّمَنُ

لا تَلْقَ دَهْرَكَ إلاّ غَيرَ مُكتَرِثٍ
ما دامَ يَصْحَبُ فيهِ رُوحَكَ البَدنُ

فَمَا يُديمُ سُرُورٌ ما سُرِرْتَ بِهِ
وَلا يَرُدّ عَلَيكَ الفَائِتَ الحَزَنُ[13]

> What to hold on to? There is no kin, no home,
> no companion, no goblet, and no refuge.

I want this time of mine to make me achieve
what time itself has not achieved.

As long as the body accompanies your soul,
prepare to meet your destiny with nonchalance

Your joy in things does not make them persist
nor does your sorrow bring back that which has passed.

Al-Mutanabbī eventually found shelter in Egypt in the Ikshided court of Kāfūr (r. 334–57/946–68) and, when he fled, his poem attacking Kāfūr was also an attack on Egypt and its people. He says:

أكُلّمَا اغتَالَ عَبدُ السّوْءِ سَيّدَهُ
أوْ خَانَهُ فَلَهُ في مصرَ تَمْهِيدُ

صَارَ الخَصِيّ إمَامَ الآبِقِينَ بِهَا
فالحُرّ مُسْتَعْبَدٌ وَالعَبْدُ مَعْبُودُ

نَامَتْ نَوَاطِيرُ مصرَ عَنْ ثَعَالِبِها
فَقَدْ بَشِمْنَ وَما تَفنى العَنَاقيدُ[14]

Whenever a wicked slave assassinates his master
or betrays him, has he to get his training in Egypt?

There, the eunuch has become the chieftain of the runaway slaves.
The free man is enslaved, and the slave is obeyed.

The gardeners of Egypt are asleep to the tricks of its foxes,
which have gotten bloated, and yet the grape-clusters are not at an end.

When al-Mutanabbī found refuge in Bawwān, a valley near Shīrāz, he still found himself a stranger:

وَلَكِنّ الفَتى العَرَبيّ فِيهَا
غَرِيبُ الوَجْهِ وَاليَدِ وَاللّسَانِ[15]

The Arab finds himself a stranger [in Bawwān]
in features, actions, and speech.

The City and its People

Natives of cities define their cities in many ways and visitors experience a city or a region not only by sightseeing or benefiting from the generosity of its ruler, but also by interacting with its inhabitants. The judge

Abū ᶜAlī al-Musabbikhī/Musabbiḥī (d. before fifth/eleventh century) did not enjoy his tenure in Sijistān and composed a few lines describing his feelings:

حُلولي سِجستان إحدى النّوبْ
وكوني بها من عجيب العَجبْ

وما بسجستان من طائلٍ
سوى حُسن نرجسها والرُّطَبْ[16]

My arrival in Sijistān is a misfortune
And my stay in it is the strangest of things.

Sijistān is of no avail
Except for its narcissus and ripe dates

Al-Musabbikhī/al-Musabbiḥī interestingly excludes the *amīr* from this attack:

يا سجستان قد بَلوناكِ دهرًا
في حراميك من كلا طَرَفيكِ

أنتِ لولا الأمير فينا لقُلنا:
لعنَ اللهُ من يَصيرُ إليكِ[17]

Sijistān, we have long been afflicted

by the protection of your spaces from one end to the other
Had the *amīr* not been with [amongst] us,
we would have cursed everyone who dwells in you

The Andalusian poet Ibn Bāqī (d. 545/1150) says, describing the city of Sevilla (Ishbīlya):

أَقَمْتُ فِيكُمْ عَلَى الإِقْتَارِ وَالعَدَمِ
لَوْ كُنْتُ حُرًّا أَبِيَّ النَّفْسِ لَمْ أُقِمِ

فَلاَ حَدِيقَتُكُمْ يُجْنَى لَهَا ثَمَرٌ
وَلاَ سَمَاءُكُمْ تَنْهَلُّ بِالدِّيَمِ

أَنَا امْرُؤٌ إِنْ نَبَتْ بِي أَرْضُ أَنْدَلُسٍ
جِئْتُ العِرَاقَ فَقَامَتْ لِي عَلَى قَدَمِ

مَا العَيْشُ بِالعِلْمِ إِلاَّ حِيلَةٌ ضَعُفَتْ
وَحِرْفَةٌ وُكِلَتْ بِالقُعْدُدِ البَرِمِ[18]

I stayed in your midst for want and destitution.
Had I been wellborn and self-respecting, I would not have stayed
Your gardens yield no fruit;
your skies pour no rain

Yet, I have merit, and if al-Andalus turns me out,
Iraq will embrace me.

Prospering here by one's intellectual abilities has become a base practice,
a craft entrusted to miserly upstarts.

Similarly Badr al-Dīn al-Ghazzī (d. 984/1577), in his travelogue about his journey from Damascus to Istanbul, describes in a few epigrams the inhospitality of the inhabitants of the city of Baᶜlabakk: they have denied him any food to break his fast in the holy month of Ramaḍān:

شهر الصيام كريم
والبخل فيكم سجيّه

هبنا نصوم نهارًا
أليس تأتي العشيّه[19]

Generous is the month of fasting,
miserliness is a nature in you.

Suppose we fast the day.
Isn't there an evening?

A city can also be attacked for the corruption of its people. Badr al-Dīn al-Ghazzī quotes the following lines in description of the Syrian city of Ḥamā:

عمّ الفساد حمى حماة فمردها
ورجالها ونسائهنّ جميعا

شبه النواعير التي يهوونها
من مسّه العاصي يدور سريعا[20]

Corruption has prevailed in Ḥamā.
Its adolescents, men, and women
are just like the noria they love.
Touched by the Orontes, they are fast to spin.

A humorous account is that of Abū Nukhayla (d. 145/762) who attacked the people of Yemen for being ugly, finding himself the most handsome amongst them despite his well-known ugliness:

لم أرَ غيري حسنا
منذ دخلت اليمنا

فيا شقاء بلدةٍ
أحسنُ من فيها أنا![21]

I have not seen a good looking person
since I entered Yemen.

How wretched is a city
in which I am the most handsome!

In Search of an Etymology

The attack on cities can take the form of humorous caricatures that play on ethnic political and social stereotypes and can become a poetic exercise for poets. Not only does an invective as such announce a poet's moving on and journeying away, it also allows him a space to perform his abilities in portraying the flaws (*masāwiʾ*) as much as he probably would have portrayed the beauties (*maḥāsin*) of a city and its court. In their attacks on cities, poets often used puns or forged etymologies that play with the city's name. The new name or the forged etymology defined the nature of the city. Bukhārā was a common target, the result of the pun on the trilateral root *kha-ra-ya* which the name of the city shares with the word *kharā* (excretion/shit). Consider for example the three lines by the Khorasanian Abū l-Ṭayyib al-Ṭāhirī (d. *ca.* 321/933), who served the Sāmānid in public and disparaged them in private, mentioned in *Yatīmat al-dahr* of al-Thaᶜālibī:

بخارى من خَرًى لا شكَّ فيه
يَعِزُّ بربعِها الشيءُ النظيفُ

فإن قُلْتَ: الأميرُ بها مقيمٌ
فذا من فَخْرِ مُفتَخِرٍ ضَعيفُ

إذا كان الأميرُ خَرًا فقل لي
أليسَ الخُرءُ موضِعُه الكنيفُ[22]

Bukhārā is derived from shit, no doubt.
Clean things are scarce in its quarters.

If you say: The *amīr* resides in it,
this boast is weak.

For if the *amīr* is shit then tell me:
Isn't the toilet the proper place for shit?

According to al-Thaᶜālibī, the motif was then picked up by Aḥmad b. Abī Bakr, who composed two lines attacking Bukhārā, saying:

لو الفرسُ العتيقُ أتى بخارى
لصارَ بطبعِه فيها حمارا

فلم تَرَ مِثلَها عيني كَنيفًا
تبوّأه أميرُ الشرق دارا[23]

If the noble horse visits Bukhārā,
his nature will become that of a donkey.

My eyes have never seen a toilet
become the mansion of the *amīr* of the east.

As an anthologist, al-Thaᶜālibī seems to have found these examples funny and he quotes several others including al-Gharbyāmī's (d. fifth/eleventh-century) lines:

ما بلدة منتنة من خرا
وأهلها في جوفها دود

تلك بخارى من بخار الخرى
يضيع فيها النَدّ والعود[24]

There is no other stinking town made of shit (*kharā*).
Its people are worms.

Bukhārā, the name is derived from the vapor of shit.
Lost in it are [the scents of] incense and agar wood.

And these lines by the Sāmānid poet Abū ᶜAlī al-Sājī (d. before 430/1038):

باءُ بخارى فاعلمنّ زائده
والألفُ الأولى بلا فائِده

فهي خرًا محضٌ وسكّانُها
كالطيرِ في أقفاصِها آبده[25]

The "b" in Bukhārā is superfluous
and the first alif has no function.

It is pure shit (*kharā*).
Its people are birds sitting in cages all year round.

Bukhārā was unfortunate with its name but other poets had more things to say about it beyond these puns. Al-Thaᶜālibī includes a number of these epigrams:

Al-Mutanabbī says:

بخارى كلّ شيء منك
يا شوهاء مقلوب

قضاة الناس ركّاب
فلم قاضيك مركوب[26]

Bukhāra, everything in you
is deformed and inverted.

Judges normally ride.
Why is your judge ridden?

While the Sāmānid poet Abū Manṣūr al-ᶜAbdūnī (d. before 430/1038) says:

إذا ما بلاد الله طاب نسيمها
وفاحت لدى الأسحار ريح البنفسج

رأيت بخارى جيفة الأرض كلّها
كأنّك منها قاعد وسط مخرج

فيا رب أصلح أهلها وانف نتنها
وإلّا فعنها ربّ حوّل وفرّج[27]

When the fresh air of God's land carries the good smell,
the scent of violet spreads at the early mornings.

I see Bukhārā's land all a corpse,
as if one is sitting in the middle of a way out

Oh Lord, amend its people and clean its rot.
Otherwise, Oh Lord, turn me away from it and set me free

This search for a new etymology was not restricted to Bukhārā. Consider the following epigram by physician Muḥammad b. ᶜAlī b. Rifāᶜā (d. seventh/thirteenth century) attacking the city of Sharīsh in al-Andalus (Jerez de la Frontera)

شريش ما أنت إلّا
تصحيف شرّ يبين

فارحل فديتك عنها
إن كنت ممن تدين

فقلّما ساد فيها
حرّ ولا من يُعين[28]

Sharīsh, you are nothing
but a distortion of *sharr yabīn* (evident evil)

Leave it! I would sacrifice myself for you
if you were one who believes.

For rarely it is ruled by a free man
or anyone of any use.

The scathing attacks on cities, as we see above, reveal what one might describe as a rivalry between poets and cities. A poet would relate to a city on an individual level, and as such, it was possible to triumph over a city. This is also why attacking a city, or even insulting it, would carry a direct and almost personal tone. The poet here still envisions his persona and that of the city as equals. That relationship, however, dramatically changes with time. The poet's persona shrinks in comparison to that of the city, which transforms from a situation that can be entered and exited into a prevailing state of mind, persistent and insurmountable.

MODERN PERSPECTIVES

The Urban Scene: From Freedom to Exile

The relative freedom poets enjoyed in the premodern period resulting from the availability of options develops into something less like freedom and more like exile in the modern era. Twentieth-century modernism in the Arabic tradition, as is the case in other traditions, exhibited a continued, likely now more urgent, questioning of the poet's role and status in society and the world. This self-interrogation posed fundamental questions that afflicted great modernist poets such as T. S. Eliot and Wallace Stevens,[29] as it did Arab modernist poets such as Adūnīs (b. 1930), Badr Shākir al-Sayyāb (1926–64), ᶜAbd al-Wahhāb al-Bayyātī (1926–99), Ṣalāḥ ᶜAbd al-Ṣabūr (1931–81) and others. The urban scene, with all its contradictions and possibilities, provided the perfect landscape for this quest for variance, for voice, and for poetry in a now "deeply *unpoetical* age."[30]

Scholars have often pointed to the centrality of the city in the formulation of a modernist poetic aesthetic.[31] The urban scene provided a space fitting for the modernist project's quest of reformulating the past and shaping it anew. The international modernist movement, whose influences on the Arab modernist experience have been extensively studied,[32] was rooted in cities,[33] in a landscape that defied the ideals of beauty and inspiration in the traditional sense. In its response to the changing cosmography of the post-industrial revolution city, the modern poetic aesthetic broke away from traditionally accepted ideals and expectations. Wordsworth bemoans this fact in his *Preface to the Lyrical Ballads*, when he describes as "generally evil" the poetry resulting from the "increasing accumulation of men in cities" and their "craving for the extraordinary incident" and the "degrading thirst for outrageous stimulation."[34] "Modernism" in literature is overwhelmingly of an urban aesthetic and the modern poet, as Santilli puts it, becomes "a participant and a protagonist in the ongoing work of constructing and deconstructing the city."[35] In the Arabic context, poetic modernism was part of a larger socio-political, intellectual, and aesthetic movement that emanated out of major urban centers such as Beirut, Cairo, Damascus, and Baghdād.[36]

The city, thus, features as one of the prominent themes of modern poetry[37] as well as a formal or architectural model upon which the modern poem is built.[38] The city, with its streets "that follow like tedious argument,"[39] its windows, the "black or luminous squares"[40] where life is lived, its comings and goings, its interplay of private and public, of old and new, provides a structural example for the modernist poem. The maze of the urban landscape, which is in constant flux, is a reflection of and an inspiration for the new forms of modernist poetry which are always in the making, as well. In that sense, the city is not only an inspiration for modern poetry, it is a manifestation of its aesthetic; an aesthetic that emerges from the ordinary, the mundane, and the man-made.

The Poet against the Corrupt City

Despite the debt the modern poem owes to the city, the relationship of the modern poet to the city is not always one of gratitude. On the contrary, the modern poets often position themselves "against" the city. The urban landscape, its noise, and its web of relationships, is the necessary backdrop against which the poets find a voice, which they then often use to attack the city, bemoaning its tyranny and complaining of its apathy. In the Arabic free verse movement, and especially in its Tammūzī[41] dimension, a poetic project that drew on ancient Near Eastern mythology to signal the urgent need for a regeneration of Arab culture, poets engaged the city as the site of the anticipated rebirth. The city therefore became a metaphor for the oppressive and corrupt world order that has to be destroyed and overcome. Al-Sayyāb expresses his loathing for the city which only suffocates him and intensifies his nostalgia for the city's Other, his childhood village, Jaykūr:

وتلتفّ حولي دروب المدينة
حبالا من الطين يمضغن قلبي
ويعطين عن جمرة فيه طينة
حبالا من النار يجلدن عرى الحقول الحزينة
يحرقن جيكور في قاع روحي
ويزرعن فيها رماد الضغينة. [42]

> The streets of the city coil around me,
> ropes of mud chewing on my heart,
> rendering its coals into mud,
> ropes of fire that whip the seams of
> grieving fields,
> scorching Jaykūr in the depth of my soul
> planting there only ashes and rancor.

Al-Sayyāb is a poet who never abandoned his childhood yearnings, remaining forever a stranger in the urban scene. His view is therefore fraught with nostalgia and a sense of loss. The city to him is a monster, a noose, a burning fire:

هنا لا طير في الأغصان تشدو غير أطيار
من الفولاذ تهدر أو تحمحم دونما خوف من المطر
و لا أزهار إلا خلف واجهة زجاجيّة
يراح إلى المقابر والسجون بهنّ والمستشفيات.[43]

Here, no birds sing in trees.
Here, only steel birds roar and snicker, fearless of rain.
Here flowers are only
in shop windows;
only flowers to be carried to graveyards, prisons,
and hospitals.

Nevertheless the awaited rebirth could only take place in the wasteland of the city. There is no road to a better world, no road to Jaykūr, that does not pass through the city, the site upon which the poet and his people will endure the pain of deliverance. The opening of al-Sayyāb's poem "*Al-masīḥ baᶜd al-ṣalb*" (Christ after the Crucifixion), delineates the poet's unavoidable relationship to the oblivious apathetic city:

بعدما أنزلوني سمعت الرياح
في نواح طويل تسف النخيل
والخطى وهي تنأى إذن فالجراح
والصليب الذي سمّروني عليه طوال الأصيل
لم تمتني وأنصتّ كان العويل
يعبر السهل بيني وبين المدينة
مثل حبل يشدّ السفينة
وهي تهوي إلى القاع كان النواح
مثل خيط من النور بين الصباح
والدجى في سماء الشتاء الحزينة
ثم تغفو على ما تحسّ المدينة.[44]

After they brought me down, I heard the winds
in a lengthy wail, lashing the palm trees,
and steps fading away. So then, my wounds,
And the cross upon which they nailed me all afternoon and evening,
did not kill me. I listened. The wailing
crossed the plain between me and the city
like a rope pulling at a ship
as it sinks to the bottom. The wailing
was a thread of light between dawn and midnight,
in the grieving winter sky.
And the city sleeps on what she senses.

The modern poet no longer inhabits the city, the city inhabits him, and it becomes an extension of his phobias and his frustrations. Robyn Creswell notes that "avoidance of the city is as characteristic of Arabic modernism as the immersion into urban life is to so many of its precursors."[45] Despite its overwhelming presence in the poems of the Arab modernist, the city is unreal, its objects are absent, and its landscape is missing. This is especially true in the poetry of Khalīl Ḥāwī, who had a propensity for the abstract and the allegorical. Beirut to Ḥāwī is "the swamp,"[46] "the whorehouse,"[47] the "bier of the drunk,"[48] "cold hell,"[49] the existentially taunting other:

نحن لم نخلع ولم نلبس وجوه
نحن من بيروت، مأساة ولدنا
بوجوه وعقول مستعاره
تولد الفكرة في السوق بغيًا
ثم تقضي العمر في لفق البكارة.[50]

We did not take off or put on faces.
We are from Beirut. We were born
a tragedy with fake faces and minds.
The idea is born a whore in the market,
then wastes her life faking virginity.

The City as Metaphor

It is worth noting here that the city in much of al-Sayyāb's work is an abstract unnamed city, a stand-in for all cities, Arab and non-Arab. It is the city as metaphor for all the dilemmas a modernist poet faces, among them his problematic place in society, his relationship with the tradition and his language's poetic memory, and his quest for a "new" poetic voice. Other modernist Arab poets have addressed specific cities by name, presenting scathing descriptions of them and expressing an overwhelming frustration with them as adversaries. The city becomes the poet's adversary, his nemesis almost. Aḥmad ʿAbd al-Muʿṭī Ḥijāzī's (b. 1935) entire collection *Madīna bilā qalb* (A Heartless City) is a case in point. In a poem titled *Al-ṭarīq ilā al-sayyida* (The Road to al-Sayyida), the poet resents Cairo, which reduces him to "nothing." Similar to al-Sayyāb in the quotations above, Ḥijāzī seeks deliverance from the city. The poem ends with a prayer-like repetition, insisting on the direction and destination of this city stroll, the mausoleum of al-Sayyida Zaynab.[51]

يا قاهرة
أيا قبابًا متخمات قاعدة
يا مئذنات ملحدة

يا كافرة
أنا هنا، لا شيء كالموتى، كرؤيا عابرة
أجرّ ساقي المجهدة
للسيده
للسيده.[52]

O Cairo!
Your overstuffed heavy domes,
your heretic minarets,
you blasphemer.
I, here, am nothing,
like the dead, like a passing vision.
I drag my tired feet
towards *al-sayyida,*
towards *al-sayyida.*

Nevertheless, escaping the city proves impossible. To be delivered from the city, the poet must ensure its deliverance as well. The city is thus no longer a physical place that the poet cannot leave but rather a metaphor that haunts the poet and travels with him. The modern poet is the seer, the prophet, the Christ-like figure, and the political activist who is no longer capable of absolving himself of the ills of the city. Its sins are his and he is on a mission to change the world or simply dream of a better one. In a poem titled "*ᶜUyūn*" (Eyes), Ḥijāzī turns the openness of a port city into a prison. The noise renders him voiceless; the masses only exaggerate his loneliness. He resigns to dreaming of life instead of living it, or envisioning a city instead of engaging with it:

لأنني أعيش في ميناء
أحار من تعدد الأجناس واللغات والأزياء
فأرقب الحياة صامتا
مكبل الحنين
كأنني بيني وبين الناس قضبان
كأني سجين
أشير، أحلم الحياة لأعيشها.[53]

Because I live in a port,
the many races, languages and fashions, confuse me.
Silently I watch life.
My nostalgia fettered,
as if iron bars keep me from others,

like a prisoner.
I point to life, I dream it
in order to live it.

Even though Ḥijāzī addresses Cairo by name, it is not only Cairo with which he is concerned. He addresses the abstract allegorical city that is at the center of his poetic experience. In fact, the city in the works of most modern Arab poets is the dream of the city. It is the hope of the city which forever clashes with its reality. This is why a poet like Adūnīs finds himself in perpetual exile. In his poem "Rīshat al-ghurāb" (The Crow's Feather), Adūnīs walks the city streets but it does not acknowledge him. He remains alone and it remains elusive and inaccessible:

من مغرب الشمس إلى ضُحاها
أعبر بيروتَ ولا أراها
أسكن بيروت ولا أراها
وحدي أنا والحبّ والثمارْ
نمضي مع النهارْ
نمضي إلى سواها.[54]

From sunset to sunrise,
I cross Beirut and I do not see it,
I inhabit Beirut and I do not see it.
Alone, with love and fruit.
We pass along with the day.
We move on to another.

The aloof and inaccessible Beirut that Adūnīs portrays above is exaggerated and allegorized in Khalīl Hāwī's (1919–82) poem "*Layālī Beirut*" (Beirut Nights). Beirut in Hāwī's poetic world is Eliot's London, Baudelaire's Paris, Sayyāb's Baghdad, and Ḥijāzī's Cairo. It is also Babel, Sodom, Rome; it is the abstract city; it is every city in its alienating effect on the poet:

"إنَّ في بيروتَ دنيا غيرَ دنيا"
"الكَدحِ والمَوتِ الرتيبْ"
"إنَّ فيها حانةً مسحورةً،"
"خمرًا، سريرًا مِن طيوبْ"
"للحيارى"
في متاهات الصحارَى،
في الدهاليزِ اللعينَهْ

ومواخيرِ المدينَهْ
(...)
مَن يقوّينا على حملِ الصليبْ
كيف نَنجُو مِن غِواياتِ الذنوبْ
والجَريمَهْ؟[55]

"In Beirut there is a world that is not the world,
toil and monotonous death.
There are enchanted taverns,
wine, and a bed of flavors,
for the confused"
In the mazes of the deserts,
in the cursed corridors
and the whorehouses of the city,
... who will give us strength to bear the cross,
Who will save us from the temptation of sin and crime?

As much as the city allows the poet freedom, anonymity, and inspiration, it also threatens and ostracizes him. The city, as Joyce puts it, is where "no-one is anything."[56] It is where the coming together of opposites, no matter how exhilarating, constantly confronts the poet with his indispensability and with the fragility and fortuity of his connection with his surroundings. In a poem titled "*Maqhā fī Bayrūt*" (A Café in Beirut), Muḥammad al-Māghūṭ (1934–2006) states: "Nothing connects me to this land but the shoe."[57] And there is no poet better at embracing the oppressive presence of the city than al-Māghūṭ. His poetic persona is the *flâneur* par excellence, the loiterer, the city hobo. In al-Māghūṭ's work the city does not offer the poet much more than the asphalt of sidewalks (*al-raṣīf)* and does not allow him the freedom to do more than loiter (*al-tasakkuᶜ*). Damascus, "the rosy caravan of women taken captive,"[58] was the homeland with which al-Māghūṭ struggled, and ultimately rejected. And, although Beirut was his exile and his haven, he was not blind to its ugly face. Both Beirut and Damascus are but two manifestations of the same abstract city with which his contemporaries were preoccupied. Despite the specific street names, a walk in Beirut is the same as a walk in any other city. It is a metaphor for the poet's perpetual marginality:

من «بلس إلى جان دارك
من «جان دارك إلى بلس»
رفعت يدي مئات المرات

محيّيًا مئات الأشخاص
باليد التي تكتب
والتي تجوع.
...
من «جان دارك إلى بلس»
ومن بلس إلى جان دارك»
سرت ملايين الكيلومترات المرصوفة فوق بعضها
رأيت أطنانا من النساء والخادمات
تأملت النقود البرية
والحلوة الهادرة تحت الجسور
تأملت أصابع النادل الرفيعة
وهي تمسح دموعي عن الطاولة كالحساء.[59]

From Bliss to Jeanne d 'Arc,
from Jeanne d 'Arc to Bliss,
I raise my hand hundreds of times
to greet hundreds of people
with the same hand that eats
and writes
and goes hungry
...
From Jeanne d'Arc to Bliss
and from Bliss to Jeanne d' Arc,
I have walked for thousands of paved kilometers
and seen tons of women and maids.
I have stared at wild currencies
and candy roaring under bridges.
I have watched the slender fingers of a waiter
as he wiped my tears off the table like soup.

Poets' relationship with the city and their perception of that relationship develop in ways that reflect their changing perception of their role and place in society. It is role that develops from that of the hero, to the group's voice and representative, to the career poet resigned to playing a circumscribed role in the social and political system, and finally to the alienated outsider looking in. The city itself, in light of this evolving perception, transforms into an ethos. The city is no longer a situation or a relationship that the poet can choose to leave. It becomes an embodiment of the modern poet's anxieties and frustrations with the world.

Notes

The decision to format the references as they appear throughout this chapter is solely that of the editors and the publishers.

1. Bencheikh (1975: 24–5). Tarif Khalidi surveys a wide spectrum of views of the Islamic city drawing from Qurʾānic and prophetic tradition material, works of geography, *adab*, philosophy, and history (1981: 265–76).
2. For the theme of lamenting cities in pre-modern Arabic literature, see Bāshā (2003) and al-Sūdānī (1999: 15–120).
3. Check, for example, al-Thaᶜālibī (2011: 2–3).
4. A model example is *al-Maḥāsin wa-l-masāwiʾ* (The Book of Beauties and Imperfections) of Ibrāhīm b. Muḥammad al-Bayhaqī (d. fourth/tenth century). Al-Thaᶜālibī's *Taḥsīn al-qabīḥ wa-taqbīḥ al-ḥasan* (Beautifying the Ugly and Uglifying the Beautiful), *al-Yawāqīt fī baᶜḍ al-mawāqīt* (The Book of the Precious Stones on Some Fixed Times and Places), and *al-Ẓarāʾif wa-l-laṭāʾif* (The Book of Amusing and Curious Stories Concerning the Praise of Things and Their Opposites) similarly treat the same topic. On this genre, see van Gelder (2003: 321–51).
5. See for example the epigrams cited in Ibn al-Marzubān (1987: 59–61).
6. Al-Thaᶜālibī (2011: 80).
7. For *al-Ḥanīn ilā l-awṭān*, see Qadi (1999: 3–31); Müller (1999: 33–58); Arazi (1993: 287–327); Rosenthal (1997: 35–75); Bauer (2001: 85–105). For a list of chapters and anthologies of *al-Ḥanīn ilā l-awṭān* with a more comprehensive list of secondary sources, see the editor's introduction of al-Thaᶜālibī (2011).
8. See Gruendler (2016: 1–41).
9. Al-Ṣūlī (1937: 146). Also see Raymond Farrin's reading of Abū Tammām's poem No. 37 and the complicated politics of apology, supplication, and praise. Farrin (2003: 221–51).
10. Abū Tammām (1997: 1: 215).
11. Based on a translation by Farrin (2003: 224).
12. See Orfali (forthcoming).
13. Al-Mutanabbī (1936: 4: 233–9). Quoted by Gruendler (2016: 20). See the same page for more examples on rejecting homeland in al-Mutanabbī's poetry.
14. Al-Mutanabbī (1936: 2: 42–3).
15. Ibid. (4: 251).
16. Al-Thaᶜālibī (1956: 4: 147).
17. Ibid. (4: 147).

18. Quoted and translated (with modification) in Farrin (2011: 216).
19. Badr al-Dīn al-Ghazzī (n. d.: 30).
20. Ibid. (40).
21. Ibn ᶜAbd Rabbih (1962: 6: 449).
22. Al-Thaᶜālibī (1956: 4: 70).
23. Ibid. (4: 70).
24. Ibid. (4: 71).
25. Ibid. (4: 71).
26. Ibid. (4: 71).
27. Ibid. (4: 71).
28. Ṣafadī (2000: 4: 115). See also, Ibn Saᶜīd al-Maghribī (1964: 306).
29. See Baker (1986: 3) and Wellek (1971: 261–3).
30. "Reflect too, as I cannot but do here more and more, in spite of all the nonsense people say, how deeply *unpoetical* the age and all of one's surroundings are. Not unprofound, not ungrand, not unmoving: *unpoetical*." Matthew Arnold (1993: 52).
31. It is worth noting here that the modernist movements in Arabic poetry, both that of the twentieth century (The Free Verse movement) and that of the ninth century (the Abbasid *muḥdath* project), are urban phenomena closely tied to and rooted in urban centers: twentieth-century Beirut and ninth-century Baghdad. For more on the urban sensibility of the Abbasid *muḥdath* poet see: Ḍayf (n. d.: 9–88) and the section titled: "L'attriance bagdadienne" (The Attraction of Baghdad) in Bencheikh (1975: 19–24). For more on the centrality of Beirut to the twentieth-century modernist movement in Arabic poetry, see for example: Creswell (2013).
32. Many studies have focused on the centrality of the Western influence on the modernist movement in Arabic literature. Here are a few examples: Azouqa (2008: 38–71); Faḍḍūl (1992); Shāhīn (1991); Moreh (1976); Abdel-Hai (1972: 72–89); El-Azma (1968: 671–8).
33. Harding (2003: x).
34. Wordsworth (1957: 117).
35. Santilli (2002: 182).
36. Shboul (2005: 61).
37. Ismāᶜīl (1967: 326).
38. Santilli (2002: 183).
39. Eliot (1954: 11).
40. Baudelaire (2009: 74).
41. For more on the ethos of this movement and its cultural project see: El-Azma (1968: 671–8).
42. al-Sayyāb (1971: 1: 41).

43. Ibid. (255).
44. Khalidi (2016: 117–19).
45. Creswell (2013: 101).
46. Ḥāwī (1972: 64).
47. Ibid. (24).
48. Ibid. (37).
49. Ibid. (43).
50. Ibid. (112–13).
51. *Al-Sayyida* is a reference to the Mosque of al-Sayyida Zaynab, named for the granddaughter of the Prophet Mohammad. The mosque and the mausoleum are located in the square in the heart of Cairo.
52. Ḥijāzī (1959: 118).
53. Ibid. (231–2).
54. Adūnīs (1970: 193).
55. Joyce (1993: 157).
56. Al-Māghūṭ (1964: 56).
57. Al-Maghūt (1959: 30).
58. Al-Māghūṭ (1964: 56–63).

Works Cited

Abdel-Hai, M. (1972), "Shelley and the Arabs: An Essay in Comparative Literature," *Journal of Arabic Literature* 3: 72–89.

Abū Tammām (1997), *Dīwān Abī Tammām*, Muḥyī al-Dīn Ṣubḥī (ed.), Beirut, Dār Ṣādir.

Adūnīs (1970), *Aghānī Mihyār al-Dimashqī*, Beirut: Manshūrāt Mawāqif.

Arazi, A. (1993), "*al-Ḥanīn ilā al-awṭān* entre la Ǧāhiliyya et l'Islam: Le Bédouin et le citadin réconciliés," *Zeitschrift der deutschen morgenländischen Gesellschaft* 143, 287–327.

Arnold, Matthew (1993), *Selected Letters of Matthew Arnold*, Clinton Machann and Forrest Burt (eds), London: Macmillan.

El-Azma, Nazeer (1968), "The Tammūzī Movement and the Influence of T. S. Eliot on Badr Shākir al-Sayyāb," *Journal of the American Oriental Society* 88.4: 671–8.

Azouqa, Aida (2008), "Metapoetry between East and West: ʿAbd al-Wahhāb al-Bayyātī and the Western composers of Metapoetry: A Study of Analogies," *Journal of Arabic Literature* 39: 38–71.

Baker, Dorothy (1986), *Mythic Masks in Self-Reflexive Poetry: A Study of Pan and Orpheus*, Chapel Hill: University of North Carolina Press.

Bāshā, Muhja Amīn (2003), *Rithā*ʾ *al-mudun wa-l-mamālik fī l-shi*ʿ*r al-andalusī*, Damascus: Shirāʿ li-l-Dirāsāt wa-l-Nashr.

Baudelaire, Charles (2009), *Paris Spleen*, trans. Keith Waldrop, Middletown CT: Wesleyan University Press.

Bauer, T. (2001), "Fremdheit in der klassischen arabischen Kultur und Sprache," in Brigitte Jostes and Jürgen Trabant (eds), *Fremdes in fremden Sprachen*, München: W. Fink, , 85–105.

Bencheikh, Jamel-Eddine (1975), "Poétique Arabe: essai sur les voies d'une creation," Paris: Éditions Anthropos.

—— (1975), *Poétique arabe: précédée de essai sur un discours critique*, Paris: Éditions Anthropos.

Creswell, Robyn (2013), *Tradition and Translation: Poetic Modernism in Beirut*, unpublished PhD thesis, New York University.

Ḍayf, Shawqī (n. d.), *al-*ʿ*Aṣr al-*ʿ*Abbāsī al-Awwal*, Cairo: Dār al-Maʿārif.

Eliot, T. S. (1954), *Selected Poems*, London: Faber.

Faḍḍūl, ʿĀṭif (1992), *The Poetics of Eliot and Adūnīs*, Beirut: Al-Ḥamrā Publishers.

Farrin, Raymond (2003), "Poetics of Persuasion: Abū Tammām's Panegyric to Ibn Abī Duʾād," *Journal of Arabic Literature* 34.3: 221–51.

—— (2011), *Abundance from the Desert*, Syracuse NY: Syracuse University Press.

Al-Ghazzī, Badr al-Dīn (n. d.), *Riḥlat Badr al-Dīn al-Ghazzī ilā Isṭanbūl*, ʿAbd al-Raḥīm Abū Ḥusayn and Ṭāriq Abū Ḥusayn (eds), Istanbul: Ghurfat Tijārat Isṭanbūl

Gruendler, Beatrice (2016), "*al-Ḥanīn ilā l-awṭān* and its Alternatives in Classical Arabic Literature," in Sebastian Günther and Stephan Milich (eds), *Representations and Visions of Homeland in Modern Arabic Literature*, Hildescheim: Olms Verlag, 1–41.

Harding, Desmond (2003), *Writing the City: Urban Visions and Literary Modernism*, New York NY: Routledge.

Ḥāwī, Khalīl (1972), *Dīwān Khalīl Ḥāwī*, Beirut: Dār al-ʿAwda.

Ḥijāzī, Aḥmad ʿAbd al-Muʿṭī (1959), *Madīna bilā qalb*, Beirut: Dār al-Ādāb.

Ibn ʿAbd Rabbih (1962), *al-*ʿ*Iqd*, Aḥmad Amīn *et al.* (eds), Cairo: Lajnat al-Taʾlīf wa-l-Tarjama wa-l-Nashr.

Ibn al-Marzubān (1987), *al-Ḥanīn ilā l-awṭān*, Jalīl al-ʿAṭiyya (ed.), Beirut: ʿĀlam al-Kutub.

Ibn Saʿīd al-Maghribī (1964), *al-Mughrib fī ḥilā al-Maghrib*, Shawqī Ḍayf (ed.), Cairo: Dār al-Maʿārif.

Ismāʿīl, ʿIzz al-Dīn (1967), *Al-Shi*ʿ*r al-*ʿ*arabī al-mu*ʿ*āṣir: qaḍāyāhu wa ẓawāhiruhu*, Cairo: Dār al-Kātib al-ʿArabī.

Joyce, James (1993), *Ulysses*, Jeri Johnson (ed.), New York NY: Oxford University Press.

Khalidi, Tarif (2016), *Anthology of Arabic Literature from Classical to Modern*, Edinburgh: Edinburgh University Press.

—— (1981), "Some Classical Views of the City," in *Studia Arabica et Islamica: Festschrift for Iḥsān ʿAbbās*, Wadād al-Qāḍī (ed.), Beirut: American University of Beirut, 265–76.

Al-Māghūṭ, Muḥammad (1959), *Ḥuzn fī ḍawʾ al-qamar*, Beirut: Dār Majallat Shiʿr.

—— (1964), *Ghurfa bi-malāyīn al-judrān*, Damascus: al-Maṭbaʿa al-Qawmiyya.

Moreh, Shmuel (1976), *Modern Arabic Poetry 1800–1970: The Development of Its Forms and Themes Under the Influence of Western Literature*, Leiden: E. J. Brill.

Müller, K. (1999), "*al-Ḥanīn ilā l-awṭān* in Early *Adab* Literature," in *Myths, Historical Archetypes and Symbolic Figures in Arabic Literature*, in Angelika Neuwirth *et al.* (eds), Beirut: Franz Steiner Verlag Stuttgart, 33–58.

Al-Mutanabbī (1936), *Dīwān al-Mutanabbī bi-sharḥ Abī l-Baqāʾ al-ʿUkbarī*, M. al-Saqqā *et al.* (eds), Cairo: al-Bābī al-Ḥalabī.

Orfali, Bilal (forthcoming), "Employment Opportunities in Literature in the 4th/10th Century Islamic Courts," in Nadia al-Baghdadi and Shady Nasser (eds), *The Arab-Muslim World in Universal History: Forms of Authority, Power and Transformation. Festschrift in Honor of Aziz Al-Azmeh*, Leiden: E. J. Brill.

Qadi, W. (1999), "Dislocation and nostalgia: *al-Ḥanīn ilā l-awṭān*: Expressions of Alienation in Early Arabic Literature," in Angelika Neuwirth *et al.* (eds), *Myths, Historical Archetypes and Symbolic Figures in Arabic Literature*, Beirut: Franz Steiner Verlag Stuttgart, 3–31.

Rosenthal, F. (1997), "The Stranger in Medieval Islam," *Arabica* 44, 35–75.

Al-Ṣafadī (2000), *al-Wāfī bi-l-wafayāt*, Aḥmad al-Arnāʾūṭ and Turkī Muṣṭafā (eds), Beirut: Dār Iḥyāʾ al-Turāth al-ʿArabī.

Santilli, N. (2002), *Such Rare Citings: The Prose Poems in English Literature*, Madison WI: Associate University Presses.

Al-Sayyāb, Badr Shākir (1971), *Dīwān Badr Shakir al-Sayyāb*, Beirut: Dār al-ʿAwda.

Shāhīn, Muḥammad (1991), *Eliot wa atharuhu ʿalạ ʿAbd al-Ṣabūr wa-l-Sayyāb*, Beirut: al-Muʾassassa al-ʿArabiyya li-l-Dirāsat wa-l-Nashr.

Shboul, Ahmad (2005), "The Arab poet and the city: Modernity and alienation," *Literature & Aesthetics* 15, 59–74.

Al-Sūdānī, ʿAbdallāh ʿAbd al-Raḥīm (1999), *Rithāʾ ghayr al-insān fī l-shiʿr al-ʿabbāsī*, Abu Dhabi: al-Mujammaʿ al-Thaqāfī.

Al-Ṣūlī, Abū Bakr (1937), *Akhbār Abī Tammām*, Muḥammad ʿAbduh ʿAzzām (ed.), Cairo: Lajnat al-Taʾlīf wa-l-Tarjama wa-l-Nashr.

Al-Thaᶜālibī, Abū Manṣūr (1956), *Yatīmat al-dahr fī maḥāsin ahl al-ᶜaṣr*, Muḥammad Muḥyī al-Dīn ᶜAbd al-Ḥamīd (ed.), Cairo: al-Maktaba al-Tijāriyya.

Al-Thaᶜālibī (2011), *Zād safar al-mulūk*, Ramzi Baalbaki and Bilal Orfali (eds), Beirut: Orient-Institut (*Bibliotheca Islamica* 52).

van Gelder, Geert Jan (2003), "Beautifying the Ugly and Uglifying the Beautiful: The Paradox in Classical Arabic Literature," *Journal of Semitic Studies* 48.2: 321–51.

Wellek, Rene (1971), *Discriminations: Further Concepts of Criticism*, New Haven CT: Yale University Press.

Wordsworth, William (1957), *Wordsworth's Preface to "Lyrical Ballads"*, W. J. Owen (ed.), Copenhagen: Rosenkilde and Bagger.

4

The Literary Geography of Meaning in the *Maqāmāt* of al-Hamadhānī and al-Ḥarīrī

Sarah R. bin Tyeer

This chapter will analyze the city/cities in the *maqāmāt* of Badīᶜ al-Zamān al-Hamadhānī (d. 395/1007) and Abū Muḥammad al-Qāsim b. ᶜAlī al-Ḥarīrī (d. 516/1122), proposing that the city plays a meaning-making role in their work, offering us interpretative strategies through their literary geographies. Both the semantic and legal geographies in the work of these two authors will be highlighted through two main foci. First, in the case of al-Hamadhānī, I propose that the text's cities belong to the geography of the "familiar," where the language use of the protagonist, Abū'l Fatḥ al-Iskandarī, would be readily comprehensible as the linguistic play that it is inside the Arabic literary geography he inhabits. His metaphors, stylistics, and inverted use of language would not be understood as literal but as a game. In this respect, the space of the familiar becomes a metonymy of semantic stability and the tools of *adab* offer us deeper insights into the *maqāmāt* and a richer reading experience. Second, I argue that the literary geography acts as a frame to both moral and legal stability in the *maqāmāt* of these authors. In al-Ḥarīrī's *maqāmāt,* the protagonist, Abū Zayd al-Sarūjī, abuses the stability of the city's legal geography for his benefit. While the legal framework of the city may not be productive for al-Iskandarī, the protagonist of al-Hamadhānī's *maqāmāt,* the city and its laws are conducive to al-Sarūjī's plans. The city therefore acts as a border in the *maqāmāt* for both semantic as well as moral and legal stability and law enforcement.

The *Maqāmāt*: One City is Not Enough

One of the most famous premodern Arabic genres, the *maqāma,* is a prosimetric genre that combines both rhymed prose known in Arabic as *saj*^{c} and poetry.[1] As Rina Drory defines it, it is a "collection of short independent narratives written in ornamental rhymed prose (*saj*^{c}) with verse insertions, and [that] share a common plot-scheme and two constant protagonists: the narrator and the hero."[2] Most *maqāmāt* follow this scheme with different adaptations according to the individual author.[3] Invented by al-Hamadhānī, the genre is partially inspired by the life of the mendicants or *al-mukaddīn* and their anecdotes.[4] Al-Hamadhānī's "interest in low life is very probably an inheritance from Ibn ^{c}Abbād who collected around him both scholars interested in low life (and obscenity, for that matter) as well as globe-trotters and witty beggars like Abū Dulaf."[5] However, these types of anecdotes are not fully comparable to the elaborate constructed metaphors, virtuosity, and subject matter covered by the protagonists Abū'l-Fatḥ al-Iskandarī and Abū Zayd al-Sarūjī in their corresponding *maqāmāt,* nor should the usage of *saj*^{c} in the *maqāmāt* be attributed to an imitation of the Bedouin mendicants.[6] As of the fourth AH/tenth AD century, *saj*^{c} was "increasingly used for official correspondence and then for historiography and other forms of prose composition."[7] The *maqāmāt* depend on accounts related to us by way of a narrator of the author's creation. Generally, in each *maqāma* the fictional narrator encounters his respective protagonist: al-Hamadhānī uses the narrator ^{c}Īsā b. Hishām, who relates his encounters with the protagonist Abū'l Fatḥ al-Iskandarī, while al-Ḥarīrī relies on the narrator al-Ḥārith b. Hammām, who describes his encounters with Abū Zayd al-Sarūjī. Integral to the *maqāmāt* as a genre is the perpetual travelling of their protagonists to different cities, which Abdelfattah Kilito (^{c}Abd al-Fattaḥ Kīlīṭū) reads as an aspect that makes the *maqāmāt* resemble contemporaneous travel accounts of geographers like al-Iṣṭakhrī (d. 346/957–8), Ibn Ḥawqal (d. after 378/988), and al-Muqaddasī (d. 380/991).[8] This also, notably, marks the *maqāmāt* as a distinctly urban genre.

One question the *maqāmāt* raise is how cities function within the narrative, whether as setting or when the names of specific cities are simply mentioned. We might ask why ^{c}Īsā b. Hishām repeatedly mentions his geographical coordinates. In a tale found in *The Thousand and One Nights,* "The Hunchback Cycle," it is related that one of the events happened in China. However, the king, the hunchback, and the protagonists, Muhsin J. al-Musawi maintains, are all under Islamic jurisdiction.[9] Setting the tale in China here serves the narrative purpose of leaving the familiar realm of Baghdad or Cairo in order to step into the unfamiliar. Yet, this unfamiliar is still familiarly Arab-Islamic as al-Musawi argues, perhaps even a literarisation of empire expansion. Unlike the foreign, mythical, mysterious, and supernatural cities in the *Nights*, the cities featured in the *maqāmāt* of both al-Hamadhānī and al-Ḥarīrī are all part of the domestic and familiar; they are not foreign. These cities are part of the authors' cartography, placed within the texts for the reader to create meaning from their literary geography.

It is instructive to ask where Abū'l Fatḥ al-Iskandarī and/or Abū Zayd al-Sarūjī are located geographically. In almost every *maqāma* by al-Hamadhānī, ᶜĪsā b. Hishām begins by justifying his travel or presence in a certain city. For instance, in *al-maqāma al-azādhiyya,* he explains his presence in Baghdad by stating that he is there to buy some dates for retail at the seasonal date market. Household or cotton trade is the reason that ᶜĪsā goes to Balkh in *al-maqāma al-balkhiyya*. In *al-maqāma al-sijistāniyya*, he justifies going to Sijistān to meet an unspecified pressing need. We know that he traveled to Yemen, Shīrāz, Damascus, and Ḥomṣ, to mention a few of the cities that comprise his geography, and that he went on the Ḥajj as well. He also twice relates that he had to escape – but does not say from where – when he was accused of theft or of earning money illegally.[10] ᶜĪsā is not just an itinerant merchant who sometimes gets into trouble while conducting business, he also relates that he was in the region of the Caspian Sea fighting with the army.[11] Thus, it seems that the figuration of these cities and the overall expanded geography that creates an image of a globetrotting charlatan and a merchant are meant to represent a believable geography for the audience of the *maqāmāt*. Al-Hamadhānī's literary creation of a verisimilitude for the audience is successful. Rather than being epistemologically barren, it could be argued that the cities' collective roles lend a sense of reality and purpose to the *maqāmāt* of both al-Hamadhānī and al-Ḥarīrī.

Writer/Reader Contract: Centers and the Literary Institutions

As ᶜĪsā travels to the different cities of the *maqāmāt*, it is acknowledged that he is a stranger amongst strangers. Yet, in each city to which he travels there is inevitably a single person he recognizes, namely al-Iskandarī. ᶜĪsā's serendipitous meetings with al-Iskandarī every time he travels tell us that al-Iskandarī occupies all of the same spaces at the same time; it may be that he is not actually anywhere in particular, but rather inhabits all of these spaces simultaneously. If indeed al-Iskandarī is everywhere, it may be useful to ask who or what is al-Iskandarī. Perhaps al-Hamadhānī's incongruent figuration of al-Iskandarī – sometimes as a young man, sometimes an adolescent, and at other times an older man with greying hair, a madman, or even an Imam – alludes to his nature. Al-Iskandarī, as he himself says, is everywhere because he is an object of deception. He refers to himself as "*jawwālat al-bilād wa jawwābat al-ufuq …*":

I am a mighty wanderer over the countries,
And a great traverser of the horizons.
I am the toy of time,
And am continually on the road.[12]

Irrespective of the city in which he is present, he lives outside the texts of the *maqāmāt.* Al-Iskandarī is what Umberto Eco calls "a fluctuating character": he "exhibits a *core of properties* that seem to be identified by everybody,"[13] ᶜĪsā and the readers included. Like other fluctuating characters across world literature (Don Quixote, Gatsby, Madame Bovary, etc.), al-Iskandarī and al-Sarūjī live independently of the text: "Being independent of the text and of the possible world where they were born, [the characters] are (so to speak) *circulating among us,* and we encounter some difficulties in not considering them real persons."[14] The literarisation of the circulation of al-Iskandarī, and later al-Sarūjī, is manifest in what both al-Hamadhānī and al-Ḥarīrī do to make these characters the travelers that they are.

The concept of the "fluctuating character" is equally evident in the *maqāmāt* of al-Ḥarīrī. In his preface to the *maqāmāt,* al-Ḥarīrī anticipates literal-minded critics and readers. He attributes the construction of his work not only to his predecessor al-Hamadhānī as the author and founder of the *maqāmāt* genre, but to the two fictional protagonists:

و بعد، فإنه قد جرى ببعض أندية الأدب الذي ركدت في هذه العصر ريحه، و خبت مصابيحه، ذكر المقامات التي إبتدعها بديع الزمان، و علامة همذان، – رحمه الله تعالى – و عزا إلى أبي الفتح الإسكندري نشأتها، و إلى عيسى ابن هشام روايتها، و كلاهما مجهول لا يعرف، و نكرة لا تتعرف. فأشار من إشارته حُكم، و طاعته غُنم، إلى أن أنشئ مقامات أتلو فيها تلو البديع […] مما أمليت جميعه على لسان أبي زيد السروجي و أسندت روايته إلى الحارث ابن همام البصري

(al-Ḥarīrī, *Maqāmāt al-ḥārīrī,* 15–16)

[…] And now to proceed, it so happened that in some belle-lettrist circles, whose energy had stagnated and light had dimmed, the *maqāmāt* that Badīᶜ al-Zamān – "the wonder of the age" and the "scholar of Hamadhān," may

> God have mercy on his soul – had created were mentioned. He attributed their origin to Abū'l Fatḥ al-Iskandarī and their narration to ᶜĪsā b. Hishām. They are both anonymous and unidentified: unknown. So he whose signal is a command and whose obedience is prized beckoned that I fashion *maqāmāt* following in the footsteps of Badīᶜ al-Zamān […] which I composed as by the tongue of Abū Zayd al-Sarūjī and attributed their narration to al-Ḥārith b. Hammām.

Al-Ḥarīrī considers Abū'l Fatḥ al-Iskandarī to be the protagonist who established the genre and ᶜĪsā b. Hishām as the one responsible for its narration.[15] Both characters are referred to as anonymous and unidentified (*majhūlun lā yuᶜraf wa nakiratun lā tataᶜarraf*), i.e. fictional characters.[16] In the quote cited above, al-Ḥarīrī does not stop at the extraordinary talent of al-Hamadhānī as an author – who he fully acknowledges and praises – but extends the success of the *maqāmāt* to the characters themselves. His emulation of al-Hamadhānī recognizes that for the genre to function and be understood as such, the characters must now be recognized as part of this convention, and so too is their globetrotting from city to city. Not only was his emulation successful, but as Wolfhart Heinrichs maintains, the *maqāmāt* of al-Ḥārīrī qualify as a "best-seller" in medieval Arabic literature despite the fact that there was not yet "a market for the masses."[17] Al-Ḥarīrī's *maqāmāt* acknowledged, classified, and participated in the literary institution of the *maqāmāt* at a specific historical moment, thereby generically grouping his work with that of al-Hamadhānī's.[18] Fredric Jameson has noted that, "[g]enres are essentially literary *institutions*, or social contracts between a writer and a specific public[.]"[19] Like any institution, people can join, participate and even reshape this institution.[20]

The literary and cultural institutions that the genre of the *maqāmāt* rest upon are a social contract that binds readers and writers/literary works. This contract stipulates that the genre depends on several "centers" for the process of meaning-making to occur. To further elaborate, al-Iskandarī's eerie presence in every city ᶜĪsā visits and their uncanny encounters tell us that Abū'l Fatḥ is not a person but an idea. When he meets Abu'l Fatḥ in Azerbaijan, a shocked ᶜĪsā wonders about the scope of the latter's deception that reaches as far as this land (*balagha hādhihi l-arḍa kayduk*).[21] The phrase serves to highlight the gravity of his deception, here measured geographically by the distance from a center in ᶜĪsā's mind as well as al-Hamadhānī's readers – a cartography of deception, so to speak. Otherwise, we could only question

Azerbaijan's far-ness in reference to what center, i.e. far from what? Is it the capital, Kufa, or the cities of Baṣra or Baghdad or Alexandria, which Abū'l Fatḥ claims as his home?[22] This imagined center, be it Kufa or Baghdad, which is as tangible in the *maqāmāt* of al-Hamadhānī as it is in the Abbasid polity, seems to be a subtle feature in the *maqāmāt*. The notion of a center is at the heart of the *maqāmāt* for al-Hamadhānī if for nothing other than ᶜĪsā's reactions to al-Iskandarī's presence in cities remote from an imagined center, perhaps the Abbasid capital. The concept of a center is not strictly limited to the geographical level as the exchanges between ᶜĪsā and al-Iskandarī show; it also translates linguistically. The idea of a "center" (semantic, linguistic, etc.) is the unspoken contract between the writer and his/her readership and it is these centers with which al-Hamadhānī plays rhetorically.

Rhetoric and the Limits of Semantic Geography

Beyond their collective role in adding a sense of reality and purpose to the narrative, cities serve a semantic purpose. ᶜĪsā b. Hishām's many encounters with the swindler Abū'l Fatḥ are marked by two paradoxical things: common language games and linguistic consistency despite the many different locations. In other words, Abū'l Fatḥ is self-described as "*jawwālat al-bilād*" (globetrotter) yet his language use and techniques are consistent in all the different places he inhabits. His metaphors, stylistics, and inverted use of language are bound to be understood within their geography. Meaning, rather than literal, his linguistic rhetoric is a game played in the cities in which he travels, inevitably meeting ᶜĪsā and other victims. But if the geography is a specifically Arabic literary geography, there is the question of what this means in terms of *adab* and/or in reference to a literary work.

The presupposition in the *maqāmāt* is that ᶜĪsā is a stranger amongst strangers in every city in which he finds himself, yet he inevitably meets the same familiar person at the end of each *maqāma* in a famous recognition scene. Jaakko Hämeen-Anttila speaks of the moment of "recognition" as characteristic of the structure of al-Hamadhānī's *maqāmāt*.[23] In an Arab-Islamic context, recognition or *anagnorisis*, Philip F. Kennedy proposes, is "… commensurate with the emergence of certain truth."[24] Al-Iskandarī is a charlatan, a master of disguise, who swindles people and ᶜĪsā knows it. ᶜĪsā only realizes the truth of al-Iskandarī during the recognition scene, which is then usually followed by the envoi of verses – lines of poetry or quotations put in the mouth of the protagonist to summarise his philosophy and explain his behavior.[25] It is thus the content of this envoi that contributes to the affirmation of al-Iskandarī's identity as a charlatan as the place within the text where the "emergence of truth" takes place. The envoi changes in every *maqāma* but what is fairly stable and fixed within it is a rhetorical technique used by al-Iskandarī: beautifying the ugly and uglifying the beautiful (*taḥsīn al-qabīḥ wa taqbīḥ al-ḥasan*).[26] The philologist Abū Manṣūr al-Thaᶜālibī (d. 429/1038), who was rightly "fascinated by al-Hamadhānī's talents,"[27] considered this technique to be the height of excellence and eloquence: "*taḥsīnu al-qabīḥi wa taqbīḥu al-ḥasani idhā humā ghāyatā l-barāᶜati wa-l-qudrati ᶜalā jazl l-kalāmi fī sirri l-balāghati wa siḥri al-ṣināᶜa.*" ([B]eautifying the ugly and uglifying the beautiful is the ultimate [marker] of skill and ability when shaping words using the secrets of rhetoric and the charm of the craft.)[28] In the final scene of almost every *maqāma*, the envoi perpetually condemns *ᶜaql* (reason and moral force) and presents it as unnecessary while deception, lies, and madness are praised. These views follow the disclosure of al-Iskandarī and immediately enable ᶜĪsā to recognize him. The truth emerges and builds what constitutes an essential aspect of recognition as al-Iskandarī speaks about madness being the only reason and states that one must "repel time with folly."[29] The very words of al-Iskandarī invite us to mistrust him even though they are charming and eloquent, according to ᶜĪsā. We, like ᶜĪsā, are bound by an unspoken semantic contract or accord established by a cognitive agreement to deem him a charlatan as per the title of this rhetorical technique (beautifying the ugly and uglifying the beautiful). This demands an implicit consensus regarding what is "beautiful" or "ugly" in the first place in order for the technique to work. His praise of madness and folly and the shunning of reason do not match this implicit semantic contract.

Despite the protagonists' constant movement, they remain in what Kīlīṭū calls "the familiar" (*al-maᵓlūf*), that is the Islamicate.[30] Abū'l Fatḥ and ᶜĪsā understand each other on both the linguistic and cultural levels, as does the anonymous third narrator who transmits their narrative to the audience, and likewise for the texts' premodern readers, as Jaakko Hämeen-Antilla argues.[31] The "familiar", Kīlīṭū suggests, is not something that creates a semantic crisis for them – as it does for Sindbad, whom Kīlīṭū uses for this example. In other words, there is a certain semantic stability in this geography that creates a linguistic and literary framework for both the protagonists and for us as readers of the *maqāmāt*. The tools offered by al-Hamadhānī through al-Iskandarī are thus in his rhetorical techniques that, despite its imagined geographical variations, are semantically stable, and despite their eloquence, are understood as deception. The envoi becomes a site for reading Abū'l Fatḥ's strategies in the same manner as it is rhetorically used to "beautify the ugly and uglify the beautiful." The limitations of this semantic stability are precisely the geography of the "familiar" from which Abū'l Fatḥ and ᶜĪsā never depart: the Islamicate or cities where semantic stability stand for the tools of *adab* that allow the detection of deception as part of this geo-semantic consensus.

At this juncture, it is pivotal to remember the question of the function of the city/cities in the *maqāmāt* by thinking about the relationship of a literary technique to the "city." As Robert Tally Jr. notes, narrative is "a spatially symbolic act in establishing a literary cartography for the reader."[32] To further explain, Emily Apter evokes the concept of "language borders" to refer to the issues ensuing from ignoring the politics of the "Untranslatable" in literary studies, meaning terms, words, or units that do not travel freely from one language to another. Because these words, Apter argues, are part of a network, part of a whole, they form relationships with each other and therefore contain complex layers within themselves. One could add that the layers are not just linguistic but also cultural and temporal.[33] The process of meaning-making in language and literature cannot be a universal process. To assert that there are defining Arab-Islamic literary terms and aesthetic features of the works should not be understood as the inability of literature to be read outside its culture, or an essentialising practice. Rather, it is an effort to enhance the reading of *adab* both inside and outside its culture and be sensitive to the alterity of this literature without denying the literary texts' aesthetic integrity. A failure to read the literary devices inside their literary geography (*adab*) would ensue in a distortion, mistranslation, or retranslation (hence rewriting) of the aesthetics and literary techniques of al-Hamadhānī specifically, the *maqāmāt* in general, and *adab* altogether.

In *What is Literature?* Jean Paul Sartre tells us that the reception of the work is not an "external" fact about it; it is an integral dimension of it and its "consumption" is part of its process of production.[34] With respect to the *maqāmāt,* al-Ḥarīrī, as one of the readers and consumers of al-Hamadhānī, understood and worked with the techniques the latter provided. The "language borders" or cities therefore function on both the narrative and meta-narrative levels. The literary geography of *adab* upholds a semantic center where the rhetorical techniques performed by the protagonists play a role in their reception. These literary devices are unveiled inside the aforementioned semantic "center" or what Kīlīṭū refers to as the "familiar." The limits of this semantic geography are the threshold of *adab* and language where the *maqāmāt* cease to work on both the fictional and referential levels, and mistranslation begins.

Like al-Hamadhānī, al-Ḥarīrī also works with the concept of the "borders" as the threshold of law and order, in the broadest sense, in the city.

The City and the Borders of the Law

Before venturing further into the use of city "borders" in the narrative of the *maqāmāt* by both authors, it is imperative to shed light on how premodern scholars defined the "city." In his *Maqāyīs al-Lugha*, Ibn Fāris tells us that a city (*madīna*) is so-called because of the jurisdiction and enforcement of the law (*li-annahā tuqāmu fiha ṭāᶜatu dhawī l-amr*).[35] He analyzes this through the root (*d.ī.n*), which he traces to its meaning that denotes "obedience" and "yielding" (*al-inqiyād wa l-dhull*).[36] Al-Fīrūzabādī adds, that to become a city-dweller or civilized (*tamadyan*) is to live a life of ease and comfort (*tanaᶜum*).[37] Al-Shirwānī explains a city (*madīna*) in terms of superlative expansion and compares it to its smaller version, town (*balad*), which is bigger than a village (*qarya*).[38]

Al-Hamadhānī uses the city skillfully in his *al-maqāma al-maḍīriyya*. The *maqāma* opens with ᶜĪsā and Abū'l Fatḥ in Baṣra where a well-loved *maḍīra* dish, a kind of meat stew, is being served. Abū'l Fatḥ reacts negatively to it and demands that it be taken away, much to the disappointment of the rest of the guests. He then relates a story that takes place in Baghdad, explaining his reaction to the *maḍīra*. One of the city's merchants had invited Abū'l Fatḥ to be a guest at his house, where the *maḍīra* dish was expected to be served – as most readers know, the meal never arrives. The host instead behaves like a typical city-dweller in al-Fīrūzabādī's definition: he indulges his guest in extended description of all the items of ease and comfort in his house. As they walk through the city, the merchant engages in small talk; he praises his wife's impeccable cooking skills, their love and devotion to each other, and her virtues. He then starts commenting on the quarter in which he lives, comparing it to other neighbourhoods in the city and the status held by each. As they reach the merchant's house, he begins by commenting on the craftsmanship of the door and its various parts that come from different cities and sellers. The merchant then calls the servant with the water basin, telling Abū'l Fatḥ about the servant's Greek origins, the ewer's Syrian brass, its Iraqi workmanship, moving on to the napkin's fabric from Jurjān, then continuing to describe all the items in his household and their cities of origin. From the outset, Abū'l Fatḥ is bored by the man's incessant talk about his wife and other pleasantries that all seem to revolve around comfort and luxury, "*wa ṣaddaᶜanī bi-ṣifāti zawjatihi ḥatta intahaynā ilā maḥallatihi*" (he bored me with his wife's virtues till we reached his quarters).[39] While the merchant revels in the craftsmanship of the table, an irritated Abū'l Fatḥ straightforwardly enquires "*hādhā al-shaklu fa-matā l-aklu*" (this is the make but when is the meal?)[40] But when he realizes that the promised meal will probably never arrive, or rather when his patience is exasperated and he cannot indulge his host in small talk any longer, Abū'l Fatḥ excuses himself to "discharge a need" in order to escape what he perceives as an empty promise on the merchant's part.

The *maqāma* highlights two salient features of life in the city and its corresponding system of laws. Throughout the merchant's descriptions, the merchant's sense of civility and cosmopolitanism is expressed through his knowledge not only of his city, its quarters, and artisans but also through the best of what other cities could offer in terms of items of luxury and comfort. Al-Hamadhānī's skill here lies in acting like a literary cartographer; he charts both the city streets and the larger regional geography, choosing which sites to include or omit in the discussion between al-Iskandarī and the host through the mention of famous or national crafts from different countries.[41] In the host's house, al-Hamadhānī essentially draws a map, which need not be a geometrical grid, for "a map may also constitute itself in words."[42] The map refers to the marks of civility and the thriving of the city of Baghdad as well as other mentioned cities as the *maqāma* traverses several cultural spaces through a single social setting.

The merchant's listing of items, their source, and excellent craftsmanship as an expression of civility are not received well by Abū'l Fatḥ, who does not reciprocate the small talk nor seem the least interested. Yet, despite Abū'l Fatḥ's boredom with the man's conversation, he must obey a certain decorum – the city's – and remain silent and nod, at least in the beginning. Even when his patience withers and he wants to escape, decorum demands that he excuse himself without embarrassing either himself or the host. He alludes to the need to relieve himself. The city here appears as a space governed by a social law that even in extreme circumstances cannot be broken. Abū'l Fatḥ cannot obey the city's decorum and prolong the niceties, pleasantries, and small talk that govern life there. His character – an outcast that thrives outside the boundaries of the city – wants to devour the meal without the social context of its emotional and intellectual investment expressed as an interest in the host's life.

The "obedience" and "yielding" about which Ibn Fāris speaks, cited above, are not to be narrowly understood as laws in the exclusively legal sense – they also translate into unspoken social laws and decorum that ought to be observed even when they stretch the limits of one's ordinary tolerance. In the *maqāma*, this is manifest in Abū'l Fatḥ's companions, who respect his aversion to the *maḍīra* because of his individual experience despite that it runs counter to their own wishes; although they outnumber him, a sense of respect for his feelings must be observed as part of an unspoken social code. It is clear that Abū'l Fatḥ, through demanding that the *madīra* be taken away, disregards the social context in the selfish and anti-social imposition of his own will over the desire of the group and spoils what could have been a pleasant gathering over a meal. His disregard for decorum, expressed as socially improper behaviour and lack of concern for the group's feelings, parallels the same tactless indifference to his host's feelings in his earlier encounter. His behaviour on both occasions serves only his own interests and needs; it reflects his borderline values that thrive outside the city's boundaries, running against the law, social integration, the observation of politesse and decorum such as the inhabitants of the city would presumably observe.

In the *maqāmāt* of al-Ḥarīrī, the city also features several times as a border governed by the law. Whereas Abū'l Fatḥ thrives outside the city in his *kudya* and does not seem able to function properly in social settings, Abū Zayd al-Sarūjī abuses the city to his benefit through *kudya*. And in this, he does not seem to be alone. Al-Ḥārith b. Hammām, al-Ḥarīrī's narrator, tells us in *al-maqāma al-Iskandariyya* that as a traveller, he is abiding by a useful piece of advice from the wise: "*annahu yalzamu l-adība l-arība idhā dakhala l-balada l-gharība an yastamīla qāḍiyahu wa yaṣtakhliṣa marāḍīyahu li-yashshudda ẓahrahu ᶜinda l-khiṣāmi wa yaʾmana fī l-ghurbati jawra l-ḥukkāmi.*" (The *adīb* should keep the company of the intelligent when venturing into a foreign city; he should befriend its judge and vie for his approval to cover his back in the event that a dispute should befall him, thus taking discretion against the ruthlessness of rulers during travel).[43] The city appears to be a benevolent ally to al-Sarūjī and his narrator.

In *al-maqāma al-Iskandariyya,* al-Sarūjī's wife goes to the judge to complain about her husband's selling of all of their furniture; she also complains about his voluntary unemployment under the pretext that his craft is no longer in demand. The judge feels for the woman and demands that the husband justify his behaviour. Al-Sarūjī, in a very long poem, explains to the judge how the likes of him, whose entire fortune is eloquence (*siḥru l-kalām*), poetry (*al-qarīḍ*), and speeches (*al-khuṭab*), are like outcasts: "*kaʾannahum fī ᶜirāṣihim jīyafun / yubᶜadu min nataniha wa yujtanabu.*" (As if there is a cadaver in their courtyard / putting off everyone with its stink)[44] People like him cannot support themselves or their families. The judge is touched by al-Sarūjī's destitute conditions so he orders that he and his wife receive money from the alms (*ṣadaqāt*) appointed for the poor. The narrator Ibn Hammām knows that it is al-Sarūjī all along but says nothing until after the couple has left. He then encourages the judge to send someone after the pair so that they can check their identity. Unlike al-Hamadhānī's narrator, al-Ḥarīrī's narrator, al-Ḥārith b. Hammām, uncovers al-Sarūjī's tricks before anyone else within the narrative, meaning the narrator is always one step ahead; al-Sarūjī's intelligence, then, is surpassed by others, namely Ibn Hammām and the readers. As a narrator, Ibn Hammām exhibits little weakness in front of al-Sarūjī's verbal seduction, rather the latter's victims do. The judge's messenger comes back confirming what the readers already know. When the judge sends for their arrest, the messenger fails to do so because they have already traveled far away from the city. The city here functions as a space of law and order. Despite this, it is not a space that is entirely avoided by al-Sarūjī, rather he uses these laws to his advantage.

In *Kitāb al-Sulṭan*, Ibn Qutayba relates an anecdote through a chain of transmission referring to a piece of advice by Kisrā (Khosrow); the latter says, "*lā tanzil fī baladin laysa fīhi khamsatu ashyāʾin: sulṭānun qāhir, wa qāḍīn ʿādil, wa ṭabībin ʿālim, wa sūqin qāʾima, wa nahrin jāri.*" (Do not reside in a country that does not have five things: a powerful ruler, a rightful judge, an expert physician, a thriving market, and a flowing river.)[45] Al-Sarūjī uses Khosrow's advice and manipulates the judge after he fabricates the dispute with his wife because of their extreme poverty. According to the law, the righteous judge ensures that they receive assistance as a result of their condition. Now that the law is enforced in al-Sarūjī's favor, the city appears to be conducive to his *kudya*. The boundaries of law and its jurisdiction are applied within the city, whereas outside the borders he is no longer within the domain of the judge or the law: the reason that the messenger informs the judge that al-Sarūjī is far away "*mukhbiran bi-naʾyihi.*"[46] The *maqāma* simply summarises the *modus operandi* of the protagonist and highlights the function of the city as a space governed by a particular social and legal system.

In another example, the same depiction of city boundaries is repeated in *al-maqāma al-shiʿriyya*. Here, al-Sarūjī fabricates a dispute with his adopted son and goes to the judge to complain that his son has plagiarised his poetry. The judge demands that the father recite both the original and the plagiarised poems to render a better judgment. After toing and froing with poetry between father and son, the judge is amazed by their talent and intelligence and gives them both money, asking them to treat each other amicably. As Ibn Hammām follows the two men, al-Sarūjī tells him to enlighten the judge about the latter's stupidity and his manipulation of the judge's emotions ("*bayyin lahu ghabāwata qalbihi wa til*ᶜ*ābī bi-lubbihi*").[47] Yet al-Sarūjī only says this once he is outside the jurisdiction of the judge ("*ajaznā ḥimā l-wālī wa afḍaynā ilā l-faḍā*ᵓ *al-khālī*") because he knows that the judge will not be able to arrest him.[48] When the judge realizes al-Sarūjī's deception, Ibn Hammām informs him that it is futile to chase after al-Sarūjī ("*ashfaqa minka li-ta*ᶜ*addī ṭūrihi fa-ẓa*ᶜ*ana* ᶜ*an baghdghada min fawrihi*").[49] The judge, however, tells us that the only reason he is not resolute in chasing al-Sarūjī until he catches him is the latter's *adab,* exhibited in the poetry that he has heard, even though he is furious and feels humiliated. He may realize that he would be overestimating his own power by demanding that al-Sarūjī be pursued wherever he is, or he may be defending his previous judgment about al-Sarūjī's poetry, i.e. that his poetry remains excellent and that he had judged well. He even urges Ibn Hammām not to relate the story to anyone lest people in the city lose respect for him, forcing him to take an oath. And though Ibn Hammām tells us that he kept the oath and was loyal to the judge – a loyalty comparable only to that of al-Samūᵓal[50] – it is he who narrates these very events.

Similarly, in al-*maqāma al-ma*ᶜ*arriyya*, al-Sarūjī and his son also deceive the judge with eloquence and manage to trick him into giving them some money. When the judge summons them after he realizes that he has been the victim of their deception, his first response upon confrontation is an expression of his admiration for al-Sarūjī's eloquence: *lillāhi darrukka fa-mā a*ᶜ*dhaba nafathāti fīka lawlā khidā*ᶜ*un fīka!* (To God be attributed your goodness, how sweet is the breath of your mouth! [...] if it were not for the deceit in you!).[51] The judge advises al-Sarūjī to mend his ways because not every judge is going to act as he did in this situation. It appears that both judges in these two *maqāmāt* have balanced al-Sarūjī's use of eloquence as an offset to his trickery. The judge refers to al-Sarūjī's mouth as the source of the sweetest words while recognizing the deception that comes out of it. Notably, the judge does not penalize him; the fact of his forgiveness is an implied confidence in his correct judgment of al-Sarūjī talent.

Conclusion: The Topography of Affective Power

Part of the literary geography charted by al-Hamadhānī and al-Ḥarīrī is their use of cities, geography, and space for their affective power. The very presence of the court of law as part of the city in the *maqāmāt* of al-Ḥarīrī is distinguished from other spaces or institutions and hence the rest of the narrative by what Robert T. Tally Jr. calls the place's "affective power" that is established within both the author's and readers' minds.[52] The affective power of the place in turn plays a role in the meaning-making tools given to the reader. The court, a metonym of law and order, and hence the city at large, contradicts the machinations of the protagonist and his enterprises. Yet he twists it to work for him. The abuse of one of the city's virtues in this case highlights both the audacity of al-Sarūjī and his inventiveness. The most unexpected place of the trick solicits a reaction that is proportional to the decorum and respect demanded by the place, and yet it does not get that respect. The reversal of expectations in this case maximises both the message and the entertainment value of the *maqāmāt.* A similar use of the dynamics of the space's affective powers is also observed in al-Hamadhānī's protagonist al-Iskandarī as a pretentious Imām who dupes people at the mosque during the day while sharing drinks at the tavern at night in *al-maqāma al-khamriyya,* for instance. The "affective power" of the place is likewise used to highlight the themes of each *maqāma.*

Both authors have employed the city and its social spaces extensively in their *maqāmāt.* Rather than featuring elaborate details of the city, the city represents a "border": a semantic space highlighted by what has been referred to earlier as the geography of the "familiar" as well as a space governed by several laws. That being said, it appears that the *maqāmāt* operate from the moral element of space. To quote Robert T. Tally Jr. again, "literary works serve a cartographic function by creating a figurative or allegorical representation of a social space, broadly understood."[53] Therefore, the role of these moral spaces in general is part of their essential meaning-making tools; they are not to be understood as conceptually vacuous geographical references in the background. Moral does not mean "moralistic" but rather what constitutes the elements of *adab.* The highly satirical nature of the *maqāmāt* feeds on these stark contrasts between actions and language, social spaces and social relations. The presence of the city, its meaning-making "borders," institutions, and other social spaces like mosques, taverns, etc. are not to be treated as an " … empty container to be filled with actions or movements[.]"[54] Rather, this literary geography offers us an opportunity for an enhanced understanding of the work on a deeper level.

Notes

1. For more on this, see Heinrichs (1997: 249–77).
2. Drory (2000: 190).

3. Ibid. (190). For more on this, see also Hämeen-Anttila (2002).
4. Bosworth (1976: 1: 30); Ḥasan (1986: 145).
5. Hämeen-Anttila (2002: 20).
6. Sources document Bedouin (*a^{c}rāb*) mendicants' eloquence that only used *saj^{c}* (rhymed prose) in their speech. One should not define real mendicants' "eloquence" here as one that is comparable to the language of Abū'l-Fatḥ, at least as seen in the examples of the Bedouin's usage of *saj^{c}*, which drew the attention of some literati such as Ibn ^{c}Abd Rabbih, for instance, because of the graceful nature of the language and the decorative and metaphorical aspects of it as such. For more on this, see Ḥasan (1986: 162–4).
7. Al-Hamadhānī, trans. Prendergast (1915: viii).
8. Kīlīṭū, *al-maqāmāt* (1993: 12).
9. Al-Musawi (2009: 152).
10. See *al-maqāma al-Asawadiyya* and *al-maqāma al-Adhirbijāniyya.*
11. *Al-maqāma al-Qazwīniyya.*
12. Al-Hamadhānī, trans. Prendergast (1915: 52).
13. Eco (2009: 87).
14. Ibid.
15. Al-Ḥarīrī (1981: 15).
16. Ibid. (15).
17. Heinrichs (1997), 262.
18. For more on the historical view of genres versus genres as institutions, see Devitt (2008: 168).
19. Ibid.
20. This is Rene Wellek and Austin Warren's statement, which precedes Jameson's, see Devitt, ibid.
21. Al-Hamadhānī (2005: 54).
22. For a discussion on Abū'l Fatḥ's name and origins and their symbolic relationship to his travels, see Birari, "Travelling in Hamadhānī's Maqāmāt".
23. Hämeen-Anttila (2002: 50). For a discussion on the entire structure of the *Maqāmāt* of al-Hamadhānī, see also ibid. (45–51).
24. Kennedy (2009: 47).
25. See Hämeen-Anttila (2002: 51). This is part of the author's explanation of the structure of the *maqāmāt.*
26. See al-Tha^{c}ālibī (1994). See also van Gelder (2003).
27. Hämeen-Anttila (2002: 27).
28. Al-Tha^{c}ālibī (1994: 21).
29. See al-Hamadhānī (2005; 96); al-Hamadhānī, trans. Prendergast (1915: 75).

30. Kīlīṭū (2001: 13).
31. Hämeen-Anttila (2002: 114).
32. Tally Jr. (2011).
33. See Apter (2013).
34. Sartre, *What is Literature?* Cited in Eagleton (2003: 72–3).
35. Ibn Fāris (1999: vol. 2, 319); al-Maqdisī (1418 AH: vol. 3, 357–8).
36. Ibn Fāris (1999: vol. 2, 319).
37. Al-Zabīdī (n. d., vol.36: 158).
38. Al-Shirwānī (n. d.: vol. 6, 346).
39. Al-Hamadhānī (2005: 125); al-Hamadhānī, trans. Prendergast (1915, 91).
40. Al-Hamadhānī (2005: 134); al-Hamadhānī, trans. Prendergast (1915: 97). In this context, Prendergast's translation choice of the word 'make' for *shakl* refers to the artistry of the finely made table.
41. See Tally Jr. (2013: 45).
42. Ibid.: 46.
43. Al-Ḥarīrī (1981: 68–9).
44. Ibid.: 72.
45. Ibn Qutayba (n. d.: vol.1, 6).
46. Al-Ḥārīrī (1981: 75).
47. Ibid.: 178.
48. Ibid.: 177.
49. Ibid.: 179.
50. Al-Samūᵓal was in his fortress, when a man came to him with the former's son as a captive. Al- Samūᵓal had Imrūᵓ al-Qays' weapons hidden with him and so the man asked Al- Samūᵓal to give him the weapons or his son would be killed. Al- Samūᵓal refused to hand over the weapons and kept his promise and so his son was killed.
51. Al-Ḥarīrī (1981: 68).
52. Tally Jr. (2013: 83).
53. Tally Jr. (2011).
54. Tally Jr. (2013: 119).

Works Cited

Apter, Emily (2013), *Against World Literature: On the Politics of Untranslatability*, London and New York NY: Verso.

Al-ᶜAskarī, Abū Hilāl (1971), *Kitāb al-Ṣināᶜatayn*, Cairo: ᶜĪsā al-Bābī al-Ḥalabī.

Birari, Mohammed (2006), "Travelling in Hamadhānī's Maqāmāt: Connotations and Significances," *Alif: Journal of Comparative Poetics*, no. 26, 138–58.

Bosworth, Clifford Edmund (1976), *The Medieval Islamic Underworld: The Banū Sāsān in Arabic Society and Literature*, Leiden: E. J. Brill, 2 vols.

Al-Dabbagh, Abdullah (2010), *Literary Orientalism, Postcolonialism, and Universalism*, New York NY: Peter Lang Publishing.

Devitt, Amy J. (2008), *Writing Genres*, Carbondale IL: Southern Illinois University Press.

Drory, Rina (2000), "The Maqama," in *The Literature of Al-Andalus,* María Rosa Menocal, Raymond P. Scheindlin, and Michael Sells (eds), Cambridge: Cambridge University Press, 190–210.

Eagleton, Terry (2003), *Literary Theory*, Minneapolis MN: Blackwell Publishing.

Eco, Umberto (2009), "On the Ontology of Fictional Characters: A Semiotic Approach," *Sign System Studies* 37: 1, 2: 82–98.

Goodman, Lenn E (1988), "Hamadhānī, Schadenfreude and Salvation Through Sin," *JAL* 19, no. 1: 27–39.

Al-Hamadhānī (1915), *The Maqāmāt of Badīᶜ al-Zamān al-Hamadhānī*, trans. W. J. Prendergast, London: Luzac.

Al-Hamadhānī (2005), *Maqāmāt*, Muḥammad ᶜAbduh (ed.), Beirut: Dār al-Kutub al-ᶜIlmiyya.

Hämeen-Anttila, Jaakko (2002), *Maqama: A History of a Genre*, Wiesbaden: Harrassowitz Verlag.

Al-Ḥarīrī (1981), *Maqāmāt al-Ḥarīrī*, Yūsuf Biqāᶜī (ed.), Beirut: Dār al-Kitāb al-Lubnānī.

Ḥasan, Aḥmad Ḥusayn (1986), *Adab al-Kudya fī l-ᶜAṣr al-ᶜAbbāsī*, Latakia: Dār Akwār li-l-Nashr wa l-Tawzīᶜ.

Heinrichs, Wolfhart (1997), "Prosimetrical Genres in Classical Arabic Literature," in *Prosimetrum: Crosscultural Perspectives on Narrative in Prose and Verse*, Joseph Harris and Karl Reichl (eds), Woodbridge: D. S. Brewer, 249–77.

Ibn Fāris (1999), *Maqāyīs al-Lugha,* ᶜAbd al-Salām Muḥammad Harūn (ed.), Beirut: Dār al-Jīl.

Ibn Qutayba (n. d.), *ᶜUyūn al-Akhbār:Kitāb al-Sulṭān*, Beirut: Dār al-Kitāb al-ᶜArabī.

Kennedy, Philip F. (2009), "Islamic Recognitions: An Overview," in *Recognition: The Poetics of Narrative: Interdisciplinary Studies on Anagnorisis*, Marilyn Lawrence and Philip Kennedy (eds), New York: Peter Lang, 26–61.

Kīlīṭū, ᶜAbd al-Fattaḥ (1993) *al-Maqāmāt: al-Sard wa l-Ansāq al-Thaqāfiyya*, trans. ᶜAbd al-Kabīr al-Sharqāwī, Casablanca: Dār Tobqāl.

Kīlīṭū, ᶜAbd al-Fattaḥ (2001), *al-Maqāmāt: al-Sard wa l-Ansāq al-Thaqāfiyya*, trans. ᶜAbdel al-Kabīr al-Sharqāwī, 2nd edition, Casablanca: Dar Tobqal.

Al-Maqdisī (1418 AH), *al-Furūc*, Abū'l Zahrā' Ḥāzim al-Qāḍī (ed.), Beirut: Dār al-Kutub al-ᶜIlmiyya.

Monroe, James T. (1983), *The Art of Badiᶜ al-Zamān al-Hamadhānī as Picaresque Narrative*, Beirut: American University of Beirut.

Al-Musawi, Muhsin J. (2009), *The Islamic Context of the Thousand and One Nights*, New York NY: Columbia University Press.

Al-Shirwānī (n. d.), *Ḥawāshī al-Shirwānī ᶜala Tuḥfat al-Miḥtāj bi-Sharḥ al-Minhāj*, Beirut: Dār al-Fikr.

Tally Jr., Robert T. (2011), "On Literary Cartography: Narrative as a Spatially Symbolic Act," *NANO: New American Notes Online*, Issue 1, https://www.nanocrit.com/issues/issue1/literary-cartography-narrative-spatially-symbolic-act (accessed 27 November 2017).

—— (2013), *Spatiality*, New York NY and London: Routledge.

Al-Thaᶜālibī (1994), *Taḥsīn al-Qabīḥ wa Taqbīḥ al-ḥasan*, ᶜAlā' ᶜAbd al-Wahhāb Muḥammad (ed.), Cairo: Dār al-Faḍīla.

van Gelder, Geert Jan (2003), "Beautifying the Ugly and Uglifying the Beautiful," *Journal of Semitic Studies* 68, no. 2: 321–51.

Al-Zabīdī (n. d.), *Tāj al-ᶜArūṣ*, Dār al-Hidāya, n. p.

5

"Woe is me for Qayrawan!" Ibn Sharaf's *Lāmiyya*, the Plight of Refugees and the Cityscape

Nizar F. Hermes

Have Qayrawan's sins grown too great,
to be forgiven? Isn't God the All-Forgiver?
Is she the only one to be afflicted with sins so serious?
hasn't terrible vice existed in the land from the beginning!

(From the *Rā ᵓiyya* of Ibn Sharaf)[1]

Why does Time punish me while I am guiltless?
as if I were the beaten ᶜAmru!
I would have deserved the function of a subject in grammar
had Time been an erudite scholar![2]

(*Dīwān Ibn Sharaf*, 101)

At least in terms of sheer number of city-elegies, Ibn Sharaf al-Qayrawānī (d. 1067) should be considered one of the most prolific city-elegists of the medieval Mediterranean world.[3] While an original *dīwān* has not survived, Maghribi and Andalusian sources have preserved no fewer than seven *marāthī* (elegies) by Ibn Sharaf to Qayrawan. In the course of his exploration of the *kharāb* (destruction) and *khalāᵓ* (desolation) of Qayrawan by the Banū Hilāl in 1057, prominent Qayrawānī chronicler al-Dabbāgh (d. 1299), for example, cited in his seminal *Maᶜālim al-īmān fī maᶜrifat ahl al-Qayrawān* (The Cornerstone of Faith in Knowing the People of Qayrawan), rather perfunctorily, two fragmented samples from Ibn Sharaf's city-elegies along with a few verses penned by Ibn Faḍḍāl (d. 1086).[4] Al-Dabbāgh did so most likely to introduce what he judged as the most Islamically inspired of *marāthī al-Qayrawan*: the *nūniyya* of Ibn Rashīq and the *tā᾽iyya* of ᶜAlī al-Ḥuṣrī (d. 1095).[5] However, it is the Andalusian anthologist Ibn Bassām al-Shantarīnī (d. 1147) who preserved Ibn Sharaf's elegiac/nostalgic corpus of *Qayrawānīyyāt*. Ibn Bassām devoted an entire section of his magnum opus *Al-Dhakhīra fī maḥāsin ahl al-jazīra* (The Treasury Concerning the Merits of the People of Iberia) to the Qayrawānī poets who emigrated to al-Andalus (*al-wāfidīna ᶜalā al-jazīra*).[6] Most suggestive perhaps is that in the lengthy chapter on Ibn Sharaf[7] Ibn Bassām opted for an extremely suggestive subtitle for Ibn Sharaf's city-elegies: "*mā akhrajtuhu min marāthīhi ilā ahli l-Qayrawān baladih*/what I have collected of his elegies for the people of Qayrawan his hometown."

All in all, Ibn Bassām cites seven city-elegies by Ibn Sharaf, providing brief critical comments on specific verses he likes or, in a few cases, of which he disapproves – especially lines burdened with what he sees as extreme *ḍajar* (angst) on the part of Ibn Sharaf. Among the seven city-elegies incorporated by Ibn Bassām, it is a *lāmiyya* that he singles out as the poetic jewel of the Maghribi émigré. Thus, he dwells at length on some of its most eloquent lines, comparing them to similar verses by the likes of Abū Tammām (d. 845) and Ibn Hānī al-Andalusī (d. 973), dubbed the al-Mutanabbī (d. 965) of al-Andalus. Compared to the *nūniyya* of Ibn Rashīq – his court arch-rival but ultimately a companion in exile – the *lāmiyya* of Ibn Sharaf has received much less attention in the Arab world, including his native country of Tunisia.[8] Likewise, in the West, Ibn Sharaf is unduly neglected and his *lāmiyya* is largely unknown; prior to this volume, he has never been the subject of a scholarly essay in English, despite his status as one of the most celebrated poets of the great Qayrawānī School.[9]

In this contribution, I offer as an appendix a full English translation of Ibn Sharaf's *lāmiyya* based on the printed *diwān* by Ḥasan Dhikrī Ḥasan, who collected it from Ibn Bassām's *Al-Dhakhīra fī maḥāsin ahl al-jazīra*. After briefly introducing the largely unstudied poet and the *fitna* of Qayrawan which led to his exile, initially to Sicily and eventually to al-Andalus, I will undertake a close reading of the *lāmiyya*'s elegiac/nostalgic verses and explore some of its most salient linguistic and rhetorical features. I will also discuss the elegiac and nostalgic representation (or lack thereof) of Qayrawan's once majestic "cityscape" and its iconic buildings. I will do so by comparing it to the *nūniyya* of Ibn Rashīq, as well as the relatively more studied city-elegies from al-Andalus and al-Mashriq that have received attention by scholars such as Zayde Antrim and Alexander Elinson.[10]

Ibn Sharaf and the *Kharāb* of Qayrawan

Muḥammad ibn Saᶜīd ibn Sharaf al-Judhāmī al-Qayrawānī (d. 1067) is one of the two most recognizable literary figures associated with Qayrawan, the second being his archrival, Ibn Rashīq. Unlike the latter, however, Ibn Sharaf was a Qayrawānī de *souche* (native-born), who is said to have been born around 1000 CE (Bouyahia, 116). During his boyhood, he received a traditional education in all branches of Islamic knowledge (*Muᶜjam al-udabāᵓ*, 2,636). In his youth, he was fortunate to have been tutored by some of Qayrawan's most influential scholars, such as Abū al-Ḥasan al-Qābisī (d. 1012), al-Qazzāz al-Qayrawānī (d. 1022), Abū ᶜImrān al-Fāsī (d. 1039), Ibrahīm al-Ḥuṣrī [the *adīb*], and Ibn Abī al-Rijāl (d. 1035), who most likely introduced him to the court of the Zīrid governor, al-Muᶜizz Ibn Bādīs (r. 1016–62), as he did Ibn Rashīq. At the Zirid court, Ibn Sharaf competed with Ibn Rashīq and reports suggest that Ibn Bādīs found enormous entertainment in fueling their poetic rivalry (*Bisāṭ al-ᶜaqīq*, 58).

As a city, Qayrawan thrived under the Zirids (972–1152) and remained the favorite destination for Maghribi scholars aspiring to fame and patronage until its invasion by the Banu Hilāl in 1057. Maghribi chronicler ᶜAbd al-Wāḥid al-Marrākushī (d. 1185) aptly explains this in *Al-Muᶜjib fī talkhīṣ akhbār al-Maghrib*, where he states that Qayrawan, "from its foundation until it was sacked by the Bedouins was the [power]house of knowledge in the West, the center of its major scholars, and the destination of the seekers of knowledge across it [the West]" (441).[11] While a comprehensive exploration of the Hilālī invasion and sacking of Qayrawan goes beyond the scope of the present chapter, it is important to note that the fate of Qayrawan dramatically changed in 1045[12] when its Zirid governor, al-Muᶜizz, decided to sever his ties with the Fatimids of Egypt. Not only did he riskily declare his principality independent of the Fatimids, but he boldly reinstated it to Sunnism by swearing allegiance to the Abbasids in Baghdad (*Kitāb al-bayān al-mughrib fī akhbār al-Andalus wa- l-Maghrib*, 397).[13] This religio-political move led indirectly to the catastrophic invasion and sacking of his capital city at the hands of nomadic tribes of Banū Hilāl and their associates in 1057. Flocking mainly from Najd and Hijaz via Upper Egypt, these tribes and others such as Banū Salīm and Banū Riyāḥ were unleashed by the Faṭimids as a vindictive retaliation against the Zirid governor al-Muᶜizz. Ibn Sharaf fled with his patron al-Muᶜizz and his archrival Ibn Rashīq to Mahdiyya (*Muᶜjam al-udabāᵓ*, 2,636).

Unlike Ibn Rashīq, who stayed with his patron until his death in Mahdiyya, Ibn Sharaf left for Mazzara in Sicily. After a few months, he emigrated to al-Andalus, where he spent the rest of his life seeking patronage in numerous courts of the *Mulūk al-ṭawāʾif*, "moving from one town to another," to quote Ibn Bassām (181). He is said to have died and been buried in Seville in 1067. Ibn Bassām lavishly praises the Qayrawānī poet, hailing him as "one of the knights of this art, who equally mastered poetry and prose, playing with both like the wind would play with the leaning branches" (170).[14] Most important to this chapter is Ibn Bassām's acute assessment of Ibn Sharaf as a poet of exceptional emotional intensity, comparable to Ibn Darrāj al-Qasṭalī (d. 1038) in his expression of "extreme complaint against Fate and the description of disasters" (171).[15] This statement, as we shall see in the *lāmiyya*, is not an exaggeration.

Truly, the *lāmiyya* is a masterpiece of elegiac and nostalgic poetry that is imbued with pathos and despair. If not a few days after fleeing Qayrawan to Mahdiyya, Ibn Sharaf most likely composed it in Sicily during the first several months after the catastrophic sack of Qayrawan. In fact, it could well be his first *marthiyya* for Qayrawan, not least because of the emotional outbursts and psychological intensity which surpass his other city-elegies. Indeed, one may confidently suggest from the outset that among all the surviving city-elegies for Qayrawan, the *lāmiyya* is by far the most pathetically hopeless and darkly pessimistic. To paraphrase Richard Chase, the tone and mode of the *lāmiyya* is pathologically desperate and Ibn Sharaf's explosive emotions never seem to subside, even in the consolatory "orders of meaning," as Chase once put it, concomitant with the acceptance of *al-qadar* (Fate) (142). The reigning gloom and despondency are masterfully initiated by a powerful *maṭlaᶜ* which, to paraphrase Ibn Rashīq, forcefully strikes the ear and touches the heart.[16] To appreciate the impact of this opening, it is worth pausing here to consider its Arabic transliteration and translation, along with the second macabre line:

āhin li-l-qayrawāni annatu shajwin
ᶜan fuʾādin bi-jāḥimi l-ḥuzni yaṣla
ḥīna ᶜādat bihi – ddiyāru qubūran
bal aqūlu – ddiyāru minunna akhla

1. Woe is me for Qayrawan! A groan of grief
   from a heart burning with the fire of sorrow.
2. After her abodes have turned into graves
   rather I'd say: her abodes are even more desolate [than graves].

The onomatopoeic/polysemic *āhin* (ah!) and the extended metaphors (*isti*ᶜ*ārāt*) that saturate the opening line capture in a dramatic way the catastrophic plight (*nakba*) of the city. Moreover, they eternalize the tortured state of mourning, given the striking absence of any gnomic or consolatory tone in face of the ineluctability of *al-qadar* (Fate), *khayrihi wa-sharrih*, both good and bad, as is commonly manifest in the introductory verses of more well-known and studied city-elegies reflecting on the Islamic virtue of *ṣabr* (patience) and contemplating the faithlessness of the Times and the vagaries of the World.[17]

Indeed, the *maṭla*ᶜ drowns the entire poem in the waters of unbearable pain and evokes a hopeless nostalgia for the city and its people.[18] The derivative root of *āhin* (ah!) – *ᵓa-waw-hāᵓ* (أ, و, ه) – mixes grief with pain and represents one of the most nostalgic terms in the Arabic lexicon. Essentially a word that combines the dual elegiac and nostalgic feelings of *taᵓawwuh* (crying woe) and that of *taḥassur* (pitying), this *annatu fuᵓādin* (a heart's groan), to use Ibn Sharaf's own words, is metaphorically intensified by the striking pun on the burning pain for the symbolically burned city. The play on *jāḥim* (vehemence) and *jaḥīm* (hellfire) in the phrase *bi-jāḥimi* (burning with the fire) conjures the tortured and pitiful cries of the poet for a dead city and its dead inhabitants.[19] In the Greek elegiac tradition, the word elegy was imagined by Hellenistic scholars to have origin in *e e legein*, "to cry woe" and express pity. As explained by Alison Keith in *Latin Elegy and Hellenistic Epigram: A Tale of Two Genres at Rome*, "the Greek etymology deriving elegia from funerary lament, ἐ ἐ λέγειν (to cry 'woe, woe'), and/or ἔλεςο (pity)" (2). Indeed, Ibn Sharaf designs a forceful "Hum(e)an scheme of affection," (142) to use Eric Parisot's suggestive phrase.[20] Seen from this vantage point, Ibn Sharaf seems to rely heavily on the efficacy of his poetic text to create a "sympathetic exchange," with his readers past and present (142). But Ibn Sharaf relies equally on a weaponry of elegiac/nostalgic classical lexicons, motifs, rhetorics, metaphors and Islamic vocabulary to perpetuate this sympathetic exchange from the very first word of his elegy to the last.

The extended metaphors and imagery brim with apocalyptic references and cataclysmic allusions borrowed from the Qurᵓānic descriptions of *ahwāl al-qiyāma* (the horrors of the Judgment Day). The striking effect of metaphorical *yawm al-ḥashr* (Day of Gathering) is obvious in this regard, especially when it comes to capturing the horrors and dreads of the inhabitants of Qayrawan. Simulating the *ṣarkha* (cry) of death as well as the individuated and communal cries of horrified human beings, the tortured cry of the poet's heart comes with a *double-entendre*: a worldly cry mimicking the announcement of death and the cries of humanity during the Gathering Day.[21] In fact, the *cri* and tortured weeping is intensified by hyperbolic *janāʾizī* /*macaberesque* vocabulary of lines (2–4).[22] While the funeralesque diction and tone inundate the first five lines directly, they also indirectly reverberate throughout the entire poem. This makes the elegy nothing short of a recitation of mourning akin to the bewailing *ḥusayniyya*,[23] without any willingness for consolatory mourning. The stirring effect is the moving description of unbearable pain and excruciating *ḥasra* (regret) over the permanent loss of the city and the never-ending plight of its people. This eternal doom is structurally and thematically captured by the striking absence of some of the most conventional motifs of the Arabic elegy, be it for humans or cities: the eulogy section, the consolatory motifs of universal mourning, the transience of human life, and the ineluctability of a deceitful Fate.[24] Between the *maṭlaᶜ* and the *khitām* (the closing line) there is a poetic exhibition of pessimism that amounts to the Islamically problematic *ḍajar*/*jazaᶜ* (existential anxiety amounting to denouncing Fate) during times of tragedies and afflictions.[25] In this regard, Ibn Bassām did not hide his annoyance at Ibn Sharaf, accusing him several times of transgression (*tajāwuz*) of Islamically legitimate *ḥuzn* (grief).[26] Ibn Sharaf recasts his elegy in a defeatist language and pessimistic imagery reminiscent of the sub-genres of *shakwā al-zamān wa-l-insān* (complaint about life and humanity), which were among his favorite themes.[27]

There is also the predominance of the traditional *aṭlāl* motif, which the elegist impressively employs in an urban setting, not surprising for a poet-critic who authored a masterful text on the balance between ancient and modern poetics.[28] By all accounts, the *aṭlāl* motif, albeit removed from its origins in the Eastern Arabian desert, was still crucial to the poet's attempt to elegiacally and nostalgically seize time, to paraphrase Jaroslav Stetkeyvych's classic *Zephyrs of Najd: The Poetics of Nostalgia in the Classical Arabic Nasīb* (116). In these contexts, the elegiac *nasīb* is stripped of the *locus classicus* of the abandoned desert campsite. The latter is effectively traded for the destroyed and desolate city. Of particular poignancy is Ibn Sharaf's reliance on widely recognizable urban images, such as candles and lamps instead of burning fire and barking dogs which would traditionally signal the existence of human life in a desert context (Verses 4–5). Even if compared to Ibn Ḥamdīs al-Ṣīqillī (d. 1133), Ibn Sharaf is second to none in the Islamic West in the intricate manipulation of the classical *aṭlāl* motif in the elegiac and nostalgic construction of his lost homeland. In this way, Ibn Sharaf's dramatic fashioning of a poetics of loss and mourning is conventional and unconventional at the same time. In doing so, he has successfully fashioned an elegiac and nostalgic "literary memorial," to Qayrawan, to borrow William Granara's description of Ibn Ḥamdīs' *Ṣiqilliyyāt* (poems on Sicily) (168). Perhaps more manifest in Ibn Sharaf are the pessimistic poetics of mourning which would be echoed in modern and postmodern elegiac productions, as will be discussed below.

The degree of the calamity is intensified by the feminization of Qayrawan, which Ibn Sharaf uses to play on the symbolic dishonoring of the city. There is nearly an equation, simultaneously latent and manifest, of the literal sacking of the city with the symbolic violation of its once protected *ḥarīm* (women), associated across the wide spectrum of medieval Arabic-Islamic texts with the safeguarding of honor. In several aspects, the poet is unique in his performative dramatization of the plight of Qayrawānī women. The *lāmiyya* is replete with moving dramatic scenes, to loosely use Beatrice Gruendler's term, which sensationalize their suffering (32):

9. A noise and clamor like the clamoring of humankind on Judgment Day
   weeping as secrets are put to the test.
10. Rises up from the widows who were left behind with orphans
    overwhelmed with grief, remorse, and bereavement.
11. And bereft mothers and pregnant widows.
    each carrying a little girl who holds an infant and a little boy.
12. And a guarded beauty as lovely as the sun,
    with wide kohl-lined eyes was now bound in rags.
13. Her covered seat was left behind,
    so she was exposed to the public in her adorned garments.
14. Time and those in authority (the rulers) oppressed them
    so they fled into the world seeking justice.
15. Leaving behind their homes, furniture, and that which would preoccupy,
    none of them carried with him any load.
16. They wore rags of coarse wool
    and the highborn among the people have become lowly.
17. The women are all weeping; ᶜAfrāᵓ aids Suᶜdā to wail
    and Suᶜād responds with a full and a long cry.

The above verses are nothing short of a "dramatic performance," as Suzanne P. Stetkevych would put it, of the plight of what was seen as the most venerable group of Qayrawānī citizens (252). All in all, Ibn Sharaf is matchless in capturing the plight of refugees and dramatically documenting the horror of forced exiles.

Most touching of all is Ibn Sharaf's sensationalization of the violation of refugees' dignity. Indeed, Ibn Bassām commented that Ibn Sharaf was unequaled in the poetic documentation of the eternal *idhlāl* (humiliation) of the Qayrawānī refugees.[29] Conjuring in our present moment the miserable treatment of Syrian refugees and the constant stream of photos and videos dramatizing their humiliation across borders, the following lines from the *lāmiyya* are worth quoting:

25. And if Fates rescue from among them
    a refugee bearing his possessions to safety,
26. He would be met with humiliation and shame
    wherever he arrives across the lands.
27. They would encounter no one but arrogant men,
    who treat him with spite and resentment.
28. You would see the noblest of men
    forced to bow their heads and oblige scoundrels.

The Qayrawānī *sharaf* (honor) is mourned by Ibn Sharaf (literally the Son of Honor) like no other honorable Qayrawānī poet. One can interpret this as a pun on the poet's name in line (27) thus leaving a space for reading the *lāmiyya* as a subtle poetic account of the poet's individual experience of forced exile. As pointed out by Michael Brett, "there is a clear autobiographical element in these verses of Ibn Sharaf" (83). In other words, more can be gleaned from this likely autobiographical segment, especially when it comes to the high human price of exile even when the exile seemingly enjoys the worldly fame and comfort of royal courts, such as those that hosted Ibn Sharaf in Sicily and al-Andalus.[30]

In this particular context, Ibn Sharaf accentuates his pessimistic view of exile by radically disregarding all conventional consolatory motifs in his *lāmiyya*. This is true of his deliberate removal of any gnomic statements about Fate as well as his disregard of the concomitant motifs of universal mourning and sympathy. These motifs were manifest in both the *nūniyya* of Ibn Rashīq and *tāʾiyya* of al-Ḥuṣrī. To quote the *nūniyya* of Ibn Rashīq:

What a horrific disaster! The grief [it brought] will never fade
  its day and night will never end.

Had Mount Thahlān been smitten with a tenth of it [the disaster]
its peak would have crumbled into dust.
All the provinces of Iraq grieved for it (Qayrawan)
and so did the towns of the Levant, Egypt, and Khurasan.
The regions of India and the Two Sinds trembled and succumbed to despair
out of sorrow for its misfortune.
After its desolation, the regions that lie,
between al-Andalus and
Ḥulwān [Irāq] were effaced.
I see the stars rise dimly on their horizon/
and the two moons [the sun and the moon] turn dark.
I see the lofty mountains brought low/ both men and jinn are trembling.
And the once stable earth, distraught on account of it, now listing precariously.

(*Dīwān Ibn Rashīq*, 210–11)

Interestingly enough, predating many modern urban elegists, Ibn Sharaf resisted the generic temptation of "turning grief into consolation," as Jahan Ramzani puts it (4). In other words, by resisting the conventional universal mourning and other consolatory motifs, Ibn Sharaf, to quote Ramzani, "vandalized the elegy's consolatory machinery" (5). The effect is a strikingly modern poetics of mourning akin to what Ramzani, employing Freud's theories of melancholia,[31] described as "the melancholic mourning" which contradicts the "normative mourning" associated with the psychological stabilizing of grief. In the context of classical Arabic elegy, the ultimate acceptance of tragedy and the final submission to Fate represents perfectly the normative consolatory grief. Ibn Bassām's comment on what he deemed as *tajāwuz* (transgression) on the part of Ibn Sharaf in his grief, is an impressive critical intervention on Ibn Sharaf's defiance of the Islamically sanctioned normative grief and the consolatory classical poetics of mourning. Ibn Bassām grasped it very well when he summarized the city-elegies as poetic documentation of the *idhlāl* (humiliation) of *ahl al-qayrawan,* the people of Qayrawan, in exile.

Perhaps most important to this volume, which explores the representation of the city in Arabic literature, is Ibn Sharaf's stunning neglect of the physical Qayrawan, its toponyms and its once majestic structural buildings and architectural icons. In contrast to what Zayde Antrim points out about elegiac and nostalgic explorations of the "urban built environment" in Andalusian and Mashriqi city-elegies, as well as Alexander Elinson's exploration of the centrality of toponyms and geographical naming of actual spaces in Andalusian city-elegies (68), the *lāmiyya* and indeed the entire corpus of Ibn Sharaf's city-elegies fail to mention any iconic structures of the metropolis that was hailed by al-Muqaddasī (d. 946) as "the pride of the Arabs," (224)[32] and by al-Idrīsī (d. 1165) as, "the greatest city in the West, the most populated, the most prosperous and thriving, with the most perfect buildings"(284).[33,34]

In *Routes and Realms: The Power of Place in the Early Islamic World*, Zayde Antrim has explored some of the earliest and most interesting specimens of *rithā᾿ al-mudun* in classical Arabic literature: al-Khuraymī, Ibn al-Rūmi, and Ibn Shuhayd, who lamented in verse the sacking of Baghdad, Basra, and Cordoba respectively. According to Antrim, these three city-elegists referred nostalgically to their cities' once majestic palaces, bustling markets, lively suburbs, thriving seaports, and river bridges and banks. Examining what she phrases as "the intersection between nostalgic representations of territory and descriptions of the urban built environment," Antrim has aptly shown the predominance of the built environment in these three Arabic city-elegies, especially in terms of the elegiac and nostalgic representation of the diminished cityscape (75). Al-Khuraymī nostalgically refers to a number of Baghdād districts and palaces such as Zandaward, al-Yāsiriyya, al-Khayzurāniyya, and the palace of ᶜAbdawayh. Ibn Shuhayd refers to the Umayyad palaces of Zāhiriyya and ᶜĀmiriyya. Ibn al-Rūmi mentions the city's bustling markets, its inbound and outbound ships, the palaces and mansions, other edifices. By contrast, Ibn Sharaf, in fact all Qayrawānī city-elegists, did not show similar interest in the actual physical spaces of their city. The only exception is Ibn Rashīq's reference to Qayrawan's most symbolic religious space and architectural icon: the Great Mosque of ᶜUqba ibn Nafiᶜ.[35] Similarly, by closely exploring the themes, images, and rhetorical strategies related to Qayrawan, it is hard not to suggest that unlike Andalusian city-elegists, Ibn Sharaf is never interested, as Elinson puts it, in "defining his lost city geographically and architecturally" ("Loss Written in Stone," 107) or in elegizing or memorializing "manmade places" and "the urban reality" (*Looking Back*, 21–2).[36]

But what is most peculiar about the *lāmiyya* is the absence overall of any rhetorical construction of a glorious past of the city as can be strongly detected in Ibn Rashīq and al-Ḥuṣrī who both constructed an idealized Islamic past for Qayrawan. They did so mainly by referring to the desolation of their city's most symbolic *mnemotopos* or site of memory, to use Pierre Nora's application, the Mosque of ʿUqba. To quote Ibn Rashīq's *nūniyya*:

As for the [once] thronged Mosque of ʿUqba,
its halls were deserted and its corners were filled with gloom.
So desolate that no congregation attended [anymore]
either to perform or call for the five prayers.
A house in which The Lord was worshiped
after the excess of idol worshipping was abolished.
A house built with The Lord's inspiration;
blessed are the building, the one who ordered its building, and the builder.

(*Dīwān Ibn Rashīq*, 209–10)

In fact, Ibn Sharaf did not shed a single tear for his city's once majestic worldly buildings and structures: its palatial seats of al-ʿAbbāsiyya, Raqqāda and Ṣabra al-Manṣūriyya, its palaces, its markets, its public baths, its gates, and cultural/scientific centers, its *bayt al-ḥikma*, hospitals, its iconic *fisqiyyāt* (cisterns) and *ḥanāyā* (aqueducts), and artificial pools and gardens. Surprisingly enough, the remembrance of the pre-Hilālī urban majesty of Qayrawan would turn into a nostalgic theme in non-Qayrawānī prose. The "prosification," of *rithāʾ al-Qayrawan*, to use Elinson's suggestive word, is indeed a topic worth studying separately. Al-Idrīsī halted literally at the *aṭlāl* of Qayarwan, a city that had once been the most majestic metropolis of the Maghrib, and described it as nothing but "erased traces and obliterated ruins" (284).[37] Echoing al-Idrīsī, al-ʿAbdarī (d. 1336) said: "We entered Qayrawan only to find a glory that was erased by the hand of Time and monuments that had existed once upon a time!"[38] In *Al-Maqāmat al-Luzūmiyya,* Andalusian Ibn Yūsuf al-Saraqūstī (d. 1143), to cite perhaps the most interesting example of the "prosification" of *rithāʾ al-Qayrawan*, devoted an entire *maqāma* to its lamentation. The opening lines, masterfully translated by James Monroe, are worth quoting:

We set up in a group, traveling in caravan, until we came to the city of Qayrawan ... Destruction had overtaken the city, Bedouin Arabs had made off with its power, diminished its cistern and pool, and shaken its

> Khawarnaq and Sadīr. I therefore halted before those ruins and tracings, and felt nostalgia for those vestiges and tattoo-like markings. (*Al-Maqāmāt al-luzūmīyah*, 302)[39]

To sum up, readers familiar with the more studied Andalusian and Mashriqi city-elegies would be surprised by the stunning absence of the cityscape that once made Qayrawan, to quote al-Idrīsī again, "the greatest metropolis of al-Maghrib" (284). This aside, what is most salient about the *lāmiyya* is the dramatization of the pain of exile and the anxiety of remembrance which Ibn Sharaf succinctly conveys with his pessimistic assessment of the doom of a fallen city and the tragic contemplation, if not condemnation, of human life itself. Echoing modern pessimism, the message seems to edge toward renouncing fatalism. In fact, like Ibn Darrāj al-Qasṭalī, as Ibn Bassām theorized, there is something Maᶜarrian in the elegiac production of Ibn Sharaf which is intensely dark, inherently pessimistic and contemplative, even existentialist. This adds to the complexity of Ibn Sharaf's poetic heritage, one that is still to be unearthed, explored, and circulated in the Western academy as well as the Arab world itself. Most important to our current world at large, Ibn Sharaf captured poetically, perhaps like no other medieval poet in my view, not only the physical but also the psychological and mental trauma of refugees.[40] The catastrophic plight of Syrian refugees and the current *kharāb* of Aleppo should add more humanistic value to the present chapter – at least this is the hope of the author, whose poetic and prosaic tears literally mix with his academic ones for the sake of the millions of suffering Syrian children. One cannot stop wondering what kind of city-elegies for Aleppo Ibn Sharaf would have composed had he witnessed what we are witnessing. For the time being, by merely changing the word Qayrawan in the *lāmiyya* fully translated in English below, we can all "cry woe" to Aleppo.

Appendix: Full English Translation of the *Lāmiyya*

1. Woe is me for Qayrawan! A groan of grief
   from a heart burning with the fire of sorrow.
2. After her abodes have turned into graves
   rather I'd say: her abodes are even more desolate [than graves].
3. There are no candles except for stars on whose
   horizon, half-asleep women tread wearily.
4. Where once the flowers of the candelabras brightly lit,
   and the threads of the lamp-wicks tightly twisted.

5. The lovely women's faces were even more dazzling [than the candles],
   surpassing them in meaning and in form.
6. Were you to look at those to whom your path was rugged
   how they have made the rugged path plain.
7. After a day when humankind appeared as if gathered [on Judgment Day],
   their feet bare, their legs naked.
8. In a crush like the throng of Judgment Day
   where books [of deeds] are recited [for reckoning].
9. A noise and clamor like the clamoring of humankind on Judgment Day
   weeping as secrets are put to the test.
10. Rise up from the widows who were left behind with orphans
    overwhelmed with grief, remorse, and bereavement.
11. And bereft mothers and pregnant widows,
    each carrying a little girl who holds an infant and a little boy.
12. And a guarded beauty as lovely as the sun,
    with wide kol-lined eyes was now bound in rags.
13. Her covered seat was left behind,
    so she was exposed to the public in her adorned garments.
14. Time and those in authority [the rulers] oppressed them
    so they fled into the world seeking justice.
15. Leaving behind their homes, furniture, and that which would preoccupy,
    none of them carried with him any load.
16. They wore rags of coarse wool
    and the highborn among the people have become plebeian [lowly].
17. The women are all weeping; ᶜAfrāᵓ aids Suᶜda to wail
    and Suᶜād responds with a full and a long cry.
18. None of the women could bid farewell to a neighbor nor could a wife see off her dead husband.
19. Separation assailed all the women so they were forced into exile group by group.
20. And if the wilderness brought them together again,
    another Fate would strike them with a different arrow,
21. Of serpents bearing fangs of bent spears,
    arrows, and sword blades.
22. And devils bearing spears coming upon
    the unarmed wretches amidst the dark wilderness.

23. The backs [of the refugees] are stripped bare and dragged off by force;
their bellies are slit and gutted clean.
24. And when they strike in the bowels one of the people they desire
they do the same to all the others.
25. And if Fates rescue from among them
a refugee bearing his possessions to safety,
26. He would be met with humiliation and shame
wherever he alights across the lands.
27. They would encounter no one but arrogant men,
who treat him with spite and resentment.
28. You would see the noblest of men
forced to bow their heads and oblige scoundrels.
29. Every time they are driven off from a land,
separately on horseback or on foot,
30. They are scattered across lands east and west
shedding tears in torrents and floods.
31. No kinsman meets a kinsman to console him,
nor does a friend meet a friend.
32. If only I knew whether I will ever return in the unknown future
to the place that has for so long caused me sorrow!

(*Dīwān Ibn Sharaf*, 89)

Notes

1. Quoted in *Al-Dhakhīra* (1979: 235).
2. A reference to the most quoted example in classical Arabic grammar: *ḍaraba zaydun ᶜamran* (ضَرَبَ زَيْدٌ عَمْرًا).
3. Unfortunately, the recent co-edited volume entitled *The Fall of Cities in the Mediterranean: Commemoration in Literature, Folk-Song, and Liturgy* (Bachvarova *et al.* 2016), which chiefly explores ancient and premodern Mediterranean and Middle Eastern city-elegies, fails to mention even in passing Ibn Sharaf or any of his compatriots who bequeathed a rich corpus of city-elegies for Qayrawan, which by all accounts was one of the most important Mediterranean medieval metropolises. In addition to Ibn Sharaf, the list includes famed poets that many would consider the greatest of Qayrawan: Ibn Rashīq (d. 1064), ᶜAlī al-Ḥuṣrī (d. 1095), and Ibn Faḍḍāl al-Qayrawānī (d. 1086). All four lived to see their beloved city ravaged, destroyed, and desolated. "Their lamentation in verse," Michael Brett notes, "is a literary monument to the disaster, couched in conventional language and imagery of poetry" (2008: 77). In fact, the four were personally impacted by

the catastrophe and were forced to flee their beloved city, to live and die in exile in various Mediterranean countries like Italy (Sicily), Spain (al-Andalus), and Morocco. Despite the fascinating interdisciplinary outlook of the essays – which mostly explore ancient and premodern Greek and Latin city-elegies for Athens, Rome, and Constantinople – there is no reference in the book whatsoever to the rich Mediterranean corpus of premodern Arabic *rithāʾ al-mudun*.

4. Ibn Faḍḍāl al-Ḥilwānī, who also emigrated to al-Andalus after the fall of his city. Ibn Bassām considered him among the major poets who moved to al-Andalus and devoted a lengthy section to his poetry.
5. To both of whom he devoted much more space and provided more comments. This is most likely because both poems seemed more suitable to his project of propagating the Islamic virtues of the city. Unlike all the pessimistic poems of Ibn Sharaf, Ibn Rashīq in particular served better the quasi-hagiographical orientation of *Maᶜālim al-īmān*. As I have shown elsewhere, Ibn Rashīq's elegy brims with Islamic themes and reads more like a eulogy for Qayrawan's *fuqahāʾ*. This is also true – although to a lesser degree – of al-Ḥuṣrī's *tāʾiyya*, which contains several verses highlighting the Islamic theme of the city and praising its scholars. For more on the *nūniyya*, see Hermes (2017).
6. Certainly, it is rather ironic that Ibn Bassām – an ultra-Andalucentrist whose gigantic project, as revealed by the title of his magnum opus, was to preserve and propagate the cultural and literary excellence of al-Andalus against the cultural and literary hegemony of not only al-Mashriq but also al-Maghrib (North Africa) – ended up preserving for posterity the competing classical Qayrawānī poetic heritage like no other Qayrawānī chronicler, including al-Dabbāgh and Ibn Nājī (d. 1435)!
7. The title of the section is "*Akhbār Abī ᶜAbdi Allāh ibn Sharaf wa-ghurarī ash ᶜ ārihi wa-dhikri kharābi baladihi al-qayrawān* (Information on Ibn Sharaf, the Crowns of his Poetry, and Mentioning the Destruction of his City Qayrawan)."
8. It was suggested to me in a private exchange with Professor Suzanne P. Stetkevych that curricular use and modern popularity of Ibn Rashīq's *nūniyya* in the Arab world relate to its nostalgic construction of a Golden Age of Arab-Islamic learning and scholarship. For a related discussion, see Suzanne P. Stetkevych (2016).
9. Nearly all English studies on premodern Arabic city-elegies fail to incorporate chapters on the Qayrawānī/Maghribi corpus of city elegy. In addition to Alexander Elinson's fascinating study on Andalusian city-elegies, I have in mind Ibrāhīm Sinjilāwī's unpublished dissertation, "The Lament for Fallen Cities: A Study of the Development of the Elegiac Genre in Classical Arabic Poetry"

(1983) and more recently, Anan Habeeb's unpublished dissertation, "Nostalgia and the East in the Arabic and Hebrew poetry of Islamic Spain" (2015).

10. Both consider the city-elegies to Baghdad, Basra, and Cordoba by al-Khuraymī (d. 821), Ibn al-Rūmī (d. 896) from the Mashriq, and Ibn Shuhayd (d. 1035) from al-Andalus as the earliest specimen of Arabic city elegy. Professor Geert van Gelder alerted me to Ibn al-Muᶜtazz's (d. 908) elegy to Samarra, Abū Nāẓira al-Sadūsī (d. 875) to Basra. I have just found a fragment of a forgotten elegy by Algerian Bakr ibn Ḥammād al-Tāhartī (d. 909) to Tahart/Tahert (Western Algeria), the capital city of the Rustamids (779–909). I am currently working on the surviving fragments of this *nūniyya* and other medieval Maghribi city-elegies in a forthcoming project entitled, *Of Cities and the Poetic Imagination in the Premodern and Modern Maghrib* (Kingston ON: McGill-Queen's University Press).
11. See also Abū al-ᶜArab al-Qayrawānī (d. 945), *Ṭaabaqāt ᶜulamāᵓ Ifrīqīyah wa-Tūnis* (al-Dār al-Tūnisīya lil-Nashr, 1968), Abū Bakr al-Mālikī (d. 1061), *Kitāb riyāḍ al-nufūs fī ṭabaqāt ᶜulamāᵓ al-Qayrawan wa-Ifriqiyya* (1983), and Muḥammad ibn Aḥmad Muᶜaskarī, *Nabaᵓ al-īwān bi-jamᶜ al-dīwān fī dhikr ṣulaḥāᵓ madīnat al-Qayrawan* (Markaz al-Dirāsāt al-Islāmiyya bi-l-Qayrawān, 2012).
12. Ibn Khaldūn's own date.
13. For a revisionist Western discussion of the Hilali invasion and its impact on Qayrawan and Ifriqiya in general, see Jacob Abadi (2013: his chapter on the Zīrīds and the Hilālīs, 103–32).
14. The modern renewal of interest in Ibn Sharaf's poetry was ushered in in the early decades of the twentieth century by Indian Arabist al-Maymanī (Rājkūtī) who published *Al-Nutaf min shiᶜr Ibn Rashīq wa-zamīlihi Ibn Sharaf al-Qayrawānīyayn* in Cairo around 1925. It seems that al-Maymanī was influenced by the assessment – however biased against the other great Qayrawani poets, especially ᶜAlī al-ḥuṣrī – of ᶜAbd al-Raḥmān ibn Khaldūn, who singled out Ibn Rashīq and Ibn Sharaf as *faḥlā al-qayrawān* (the two giants of Qayrawan). Of course, many would not agree with Ibn Khaldun's assessment, not least because it does not give credit to ᶜAlī al-ḥuṣrī (*al- ḍarīr/al-makfūf,* the blind), whom many would see as the greatest poet of Qayrawan. Ḥasan Ḥusnī ᶜAbd al-Wahhāb (d. 1968), Tunisia's most renowned modern historian and literary critic, dubs al-ḥuṣrī, Ibn Sharaf, and Ibn Rashīq the Qayrawānī *thālūth* (trinity), a clever response to Ibn Khaldūn.
15. *"inḥanā manḥā al-qasṭalī fi-shakwā al-zaman wa-l- ḥadīthi ᶜani l-fitan"*
16. While a talented and independent critic on his own, Ibn Sharaf placed an importance on the *maṭlaᶜ* reflective of his arch-rival Ibn Rashīq's recommendation: "poetry is a lock the first (part) of which is the key. A poet ought to make

the beginning of his poem good, for it is the first thing to strike the ear; and from it one can infer, from the first instant, what he has to say" (*mā^cindahū*) (Van Gelder 1982: 116).

17. Dubbed in the Arab world, "*ummu al-marāthī wa-sayyidat al-qawāfi* / the mother of elegies and the queen of poems," one is, of course, referring here to al-Sharīf al-Rundī's classic "*Nuniyya fi-Rithā*ᵓ *al-Andalus*." The *maṭla*ᶜ of this Andalusian elegiac masterpiece has attained an unequaled fame and is one of the most quoted verses in the Arabic-Islamic world. As masterfully translated by James T. Monroe, the *maṭla*ᶜ is as follows: "Everything declines after reaching perfection,/therefore let no man be beguiled by the sweetness of a pleasant life"(1974: 336).
18. While the discussion of the nostalgic modes of the *lāmiyya* goes beyond the scope of this chapter, not least because of word-limit, one can briefly argue that there is a predominance of what the late Svetlana Boym termed "reflective nostalgia," over "restorative nostalgia." While Boym does not perceive them as "absolute binaries," she maintains that restorative nostalgia focuses on the *nostos* (home), endeavoring to "rebuild the lost home and patch up the memory gap." Restorative nostalgia is predominantly characteristic of nationalistic and religious projects that physically and rhetorically aim to rebuild a mythologized 'golden age.' Reflective nostalgia de-emphasizes the *regainability* of the past in favor of *algia* (longing). "*Algia*," to quote Boym, "lingers on ruins, the patina of time and history, in the dreams of another place and another time" (2001: 41).
19. The turn from life into death is metaphorically captured through the *ṭibāq* (paradox) between light and darkness. This is intensified by the allusions to the candles as flowers to represent the bygone brilliance and grace of the city. Remarkable is also the grave imagery which is intensified through the *istiᶜārah* (metaphor) "*bal aqūlu – diyāru minunna akhla.*"
20. This is a recently coined phrase by Eric Parisot to delineate what he describes as the broadening of sympathetic horizons in elegiac poetry from the elegist (actor) and reader (spectator) to different mourning communities at large (2016: 142).
21. There is a striking absence of the Qurᵓān's apocalyptic references and cataclysmic allusions in Ibn Rashīq's *nūniyya*. Ibn Rashīq opted for the more conventional cosmic mourning and universal sympathy.
22. There is always a strong possibility that the word "*macabre*" is etymologically rooted in the Arabic *maqābir* (مقابر), plural of *maqbara* (graveyard). "Macaberesque" is my own approximation.
23. A Shiᶜi Mourning performance commemorating the martyrdom of Imām al-Ḥusayn.

24. The most conventional motifs of classical Arabic elegy are ably discussed by Arie Schippers (1988).
25. Most likely, it is the predominance of *ḍajar* and *jaza*ᶜ that discouraged al-Dabbāgh from incorporating the *lāmīyya* in the introduction to *Ma*ᶜ*ālim al-īmān.*
26. For example, commenting on the prefatory lines of the present study, Ibn Bassām commented: *ḍajara abū* ᶜ*abdillāh* ᶜ*afaā allāhu* ᶜ*anh* (Abū ᶜAbd Allah has expressed his vexation may God forgive him) (*Al-Dhakhīra*, 1979: 235). Of course, we have to relate this to the Islamic tenet of *al-riḍā bi-l-qadari khayrihi wa-sharrih* in order to understand the statement of Ibn Bassām and his *du*ᶜ*ā* of forgiveness for Ibn Sharaf.
27. Indeed, in addition to the second prefatory quotation, some of his moving lines are worth quoting in this regard: "If you ask about my satisfaction with Fate, it is similar to the view of al-Farazdaq of the Banū Yarbūᶜ"; "What are these frauds that you have committed?/ by calling the traitors brothers!"; "By God, the treason of the envious foe is nothing/ Compared to the treason of the brother and the friend!" (*Dīwān*, 101–8).
28. Ibn Sharaf is among the classical critics who opted for a balanced and moderate position on the heated debate between *al-qadīm wa-l- ḥadīth* (the ancient and the modern). See Pellat (ed.) (1953).
29. Again, this can be corroborated by Ibn Bassām's reference to the *idhlāl* (humiliation) of Qayrawanīs in the cities they fled to, especially Sousse, on the coast of Tunisia.
30. Sadly enough, the ongoing human plight of Syrian refugees seems to corroborate Ibn Sharaf. Indeed, François Crépeau, the UN Special Rapporteur on the Human Rights of Migrants, would describe – quite romantically – asylum-seeking and migration, as "an exercise in dignity seeking." Ibn Sharaf centuries earlier was more realistic when he, not without proof, described them as an exercise in dishonor seeking.
31. Freud (1915: 277–87).
32. "*mafkharatu al-*ᶜ*arabi wa-markazu al-sulṭāni wa-aḥadu al-arkān.*"
33. "*kānat a*ᶜ*ḍama muduni al-maghribi quṭran wa-aktharaha basharan wa-aysaraha amwālan wa-awsa*ᶜ*aha aḥwālan wa-atqanaha binā*ᵓ*an …*"
34. There is a large unstudied corpus of *Qayrawāniyyāt* both in prose and poetry bound with effusive praise for Pre-Hilālī Qayrawan. This corpus comprises texts and poems on the foundation and early growth of Qayrawan, as well as the city's golden age, which is usually equated with the Aghlabid dynasty (800–909).

35. In the entire surviving corpus of Qayrawānī city-elegies, only al-Ḥuṣrī in his 69-verse *tāʾiyya* mentions, albeit briefly, two of the iconic physical buildings of Qayrawan: the palatial seat of Ṣabra and the famous *ḥanāyā* (aqueducts):

    Since it is in God's power to decree a relief for
    those afflicted across this world,
    So why not hope that Qayrawan will return to us
    and so will Ṣabra, its mosque, and aqueducts?

    (*ᶜAlī al-Ḥuṣrī*, 158)

    Echoing al-Ḥuṣrī, Ibn Sharaf briefly refers to *qibābu ṣabra wa-l-muṣalla* (the domes of Ṣabra and the mosque) but in a panegyric he composed to praise Ibn al- Saqqāʾ (d. 1063), the competent *wazīr* of Abū al-Walīd ibn Jahwar, (petty) king of Cordoba (r. 1043–59).

36. This is so true because of the conventional absence of any eulogistic component or, in the specific context of city-elegies, even a brief reference to its virtues (*faḍāʾil*) as strikingly dominant in the *nūniyya* of Ibn Rashīq. These illustrative lines from the *nūniyya* tell much in this regard:

    Thanks to them – if *minbars* were counted – Qayrawan
    was counted the flower of all cities.
    As it proudly boasted of them, it so deservedly
    eclipsed Cairo and it outshone Baghdad.
    It became so beautiful. Then, its beauty reached perfection
    and every gazing eye was raised to it.

    (*Diwān Ibn Rashīq*, 206–7)

37. "*aṭlālun dārisatun wa-athārun ṭāmisa.*"
38. "*fa-khiltuhā majdan maḥathā yadu az-zamān wa-āthā rān yuqalu* ᶜanhā kāna *wa-kān.*"
39. For an insightful discussion of this work, see Alexander E. Elinson (2005).
40. There is something of a postmodern "elegiac humanism," to quote Ken Seigneurie (2011), in the poetic lamentation of Ibn Sharaf that is yet to be explored.

Works Cited

Abadi, Jacob (2013), *Tunisia Since the Arab Conquest: The Saga of a Westernized Muslim State*, Reading: Ithaca Press.

ᶜAbd al-Wahhāb, Ḥasan Ḥusnī (1970), *Bisāṭ al-ᶜaqīq fi ḥaḍārat al-Qayrawan wa-shāᶜirihā Ibn Rashīq*, Tunis: Maktabat al-Manār.

Al-ᶜAbdarī, *Riḥlat al-ᶜAbdarī* (1999), ᶜAlī Ibrāhīm Kurdī (ed.), Damascus: Dār Saᶜd al-Dīn.

Abū al-ᶜArab al-Qayrawānī (1968), *Ṭabaqāt ᶜulamāᵓ Ifrīqiyya wa-Tūnis,* Tunis: al-Dār al-Tūnisiyya lil-Nashr.

Antrim, Zayde (2012), *Routes and Realms: The Power of Place in the Early Islamic World,* Oxford: Oxford University Press.

Bachvarova, Mary, Dorota Dutsch and Ann Suter (eds) (2016), *The Fall of Cities in the Mediterranean: Commemoration in Literature, Folk-song, and Liturgy,* Cambridge: Cambridge University Press.

Bouyahia, Ch. (1972), *La vie littéraire en Ifriqiya sous les Zirides (362–555 de l'H./972–1160 de J.-C.*), Paris: Sorbonne.

Boym, Svetlana (2001), *The Future of Nostalgia,* New York NY: Basic Books.

Brett, Michael (2008), "The Poetry of Disaster: the Tragedy of Qayrawān 1052–1057 CE," in *Continuity and Change in the Realms of Islam: Studies in Honour of Professor Urbain Vermeulen,* K. d'Hulster and Jo van Steenbergen (eds), Leuven: Peeters, 73–89.

Chase, V. Richard (1955), *Walt Whitman Reconsidered,* London: Gollancz.

Al-Dabbāgh, Abd al-Raḥmān (1968), *Maᶜālim al-īmān fī maʿrifat ahl al-Qayrawan,* Cairo: Maktabat al-Khānji.

Elinson, Alexander E. (2005), "Tears Shed over the Poetic Past: The Prosification of *Rithāᵓ Al-mudun* in Al-Saraqustī's *Maqāma Qayrawāniyya,*" *Journal of Arabic Literature* 36: 1–27.

—— (2008), "Loss Written in Stone: Ibn Shuhayd's Rithāᵓ' for Cordoba and its Place in the Arabic Elegiac Tradition," in *Transforming Loss into Beauty: Essays on Arabic Literature and Culture in Honor of Magda al-Nowaihi,* Marlé Hammond and Dana Sajdi, (eds), Cairo: American University in Cairo Press, 79–114.

—— (2009), *Looking Back at al-Andalus: The Poetics of Loss and Nostalgia in Medieval Arabic and Hebrew Literature,* Leiden: E. J. Brill.

Freud, Sigmund (1915), "Trauer und Melancholie," *Psychoanal* 4: 277–87.

Granara, William (1999), "Remaking Muslim Sicily: Ibn Ḥamdīs and the Poetics of Exile," *Edebiyāt* 9: 167–98.

Gruendler, Beatrice (2013), *Medieval Arabic Praise Poetry: Ibn Al-Rumi and the Patron's Redemption,* New York NY: Routledge.

Habeeb, Anan (2015), "Nostalgia and the East in the Arabic and Hebrew poetry of Islamic Spain," unpublished dissertation, Bloomington: Indiana University.

Al-Ḥamawī, Yāqūt (1993), *Muᶜjam al-udabāᵓ*, Beirut: Dār al-Gharb al-Islāmī.

Hermes, Nizar F. (2017), "'It Eclipsed Cairo and Outshone Baghdad!' Ibn Rashīq's Elegy for the City of Qayrawan", *Journal of Arabic Literature* 17.3: 1–28.

Ibn Bassām, Abū al-Ḥasan (1979), *Al-Dhakhīra fī maḥāsin ahl al-jazīra*, Beirut: Dār al-Thaqāfa.

Ibn Khaldūn (2000), ᶜAbd al-Raḥmān, *Kitāb al-ᶜibar wa-dīwān al-mubtadá wa-al-khabar fī ayyām al-ᶜArab wa-al-ᶜAjam wa-al-Barbar*, vol. 6, Beirut: Dār al-Fikr.

Ibn Sharaf (1983), *Dīwān ibn Sharaf al-Qayrawani*, Ḥasan Dhikrī Ḥasan (ed.), Cairo: Maktabat al-Kullīyāt al-Azharīyya.

Al-Idrīsī, Muḥammad (1990), *Nuzhat al-mushtāq fī ikhtirāq al-āfāq*, Cairo: Maktabat al-Thaqāfah al- Dīniyya.

Keith, Alison (2011), *Latin Elegy and Hellenistic Epigram: A Tale of Two Genres at Rome*, Newcastle: Cambridge Scholars.

Al-Mālikī, Abū Bakr (1983), *Kitāb riyāḍ al-nufūs fī ṭabaqāt ᶜulamāᵓ al-Qayrawan wa-Ifriqiyya*, vol. 2, Beirut: Dār al-Gharb al-Islāmī.

Al-Marrākushī (1881), ᶜAbd al-Wāḥid, *Kitāb al-Muᶜjib fī talkhīṣ akhbār al-Maghrib*, Leiden: E. J. Brill.

Al-Marzūqī, Muḥammad and Jīlānī Ibn al-Ḥajj Yaḥya (eds) (2009), *Alī al-Ḥuṣrī al-Qayrawānī,* Tunis: Bayt al-Ḥikma.

Al-Maymanī, ᶜAbd al-ᶜAzīz (1925), *Al-Nutaf min shiᶜr Ibn Rashīq wa zamīlihi Ibn Sharaf al-Qayrawāniyyayn*, Cairo: al-Maṭba'a al-Salafīyya.

Monroe, James T. (1974), *Hispano-Arabic Poetry: A Student Anthology*, Berkeley CA: University of California Press.

Al-Muqaddasī, Muḥammad(1967), *Kitāb Aḥsan al-taqāsīm fī maᶜrifat al-aqālīm*, Leiden: E. J. Brill.

Nora, Pierre (1989), "Between Memory and History: Les Lieux de mémoire," *Representations* 26: 7–25.

Parisot, Eric (2016), *Graveyard Poetry: Religion, Aesthetics and the Mid-Eighteenth-Century Poetic Condition,* New York NY: Routledge.

Pellat, Charles (ed.) (1953), *Questions de critique littéraire, Masā ᵓil al-intiqād: texte arabe établi d'après deux éditions et traduction française*, Alger: Éditions Carbonel.

Ramzani, Jahan (1994), *Poetry of Mourning: The Modern Elegy from Hardy to Heaney*, Chicago IL: University of Chicago Press.

Al-Saraquṣṭī, Abū l-Tāhir (2002), *Al-Maqāmāt al-luzūmīyah*, trans. James T. Monroe, Leiden: E. J. Brill.

Schippers, Arie (1988), "Introduction," to "Hebrew Andalusian Elegies and the Arabic Literary Tradition," *Near Eastern Studies*: 290–338.

Seigneurie, Ken (2011), *Standing by the Ruins: Elegiac Humanism in Wartime and Postwar Lebanon*, New York NY: Fordham University Press.

Sinjilāwī, Ibrāhīm (1983), "The Lament for Fallen Cities: A Study of the Development of the Elegiac Genre in Classical Arabic Poetry," unpublished dissertation, Chicago IL: University of Chicago.

Stetkevych, Jaroslav (1993), *The Zephyrs of Najd: the Poetics of Nostalgia in the Classical Arabic Nasīb*, Chicago IL: University of Chicago Press.

—— (1994), "Toward an Arabic Elegiac Lexicon: The Seven Words of the Nasīb," in Suzanne Pinckney Stetkevych (ed.), *Reorientations: Arabic and Persian Poetry*, Bloomington IN: Indiana University Press.

Stetkevych, Suzanne Pinckney (2002), *The Poetics of Islamic Legitimacy: Myth, Gender, and Ceremony in the Classical Arabic Ode*, Bloomington IN: Indiana University Press.

—— (2016), "Abbasid Panegyric: *Badīc* Poetry and the Invention of the Arab Golden Age," *British Journal of Middle Eastern Studies*, May: 1–25, online edition.

Van Gelder, Geert (1982), *Beyond the Line, Classical Arabic Literary Critics on the Coherence and Unity of the Poem,* Leiden: E. J. Brill, 116.

Yāghī, cAbd al-Raḥmān (1961), *Dīwān Ibn Rashīq al-Qayrawānī*, Beirut: Dār al-Thaqāfa.

6

In Memory of al-Andalus: Using the Elegy to Reimagine the Literary and Literal Geography of Cordoba

Anna C. Cruz

This chapter will examine the manifestation and transformation of the genre *rithā᾽ al-mudun* (the city elegy) in the poetry of Ibn Zaydūn (d. 463/1071), a fifth/eleventh-century poet who experienced the disintegration of his home, the city of Cordoba, from afar. While Ibn Zaydūn composed numerous poems lamenting his bygone relationship with his beloved, the Umayyad princess Wallāda bint al-Mustakfī (d. 484/1091), he also wrote a number of poems elegising his beloved city. Throughout the course of his poems, his exile unfolds in temporal and spatial ways as he creates his version of Cordoba based on memories from his youth. The result is an exhaustive mapping and memorialization of Cordoba and the palace-city Madīnat al-Zahrā᾽ as a Paradise Lost. By plotting the sites mentioned by Ibn Zaydūn in consultation with archaeological, art historical, and landscape architectural sources, the goal is to present an idea of the Cordoba that once was, fusing the task of the poet and historian into a single role of connecting the past city space with the patterns of a quotidian life long gone.

Ibn Zaydūn attempts to compensate for his loss of time, space, and identity through his distinctive rendition of the *rithā᾽ al-mudun* and many of the sites, which are no longer in existence, are revivified to serve as personal repositories of memory for the exiled Cordoban. The *rithā᾽ al-mudun* genre is traditional in form and style, utilising a series of stock tropes and patterns for a twofold purpose: as a medium for one's own mourning while simultaneously immortalising the lost city as remembered by the poet. While the city elegy provides a specific framework with which one can lament the loss of a homeland, Ibn Zaydūn reformulates the elegy's existing characteristics in his *mukhammas* to evoke the same feelings of mourning, remembrance, and nostalgia.

The *rithāʾ al-mudun* emerged in al-Andalus in the fifth/eleventh century after the fall of Cordoba in 1013 due to the Berber *fitna* and remained an important Andalusian form until the Capitulation of Granada in 1492. The losses throughout al-Andalus did not originate from a single cause and thus, in each city elegy, the poets differ in their approach to both extolling and lamenting the virtues of Andalusī cities as a result of specific political and social circumstances. Their elegies fuse the beloved and the city into a single object of mourning, allowing "for a new method of altering and blending such themes as *al-aṭlāl* (the abandoned campsite), geographic description, rumination of the vicissitudes of fate, the inevitability of death, and so on."[1] The intrinsic relationship between resident and residence is clear as poets present their subjective experiences, which are tied to familiar places and memories. Similar to the Arabic elegiac tradition, the city elegy allows the poet to mourn and lament a lost beloved while providing a space to discuss the inescapable nature of Fate and the vicissitudes of time before transitioning into panegyrics of his subject. In the *nasīb*, or nostalgic prelude, per Jaroslav Stetkevych's description found in *The Zephyrs of Najd: The Poetics of Nostalgia in the Classical Arabic Nasīb*, "the male poet bemoans the loss of a female beloved, who has departed from a campsite upon whose 'traces' the poet now gazes."[2] In the city elegy, however, the beloved has become the city in ruins, or as seen in the *mukhammas* of Ibn Zaydūn, the city on the verge of or in the process of becoming ruins. "[T]he city, just like the *dār*, embodies the poet's sense of lost happiness and is the locus of a nostalgia that both triggers and anchors the melancholic poetic expression."[3]

The city elegy is representative of the loss felt by the individual, yet also becomes a historical archive for poets to record the various losses and catastrophes that occurred before their eyes. I will examine how Ibn Zaydūn remembers the city in much the same way pre-Islamic and classical Arabic poets remember the time spent with their beloveds. The obliterated abodes in the desert that once sparked nostalgic memories have been replaced with urban landscapes and palatial estates. Regardless of location, memory, in the words of Gaston Bachelard, requires a physical space in order to function, for "memories are motionless and the more securely they are fixed in space, the sounder they are."[4] According to Alexander Elinson, the city elegy includes three main characteristics: the typical elegy written in praise and honor of a fallen loved one or companion, repetitive words or phrases, and finally the use of toponyms, which is a practice that has existed since pre-Islamic times.[5] If we take these characteristics to be the "requirements" for the city elegy, the *mukhammas* of Ibn Zaydūn, I argue, is in fact part of the Andalusī *rithā᾽ al-mudun* genre. The poet's subjective experiences create an affective map of the city with the landscape and built environment serving a dual purpose: they act as the poet's personal memory devices to amplify and project back his emotion while also providing a phenomenology of the Cordoban caliphate during the tenth and eleventh centuries.

The nostalgic ode had been a tradition in al-Andalus since the establishment of Cordoba as an Umayyad emirate by ᶜAbd al-Raḥmān I (d. 172/788) in the second/eighth century. Reportedly written by the Umayyad emir himself due to his homesickness for his grandfather's estate in Syria, his ode to a palm tree is representative of a longstanding tradition of writing on exile, separation, and longing:

> A palm tree stands in the middle of Ruṣāfa,
> Born in the West, far from the land of palms.
> I said to it: How like me you are, far away and in exile,
> In long separation from family and friends.
> You have sprung from soil in which you are a stranger;
> And I, like you, am far from home.[6]

Ibn Zaydūn was only eight years old when a Berber revolt led to the destruction of Madīnat al-Zahrā᾽, the former palace-city of the Caliph ᶜAbd al-Raḥmān III (d. 355/961). The city, which took nearly forty years to construct, was sacked in 1010, leaving a dynastic legacy that lasted for approximately seventy-four years. The marble and precious stones were looted and used for other structures, leaving "the ruins of the palaces and gardens of Madīnat al-Zahra [to become] the touchstones in Andalusian memory for human grandeur – and its ultimate fragility."[7] From then on, the caliphal city became another site upon which poets would stop and weep. The sixth/eleventh-century poet al-Sumaysir is just one of the many poets who observed the pre-Islamic practice of *al-bukā᾽ ᶜalā-l-aṭlāl* (weeping at the ruins). He writes:

> I stopped at al-Zahrā᾽ weeping,
>   taking it in, lamenting its fragments.
> And I said: "Oh Zahrā᾽, won't you come back?"
>   and she replied: "Does one ever come back from death?"

I didn't stop weeping, weeping there,
the tears were of no avail, none at all.
As though they were traces shed
by the mourners who lament the dead.[8]

Although Madīnat al-Zahrāᵓ became a landscape of desolation, the space became intimately and favorably tied to Ibn Zaydūn as a result of his trysts with Wallāda. Stetkevych observes that in Ibn Zaydūn's poetry, "all ruins become abodes of beauty and happiness, and indeed of perfection … The remembering heart seems to know no ruins."[9] The poet transforms the architectural ruins of Madīnat al-Zahrāᵓ into an earthly paradise and the comparison of the garden to a Qurᵓānic paradise is a common device in his poetry. His *Nūniyya*, or *Ode Rhyming in Nūn*, is considered to be his best work as he reflects nostalgically on his lost love. In his discussion of this poem, Devin Stewart cites the eighth/fourteenth-century philologist al-Ṣafadī as declaring the *Nūniyya* to be "so emblematic of longing and exile that anyone who memorized the poem, it was rumored, would surely die far from home."[10]

The eleventh/seventeenth-century historian Aḥmad ibn Muḥammad al-Maqqarī composed a two-part history of al-Andalus, with the first part constructed as a compilation of many authors' work on the history of Muslim Spain, with descriptions of its many cities and the second part focusing on Ibn al-Khaṭīb, the eighth/fourteenth-century scholar from Granada. In Part One: Book Three, there is a detailed description of Cordoba, beginning with its ancient history and detailing the construction of buildings and palaces, including Madīnat al-Zahrāᵓ. Al-Maqqarī cites various authors in his section on Cordoba and descriptions include Cordoba as "the largest city in all Andalus, and one which had no rival either in the East or the West."[11] Currently, however, archaeological evidence has only been able to account for approximately 10 per cent of this total area, causing historical and literary texts to account for the rest of the space. The textual evidence provides a glimpse into how Andalusī society functioned and utilized the spaces around them. Ibn Zaydūn's vision of Cordoba is classified, organized, and partitioned strophically and spatially, thus creating a multidimensional system to capture the poet's memories.

The *mukhammas* of Ibn Zaydūn is interesting for its *nasīb* within a *nasīb* and lack of a traditional *raḥīl* section. The first two strophes follow convention as the poet speaks of weeping and calls upon his two companions while he comments upon Fate's ability to bestow disaster. However, his response to handling said disaster is cavalier, even going so far as to imitate the now proverbial line attributed to Imruʾ al-Qays when he learned of the death of his father while drinking, *al-yawma khamrun wa ghadan amrun* ("wine today, business tomorrow").[12]

1 Breathing in the fragrance of the zephyrs
And [the] longing for the memories of youth returns time after time
The flash of lightning does not cease to radiate
Calling upon tears until they gush forth
For does youthful longing even possess tears?

2 Oh my two friends, if I worry then the cause is evident
If I can be patient it is because patience is in my nature
If Fate bestows disaster
Then our today has wine and tomorrow is another matter
It is no wonder that the noble are generous.[13]

The poem takes on an elegiac tone immediately thereafter as he complains about the vicissitudes of fate and the watchful stars before entering into a dialogue with his beloved, the city of Cordoba, as seen in Figure 6.1.[14] The dialogic nature of this section shifts from addressing his two companions (*khalīlayya*), to the second-person singular feminine, as seen with the poet's use of the possessive pronoun (*-ki*):

3 The nights shot me from the bow of misfortune
For calamities' messages didn't miss me
I spent my day nursing false hopes
At night I sought refuge under slow-moving stars
For the slowest night traveller is a star with eyes upon it

4 Oh beautiful Cordoba! Is there desire in you?
Is the heart that burns with desire due to your distance doused?
Will your famous nights have a place to return to?
Where beauty is seen in you and leisure is heard?
Where all the world's pleasures are pleasant?

5 Isn't it strange that parting has gone too far?
So I live as if I hadn't forgotten the scent of your surroundings
As if my parts were tied to yours?
As if I weren't first created out of your soil?
As if I weren't safely cradled in your districts?

The poet's grief in the fourth and fifth strophes is highlighted through the repetitive use of interrogative particles, one of three elements that Alexander Elinson has identified as being a characteristic of the city elegy.[15] These strophes provide insight into the poet's relationship to Cordoba while fostering feelings of sadness at the current and degenerating state of the city. In expressing his angst at being separated from the city, he declares his Cordoban identity: he is a direct product of everything that constitutes the natural and urban environment.

Jaroslav Stetkevych observes that Ibn Zaydūn's relationship to Cordoba is akin to Adam's claim to Paradise.[16] This foreshadows two things to come: the poet will inevitably face the same fate as Adam but until then, Cordoba remains the poet's Garden of Eden. Thus his ode to the city begins in the sixth strophe with descriptions that excite all the senses.

> 6 Your days are luminous, your nights are radiant
> Your soil is morning rain, your branches are intoxication
> Your earth is clothed in green when your sky is bare
> Your aroma and myrtles are refreshing to the soul
> Your pleasant shade is sufficient for wishes

This strophe could be interpreted as the *takhalluṣ*, or disengagement from his sadness, as he embarks on his *raḥīl.* Unlike the desert journey, however, which the poet typically undertakes on a she-camel, Ibn Zaydūn travels by foot through Cordoba and Madīnat al-Zahrā'. While these detailed peregrinations are clearly the poet's attempt to restore an idealized past, they also provide a layout of fifth/eleventh-century Cordoba that no longer exists. These topographical spaces are each invested with a number of cultural connotations, thus charging the text's spaces with historical and cultural content. French literary theorist Philippe Hamon dedicates an entire chapter in his work *Expositions: Literature and Architecture in Nineteenth-Century France* to the use of architecture in the French lyric poem. Hamon's argument in this chapter is that the inclusion of architecture in the lyric allows the writer to believe that he is controlling both space and time.[17] In the case of Ibn Zaydūn and his Andalusī city elegy, by controlling his environment through the detailing and placement of architectural sites, he in turn establishes his identity as a member of Cordoban aristocracy.

As he calls out to Cordoba, with its celebrated nights and pleasures, he positions his current self as merely an observer of the past. The fragrant streets are now only present in his memories and the city's calm, clear days and mirth-filled evenings, once common experiences for Ibn Zaydūn, are now out of reach for the poet in exile. His depiction of the space of Cordoba and in particular Madīnat al-Zahrāʾ is based on his recollections of time spent in the city, and these descriptions constitute a large portion of the poem. The poet's desire to regenerate the city is clear as he spends nearly two-thirds of his one hundred-line poem on space, landscape, and architecture, with descriptions ranging from grand, caliphal estates to small paths along the riverbanks. This ekphrastic description via architectural and topographical spaces creates a symbiotic relationship between objects and poetry.[18] The reader is unable to grasp the full meaning of the poem with its emotional valences without also imagining the spatial layout of Cordoba, and vice versa.

Starting with the seventh strophe, Ibn Zaydūn creates his own city districts comprising specific buildings, landscapes, and toponyms that generate a recollection of specific events either in his personal history or that of the city. The poet continues his description of the city for six strophes, resulting in thirty lines detailing his previous activities in Cordoba and Madīnat al-Zahrāʾ. His first district contains perhaps the most emotionally evocative site in all of Cordoba – Ruṣāfa:

7 How could I forget the time of leisure in the hills,
A pleasant life under the cover of Ruṣāfa,
A villa facing the Jaᶜfariyya,
Enjoying the places of the soul: the gardens and streams
Enjoying the places of youth and pleasure

In her book *The Ornament of the World: How Muslims, Jews, and Christians Created A Culture of Tolerance in Medieval Spain*, Maria Rosa Menocal (2002) details the history of Cordoba as a site of refuge for ᶜAbd al-Raḥmān I, the first Emir of Cordoba, after years in exile following the Umayyad fall in Damascus in 132/750. Menocal states, "among the memory palaces built by the exiled Umayyad prince in al-Andalus, none was more personal and poignant than a place called Rusafa. Located in Syria, the Umayyads turned a walled city into their family retreat … Outside Cordoba, Abd al-Rahman built his new Rusafa … a place where he could collect and cultivate the living things that had been so central to beauty and delight in Syria."[19]

The poet's choice to begin with this acclaimed estate over all others is a deliberate effort to showcase his former status in Cordoban society. Philippe

Hamon writes, "since all architecture is social and human … [it] thus functions as an ostensive (or ostentatious) way of displaying the signs of private social vanity or of flaunting official power."[20] The Cordoban Ruṣāfa became the material way of displaying political authority and authenticity as this estate was "a marker for the capital of the Umayyad Empire, first in Syria and now in the West."[21] The gardens and surrounding flora as representative of the poet's *locus amoenus* continue into the eighth strophe, where he introduces a long-standing poetic convention of geographic uncertainty: the ᶜAqīq:

8 Oh many a gathering and festivity at the ᶜAqīq
At a canal filled with peeking narcissus
A setting of breezes, mixing desire with despair
Cloudy yet sunnied by the resplendence of wine
Which when wine appears in its glass, it shines

Jaroslav Stetkevych traces the usage of this symbolic place to the *muᶜallqāt* of pre-Islamic poets Imruᵓ al-Qays and Hārith Ibn Hillizah. In both cases, its usage occurs in the *nasīb* to position the poet's elegiac landscape. While little is known about the geographical identity of the ᶜAqīq, Stetkevych argues that this point is of little relevance because its primary role is metaphorical, as it undergoes a symbolic transformation in Bedouin and courtly elegies to nostalgic idylls in the Andalusī tradition.[22] Stetkevych hypothesizes that the ᶜAqīq found in the poems of Ibn Zaydūn may in fact be the Guadalquivir River (Figure 6.3), but he emphasizes that the ritual and symbolic aspect of invoking the ᶜAqīq as the "river is now epitomized and where poets everywhere take delight."[23]

Continuing with the theme of water, the next strophe details one of the poet's first meetings with his beloved at the "Honeycomb" fountain (ᶜAyn Shuhda). This is also the first instance where Ibn Zaydūn provides physical characteristics of his beloved:

9 At ᶜAyn Shuhda, a scene brought us together
We went back and forth and the return was more worthy
A fair-skinned, dark-eyed one announces a bride of pleasure
With a sweet mouth and rosy cheeks
And hennaed palms dyed with wine

The poet continues his cataloging of ruins and topographical minutiae with the naming of streets, paths, and streams. On numerous occasions, he describes walking along a path to the Nāṣir Palace located between white hills (Figure 6.4).

Where we crossed the bridge upstream
To the Nāṣir Palace between the white hills
We went from the shores of the riverbank to the hills
Where the winds play and spread perfume
Along branches of flowers fluttering from side to side

It is clear that this particular path holds special significance to the poet and as he describes it, he makes note of certain landmarks and landscapes that are visible from this area. D. Fairchild Ruggles notes that Ibn Zaydūn's name for this palace is especially interesting due to two factors: the unusual word-choice for palace, *jawsaq*, and the adjective used to describe the palace, *naṣriyy*. Edward Lane defines *jawsaq* as an Arabicized form of the Persian كوشك[24] and Ruggles provides an architectural historical context to this term for "although the word *jawsaq* was seldom used in relation to Hispano-Islamic palaces, in the east this Persian word had the meaning of 'palace' or 'villa.'"[25] This is also the only instance in the poem where Ibn Zaydūn does not use the Arabic word for palace, *qaṣr*. In 317/929, the emir ᶜAbd al-Raḥmān III "declared himself caliph of al-Andalus … and adopted the throne name al-Nāṣir (The Victorious One)."[26] Maribel Fierro provides a thorough detailing of the caliphal names assumed by ᶜAbd al-Raḥmān III and states that al-Nāṣir was the title "most used in the literary sources as well as in the epigraphy and numismatics of the time."[27] Based on the adjective used by the poet to describe the palace, along with the historical record, this palace was likely the former residence of Caliph ᶜAbd al-Raḥmān III. Elinson argues that the authenticity of such places in the Arabic poetic tradition is inconsequential, because "rather than presenting a description or demarcation of an actual location, the poet uses the emotionally evocative *nasīb* and the metaphor of place to express the universally familiar and ineffaceable feelings of desolation, loss, and nostalgia."[28] However, while these toponyms do hold immense evocative power, I will later show that by verifying the existence of these places and their geographical locations, the poet has a secondary role as a cartographer, detailing the urban layout of fifth/eleventh-century Cordoba, a site for which scant contemporaneous cartographic evidence survives.

Returning again to the path that leads to the caliphal palace, Ibn Zaydūn identifies the surrounding landscapes and additional palaces located in Cordoba. Paths, according to urban planner Kevin Lynch, are vital in the creation of one's mental map for "paths with clear and well-known origins and destinations ha[ve] stronger identities, help[] tie the city together, and g[ive] the observer a sense of his bearings whenever he crosse[s] them."[29] This last statement is especially useful in analyzing Ibn Zaydūn's reconstruction of the city. Even though he composed this poem while in prison, his recollection of this path allowed him to once again position himself in a certain sector of the city.

The eleventh strophe provides much more information on the makeup of the city:

> 11 The best days have passed
> Either at the waterwheel or the Nāṣiḥ palace
> The winds tremble within those valleys
> Rippling the surface of the springs and canals
> Where one sees the sun shining its rust-coloured spears

In an article on the Arab monuments of Cordoba, Rafael Castejón suggests that the Cortijo Del Alcaide, a Spanish site along the Guadalquivir River, contains remnants and fragments that lead him, along with other archaeologists, to believe that the location was once the site of Dār al-Nāᶜūra, the Palace of the Waterwheel.[30] Dār al-Nāᶜūra was the country home of the caliph and after construction began at Madīnat al-Zahrā°, he had a path that connected the two residences.[31] The other site mentioned in this strophe is the Nāṣiḥ Palace, plotted in Figure 6.5; it may correspond to another villa, the munyat Arḥā° Nāṣiḥ. This villa, according to Ruggles, was the favorite residence of the caliph al-Ḥakam II. This estate was "situated on the right bank of the Guadalquivir River on the Seville–Cordoba road just before the entrance to the city."[32] Referencing medieval Arabic texts and historical documents, Ruggles details how the caliph left Madīnat al-Zahrā° after suffering a stroke and, accompanied by his dignitaries, spent the night at Arḥā° Nāṣiḥ. The next day, they traveled to Munyat al-Nāᶜūra and proceeded on to Cordoba, where the caliph passed away a few months later.[33]

This strophe also includes a vivid description of the winds blowing across streams and canals. In his mention of the canals, Ibn Zaydūn lays the foundation for turning his attention back to Madīnat al-Zahrā°. This location, as highlighted in Figure 6.6, was known for its verdant gardens and aqueducts that allowed for the maintenance of its lush vegetation throughout the year. Excavation reports show that these canals ran through the caliphal palace and the central buildings of Madīnat al-Zahrā°.[34] This system allowed for the gardens that helped to solidify this area as the "ornament of the world.'[35] The environment in the palace city was so beautiful that Ibn Zaydūn likens it to heaven on Earth. In the twelfth strophe, he praises the former beauty of the palace city as even surpassing the qualities of the Garden of Eden and al-Kawthar, the river in Paradise:

12 Oh how lovely Zahrāʾ is! A welcomed sight!
With delicate winds and jewel-like perfection
How remarkable it is in beauty and presence
The Garden of Eden and River Kawthar marvel at you
With a single look, life is extended

This strophe is the end of the poet's praise (*madḥ*) and description (*waṣf)* of Cordoba and Madīnat al-Zahrāʾ. From this point forward, we are presented with insight into the poet's psyche as he laments the loss of his beloved city and begins to surrender to the inevitability of Fate. In the 1964 edition of *Dīwan Ibn Zaydūn*, the editor states that the poet composed this work while in prison,[36] yet the poet's vivid and nostalgic reflections allow one to forget that he is confined to a small space as he reconstructs the capital of the Umayyad caliphate. It is only after he has completed his re-creation of the city that we are once again reminded of the poet's circumstances. Memories of trysts with Wallāda are presented without any indication of time since the poem has frozen their encounters in a vacuum, with the environment of his treasured city as their backdrop. The city becomes a symbol of his existence as he blends his nostalgia for his youthful days of leisure with architectural, natural, and topographical details.[37] Now that he has completed both the recollection of his past and his mental map of the city, the ostracized poet struggles to come to terms with his current status:

13 Places where I weep for lost love
More tender and fine than a plucked rose
We clad ourselves in the embellished dress of youthfulness
Leading a huge army to bliss
Safety has an ally and enmity a watchtower

14 The calm spring dressed her in a brocade of meadows
She has days of contentment among the tender winds
Her sons anticipate a life of sweet disposition
Continuing within us at morning and afternoon
To send love and greetings to those places

15 Oh brothers! Do those who return ever come back?
There is no first that the last will not follow

Verily I glance upon the goodwill of Fate
For fortune has brought new life and is unsuccessful
The outcome of the matter is approved yet still detested

In *The Poetics of Space*, Gaston Bachelard writes that "memory encumber[s] [an] image by stocking it with composite memories from several periods of time. Here everything is simpler, radically simpler."[38] The city of Cordoba is transformed into a familiar and intimate space because it is created entirely from Ibn Zaydūn's practice of these very spaces.[39] Up until now, the city has been filled with joyous memories from the poet's former life. However, the final five strophes of the poem deviate from this pattern as the poet's angst and despair over his existing situation is accentuated. The poet abandons the use of architectural references, which coincides with his feeling of helplessness amidst his exclusion from the very spaces he describes. His feelings and memories are no longer tied to locations throughout Cordoba, thus his status as it currently stands has become less certain and distinguishable. The sixteenth strophe highlights Ibn Zaydūn's awareness of his situation by plainly stating that he is no longer of any importance to his homeland as he expounds on his feelings of being a *persona non grata*. He finally acknowledges his current location in the seventeenth strophe and when he does, there is absolutely no depiction of his surroundings nor any mention of the city in which he resides at the time he composes this poem:

16 I left, for as it is the case when the free are oppressed and depart
I found solace in grief when I was saddened
The readied heart became accustomed to despair
And a country where I am of little importance is more despicable
And whoever desires something disgraceful like me is even viler

17 My enemies won't succeed in erasing my presence with imprisonment
I saw the sun hiding among the gloomy clouds
For I am nothing but a sword in its sheath
Or a lion in its cave or a falcon in its nest
Or a precious object hidden in a perfume jar

These strophes are the first in which the poet reveals himself to be vulnerable to a force other than Fate. All he can do is acknowledge his seclusion at the hands of his enemies as he likens himself to "a lion in its cave," "a falcon in its nest," and a "sword in its sheath." These elements are all potentially deadly, but Ibn Zaydūn relegates them to their abodes, unable to truly be a fierce adversary against any enemy. While it is clear that the poet feels helpless in his current situation, he remains a proud aristocrat and is unwilling to be disgraced or to relinquish his dignity. These two contrasting sections of the poem create a paradox of sorts: while Ibn Zaydūn narrates his experiences inside Cordoba, this is also the place where he is excluded and unwelcome.

The poem ends with an *ubi sunt* motif as the poet contemplates life's transience. He ultimately accepts his fate and his inability ever to reintegrate into Cordoban society as a result of political and cultural strife:

18 My path is distressed with all forms of longing
To every free-minded and urbane one among you
May the silver of your glittering features be gilded gold
For the moon rivals the finest stars
Knowing that she is the most splendid and brilliant light

19 I grieve for I am despondent and wine becomes sour
I don't perform songs even though they captivate the heart
I don't abstain from sighing when I am censured
I have no diversion since I am separated from you all
Save for news that comes from you unexpectedly from afar

20 You praised the tenderness of her friendship
The world delights you all with the beauty of her coquetry
When it's free from reproach and boredom
There is still one among you clothed in her protection
Allowing the best of hopes and well wishes to be bestowed

Through the poet's cognitive mapping of Cordoba, he explicitly and implicitly presents insight into a specific identity felt and expressed by an individual, a cultural identity representative of a socio-economic class, and a social identity reflective of the customs and behaviors present in fifth/eleventh-century Islamic Spain.[40]

In 422/1031, the caliphate of Cordoba disintegrated into a number of *taifas*, or petty kingdoms. Nevertheless, the history and legacy of Cordoba endured and influenced the literary and visual production of the Mediterranean and beyond. Maps of the region comprised an illustrated tradition known by the general title *Kitāb al-masālik wa-l-mamālik* (Book of Roads and Kingdoms), the first known geographic atlases of maps. Cordoba is positioned in the center of the Iberian Peninsula even though Seville had become more important in the region by that time, as seen in the Leiden manuscript Orientalis 3101 (Figure 6.8) from the late sixth/twelfth century. According to Karen Pinto, the cartographer of this manuscript suspends time and history through their depiction of late fourth/tenth-century Cordoba when it was at the height of its cultural and political eminence.[41] This action reflects the lasting romanticized memory of Cordoba in the medieval Arab artistic imagination and its continuing role as the subject of loss and unrequited affection.

The *mukhammas* of Ibn Zaydūn, while departing from the traditional structure of the city elegy, is in fact part of the genre based on its formal characteristics and thematic content: al-Andalus is both the lost beloved and the idealized site for mourning. The poet is aware that his beloved homeland has disintegrated yet he uses his city elegy to revive Cordoba and long for the life of love and leisure he once had. The role of memory in this elegy is significant as "memory is often more powerful than reality because it engages the imagination: ruins remind us of what was, allowing the mind's recollection to reconstruct the place as it might have been and as it ought to have been."[42] The obliterated abodes in the desert that once sparked nostalgic memories within pre-Islamic and classical Arabic poets have been replaced with urban landscapes and palatial estates. Ibn Zaydūn's city elegy becomes a multi-faceted memorial to a city in ruins which he textually reconstructs, while also becoming a historical archive to record loss and catastrophe at once personal and collective.

Figure 6.1 Cordoba, in dotted box.

Figure 6.2 Ruṣāfa and Palace of Ja^cfar, in boxes with rounded edges.

Figure 6.3 The ^cAqīq, as represented by the Guadalquivir River, highlighted in black.

Figure 6.4 The Nāṣir Palace and the bridge, circled.

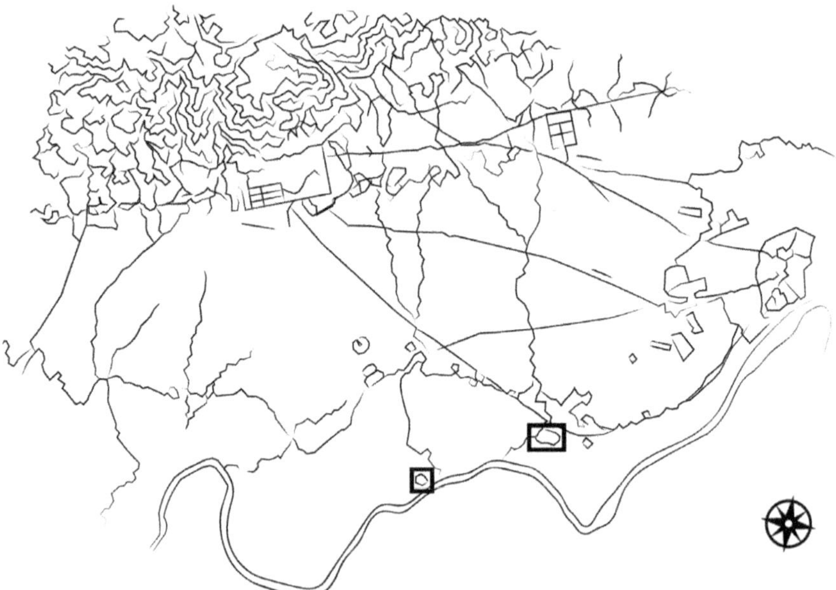

Figure 6.5 The Nāṣiḥ Palace and the Palace of the Waterwheel, in boxes with square edges.

Figure 6.6 Madīnat al-Zahrāʾ, in dashed box.

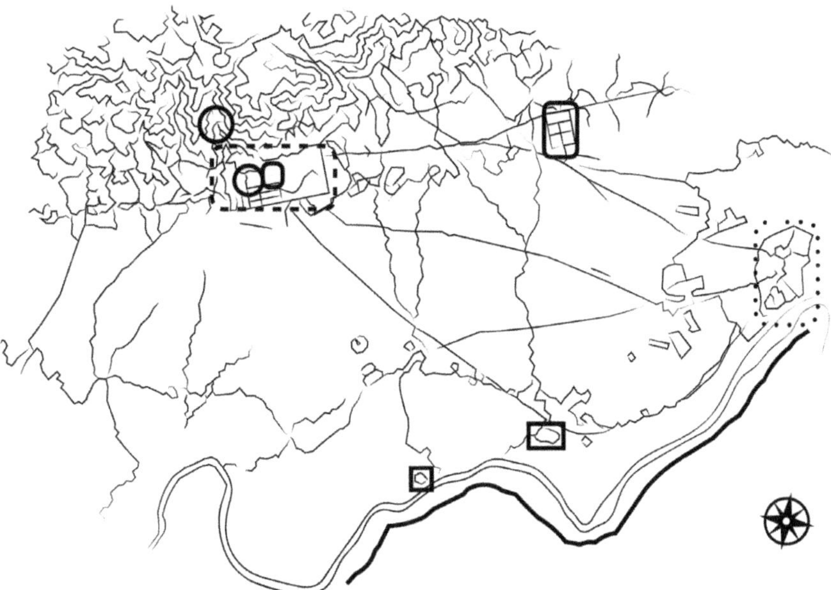

Figure 6.7 Ibn Zaydūn's completed map of the city of Cordoba and Madīnat al-Zahrāʾ.

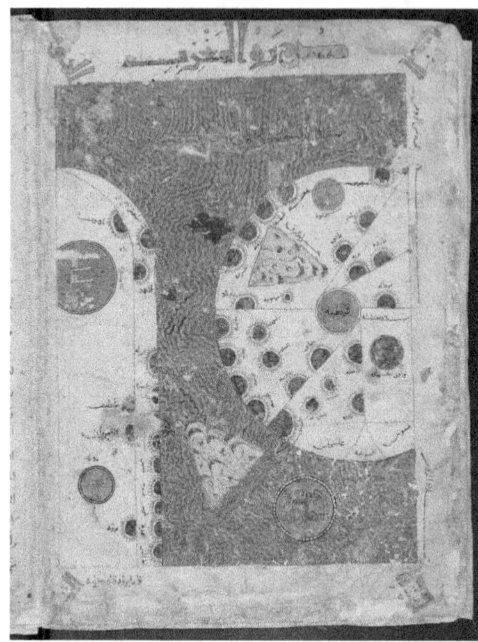

Figure 6.8 *Ṣūrat al-Maghrib*, Leiden University Library, ms. Or. 3101, fol. 20, *ca.* late twelfth century. The city of Cordoba is the circle centered within the half-circle identified as the Iberian Peninsula.

Notes

1. Elinson (2008: 84).
2. Hammond (2008: 145).
3. Vázquez and Havard (2003: 129).
4. Bachelard (1994: 9).
5. Elinson (2008: 81).
6. Ruggles (2000: 138).
7. Menocal (2002: 37).
8. Al-Zayyāt (1990: 665). Translation my own.
9. J. Stetkevych (1993: 193).
10. Stewart (2000: 312).
11. Al-Maqqarī (1840: vol. 1, 201).
12. S. P. Stetkevych (1993: 245).
13. Ibn Zaydūn (1964: 37–45). All translations are my own unless otherwise noted. I also relied upon a Spanish translation of this poem by Mata, *Literatura hispanoárabe* (University of Alicante 2004: 76–9).

14. I would like to thank Christian Go for generously recreating the maps used in this chapter.
15. Elinson (2008: 81).
16. J. Stetkevych (1993: 198).
17. Hamon (1992: 191–208).
18. For the purpose of this paper, I am using the Ancient Greek rhetoric of ekphrasis and not the modern definition of the term, which is a poetic description of a work of art. For a detailed discussion of this term, see Webb (1999: 7–18).
19. Menocal (2002: 64).
20. Hamon (1992: 43).
21. Safran (2000: 176).
22. J. Stetkevych (1993: 113).
23. Ibid.
24. Lane (2015: 486).
25. Ruggles (2000: 128).
26. Higbee Walker (2003: 7).
27. Fierro (2011: 95).
28. Elinson (2008: 81).
29. Lynch (1960: 54).
30. Castejón (1959–60: 163–6).
31. Vallejo Triano (2007: 29).
32. Ruggles (2000: 122).
33. Ibid.
34. Vallejo Triano (2007: 8–12).
35. This phrase is attributed to the tenth-century Saxon nun Hroswitha, as cited in Dozy (1913: 446).
36. Ibn Zaydūn (1964: 40).
37. Ṭaḥṭaḥ (1993: 77).
38. Bachelard (1994: 229.)
39. By "practice," I refer to the topoanalysis of the city undertaken by Zaydūn here. Topoanalysis, defined by Bachelard, is "the systematic psychological study of our intimate lives" (1994: 8).
40. I am borrowing Tara Welch's tripartite classification of identity as presented in her book *The Elegiac Cityscape* (2005: 8–9).
42. Pinto (2013: 208–9).
43. Ruggles (1993: 171–8 ;172).

Works Cited

Bachelard, Gaston (1994), *The Poetics of Space: The Classic Look at How We Experience Intimate Place,* trans. Maria Jolas, Boston MA: Beacon Press.

Castejón, Rafael (1959–60), "Los Monumentos Árabes de Córdoba: Excavaciones en el cortijo El Alcaide. Dar al-Naura?" *Al-Mulk: Anuario de Estudios Arabistas* 1, 163–7.

Dozy, Reinhart (1913), *Spanish Islam: A History of the Moslems in Spain,* trans. Francis Griffin Stokes, London: Chatto & Windus.

Elinson, Alexander E. (2008), "Loss Written in Stone: Ibn Shuhayd's Ritha᾽ for Cordoba and Its Place in the Arabic Elegiac Tradition," in Marlé Hammond and Dana Sajdi (eds), *Transforming Loss into Beauty: Essays on Arabic Literature and Culture in Honor of Magda al-Nowaihi,* Cairo: American University in Cairo Press, 79–114.

Fierro, Maribel (2011), *Abderramán III y el califato omeya de Córdoba,* Donostia-San Sebastián: Editorial Nerea, S. A.

Hammond, Marlé (2008), "*Qasida, Marthiya,* and *Différance,*" in Marlé Hammond and Dana Sajdi (eds), *Transforming Loss into Beauty: Essays on Arabic Literature and Culture in Honor of Magda al-Nowaihi,* Cairo: American University in Cairo Press, 143–84.

Hamon, Phillippe (1992), *Expositions: Literature and Architecture in Nineteenth-Century France,* trans. Katia Sainson-Frank and Lisa Maguire, Berkeley CA: University of California Press.

Higbee Walker, Marilyn (2003), "ᶜAbd al-Raḥmān III, Caliph of Córdoba," in E. Michael Gerli (ed.), *Medieval Iberia: An Encyclopedia,* New York NY: Routledge, 6–8.

Ibn Zaydūn, Aḥmad ibn ᶜAbd Allāh (1964), *Diwān,* Karam al-Bustānī (ed.), Beirut: Dār Ṣādir.

Lane, Edward (2015), *Arabic–English Lexicon,* book I, 486, www.ejtaal.net (accessed 16 May 2015).

Lynch, Kevin (1960), *The Image of the City,* Cambridge MA: MIT Press.

Al-Maqqarī, Aḥmad Ibn Muḥammad (1840), *Nafḥ al-ṭīb ghuṣn al-Andalus al-raṭīb, wa-dhikr Lisān al-Dīn ibn al-Khaṭīb,* trans. Pascual de Gayangos as *The History of the Mohammedan Dynasties in Spain,* London: Oriental Translation Fund, vol. 1.

Menocal, Maria Rosa (2002), *The Ornament of the World: How Muslims, Jews, and Christians Created A Culture of Tolerance in Medieval Spain,* Boston MA: Little, Brown and Company.

Pinto, Karen (2013), "Passion and Conflict: Medieval Islamic Views of the West," in Keith D. Lilley (ed.), *Mapping Medieval Geographies: Geographical Encounters in the Latin West and Beyond, 300–1600*, New York NY: Cambridge University Press, 201–24.

Ruggles, D. Fairchild (1993), "Arabic Poetry and Architectural Memory in al-Andalus," *Ars Orientalis*, vol. 23: Pre-Modern Islamic Palaces, 171–8.

—— (2000), *Gardens, Landscape, and Vision in the Palaces of Islamic Spain*, University Park PA: Pennsylvania State University Press.

Safran, Janina M. (2000), *The Second Umayyad Caliphate: The Articulation of Caliphal Legitimacy in Al-Andalus*, Cambridge MA: Harvard University Press.

Stetkevych, Jaroslav (1993), *Zephyrs of Najd: The Poetics of Nostalgia in the Classical Arabic Nasib*, Chicago IL: University of Chicago Press.

Stetkevych, Suzanne Pinckney (1993), *The Mute Immortals Speak: Pre-Islamic Poetry and the Poetics of Ritual*, Ithaca NY: Cornell University Press.

Stewart, Devin J. (2000), "Ibn Zaydun," in Maria Rosa Menocal, Raymond P Scheindlin, and Michael Anthony Sells (eds), *The Literature of Al-Andalus*, New York NY: Cambridge University Press, 306–17.

Ṭaḥṭaḥ, Fāṭimah (1993), *al-Ghurbah wa-al-ḥanīn fī -l-shiᶜr al-Andalusī,* Rabat: al-Mamlakah al-Maghribīyah, Jāmiᶜat Muḥammad al-Khāmis, Kullīyat al-Ādāb wa-al-ᶜUlūm al-Insānīyah.

Vallejo Triano, Antonio (2007), "Madīnat al-Zahrāᵓ: Transformation of a Caliphal City," in Glaire D. Anderson and Mariam Rosser-Owen (eds), trans. Mariam Rosser-Owen, *Revisiting al-Andalus: Perspectives on the Material Culture of Islamic Iberia and Beyond*, Leiden: E. J. Brill, 3–26.

Vazquez, Miguel Ángel and Robert G. Havard (2003), "Poetic Pilgrimages: From Baghdad to Andalucía, Abū Tammām's Lā anta anta wa-lā al-diyāru diyāru," *Journal of Arabic Literature* 34: 1/2, 122–37.

Webb, Ruth (1999), "*Ekphrasis* ancient and modern: the invention of a genre," *Word & Image: A Journal of Verbal/Visual Enquiry*, vol. 15, 7–18.

Welch, Tara (2005), *The Elegiac Cityscape: Propertius and the Meaning of Roman Monuments*, Columbus OH: Ohio State University Press.

Al-Zayyāt, Abd Allāh Muḥammad (1990), *Rithāᵓ al-mudun fī-l-shᶜir al-Andalusī*, Benghazi: Manshūrāt jāmiᶜat Qaryūns.

7

The Mamluk City as Overlapping Personal Networks

Kelly Tuttle

During the Mamluk sultanate (1250–1517) in Egypt and the Levant, the ruling military elite built monumental public works, gave patronage and endowments to support cultural production, and employed a wide-ranging bureaucracy, all while maintaining a near-constant power struggle amongst themselves. Their development of the area's cities also meant that the Mamluk bureaucracy employed a large number of scholars throughout the two and a half centuries of rule. These bureaucrats produced vast amounts of writing, much of which has survived in manuscript and is currently being studied with renewed interest. In addition to collections of poetry, letters, anecdotes, analyses, commentaries and religious works, there were also a number of significant compositions written that describe the people and structures of the time. These texts include histories, scribal manuals, analyses of state organization, and biographical dictionaries, among other works.[1]

As a form, biographical dictionaries can themselves contain other genres. Histories, genealogies, annals, chronologies, all of these may fit into the umbrella form of biographical dictionary. If the work is arranged as a series of entries about individual people, then it is a biographical dictionary.[2] The intersection of the social, cultural, and political is made manifest in this genre, since the authors can list everything in which a person has participated. Naturally, some authors are more anecdotal and conversational than others in this regard and include a wider range of reported experiences for each entry. By reading a biographical dictionary and tracing the connections among the subjects of the entries, a reader gains a fuller understanding of how the cultural, social, and political webs of subjects and rulers of the Mamluk period interconnected. If we take this a step further, and borrow from Nimrod Luz's book on the Mamluk city in which he argues that Mamluk "cities should be viewed, above all, as socio-cultural-political processes, rather than inert localities,"[3] then we can view the biographical dictionary as a way to describe the city.

Turning now to a specific example from the Mamluk period, we find the dictionary called *Aᶜyān al-ᶜAṣr wa-Aᶜwān al-Naṣr.* This dictionary lists, in six volumes, just over two thousand contemporaries of its author, Ṣalāḥ al-Dīn Khalīl b. Aybak al-Ṣafadī (d. 1363).[4] What makes the *Aᶜyān* different from other biographical dictionaries is its focus on al-Ṣafadī's contemporaries.[5] In his introduction to the dictionary, al-Ṣafadī says he is drawing from his larger biographical collection, *al-Wāfī b'il-Wafayāt.* Nonetheless, Donald P. Little has estimated that there are about twice as many contemporaries of al-Ṣafadī listed in the *Aᶜyān* as in his larger collection.[6] Therefore, al-Ṣafadī was not just republishing an excerpt of his earlier text; he was writing new entries for the *Aᶜyān*, expanding on the description of his contemporaries. Distinctive among biographical dictionaries, al-Ṣafadī's *Aᶜyān* is broad in the sense that it does not treat a particular group of people, adherents of a particular legal school (*madhhab*), for example, or residents of a specific town. Instead it is limited by its timeframe, which is confined to the lifetime of al-Ṣafadī himself. The collection includes entries on people from many different professions including rulers, the military, financial and diplomatic bureaucrats, judges and other political appointees, merchants, religious scholars, writers, and others from an array of locations, though largely focused on Egypt and the Levant. The subjects of entries range from the year 1297, when al-Ṣafadī was born, to 1362 which is the last date that he mentions in the *Aᶜyān*. Al-Ṣafadī died only one year later, in 1363, which means he was revising the collection almost until the end of his life. This dictionary provides a snapshot of peoples' public interactions over the course of about sixty years. The collection focuses on the cities and the circulation of people among those cities as their lives dictate.[7] Each entry furthermore shows how the various individual networks intersect with each other to create a much larger network, a socio-cultural-political process that in turn makes up the Mamluk city.

Aᶜyān al-ᶜAṣr as Descriptive of Networked Cities

In contradistinction to location-specific books that describe the geographical or imagined layout of a town,[8] the biographical dictionary describes the city as a network. To put it differently, in a biographical dictionary people are described in terms of their public interactions, and these interactions make up their functional city. If we consider also that biographical dictionaries were read aloud in public, as indeed were many other types of works, then the descriptions of the interactions that are recorded in the book are then also performed publicly, which opens them to possible public revision.[9] The *Aᶜyān* was read publicly in the Umayyad Mosque in Damascus between November 1356 and May 1357.[10] Public performance validates the veracity of the connections between people that are described in the dictionary. Much cultural, social, and political influence could be gained through a network, especially one that was well-maintained, and publicly known.[11] Al-Ṣafadī, as an author, was quite comprehensive in recording details about when and where he had met someone or heard something, and was also meticulous about checking his sources.[12] It has been rightly observed that this attention to detail in his works has not only let scholars reconstruct his movements more easily than for some others of his contemporaries, but also makes his own network more easily visible in many of his works.[13] Al-Ṣafadī pays such careful attention to where and when he met someone or received knowledge for at least two possible reasons. First, the information could then be more easily corroborated and thus be seen as accurate, or collectively acknowledged. Second, such meticulousness also simply let him exhibit his network for what it was – a vast and interconnected web that allowed him to travel around the area and communicate across it regardless of his location. Such a network also made him look good – well-connected and well-educated. This type of cultural and social capital could in turn bring economic or political capital, too.

Biographical dictionaries are not the only descriptor of networks. The importance of different types of networks has been recently analyzed in a volume edited by Stephan Conermann.[14] In its introduction Conermann, drawing on Bourdieu, says the purpose of the exchange of economic, social, and cultural capital, "is the costly accumulation of symbolic capital, which can be ambiguously defined as honor or prestige. Social capital for example can consist of being 'well interconnected' or part of a status group, whereas cultural capital corresponds to education."[15] For a bureaucrat in the Mamluk Empire, social well-connectedness and cultural education are capital of vital importance for finding work and being successful. It matters less the city in which one lives, than the cultural capital one has to wield. This seems to be especially true during the period that the *Aᶜyān* covers, since the subjects of entries are reported to have traveled around the Mamluk-ruled area extensively and often.

Looking simply at the biography of al-Ṣafadī himself, as reconstructed from comments in his works, we find that he traveled extensively in the region and was often moving around as part of his job. He lived and worked in Ṣafad, Aleppo, al-Raḥbah, Damascus, and Cairo and traveled among them fairly frequently. For example, when he was working for the governor of Damascus, Tankiz,[16] from 1331 until Tankiz was arrested in 1340, al-Ṣafadī traveled with him. This included trips to northern Syria for hunting, trips to provincial towns like Ṣafad for political reasons, as well as at least five, if not yearly, trips to Cairo so that Tankiz could meet with the Sultan.[17] Al-Ṣafadī was not unique in this extensive travel, by any means. Travel around the region governed by the Mamluk sultanate was quite common.[18] Not even villages can be thought of as entirely separate one from another[19] during this time period, to say nothing of provincial capitals and the regional capitals of Damascus and Cairo. The ways in which traders and scholars moved around for work and education, the ways in which correspondence could pass relatively easily among cities, and the importance of letter-writing and the bureaucracy in general kept the various cities in communication with one another quite effectively.[20]

In the *A*ᶜ*yān*, al-Ṣafadī often highlights a subject's travels by the way that he structures the entries. He begins with a short summary of the person in rhyming prose (*saj*ᶜ), which is followed by a list of teachers and sometimes students with whom the subject has worked. Next is a more detailed account of the subject's professional development and work life, which is often closely tied to travel around the region. A final section in the entry often records examples of the subject's poetry, letters, or other literary output. This style of entry makes networks more obvious in several ways, particularly since this is a dictionary of al-Ṣafadī's contemporaries. First, connections are made among sources and subjects since al-Ṣafadī's sources are also his subjects; they are all treated in the dictionary. A source for one entry will be the subject for another. Naturally, there are many more subjects than sources. Even so, this connection is present throughout the dictionary. Second, al-Ṣafadī is also more anecdotal in his biographical dictionaries than are some other authors.[21] This means that he not only connects himself into the entries whenever he can, for example by mentioning when and how a source told him the cited story, but also that he simply includes more stories (*nukat*) in his entries.[22] In short, the *A*ᶜ*yān* describes personal networks while also showing why they are important to maintain. Additionally, since the center of each personal network moves around, between and among cities in the Mamluk Sultanate, the city itself loses its boundaries and becomes portable. Finally, by reading the dictionary as a whole, we have an idea of the socio-cultural-political processes that can be considered to define the city during this time period, since this dictionary lists only people who were contemporaries of al-Ṣafadī himself.

Personal Networks and a Borderless City

Before looking at a longer entry for a subject that illustrates the extensive personal network, the reasons for it, and the fact that it spanned several cities, let us first look at a shorter example that is nonetheless illustrative of the pattern entries generally take:

> Aḥmad b. Ibrahīm b. Saru Shihāb al-Dīn Abū al-Abbās al-Baᶜalbakī, a resident of Ḥamā. He sought excellence in *ḥadīth* (Prophetic traditions) instruction and studied under al-Mizzī,[23] Zaynab,[24] Abū al-Abbās al-Jazarī,[25] and several others. He then studied the seven readings of the Qurʾān under al-Jaᶜbarī.[26] He was naturally capable in his knowledge, deliberate in his ability, and enchanting in his poetic compositions. After Baᶜalbak, he lived in Ḥamā making it his sanctuary (*ḥamāhu*). He continued to live his life, sipping both its sweetness and its bitterness until death came to take him. He died in Ḥamā in 747, may God have mercy on him. And he was born in the year 710. And from his poetry …[27]

Even in this short entry, we see that al-Ṣafadī assumes a reader of this text will know, if not necessarily where cities are located in relation to each other, at least the names of larger cities without extra descriptions. Baᶜalbak and Ḥamā are cities with which the readership would have been familiar and thus they do not need to be situated in any descriptive geographical landscape the way some of the less well-known towns might need to be. Only rarely does al-Ṣafadī give geographical indications as to where a town is located. When the town is small enough that readers might not know it by name, he generally provides another town nearby for orientation. For example, in the entry for Ibrahīm b. Sulayman al-Mantiqī (d. 1331), al-Ṣafadī describes his hometown of Āb Karam as being "a tiny town close to the village of Qūnyah, a place with many fruit trees."[28] That description combined with the subject's other *nisba* of "al-Rūmī" would be enough to indicate to the reader that he originally came from Anatolia.

Another aspect of Shihāb al-Dīn al-Baᶜalbakī's entry worth noting is that he died fairly young, according to al-Ṣafadī's calculations; he was born in 1310 and died in 1346, making him only thirty-six years old. The subject's occupation is nowhere listed except to say that he had been studying *ḥadīth* and the various readings of the Qurʾān with his teachers, and that he was a gifted poet. Although there is a space left for quotations to be added following the main entry and headed by "and from his poetry …" (*wa-min shiᶜrihi …*), the additions never made it into the revisions. Regardless, even in an entry of this brevity, we can see evidence of a network, in this case one made up of teachers. That Shihāb al-Dīn al-Baᶜalbakī decided to move from his place of origin to Ḥamā implies some reason for the move. In his case, it was likely in order to have access to more teachers.

The city, in this short example, appears as a desirable place to be. Ḥamā itself is not described in any detail, except as it appears with the wordplay. Since virtually any word is free to be made a locus of wordplay for al-Ṣafadī, as for many of his contemporaries, we may be tempted to write this comparison of Ḥamā to *ḥamà* off as rhyming exuberance. Yet, given that plays on words are deliberate, and that a word meaning sanctuary or protection was chosen to be associated in the reader's mind with Hama, the name of the city, one cannot help but make a positive association with the city. A migration to a bigger city that will provide more opportunity for networking and potentially more opportunity for work is a common theme among the entries, as is a somewhat circular trajectory towards Damascus and Cairo as one advances through the ranks of the chancery.

A longer, and rather representative entry in the *Aᶜyān* that goes into more detail about the subject and his network is the entry for Zayn al-Dīn Abu Ḥafṣ ᶜUmar b. Dawūd, al-Ṣafadī (d. 1349), which we will look at in some detail.[29] This entry illustrates not only how the citing of source material creates a network between al-Ṣafadī (the author) and the source, but also between the author and the subject since they were friends.[30] Additionally, this entry makes explicit rather than implicit the connections between Zayn al-Dīn ᶜUmar and other people who appear in the dictionary not as sources.

Zayn al-Dīn ᶜUmar, according to the entry in the *Aᶜyān*, was born in 1294 in the town of Nayn, which al-Ṣafadī describes as "a village in the Bani ᶜĀmir plains surrounding Ṣafad, [spelled] with two of the letter *nūn*, and between them the letter *yāʾ*, and structured on the same pattern as the words '*bayn*' and '*dayn*.'"[31] ᶜUmar held a number of different positions over the course of his life, mostly linked to the chancery. When summing him up in the collection of correspondence, al-Ṣafadī refers to him simply as a chancery secretary (*kātib al-inshāʾ*).[32] Before delving into the detail of the subject's work, however, al-Ṣafadī sets out a short summary of all the places the subject has lived. He says,

> He was transferred from Ṣafad to Damascus to Gaza to al-Raḥbah, then to Damascus, then to Cairo, to Damascus, to Cairo two times, departing time after time, with a break that came in between. The situation almost continued in that way without stopping, but then fate would be kind to him and return his name to the rolls [*al-dasātīr*].[33]

Zayn al-Dīn ᶜUmar was transferred from place to place many times, and his life was characterized by periods of work followed by sometimes lengthy periods of unemployment. Sometimes the periods of unemployment were so long that it seemed they might not end, but they always did. Zayn al-Dīn ᶜUmar received quite a bit of help from other members of the chancery, who suggested him for positions when they opened. In a similar way, when he lost a post it was often tied to a political event rather than his poor performance at his job. In fact, he was clever and good at his job, though extremely curious about people, al-Ṣafadī reports.

From the middle of the entry comes this longer extract, which shows in greater detail the ways in which Zayn al-Dīn ᶜUmar found work and was moved around because of it. The selection starts just after Zayn al-Dīn ᶜUmar had been living in Damascus unemployed for a long period of time.

> The amir Sayf al-Dīn Tankiz then sent him [Zayn al-Dīn ᶜUmar] to al-Raḥbah, appointed on the suggestion of Shams al-Dīn Muḥammad[34] the son of our teacher Shihāb al-Dīn Maḥmūd[35] after he lived in Damascus unemployed for nine years. He lived there [in al-Raḥbah] for two years.
>
> When the judge Muḥyī al-Dīn[36] and his son the judge Shihāb al-Dīn[37] went to Egypt the emir Sayf al-Dīn Tankiz said to them "there is no one left in the chancery." They both reminded him of him [Zayn al-Dīn] and they said, "O Master, the secretary in al-Raḥbah Zayn al-Dīn al-Ṣafadī is suited to be in the palace of our lord, head of the amirs." And the judge Jamal al-Dīn Ibn Rizq Allāh[38] had left his place in the Damascus chancery for an appointment in Gaza, so Zayn al-Dīn was told to present himself in Damascus, so he came there and lived there for not quite a year. Then, the judge Shihāb al-Dīn bin Faḍl Allāh asked for him [to come] to Egypt. So he went and lived there working as a secretary for him almost eight years until the sultan, al-Malik al-Nāṣir Muḥammad, ordered the judge Shihāb al-Dīn bin Faḍl Allāh to remain in his house. Since he [Zayn al-Dīn ᶜUmar] was

> working in his service, the sultan took him out of the chancery and he then stayed in Cairo for a while confined to his house. Then, Ṭājār al-Dawādār[39] made him leave Cairo for Ṣafad unemployed. He stayed there until the judge Shihāb al-Dīn bin Faḍl Allāh came to Damascus after the arrest of the amir Sayf al-Dīn Tankiz. The judge Shihāb al-Dīn talked to him [Zayn al-Dīn] and ordered him from Ṣafad to Damascus, where he stayed unemployed until the Sultan al-Malik al-Nāṣir Muḥammad died. Then the judge Shihāb al-Dīn bin Faḍl Allāh talked to the amir ᶜAlā ᵓ al-Dīn Altunbugha,[40] the governor of Damascus, and then ordered him [Zayn al-Dīn] to enter the Damascus chancery. So [Zayn al-Dīn] remained there until al-Malik al-Ṣāliḥ[41] ordered the firing of everyone who had been newly employed after [the death of] his father al-Malik al-Nāṣir. He was fired and remained confined to his house for a period of time. Then, he was reemployed with everyone else who was reemployed later.[42]

As is easy to see, even this short excerpt is peppered with names, all of which can be found in the *Aᶜyān al-ᶜAṣr*. Furthermore, since all of the people in the *Aᶜyān* lived at the same time, the descriptive network as socio-cultural-political process is made that much clearer to a reader. A reader still needs to spend some time working out how the named people fit together, but of course the dictionary itself helps in this regard. In this excerpt, for example, Zayn al-Dīn ᶜUmar is helped several times by Ibn Faḍl Allāh al-ᶜUmarī, who was also one of al-Ṣafadī's good sources for the compilation of this dictionary. He is connected to both the writer and the subject of this entry. Then, since he was a major figure both in the chancery and as a writer during this time period, as readers, we know that his network is much larger, even if in this particular entry the details are not all mentioned. Naturally, Ibn Faḍl Allāh al-ᶜUmarī also has his own entry in the dictionary, and if one wanted to, rather than reading from beginning to end, a reader could stop and look up the names mentioned as they appear. Reading back and forth or around in the entries fills out the idea of the city that is generated by the overlapping personal networks.

As mentioned above, people's mobility among cities is pronounced while at the same time a person's general type of employment will not necessarily change. Zayn al-Dīn ᶜUmar and Ibn Faḍl Allāh al-ᶜUmarī both remained working in the bureaucracy over the course of their lives. At the same time, though, they both moved around several times throughout their lives. Furthermore, since Ibn Faḍl Allāh al-ᶜUmarī was from a well-known family of administrators, he started out with a more complete and effective network than did Zayn al-Dīn ᶜUmar who, as mentioned, was from a small village outside of Ṣafad. Clearly, it took Zayn al-Dīn ᶜUmar some time to gain the connections necessary to find better placements. As with al-Ṣafadī himself, the posting of Zayn al-Dīn ᶜUmar to al-Raḥbah, a frontier town that was quite removed from other cities, seems to have been helpful for gaining future positions and transferring back towards the center.

Although movement towards one of the bigger cities of Damascus or Cairo could mean promotion and continued employment, as we see in this excerpt, it could also mean waiting around for an opportunity or until someone else put in a good word. Furthermore, political upheavals had repercussions. We see a small example of that here when the sultan places Ibn Faḍl Allāh al-ᶜUmarī under house arrest. Because Zayn al-Dīn ᶜUmar is working for him at his request, he, too, is confined to his house and then sent back to Ṣafad. We see it again when the Sultan al-Malik al-Ṣāliḥ decides that anyone new in the chancery should be let go. In both cases Zayn al-Dīn ᶜUmar returned to working for the chancery, but this kind of event is not unusual in this dictionary.

Taken together, the links created by the structures of this particular biographical dictionary along with the many anecdotes that al-Ṣafadī spreads through all of the entries, create an image of a connected, vibrant, but often unpredictable city life during this period. Using the connections described by *Aᶜyān al-ᶜAṣr*, a reader can trace the intersecting networks, noting that most of the subjects move around the area of the Mamluk sultanate, entering and leaving cities and positions, all without leaving their networks. The city becomes larger than its geographic boundaries. A biographical dictionary such as the *Aᶜyān*, especially if read by following strands of connections, paints the city as vast, but portable. It paints success as the creation of a network that extended around the region, and would expand in response to growing success, but also expanded as a means of bringing success. The relatively free movement and help that such networks provided for those working in the bureaucracy is a manifestation of the social and cultural capital necessary for success in the city.

Notes

1. For introductions to this last genre see Auchterlonie (2004: 186–200); Gilliot (2002: 19–54); Marín (2002: 1–17); al-Qadi (1995: 93–122).
2. Al-Qadi (1995: 94).
3. Luz (2014: 227).

4. Al-Ṣafadī (1998).
5. Little (1976: 190–210, 209).
6. Ibid.: 198. The *Wāfī* is al-Ṣafadī's most well-known work. It lists thousands of scholars and has been used for years as a resource when researching scholars, their lives, and their networks. In fact, we might say that its impact on al-Ṣafadī-related research has been somewhat oversized. Al-Ṣafadī was prolific. His literary output numbers in the hundreds of volumes, but much of his other work has been overlooked. His other works are beginning to be reassessed now, with the renewed interest in literature of the Mamluk period. Additionally, however, al-Ṣafadī's own writing has sometimes been deemed prolix, repetitive, and derivative in a negative way in comparison to other writers of the period. See Bauer (2009) in *Essays in Arabic Literary Biography: 1350–1850*, and also Rowson from the same volume. Each essay talks briefly about the opinions of al-Ṣafadī's contemporaries about his writing.
7. This was a point of prosperity and expansion in the Mamluk empire during the third reign of the Sultan al-Nasir Ibn Qalawun (1310–41). Under his rule, much building activity happened and what had been provincial towns, even including Damascus, were developed and came to be more politically important. See Levanoni (1995).
8. By "imagined layout," I mean the way in which people remember a town as opposed to how it actually exists in the world at the time. In memory, streets may be different or connect differently; structures may be remembered in different places, etc. For a more detailed analysis of this kind of geographic misremembering and how it interacts with archaeological evidence, see Luz's analysis of a description of Ṣafad in his book "The Mamluk City," especially 175–99 (2014).
9. For an analysis of the importance of public reading, see Hirschler (2012), particularly Chapter 2.
10. Little (1976: 209). In a marginal note in the manuscript that Little worked with, al-Ṣafadī says that all twelve manuscript volumes were read in the mosque over the course of those seven months.
11. For a specific example tracing why hearing a public reading was important for one's social network, see Gharaibeh (2014: 223–66).
12. Little (1976: 204). This meticulousness in source-checking and note-taking does not equate to historical, factual correctness, but it does equate to representation of a general opinion seen as correct. For an article that treats this idea with regard to al-Ṣafadī's biographical entry on the governor of Damascus, Tankiz, see Conermann (2008: 1–24).

13. Little (1976: 206). It is thanks to these references to people and place which Little traces through the *ᶜAyan*, that he was able to put together a more complete biography of al-Ṣafadī than had previously been available.
14. Conermann (2014).
15. Ibid. (13).
16. This is Tankiz ibn ᶜAbd Allāh al-Ḥusāmī al-Nāṣirī (d. 1340), governor of Damascus and close consultant of Sultan al-Malik al-Nāṣir Muḥammad (d. 1341) until his arrest and subsequent execution was ordered in 1340. Again, see Conermann (2012) for his history. An entry for Tankiz is also included in the *ᶜAyan*, v. 1, 116–38, no. 255.
17. Little (1976: 208).
18. See Petry (1981), which uses quantitative methodology and biographical dictionaries to assess the numbers of people from Cairo who travelled outside the Cairo metro area. He finds that most of the travel went to the Levant. See also his more recent article (2014: 157–72), in which he studies the biographies of two extremely well-travelled individuals in much closer detail.
19. Walker (2014: 326–48). She argues that

> "One cannot speak of the 'isolated village' of the Mamluk period – peasants lived in a world of connectedness and movement. New peoples, ideas and goods came in and out of local communities with regularity. The borders between villages – determining where the lands of one village ended and the next began – were even in flux," 326.

20. For a study of letter-writing in the eleventh to fifteenth centuries, which includes the Mamluk period, see Gully (2008). Similarly, the frequency with which al-Ṣafadī mentions people traveling by messenger route (*al-barīd*) in his dictionaries attests to the connectedness of the cities during this time.
21. Al-Ṣafadī's tendency to be conversational in his writing has been remarked on in Rowson (2009: 341–57).
22. For example Ibn Ḥajar al-ᶜAsqalānī (d. 1449) in his dictionary *al-Durar al-Kāminah fī Aᶜyān al-Miᵓah al-Thāminah* (1966–7), which also focuses on the Mamluk period, writes about many of the same people who are found in al-Ṣafadī's *Aᶜyān*, but the entries are less anecdotal, do not include as much detail, and cite less poetry or other literary output by the subject of the entry. Of course, Ibn Ḥajar's dictionary also has more than twice the number of entries and covers a longer timespan, which may have dictated the form it took.
23. Jamāl al-Dīn, Yūsuf b. Abd al-Raḥmān Abū al-Hajjāj al-Mizzī (d. 1341). Al-Ṣafadī (1998: vol. 5, 644–57).

24. Zaynab bint al-Kamāl (d. 1340). Al-Ṣafadī (1998: vol. 2, 390).
25. Aḥmad b. Yaḥyā b. Muḥammad al-Jazarī (d. 1328).
26. Burhan al-Dīn Ibrahīm b. ᶜUmar al-Jaᶜbarī al-Muqriᶜ (d. 1332).
27. Al-Ṣafadī (1998: vol. 1, 158–9, no. 69).
28. Ibid. (vol. 1, 73, no. 235).
29. He is also listed in al-Ṣafadī's collection of letters, although interestingly most of the letters published there are the same as the letters at the end of his entry in the *Aᶜyān*. See al-Ṣafadī (2004: vol. 2, 26–40, no. 61).
30. Their friendship can be seen in the letters that are written between the two. Almost the same letters are published in the *Aᶜyān* as in the *Alḥān*, though the latter contains some extra lines of poetry that were recited directly to al-Ṣafadī. See al-Ṣafadī (2004: vol. 2, 26–40).
31. Al-Ṣafadī (1998: vol. 3, 610–29, no. 1267, 610).
32. Al-Ṣafadī (2004: vol. 2, 27).
33. Al-Ṣafadī (1998: vol. 3, 610).
34. Shams al-Dīn Muḥammad b. Maḥmūd Ibn Fahd (d. 1327), Al-Ṣafadī (1998: vol. 5, 254–6, no. 1780). He was a judge and also the head of the chancery in Damascus.
35. Shihāb al-Dīn Abū al-Thanāᵓ Maḥmūd b. Sulaymān Ibn Fahd (d. 1325), Al-Ṣafadī (1998: vol. 5, 372–99, no. 1840). He was the head of the chancery in Damascus and in Cairo and had served for a time as a Hanbali judge in Cairo.
36. Muḥyī al-Dīn Abū al-Maᶜālī Yaḥyā Ibn Faḍl Allāh (d. 1337), Al-Ṣafadī (1998: vol. 5, 571–6, no. 1946). At this time, he was the head of the famous Faḍl Allāh family of administrators who oversaw the Damascus and Cairo chanceries. He was first the head of the Damascus chancery and then of the Cairo one at the end of his life.
37. Shihāb al-Dīn Abū al-ᶜAbbās Aḥmad Ibn Faḍl Allāh al-ᶜUmarī (d. 1349), perhaps the most well-known of the Faḍl Allāh brothers for his books on Mamluk administration and organization such as *Masālik al-Abṣār fī Mamālik al-Amṣār*. He was a *kātib al-sirr* in both Damascus and Cairo. He was also a colleague of al-Ṣafadī's and a source for much of what appears in the *Aᶜyān*. The other brothers, Badr al-Dīn Muḥammad (d. 1345) and ᶜAlaᵓ al- Dīn ᶜAlī (d. 1368), both also worked as head of the chancery in Cairo and Damascus and appear later in the entry to place Zayn al-DīnᶜUmar again into a position in the chancery in Egypt.
38. The judge Jamāl al-Dīn Yūsuf b. Rizq Allāh (d. 1344), Al-Ṣafadī (1998: vol. 5, 624, no. 1981). He was the son of the sister of Sharaf al-Dīn bin Faḍl Allāh. He was a chancery secretary in Damascus, Gaza, and Ṣafad.

39. The emir Sayf al-Dīn Ṭājār al-Dawādār (d. 1342). Al-Ṣafadī (1998: vol. 2, 564–6, no. 897).
40. [c]Ala[ɔ] al-Dīn Altunbugha (d. 1356). He was an emir, seen favorably by the sultan, according to al-Ṣafadī, and given governance over Gaza. Al-Ṣafadī (1998: vol. 1, 614–15, no. 331).
41. [c]Imād al-Dīn Ismā[c]īl, (r. 1342–5). A son of al-Malik al-Nāṣir Muḥammad who became sultan about a year after his death and after his brother, who had been ruling, absconded.
42. Al-Ṣafadī (1998: vol. 3, 612–13).

Works Cited

Auchterlonie, Paul (2004), "Historians and the Arabic Biographical Dictionary: Some New Approaches," in Robert G. Hoyland and Philip F. Kennedy (eds), *Islamic Reflections, Arabic Musings: Studies in Honour of Professor Alan Jones*, Cambridge: Gibb Memorial Trust, 186–200.

Bauer, Thomas (2009), "Jamāl al-Dīn Ibn Nubātah," in Devin Stewart and Joseph Lowry (eds), *Essays in Arabic Literary Biography: 1350–1850*, Wiesbaden: Harrassowitz, 184–202.

Conermann, Stephan (2008), "Tankiz ibn [c]Abd Allāh al-Ḥusāmī al-Nāṣirī (d. 740/1340) As Seen by His Contemporary al-Ṣafadī (d. 764/1363)," in *Mamlūk Studies Review* XII.2: 1–24.

—— (ed.) (2014), *Everything is on the Move: The Mamluk Empire as a Node in (Trans-) Regional Networks*, Goettingen: V. & R.

Gharaibeh, Mohammad (2014), "Brokerage and Interpersonal Relationships in Scholarly Networks," in Conermann (ed.), *Everything is on the Move*, Goettingen: V. & R., 223–66.

Gilliot, Claude (2002), "Prosopography in Islam. An Essay of Classification," *Medieval Prosopography* 23: 19–54.

Gully, Adrian (2008), *The Culture of Letter-writing in Pre-modern Islamic Society*, Edinburgh: Edinburgh University Press.

Hirschler, Konrad (2012), *The Written Word in the Medieval Arabic Lands: A Social and Cultural History of Reading Practices*, Edinburgh: Edinburgh University Press.

Ibn Ḥajar al-[c]Asqalānī, Aḥmad Shihāb (1966–7), *Al-Durar al-kāminah fī a[c]yān al-mia[ɔ]ah al-thaminah*, 5 vols, Cairo: Dar al-kutub al-ḥadithah.

Levanoni, Amalia (1995), *A Turning Point in Mamluk History: The Third Reign of al-Nasir Muḥammad Ibn Qalawun (1310–1341)*, Leiden: E. J. Brill.

Little, Donald (1976), "Al-Ṣafadī as Biographer of His Contemporaries," in Donald P. Little (ed.), *Essays on Islamic Civilization Presented to Niyazi Berkes*, Leiden: E. J. Brill, 190–210, 209.

Luz, Nimrod (2014), *The Mamluk City in the Middle East: History, Culture, and the Urban Landscape*, New York NY: Cambridge University Press.

Marín, Manuela (2002), "Biography and Prosopography in Arab-Islamic Medieval Culture," *Medieval Prosopography* 23: 1–17.

Petry, Carl (1981), *The Civilian Elite of Cairo in the Later Middle Ages*, Princeton: Princeton University Press.

—— (2014), "'Travel Patterns of Medieval Notables in the Near East' Reconsidered: Trajectories, Interconnected Networks," in Conermann (ed.), *Everything is on the Move*, Goettingen: V. & R., 157–72.

Al-Qadi, Wadad (1995), "Biographical Dictionaries: Inner Structure and Cultural Significance," in G. N. Atiyeh (ed.), *The Book in the Islamic World: The Written Word and Communication in the Middle East*, Albany NY: State University of New York Press, 93–122.

Rowson, Everett (2009), "al-Ṣafadī," in Devin Stewart and Joseph Lowry (eds), *Essays in Arabic Literary Biography: 1350–1850*, Wiesbaden: Harrassowitz, 341–57.

Al-Ṣafadī, Ṣalāḥ al-Dīn Khalīl ibn Aybak (1998), *Aᶜyān al-aṣr wa-aᶜwān al-naṣr*, 6 vols, ᶜAlī Abū Zayd, Nabīl Abū ᶜAmshah, Muḥammad Mawᶜid, Maḥmūd Sālim Muḥammad (eds), Beirut: Dār al-Fikr al-Muᶜāṣir.

—— (2004), *Alḥān al-sawājiᶜ bayna al-bādī wa-al-murājiᶜ*, 2 vols, Ibrahīm Ṣāliḥ (ed.), Damascus: Dār al-Bashāʾir.

Walker, Bethany (2014), "Mobility and Migration in Mamluk Syria: The Dynamism of Villagers on the Move," in Conermann (ed.), *Everything is on the Move*, Goettingen: V. & R., 326–48.

8

Citystruck

Adam Talib

The cities of premodern Arabic literature are erotic playgrounds. The proximity engendered by urban life and the opportunity to encounter, seduce, and manipulate strangers afforded by the imperative of economic exchange are key themes in Arabic narratives and lyrics about cities. In poetry especially, all social interactions in the urban sphere are given an erotic gloss. Sexual opportunity, the vulnerability of women and young men, elite prerogative, and anonymous encounters can appear rather fun and titillating from the perspective of most poets in the Arabic literary tradition, which has generally been the preferred point of view adopted by most scholars, but the outlines of another city can be detected beneath the façade of the erotic playground so often encountered in literature and recreated in scholarship. It is the predatory city, an exhaustingly erotic, frighteningly promiscuous, and diverse and dangerous arena in which eloquent objectification and amusing assaults have not yet lost their sting.

Smooth Trade

في غلام خيَّاط: [من المنسرح]

[١] لَمَّا أتَى والمِقَصُّ في يَدِهِ وفَصَّلَ العاتِقَيْنِ والبَدَنا

[٢] فقالَ وصْلاً أعُوزُ قُلْتُ لَهُ ألعائِزُ الوصْلَ يا حبيبِ أنا

On a young tailor / tailor-slave:

He came to me, shears in hand,
and measured my shoulders and torso.

"I need to take a receipt [*waṣl*]," he said, but I replied,
"It's me who needs union [*waṣl*] with you, my love."

A scene so familiar it has become a film cliché. A wealthy and powerful man – perhaps a mafia don or king, or a poor man in the company of a wealthy sponsor, or in some cases a secret agent – stands in the center of the tableau, often several centimeters off the ground, and usually in front of an array of mirrors, as another man – hunching and obsequious – moves around him silently, taking measurements, running his hands over the other man's body, pinning, pleating, and chalking. The poem quoted above is at least as old as the mid-fifteenth century so the scene being depicted and the clothes being tailored are, of course, radically different from the familiar film scenes set in Savile Row – radically different from the few old-fashioned tailors left in downtown Cairo, too – but the power imbalance, peacocking, and unusual intimacy inherent in such scenes has not diminished much over the past five centuries. The homoeroticism in modern and contemporary depictions of scenes like this is hardly hinted at, however, whereas in the premodern literary depiction presented above, homoeroticism is the whole point. It is the subject of the poem as well as the point of the poem's epigrammatic structure (premise-exposition-resolution).

Premise: Tailor comes to perform a fitting (heading and l. la)
Exposition: Tailor performs fitting and asks for a receipt or promissory note (ll. 1b, 2a)
Resolution: The resolution hinges on a point, in this case a pun (or *jinās mumāthil*) in l. 2b.[2] The word *waṣl*, by which the tailor character means "receipt" or "promissory note" (l. 2a), is used by the poet-persona in his antanaclastic reply to mean "union," either the union of souls or spiritual union with the Godhead, and often a euphemism for sex.[3] The word can also mean "an act of kindness, favor."

This poem is one of hundreds, if not thousands, in Arabic about the various professions and trades encountered in the life of a premodern city. In addition to individual lyric poems, there are whole collections devoted to trades and artisans, including encyclopedias, dialogues, etc. and these have drawn the attention of social and cultural historians alike.[4] Similar concerns about urban space and social interaction are also reflected in the *shahr-angīz (şehrengiz)* genre in Persian, Turkish, and Urdu literatures.[5] Yehuda al-Ḥarīzī's (d. 1225) *maqāmah*-esque *Sefer Tahkemoni* is an example of the same urban genre in

Hebrew literature as can be seen in the following poem on a miser the poet met in Mosul (trans. Peter Cole):

In Mosul I praised a miserable man
with a poem that was sheer invention;
and he made me a vow as full as my song
of wind and utter pretension.
From Baghdad to Spain, I've never known
an oath even half as vain—
and when his friends objected, "Lord,
your hands were taught to be open!"—

he answered them: "I've got nothing left,
and don't know what I can say.
Every day I've bills to pay
and so, it seems, I'm stuck:
I've got a boy who does my will
—our bed is always fresh—
but I'm obliged by law to provide him
with clothing, food, and a fuck."[6]

Al-Ḥarīzī's poem is a lampoon of a man whose miserliness, it emerges, is the result of his sexual profligacy – a humorous juxtaposition of vices. It is also a reflection of potent social anxieties about urban living.

Fish-out-of-water

The Arabic tradition is by no means unique in exhibiting mixed feelings about the relative merits of rural and urban life, but there is a good case to be made that it is predominantly anti-rustic. Consider the modern Levantine proverbs "*zabbāli l-mudun wa-lā sulṭāni l-qarāyā*" (Better a city garbage-collector than a rural sultan), "*ᶜīshat il-qarāyā min il-balāyā*" (To live in a village is to be cursed), and "*in jāra ᶜalayk iz-zamān lā tiskun illā l-mudun*" (If fate turns against you, live only in a city).[7] This fact notwithstanding, cities are themselves often depicted as dangerous places. One of the most anti-rustic texts in the Arabic tradition is the seventeenth-century *tour de force Kitāb Hazz al-quḥūf bi-sharḥ qaṣīd Abī Shādūf* (*Brains Confounded by the Ode of Abū Shādūf Expounded*) by Yūsuf al-Shirbīnī in which the author mischievously excoriates country folk and their uncouth customs and lifestyles for the amusement of an urban readership. Even in that work, however, the city is depicted as a threatening, inhospitable environment whose foundation has been corrupted by money (trans. Humphrey Davies):[8]

> [A]nother man from the countryside went up to the city and was overtaken by the need to defecate, but found himself at a loss, not knowing of an alley in which he could take a shit. When things became unbearable he complained to a citizen of Cairo, may the Almighty protect it, and told him, "I can't go any longer without taking a leak and a crap, but whenever I try to piss in front of a shop, the people stop me and abuse me!" Said the man, "Peasant, in the city no one shits without paying. If you have money on you, I'll show you an alley or a hole where you can shit. If not, you can shit on yourself."

The fish-out-of-water peasant is the butt of the joke as the rest of the story makes clear. The depiction of a clueless tyro in an urban environment allowed urban audiences to question the patterns of life they took for granted. This is the same genre of social criticism presented in, *inter alia*, al-Muwayliḥī's novel *Ḥadīth ᶜĪsā ibn Hishām* (*What ᶜĪsā ibn Hishām Told Us, or A Period of Time*, 1907), the Egyptian film *Ṣaᶜīdī fī l-jāmiᶜa al-amrīkiyya* (*An Upper Egyptian Attends the American University [in Cairo]*, 1998) and a number of early Eddie Murphy films: *Trading Places* (1983), *Beverly Hills Cop* (1984), and *Coming to America* (1988), as well as Murphy's groundbreaking *Saturday Night Live* sketch "White Like Me." In the fictional sketch, broadcast on NBC on 15 December 1984, Murphy masquerades as a white man in order to conduct an undercover journalistic investigation of white urban spaces. In one of the first scenes, a white cashier lets Murphy take a newspaper without paying, which causes momentary confusion until Murphy realizes – as he explains in a voiceover – that "when white people are alone, they give things to each other for free." In Murphy's sketch, the money saved on a newspaper is a synecdoche for white privilege, just as in many fish-out-of-water tales, money acts a central and mystifying criterion of difference. Language, too.

Al-Shirbīnī tells another humorous story about three bumpkins travelling to Cairo that manages to incorporate all three of these dimensions of alterity: milieu, money, and language:[9]

> When they were almost there [i.e. Cairo], their leader and counselor said, "The City of Cairo is all troopers and foot-soldiers that cut off people's

> heads, and we are peasants, and if we don't do as they do and gabble at them in Turkish, they'll chop off our heads." "Abū Daᶜmūm," said his companions, "we know nothing about Turkish or anything else!" [...] "When we get to the city," he said, "we'll go to the bathhouse, which people call the Sweetness of This World, and take a bath and wash our hides – they say it has a deep hole that they shit and piss in! As we're leaving the Sweetness of This World, and standing wrapping ourselves in our cloaks and about to be on our way, I say to you, '*Kardeş Mehmet!*' ('Brother Mehmet!') and you say, 'At your command!' and '*Hah! Ne var?*' ('Huh! What's up?'). Then I ask you, 'Do you have *bir munqār*?' meaning one *jadīd*, and you say '*Yok yok!*' meaning 'No, we don't.' Then the bathhouse keeper will get scared and say to himself, 'These are foreign troopers who chop off people's heads!' and he'll let us leave without paying and everyone will stand in awe of us and we'll be treated in Cairo like *amīrs*.

Needless to say, the bathhouse keeper sees right through the bumpkins' ploy and they end up paying the price in more ways than one. It is no coincidence that a story such as this should be set in a bathhouse. For all that they were ubiquitous and functional features of premodern Islamic cities, bathhouses were also sites of moral and erotic anxiety.[10] This notoriety is mirrored in early-modern English culture as words that originally meant bathhouse – "stew" and "bagnio" – later came to mean brothel.[11]

Hot and Steamy

The Yemeni scholar Shihāb al-Dīn Aḥmad b. Muḥammad al-Ḥaymī al-Kawkabānī's (1073–*ca.* 1151/1663–*ca.* 1738) treatise *Ḥadāʾiq al-nammām fī l-kalām ᶜalā mā yataᶜallaq bi-l-ḥammām* (*Gardens of Wild Thyme: Everything there is to know about the Bathhouse*) is an overview of the bathhouse and socio-cultural elements related to it, including mores.[12] Al-Ḥaymī cites Prophetic traditions and legal opinions pertaining to the subject of public bathing and gives quite a comprehensive set of instructions for the virtuous bather. These include rules about nudity, bodily contact, cleanliness, Qurʾān recitation, when to visit the bath, what to do at the bath, economic use of water, hygiene, etc. While al-Ḥaymī does address issues of nudity and bodily contact, they do not seem to preoccupy him greatly.[13] He makes it clear, however, that one should not be nude in the bathhouse and that one should leave if other people present there are nude. One should also reprimand nude bathers. Ibn Baṭṭūṭah actually went a step further when he found men bathing in the nude at a bathhouse in Minya in Upper Egypt; he reported the incident to the governor.[14] One is allowed to be massaged by the bathhouse attendant only if the attendant is wearing a *ḥāyil* (a washcloth glove called *kīs* or *kassa* in North Africa today) and one should not allow the attendant to touch one's thighs or pelvic region.[15] One should also avoid lying prone when being massaged.[16] Al-Ḥaymī's straightforward guidelines about bathhouse behavior are literarily subverted by the poems he includes in his treatise, however.[17]

Al-Ḥaymī includes a selection of poems about the sight of handsome young men entering the bathhouse:[18]

لا شكّ أنّ داخِل الحمّام قد يكون جميلًا يجرّد من طرفه صارمًا صقيلًا فهو من الحسان الذين «شدّوا مآزرهم من الأرداف على الكثبان»

> Of course, the person entering the bathhouse may be handsome and may unsheath the sharp and polished sword of his glance[19] for he is one of the pretty ones who "gird[s] their loincloths over their buttocks atop the sand-dunes."[20]

The quotation in al-Ḥaymī's hearing refers to the first poem he cites, a poem by Maḥāsin al-Shawwāʾ (d. 635/1237) on a group of handsome young men entering the bathhouse (*fī zumrah min al-ḥisān dakhalū l-ḥammām*):[21]

[من الكامل]

[١] شَدُّوا ٱلمآزِرَ فوقَ كُثْبانِ ٱلنَقا   بأناملٍ حَلُّوا بِها عَقْدَ ٱلتُقَى
[٢] وتجرَّدوا فرأيتُ بانَ معاطِفٍ   نَشَروا ذؤابتَهُمْ عَلَيْهِ فأوْرَقا
[٣] وبَدَوْا فأطْلَعَ كُلُّ وجْهٍ مِنْهُمُ   بدْرًا فأضْحى كُلُّ بدْرٍ مُشْرِقا
[٤] وتَضَوَّعَ ٱلحَمَّامُ مِسْكًا عِنْدَما   نَثَروا مِنَ ٱلأصْداغِ نَظْمًا مُعْبِقا
[٥] مِنْ كُلِّ أهْيَفَ حَلَّ عُقْدَةَ بَنْدِهِ   أضْحَى بِلَحْظِ عُيونِنا مُتَمَنْطِقا

They girded their loincloths atop the sandy hillock,
with the [same] fingertips they used to untie the knots of piety.
When they undressed, I saw the ben-tree of bending bodies;[22]
then they loosened their locks and it burst into leaf.
When they appeared, each of their faces revealed
a full moon, so every full moon became resplendent.
The scent of musk filled the bathhouse when
they scattered the fragrant pearl-strings of their temples.
Each slender one who undid the knot of his belt
was girdled by the side-glance of our gaze.

This highly erotic poem is primarily ekphrastic and its use of natural comparisons to describe features of the men's bodies is a well-known convention of Arabic erotic poetry. In this poem, the beautiful young men are blameless, though they are said to have "untie[d] the knots of piety," and it is the onlookers whose gaze violates appropriate bathhouse behavior. In the following poem by Jamāl al-Dīn Yūsuf (d. 750/1349) many of the same natural comparisons are deployed to depict an entirely more disreputable scenario.[23]

وقال جمال الدين يوسف الصوفي رحمه الله تعالى في مليح تركيّ دخل الحمّام ورشّ مَنْ به بماء الورد وجعل يتّجه عليهم

[من الطويل]

[١] وجازَ إلى حمَّامِهِ يَتَخَطَّرُ   ولَمْ أَنْسَهُ لَمَّا تَعَرَّى ثِيابَهُ
[٢] وفي وَجْهِهِ نورٌ مِنَ ٱلحُسْنِ يَظْهَرُ   ولمَّا أفاضَ ٱلماءَ فوقَ قَوامِهِ
[٣] يلوحُ عَلَيْهِ لؤْلؤٌ يَتَحَدَّرُ   رأيتُ هِلالاً تَحْتَهُ غُصْنِ فَضَّةٍ
[٤] بِثَغْرٍ لَهُ كالمِسْكِ بَلْ هو أعْطَرُ   أتانا بِما وَرْدٍ ذكيٍّ فبَخَّهُ
[٥] أَمَ ٱلوَرْدُ مِنْ خَدَّيْهِ يَحْمَى فيقْطُرُ   فقُلْتُ أَظَبْيُ ٱلتُّرْكِ قَدْ فاحَ مِسْكُهُ

Jamāl al-Dīn Yūsuf al-Ṣūfī, God rest his soul, wrote [this poem] about a handsome young Turk who entered a bathhouse and sprayed rose-water on those present and proceeded to go up to them:

> I'll never forget him: when he stripped off his clothes,
> and walked into the bathing chamber, swaying his hips,
> and when he poured the water over his body,
> while the light of beauty in his face shone out:
> I saw a crescent moon above a branch of silver,
> glinting pearls sliding down over him.
> He came to us, [bearing] fragrant rose-water, which he sprayed
> from his mouth. It was like musk, only more fragrant.
> So I said: has this Turkish deer sprayed his musk
> or has the rose on his cheeks warmed and begun to drip?

In this poem, the handsome young man – who, in the world of classical Arabic poetry, calls to mind the figure of the wine-server – pours liquid all over his own body, and the kind of language that is used to describe wine and goblets in a *khamriyya*-poem is used to describe the liquid that glistens against the surface of his skin.[24] The image of his scent wafting over the other men assembled in the bathhouse renders the titillatingly close quarters of the setting almost palpable.

We find the same eroticization of the bathhouse environment in a poem from Ṣafī ad-Dīn al-Ḥillī's (d. *ca.* 750/1350) *Dīwān*.[25] The cluster of double-entendres (*tawriya*) in the second hemistich of line three necessitates an expanded translation:

[من البسيط]

[١]	لَمْ أَنْسَ ما عِشْتُ حمَّامًا حَلَلْتُ بِهِ	ما بَيْنَ كُلِّ رَخيمِ ٱلدَّلِّ فَتَّانِ
[٢]	في جَنَّةٍ مِنْ طِباعٍ أَرْبَعٍ جُمِعَتْ	أَرْضٍ وماءٍ وأَهْواءٍ ونيرانِ
[٣]	فَنِلْتُ مِنْ حَرِّها بَرْدًا عَلَى كَبَدي	وفُزْتُ مِن مالِكٍ فيها بِرِضْوانِ
[٤]	فأَعْجَبْ لَها جَنَّةٌ فيها جَحيمُ لُظىً	تُذكي ولَمْ تَخْلُ مِنْ حُورٍ ووِلْدانِ

1. I'll never forget, so long as I live, a bathhouse I once visited:
   it was full of heartbreakers, easy on both the ears and the eyes.
2. It was a heaven that brought together all four of the elements:
   Earth and Water, Air and Fire.
3. I took from its heat a cool salve for my distressed liver
   (i) and I won a slave called Riḍwān from his owner there.
   (ii) I had the better of a man named Mālik there and took my [sexual?] satisfaction (*riḍwān*, *ruḍwān*) from him.
   (iii) I defeated the angel Mālik, the Guardian of Hell, so that I could reach the angel Riḍwān, the Guardian of Paradise.
4. Marvel at that Paradise where Hellfire
   rages, and beautiful young women (*ḥūr*) and men (*wildān*) are found.

This poem, suffused as it is with same-sex desire, is not particularly transgressive, not even with its explicit references to the divine text in ll. 3–4, but it is not morally inert either. Nevertheless, poems such as this represent the mainstream of elite Arabic cultural aesthetics in the premodern period. Recent interventions by Thomas Bauer and Shahab Ahmed have delved into this culture of normative heterodoxy with more detail and erudition than I can offer here and all interested readers should consult them.[26] The implicit and explicit transgressions in the poems discussed above reflect the erotic dimension of proximity; an urban condition that engendered much discomfort in premodern Arabic literature. Sinan Antoon connects the utility of *sukhf* poetry to the sometimes fragile divide between the elite and the hoi polloi:[27]

> Ibn al-Ḥajjāj's "wallowing in filth," for which he and other scatologues are condemned, was, on one level, a performance that allowed his audience to symbolically cleanse themselves of unwanted nearness implied in

> expressions of disgust. Needless to say, this reinforcing of boundaries justified and legitimized, unconsciously, the way the world was configured and naturalized socioeconomic and other inequities by linking them to nature and the body.

This discomfort does not belong exclusively to the premodern period, as the United States' recent legislative trans-panic most eloquently demonstrates. The eroticization of anxiety-causing proximity – rather than diminishing the sanctimony of a treatise such as al-Ḥaymī's – complements it, by demonstrating mimetically what moral instruction aims to prevent. By eroticizing urban spaces such as bathhouses, and indeed the entirety of a city's public and semi-public spaces, these mimetic works reinforce social strictures that regulate proximity (the predecessor of what Michel Foucault called "disciplinary power").

Goods for Sale

Urban economic exchange was no less regulated, and the activity of the buying of goods and services also provided the material for much erotic creativity.[28] The protagonist or narrator of these literary exchange-encounters is almost always the purchaser, while the vendor is cast as the erotic object, as in the poem with which this article began. This dyad of exchange maps cleanly onto the more ancient dyad of lover–beloved in Arabic erotic verse. The sexual thrill of economic exchange often takes the place of the commodity being traded as in the following poem on a handsome young druggist (*malīḥ ᶜaṭṭār*) by Ṣalāḥ ad-Dīn aṣ-Ṣafadī (d. 764/1363):[29]

[من الطويل]

[١] كَلِفْتُ بِعَطَّارٍ حَكَى ٱلبَدْرَ في ٱلسَّنَا وظبي ٱلفلا في جيده ونفاره

[٢] دَوَا أَلَمي ٱلوردُ ٱلمربَّى بِخَدِّهِ يَذُرُّ عَلَيْهِ آنسونَ عِذارِهِ

> I've fallen for a druggist, who resembles the moon in the sky
> and a desert gazelle, fine-necked and skittish.
> He cured my pain with the rose growing on his cheek,
> he sprinkled on top of it the anise flowers – or, rather: the intimates of his cheek-down.[31]

The same erotic conflation of a commodity for sale and the body of the person selling it is central to this modern song (*mawwāl*) from Aleppo by Muḥammad al-ᶜĀṣī.[32] In this case, the object of desire is a woman selling roses in the street.

[من البسيط]

[١] ذاتَ ٱللَّيالي سَرَيْنا نَبْتَغي وَرْدا
[٢] مِن خَمْرَةِ ٱلحُبِّ أوْ مِن ناهِدٍ وَرْدا
[٣] شُفنا ٱلعَجايِبْ عُيون تْصدِّنا وَرْدا
[٤] تَصرعْ ذَوي ٱللّبِّ مِنْ راش ٱلسَّهِمْ خَدّها
[٥] هاروتُ لَوْ شافَها ضَلَّ بْشَرَكْ خَدِّها
[٦] غَيْدا تَبيع ٱلوَرْدْ والوَرْدُ في خَدِّها
[٧] وتْصيحِ ياهل ٱلهَوَى مَنْ يِشْتِري وَرْدا[33]

We went out one night in search of a drink
of the wine of love, or from the buxom girl who crossed our path.
What a vision! Her glances parry and strike back!
Discerning men are cut down by the arrows [of her glance].
Even Hārūt, the king of magic, would get stuck in her trap if he saw her.
The young woman sells roses, but true roses are her cheeks,
and calls out: "Come on, all you lovers, who wants to buy a rose?"

The persona of the poem comes upon a beautiful woman, by chance, though it is clear that he and his companion(s) are in the mood for a romantic encounter, not simply an intoxicating drink. The man does not speak to the woman, but to the audience, and his only interaction with her, according to the text of the song, is through glances; in her case, these glances are hostile and deadly. In fact, the woman seems not to entertain the man's interest at all: she is described as parrying men's glances, slaying them with her eyes, and setting traps for them. Why should the poet, or singer, accept the woman's predatory supremacy in this scene? The answer lies in the simple reality communicated by the final two lines: the beautiful, able, and fierce woman who has been described in lines 2–5 is a vendor of roses, though we are told that the real roses are her cheeks. The beloveds of Arabic poetry are often cruel and deadly – and this woman is no exception – but in this case, the persona need not outperform her or suffer at her hand. He has another means of defeating her: economic exchange. The rose-cheeked woman addresses "romantics" in the final line of the song and offers her roses for sale, but by now the border between commodity and body has been blurred. The woman is ferocious because she is vulnerable. The man is stoical because he has purchasing power. Their urban interaction has already been economically determined.

It has become a scholarly cliché to cite wine-drinking at a monastery, tavern, or private gathering as the most prominent representation of illicit behavior or moral transgression in premodern Arabic literature, but the economic exchange implicit in this topos makes it relevant to the present discussion. That these settings are equally popular in other Islamicate literatures points to a broader trend toward an eroticization of urban space.[34] In the following poem by ᶜUbayd-i Zākānī (d. *ca.* 1370), wine-drinking is not simply the passtime of social outcasts, it is an anti-materialist rejection of wealth accumulation:[35]

[۱] دَر خانه تا قَرابه ما پر شراب نیست   ما را قرار و راحت و آرام و خواب نیست
[۲] در خلوتی که باده و ساقی و شاهد است   حاجت به شمع و مطرب و چنگ و رَباب نیست
عمری که خوش نمی گذرد در حساب نیست
[۳] خوش کن به باده وقت عزیزان که پیش ما   در آفتابه کن که در این خانه آب نیست
[۴] اینک شراب اگر هوست می کند وُضو   حاجت به جود خسرو مالِکِ رِقاب نیست
[۵] ما را که ملک فقر و قِناعت مسلَّم است   بالله چو نیک در نگری جز عذاب نیست
[۶] این مال و جاه را که غَنیمت شمرده ای
[۷] همچون عبید خانه هستی خراب کن
[۸] زیرا که جای گنج بغیر از خراب نیست

If the flagon at home
isn't full of wine,
there'll be no rest, or calm,
or sleep, or ease of mind.
In seclusion, with wine and a serving-boy
and a beauty at one's side,
who needs candles or music,
or to hear a singer whine?
Enjoy drink in company with friends—
delight in leisure!
The only days that count for us
are days of pleasure.
Take this wine, if you want
to wash in time for prayer.
Pour it in the basin.
We keep no water here.
We, who've been promised the reign
of poverty and austerity
have no need of slave-master
Khosrow's generosity.

This wealth and this status
    that you cherish so dearly
    may please the eye
    but how it makes the soul weary.
Follow ᶜUbayd and lay ruin to the world!
    You'll only find treasure in the ruins of the city.

An Urban Encounter

I know of no text that more perfectly combines the anxieties of proximity and exchange with the erotic possibilities of an urban environment than the following song, which was first published in 1893. It was published by Urbain Bouriant in his *Chansons populaires arabes*, which he claimed to have taken from the manuscripts of an unnamed Cairene balladeer, and was again published in a revised and annotated edition along with a translation by Pierre Cachia in 1989.[36] The song is set in Cairo's Izbikiyyah district, an area famous at the turn of the twentieth century for its licit and illicit pleasures; there the protagonist encounters a beautiful maiden (*ᶜadhrā*) being escorted by a donkey-driver (*ḥammār*). The protagonist proceeds to convince the woman, through far-fetched lies, to abandon her escort and to accompany him back to his palace. When they arrive at the man's shabby dwelling and his dishonesty is exposed, she gives him another chance to win her affection: he must use his eloquence to do justice to her beauty (l. 94). He succeeds in doing this and the poem ends just as the couple begin to kiss (l. 107), but not before a final stanza: a stanza of praise for the Prophet (*dawr al-madīḥ*) in which the poet begs forgiveness for his sins and shortcomings and those of all believers (ll. 108–12).

The poem begins with an erotic couplet (*maṭlaᶜ*) in which the object of beauty is grammatically masculine, but the gender of this figure is soon made ambiguous by its juxtaposition with the character of the beloved, who makes her appearance in the stanza that immediately follows:[37]

[*al-Maṭlaᶜ*, ll. 1–2]
I fell for a boy,
lithe and lively,[38]
how dark his glance,
how plump his ass.

Good sense abandoned me
when I laid eyes on him.

All I wanted was to have him,
even if it cost me a thousand gold pieces.[39]

[Stanza (*dawr*), ll. 3–7]
All that came to pass one day—
oh, how the heart suffered—
on one of Cairo's streets,
down in Izbikiyyah.

It was fate, not even luck,
that caused me to look up
and see a donkey-driver
escorting a radiant maiden.

Her ass stuck out
a full cubit, no less,
and her waist and her breasts—
Have Mercy, Lord, our Savior.

Her mouth was a ring of gold,
adorned by shining teeth,
her fair cheeks
were crowned by red roses.

She shipped me off
over seas of love
when my eyes fell upon
her marble chest.

By the second line, it is obvious that the protagonist has internalized a price system for sexual exchange. In this case, we understand that one thousand *dīnār* (itself a classicizing topos) would be an awful lot to pay for sex, and that this extravagance reflects the young man's beauty. Other marketplace references are used to describe the female beloved, who is the main object of desire in the poem: her rear measures a cubit and her mouth is like a golden ring adorned with pearls.

Having been struck by the woman's beauty, the protagonist decides to follow her and her companion to see what may happen between them (l. 8: "*ḥattā tanẓur aysh yaqa*^{c} *baynak wa-baynuh*"). This is the key moment in narratives of urban seduction. The city holds secrets: one never knows when one will encounter another city-dweller whom one does not know, has never seen, and may never see again. The chance encounter in the anonymous city is loaded with an urgency that other erotic settings simply lack. The protagonist follows them, but is soon spotted by the donkey-driver, who addresses him, first in a neighborly fashion and then suspiciously (ll. 11–12):[40]

> "What's up with you?" he said.
> "What's the matter?
> "Come, I'll show you the way,
> "If the sun's got you blinded."
>
> "Or are you a thief?
> "Or a rascal that's trailing us?
> "Scouting the place so you can come
> "at night with the rest of your gang?"

The donkey-driver's reaction makes clear a fundamental tension at the heart of urban life: cities are large and confusing and people may need one another's help to find their way, but cities are also crowded and full of strange people, some of whom have nefarious intentions. When the female beloved speaks for the first time it is to resolve this tension. She asks the protagonist to identify himself: by name, neighborhood, and profession (ll. 13–14).[41] The protagonist ignores most of the woman's questions and answers the final question about his five trades in a clever and florid recital of sexual innuendo. He is a cannoneer whose cannon "knocks and crashes and demolishes walls and castle gates" (l. 17), and a chicken-hatcher whose three-quarter cubit-long, red-crested cock rests "shrunken and curled-up over its eggs" (l. 22).[42] He is a potter, who works "from the inside out" (l. 23) and who strips off his clothes when he is working (l. 24), presumably on account of the heat of the kiln.[43] "If I get caught up in work," he says in line 25, "stay up for me. I'll make you a thousand jars [or give you a thousand strokes] each night." He is also a lancer who "never stops thrusting" (l. 30) and the captain of a boat, whose "furling rope moves back and forth between us" (l. 36). "When [he] lets go of the tiller, it gets thrown about, but then [he] pulls out the punt-pole and nails it in the rear" (l. 37). The recitation makes an impression on the woman, who then asks the protagonist about his possessions (l. 38).

This prompts a rare moment of introspection: after nearly telling her the truth of his penury, the protagonist decides he is better off lying to the woman in the hope that he may enjoy the "spoils" (*maghnam*) of sexual union with her (l. 40). He then proceeds to dazzle her with a litany of fantastic treasures, including precious metals and jewels, but the showpiece is certainly his house, which the woman is very eager to see (ll. 43–68). The protagonist convinces the woman to ditch her donkey-driving chaperone and then escorts her back to his hovel (ll. 69–71). When they arrive there, the woman is understandably irritated but the protagonist manages, through the same verbal cunning, to get her to go inside the "ruin" (*kharāba*) that is his home (ll. 72–6). On the inside, however, there is no hiding the protagonist's deception and the woman throws the grandiloquent descriptions of wealth back in his face (ll. 77–85). It is at this point that the protagonist comes clean. He admits that he was lying the entire time and that he is dirt-poor. He owns nothing, he says, except his love for her and it was her beauty that drove him to invent his tale in the first place (ll. 86–91). Both characters at this point refer to the protagonist's aspiration as "union" (*waṣl*) (ll. 91–2):

> I composed those words
> so that I could be with you
> when I saw your beautiful
> lamp-bright face.
>
> And she said, "If what you want
> "is to be with me,
> "describe my beauty,
> "if you think you can."

Having demonstrated his rhetorical talents, it is no surprise that the protagonist should accomplish this feat with minimal suspense (ll. 93–106). He even ends his masterful description with the ironic claim: "You've now been a quarter-described, my lovely, but in rhetoric it's always better – and more clever – to hold back" (l. 106). The protagonist – the rightful hero of the song – is rewarded for his eloquence with "union" (*talāqī*) but by this point his accomplishment is already a foregone conclusion (l. 107). The audience is perhaps still pruriently curious, but they have already been won over by the protagonist's victory in the urban arena. A man with no money, connections, or prospects managed through eloquent trickery alone to meet a stranger in the street, convince her to abandon her chaperone, and take her back to his abode.[44] Whether or not the woman and the man ultimately unite – and the degree of sexual contact beyond kissing is ambiguous – the protagonist has won the game of urban erotic opportunity.[45]

These erotic opportunities are often framed as zero-sum conflicts, in which the lover can only gain sexual pleasure at the expense of the beloved's chastity. That the lover is often the beloved's social superior (whether in terms of class, gender, or economic status and personal liberty) means that the beloved is frequently in the position of weighing economic gain against sexual coercion. The urban enviroment of the premodern Arabic literary imaginary may best be described as the predatory city: an environment in which adult men use their social and economic prerogatives to coerce women and younger men into sexualized interactions wherever and whenever they choose.[46] This literary environment resembles that of songs in the English folk tradition in which cautionary tales are told of handsome and charming strangers who take advantage of a naive girl's generosity ("Soldier, won't you marry me?") or a sailor's wages ("Young Sailor Cut Down").[47] The villains or the victims in these songs are often out of place, like the unlucky peasants in al-Shirbīnī's *Hazz al-quḥūf*. In other songs, like "Young Ramble Away" and "Let No Man Steal Your Thyme," the threat is specifically sexual.[48]

Another Urban Encounter

Rather than warn young unmarried women about predatory men, the following song, a *ṭaqṭūqa* by Zakariyyā Aḥmad (1896–1961), directly rebukes young men for harassing women in the streets of Egyptian cities.[49] The song is sung from the perspective of a young woman and exploits concerns related to class and national pride to shame men into behaving better.

ما يِصَحّش تِعاكِسْني

[مذهب]

[١] ما يِصَحّش تِعاكِسْني يأخينا — ولا تِمْشي كِدَهْ سَكْران طينه
[٢] عامِل خِفَّه وجِنْتِلْمان — ليه تِتْمَحَك في ٱلنِّسوان
[٣] وماشي تعط — وانت برط
[٤] يِجْرى إيه لو تِمْشي تَمَّام — هو مَشِي الحِشْمَه حَرام

ما يِصَحّشْ

[دور]

[٥] الطَّرْبوش أربع قَراريط — ولابِس بَدْلَه بايط الاِيط
[٦] دم يا سِمْ — تِبْقى مِتْرَم
[٧] ما يِجيبَكْش اِتْنَيْن مِلِّيم — وتِعاكِسْلي كَمان في حَريم

ما يِصَحّشْ

[دور]

[٨] النَّار تِدْخُلْها بِرِجْلَيْك   والنَّاس كُلَّها ناقْدَهْ عَلَيْك
[٩] إمتى تْحِسّ   يَعْني تْخِس
[٠١] لَمَّا تِتْجَوِّز وتْعيش   عِيشه عال ما فيهاش يِغْنيش

ما يِصَحِّش

[دور]

[١١] عاوِز تِبْقَى صَحيح إنْسان   صُون أعْراض ٱلنَّاس تِنْصان
[٢١] ما تْحَوِّدش   ما تْلَوِّدش
[٣١] ليه تِدوس شَرَفَكْ وتْخون   وانْتَ أبوكْ توت عَنْخ آمون

ما يِصَحِّش

You shouldn't harass me
Brother, you shouldn't harass me[51]
And you shouldn't stroll around like that sozzled.
You dress up classy, like a gentleman
So why are you out wheedling ladies?
Walking around like a tramp,
You're just a piece of shit [?].
What's wrong with minding your own business?
When did modesty become a sin?

It just won't do.

You're wearing a four-inch fez
and a "Buy it Elite" [?] suit.
You're a bore [?]
and you'd better straighten up!
As soon as you get your hands on a couple of bucks
you think you can start chatting up women in the street?

It just won't do.

You're going to hell head-first.
No one can abide what you do.
When will you wise up,
by which I mean get lost?
After you get married
and start your great life, lacking for nothing?

It just won't do.

If you want to be a proper human,
then respect people's dignity and preserve your own.
Don't swivel,
Don't swerve.
Why would you crush your honor and betray it?
Aren't you the son of Tutankhamun?

The putative harasser is not indigent, rather he has sufficient disposable income to dress nicely and can look forward to marrying without financial difficulty. Despite her harsh condemnation of the man's behavior, the woman narrating the song is invested in the man's redemption. This is apparent in her appeals to the man's class background, personal dignity, and potential perdition, as well as Egyptian national pride.[52] There is no romanticization of street harassment here, unlike in the opening of Cheb Khaled's hit song "Aïcha" (1996). The tone of the admonishment "It just won't do" (*mā yiṣaḥḥish*) is itself rather subdued. Nevertheless, we cannot mistake the fact that this scene – a man using the presence of a woman or young man in public as an opportunity to objectify them – is one that we have seen over and over again in the examples above, although in this case the story is told by a woman rebuking the man who has accosted her. I do not mean to say that every proposition in the history of premodern Arabic literature was unwelcome – that is demonstrably false – but this song may induce us to see the tradition in a different light.

The Predatory City

It may strike some as dour or literal-minded to characterize the urban setting of much premodern Arabic literature as the predatory city. Indeed, humor is integral to much of this literature, but that humor often depends on an uncanny and discomfiting schadenfreude that we must recognize, even as we acknowledge that these works were intended to push social boundaries and tickle the sublimated anxieties and desires of their urban audience. One of the ways in which authors achieved this was by eroticizing everything: the promiscuity of public space, semi-public semi-nudity, social stratification, slavery, and the commodification of bodies. No setting was too sacred or somber for erotic exploits, be it the Kaᶜbah or a funeral, as in this last example, a poem by Ibn Qalāqis (d. 567/1172).[53]

قال أيضًا وقد رأى صبيًا في بعض المآتم يبكي

[من الرجز]

[١] وابأبي مَنْ لَمْ يَدَعْ فيَّ مكانًا لِلأَلَمْ
[٢] بَدْرٌ أَبَى ضِياؤُهُ أَنْ تَتَغَشَّاه ٱلظُّلَمْ
[٣] أَبْصَرْتُهُ في مَأْتَمٍ يا مَأْتَمًا عَلَيَّ تَمْ
[٤] وقُلْتُ لَمَّا أَنْ بَكَى كَأَنَّهُ قَدِ ٱبْتَسَمْ
[٥] لِلّٰهِ فيهِ جامعًا أَحْسَنَ أَوْصافِ ٱلقَلَمْ

On a young boy crying at a funeral
I'd ransom my father's life for one who doesn't
leave any space in me for pain,
A moon-faced one whose splendor refuses
to be covered by gloom
I saw him at a funeral,
oh what a funeral that brought me to my end!
I said – when he cried,
and in crying it was as though he were smiling—
God has gathered in him
the finest descriptions of the pen.

Let us, for the purposes of argument, stipulate that the scene described in the poem never happened, that it is a conceit and entirely a product of the poet's imagination. These assumptions – good scholarly, critical hygiene though they may be – do not actually help us understand whether these urban literary encounters were understood as hypothetical, impossible, or absurd. We must not allow ourselves to be so seduced by ego-affinity that we can only read these encounters from the perspective of the poet-persona, the I. Would it be overdetermined, or anachronistic, to read this poem from the perspective of the boy being described? A pre-adolescent, grieving in the company of adult men. This imaginary moon-faced boy may never have known that he was the object of the poetic I's narcissistic desire. The poem only mentions the boy's beauty and his grief. It is not even clear that the persona's desire for the boy is sexual. One of the most vexing aspects of classical Islamicate poetry for the modern reader is that we struggle to understand the apparent distinction between the erotic and the libidinous. How would one even begin to express libido in a society in which all social interactions were routinely eroticized? A lack of imagination leads us to fill in unfamiliar and blurry spaces in our schemata of literary encounters with our own anti-erotic society's dominant preoccupation, libido. This scene is perforce fictional, and perhaps even comic – and we understand that lyric poetry intends to express and stimulate individual and communal emotion – but what must it have been like to live in a society whose culture celebrated and encouraged the eroticization of every form of social interaction? What must it have been like to inhabit the body of a woman or a pubescent male in a premodern Arab city? It would be wrong to assume from these texts that all social encounters in premodern Arab cities were eroticized in reality, that women and young men would have always felt themselves to be the object of erotic attention or desire in every social interaction with an adult male, or indeed that this erotic attention or desire would have always been unwelcome. But it is no less wrong to assume that it was always fun and games just because the poets tell us it was.

Notes

1. This anonymous poem is edited in Talib (2012: 648, no. 94). When that article was published, I enjoyed discussing the poem and its puns with my colleague and mentor Humphrey Davies, a paragon of urbanity (in both senses of the word) and an inspiration to all who take this megalopolis as our muse. I dedicate this article to him. I would like to thank Samah Selim for her incisive and supportive comments on this article. Thanks are owed as well to Domenico Ingenito, Katharine Halls, and the anonymous reviewers for their corrections and suggestions. Nizar F. Hermes and Gretchen Head kindly invited me to contribute to this volume and were more patient and good-humored than I had any right to expect.
2. Pierre Cachia terms this form of perfect paronomasia (*jinās tāmm*) "congruent paronomasia" (see Cachia 1998, no. 19).
3. The caesura in the second line is interesting linguistically. I have edited the dialogue according to the conventions of classical Arabic:

   [...] *qultu lahū* || *ʾal-ʿāʾizu l-waṣla yā ḥabībi ʾanā*
   [...] ⏑ – ⏑⏑ – || – – ⏑ – – ⏑ – ⏑ – ⏑⏑ –

   but one could read it as a case of mixed Arabic, in which what appears as the definite article in the word *al-ʿāʾiz* is actually a relative pronoun:

   [...] *qultu lahūl-* || *lī-ʿāʾyizə l-waṣlə yā ḥabībi ʾanā*
   [...] – ⏑⏑ – || – – ⏑ – – ⏑ – ⏑ – ⏑⏑ –

   This is not, as far as we know, how the relative pronoun *illī* was written in premodern Arabic – that would be الي or اللي – but it is one of the orthographic forms that it takes in contemporary Cairene Arabic. Compare the preposition *fi*, which is often written as the letter *fā*ʾ prepended to an indefinite or definite (*fā*ʾ*-lām*) substantive when proclitic, as distinct from "*fī*" ("there is"), which is often written *fīh*. There is a slight possibility that scholars may mistake the relative pronoun for the definite article in indistinct cases.

4. See Ibn Makānis (d. 794/1393), *Muḥāwarah bayn ahl al-ḥiraf*; al-Bilbaysī, *Kitāb al-Mulaḥ wa-ṭ-ṭuraf min munādamat arbāb al-ḥiraf* (Unseen. On this work and author, see *EI*², "al-Bilbaysī" (Joseph Sadan). NB: Ibn Baṭṭūṭah specifies the vocalization Balbays.) See also Muḥammad Saᶜīd al-Qāsimī, which includes literary material. See also relevant discussions in Hirschler (2012: 44–6 and *passim*), and in al-Musawi (2015: 172).
5. See, *inter alia, EI*², *"Shahrangīz"* (J. T. P. de Bruijn; Talat Sait; Munibur Rahman); Sharma (2000: 107–16); Gulchīn Maᶜānī; Glünz; Tuğcu. Oṇ Urdu Rekhti poetry see Vanita.
6. Cole (2007: 210–11). See also Decter, "Judah al-Harizi's Book of Tahkemoni" (2004). On another "sodomite" in medieval Hebrew literature, see Decter, "A Hebrew 'sodomite' tale from thirteenth-century Toledo" (2011).
7. The first of these is recorded in Freyha (1974: 338); the last two are from Feghali (1938: 441, 438). A particularly nasty example of this is another proverb also recorded by Feghali: "Feed a peasant milk for forty years and his shit will still be black" (اطعم الفلاح اربعين سنة حليب بتضل خريته سودا) (440).
8. Al-Shirbīnī, 2: 57–8, 1: 53 (Arabic text) (2005–13 ed.); 1: 86–7 (2016 ed.).
9. Al-Shirbīnī, tr.2: 48–9; 1: 41–2 (Arabic text) (2005–13 ed.); 1: 72–5 (2016 ed.).
10. See two important articles by Semerdjian (2015), "Naked Anxiety" and "Sexing the *Hammam*"; and Schick (2004), "Representation of Gender and Sexuality in Ottoman and Turkish Erotic Literature." See, too, reporting in *Mada Masr* <www.madamasr.com> on the case of a televized raid on the Bāb al-Baḥr bathhouse in Cairo in 2015. More generally on bathhouses in premodern Arab cities, see *EI*² (1960–2009), "Ḥammām" (J. Sourdel-Thomine and A. Louis) and Grotzfeld. See also Dunbabin (1989).
11. Partridge (1968: 191).
12. In his anthology *Classical Arabic Literature*, Geert Jan van Gelder has translated part of the same author's *ᶜIṭr nasīm aṣ-ṣabā*, which also has to do with the bathhouse (2013: 345–51).
13. Al-Ḥaymī al-Kawkabānī (1986: 76–8).
14. Ibn Baṭṭūṭah (1997: 1: 225).
15. Al-Ḥaymī al-Kawkabānī (1986: 77). It is tempting to interpret the word *ḥāyil* as deriving from the verb *ḥāla* [*dūna*] "to come between" (root *ḥ-w-l*), scil. *ḥā*ʾ*il*. The city in Najd is known variously as Ḥāyil and Ḥāʾil.

16. If the reader will indulge a weak generalization, I would note that sleeping face down is also frowned upon in popular culture and religious discourse in the Arab world today. One can point to *ḥadīth* reports, including one narrated by Ibn Mājah in which the Prophet Muḥammad remarked that sleeping on one's front "[...] is how people in Hell sleep" (*innamā hiyya ḍajᶜat ahl an-nār*). I was once told by a middle-aged woman whom I knew from the Mubtadayān neighborhood in Cairo that: *illī bi-yənām ᶜalā baṭnuh ᶜāyiz yitnāk* ("Whoever sleeps on their front is asking to get fucked").
17. The passage by al-Ḥaymī, which G. J. van Gelder translated, is also highly homoerotic (see note 12 above).
18. Al-Ḥaymī al-Kawkabānī (1986: 103). I reproduce here the earlier recension of the text; the editor al-Ḥibshī includes additions from the expanded recension between brackets in his edition.
19. The verb *jarrada* can also mean "to undress" and the adjective *ṣaqīl* ("polished") is also used to describe gleaming skin.
20. *Shaddū maʾāzirahum* (prepare for battle): compare "to gird one's loins."
21. Al-Ḥaymī al-Kawkabānī (1986: 103). The active participle *muᶜbiq* in l. 4 is not attested, but I assume it to be a synonym of the attested active participle *muᶜabbiq*: (of a fragrance) permeating.
22. *bāna maᶜāṭifin*: the last word in this line makes it clear that the intended meaning of the word *bāna* is the ben-tree, and not the verb "to appear" (*bāna*), but the use of the verb "to undress" (*tajarradū*) in the beginning of the line may prompt an initial, intentional misperception. See Cachia (1998: no. 108).
23. Al-Ḥaymī al-Kawkabānī (1986: 105).
24. Compare lines 2–3 of a very well-known poem by Abū Nuwāsʾ (1958–2006: *Dīwān*, 3: 106–8, Poem 82).
25. Al-Ḥillī (2000: 1: 456; 2016: 1: 317–18 (slightly different reading)) (meter: *al-Basīṭ*).
26. Bauer (2011); Ahmed (2016).
27. Antoon (2014: 131).
28. On this regulatory environment, see Stilt (2012) and Ghabin (2009).
29. Al-Ṣafadī (Princeton MS Garrett Yahuda 935: ff. 78b–79a); and in the al-Hayb edition of this work (2003: 73).
30. *as-sanā*: reading with Princeton MS, rather than al-Hayb's editon: *as-samā*.
31. The double entendre in this final hemistich has to do with the near homophony in the words for anise (*yānisūn*) and intimate companions (*ānisūn*). The rose in the preceding hemistich would lead the reader to assume what is meant is another type of flower, but this is a feint.
32. Khayyāṭah (2009: 319–20).

33. *tṣīḥ*: emended from printed edition "*t-ṣ-b-ḥ*."
34. See, for example, a poem by Nefᶜī (d. 1635) in Andrews *et al.* (2006: 109).
35. ᶜUbayd-i Zākānī, 76, no. 27 (meter: *możāre*ᶜ).
36. Bouriant (1893: 126–33); Cachia (1989: 103–20). See also the non-erotic genre of Turkish "street-*destan*" as described in Özkul Çobanoğlu (2001).
37. I have re-translated extracts from the song for this article but I would not have been able to do so without reference to Cachia's excellent edition and translation. NB: the object of desire in my translation of the refrain is male, in Cachia's it is female. The grammatical gender is masculine in the Arabic. I maintain the gender of the Arabic in my translation. For a discussion of this thorny issue in translation, see Selim Kuru's remarks in his review of *Ottoman Lyric Poetry* (1999).
38. Cachia also translates the word *miṭaqṭaq* as "lively," but he links the word to contemporary meanings of "cracking" and "smartening up"(see Hinds and Badawi, *Dictionary of Egyptian Arabic*, s. r. "*ṭ-q-ṭ-q*" in Cachia 1989: 120). I prefer to link it to Lane's definition based on az-Zabīdī: "in the language of the common people, *Light in person*; and *light*, or *prompt, in speech*" (Lane 1863–93, s. r. "*ṭ-q-ṭ-q*").
39. Reading with MS and Cachia (1989), "*wi-qaṣdī yiwāṣilnī*" *contra* Bouriant's (1893) emendation: "*wa-aṣadt innuh yiwāṣilnī.*"
40. In l. 10, I read "*tābi*ᶜ *khaṭwithum*" or *Khaṭrithum contra* Cachia (1989) and Bouriant (1893): "*tābi*ᶜ *khaṭirhum.*"
41. Add to this list age, religion, and marital status, and you have exactly the same information that is present on an Egyptian personal identity card (*biṭāqah shakhṣiyyah*) today.
42. Cachia (1989) translates *yadak* as "ramrod," but it means something like wick or botefeux.
43. "From the inside out" (l. 23): I read "*min guwwa li-barra,*" *contra* Cachia and Bouriant: "*min guwwa l-mibarra.*" It may rather mean, "I work inside the kiln area, [firing the ceramic], and outside it, [sculpting it]."
44. There is overlap here with the character-type detailed in Lyons (2012).
45. One can compare this song with a Persian poem by Sūzanī Samarqandī (d. *ca.* 1173) that depicts a similar scenario to perceive better the different mores of the *ghazal* and *mujūn* genres (translated in Zipoli 2015: 156–9).
46. For a different perspective on cities in classical Arabic literature, see Bayyud (1988).
47. "Soldier, won't you marry me?" published in Auden (1938: 363–4). The song was first published in Campbell and Sharp (1917: 262). "Young Sailor Cut

Down" published in Roud and Bishop (2014: 217–18). On the history of the song, see the latter: 455.

48. "Young Ramble Away," published in Roud and Bishop (2014: 215–16). On the history of the song, see Ibid. (454–5).
49. Reprinted in Īzīs Fatḥ Allāh, *Zakariyyā Aḥmad*, 1: 238. In early twentieth-century American English, men who verbally harassed women on the street were called "mashers" (see Freedman (2013: ch. 10).
50. Emended from *m-r-m*.
51. I have chosen to translate the Form III verb *ᶜākis / yəᶜākis / muᶜāksah* as "to harass." Over the past decade, the term *muᶜāksah* has been the subject of much public debate as part of the larger issue of street harassment in Egyptian cities. A broad swathe of activists and feminists, and here I include myself, reject the term *muᶜāksah* and insist that verbal street harassment be described as *taḥarrush* or *taḥarrush lafẓī*. This new, politically astute usage has since entered the mainstream but *muᶜāksah* continues to be used to refer to a spectrum of sexually suggestive speech including consensual flirting between acquaintances or strangers. Some commentators specify this is as *il-muᶜāksah ig-gamīlah bitāᶜət zamān* (old-fashioned polite flirting). The word *muᶜāksah* is even used – but in this case only by the men doing it – to describe making vulgar, sexually explicit, threatening, and objectifying comments to women in public. Some feminists continue to describe consensual, or at least respectful, flirting as *muᶜāksah*, though the verb *kān bi-yəflirt / bi-yəflirt* is also lately being used. The use of the term *taḥarrush* or *taḥarrush lafẓī* in the place of *muᶜāksah* is part of a political campaign to link verbal street harassment to the wider phenomena of hostility and violence directed towards women in public and semi-public spaces. It is clear from this song that the term *muᶜāksah* has been used to refer to verbal sexual harassment for at least a century.
52. There are a few allusions in the song to religious diction, for instance modesty (*ḥishmah* in l. 4b) and sin and hellfire (*ḥarām* in l. 4b, *an-nār* in l. 8a).
53. Ibn Qalāqis (1988: 529–30, no. 417). This motif predates Ibn Qalāqis, of course. See, for example, al-Mihzamī (2011: 42).

Works Cited

Abū Nuwās (1958–2006), *Dīwān*, Ewald Wagner and Gregor Schoeler (ed.), 7 vols (vol. 4), Vienna: Bibliotheca Islamica.

Ahmed, Shahab (2016), *What is Islam? The Importance of Being Islamic*, Princeton NJ: Princeton University Press.

Andrews, Walter G. (2006), Najaat Black, Mehmet Kalpaklı, *Ottoman Lyric Poetry: an Anthology*, Seattle WA: University of Washington Press.

Antoon, Sinan (2014) *The Poetics of the Obscene in Premodern Arabic Poetry: Ibn al-Ḥajjāj and* Sukhf, New York NY: Palgrave Macmillan.

Auden, W. H. (ed.) (2004), *W. H. Auden's Book of Light Verse,* rev. ed. of *The Oxford Book of Light Verse* (1938), New York NY: The New York Review of Books.

Bauer, Thomas (2011), *Die Kultur der Ambiguität*, Berlin: Verlag der Weltreligionen.

Bayyud, Hussein (1988), *Die Stadt in der arabischen Poesie, bis 1258 n. Chr.* Berlin: Klaus Schwarz.

Bearman, P., Th. Bianquis, C. E. Bosworth, E. van Donzel, and W. P. Heinrichs (eds) (1960–2009), *EI²: The Encyclopaedia of Islam. New Edition*, 11 vols, Leiden: Brill.

Bouriant, U. (1893), *Chansons populaires arabes en dialecte du Caire d'après les manuscrits d'un chanteur des rues*, Paris: Ernest Leroux.

Cachia, Pierre (1989), *Popular Narrative Ballads of Modern Egypt*, Oxford: Clarendon Press.

—— (1998), *The Arch Rhetorician. Or, The Schemer's Skimmer: a handbook of late Arabic badīᶜ drawn from ᶜAbd al-Ghanī al-Nābulsī's Nafaḥāt al-azhār ᶜalā nasamāt al-asḥār*, Wiesbaden: Harrassowitz Verlag.

Campbell, Olivia Dame and Cecil Sharp (1917), *English Folk Songs from the Southern Appalachians*, New York NY and London: G. P. Putnam's Sons.

Çobanoğlu, Özkul (2001), "Street-*Destans* in the Turkish Minstrel Tradition," *The Turkish Studies Association Bulletin*, 25: 1 (Spring), 1–20.

Cole, Peter (2007), *The Dream of the Poem: Hebrew poetry from Muslim and Christian Spain, 950–1492*, Princeton NJ: Princeton University Press.

Decter, Jonathan P. (2004), "Judah al-Harizi's Book of Tahkemoni," in Joyce Moss (ed.), *Middle Eastern Literatures and Their Times*, Santa Monica: Moss Publishing, 68–75.

—— (2011), "A Hebrew 'sodomite' tale from thirteenth-century Toledo: Jacob Ben Elᶜazar's story of Sapir, Shapir, and Birsha," *Journal of Medieval Iberian Studies*, 3: 2, 187–202.

Dunbabin, Katherine M. D. (1989), "Baiarum Grata Voluptas: Pleasures and Dangers of the Bath," *Papers of the British School at Rome*, 57, 6–46.

Fatḥ Allāh, Īzīs (2011), *Zakariyyā Aḥmad.* 2 vols. Ser. *Mawsūᶜat aᶜlām al-mūsīqā al-ᶜarabiyyah*, vol. 5, Cairo: Dār al-Shurūq.

Feghali, Michel T. (1938), *Proverbes et dictons syro-libanais. Texte arabe, transcription, traduction, commentaire et index analytique*, Paris: Institut d'ethnologie.

Freedman, Estelle B. (2013), *Redefining Rape: Sexual Violence in the Era of Suffrage and Segregation*, Cambridge MA: Harvard University Press.

Freyha, Anis (1974), *A Dictionary of Modern Lebanese Proverbs,* Beirut: Librairie du Liban.

van Gelder, Geert Jan (2013), *Classical Arabic Literature. A Library of Arabic Literature Anthology*, New York NY: New York University Press.

Ghabin, Ahmad (2009), *Ḥisba, Arts and Craft in Islam*, Wiesbaden: Harrassowitz.

Glünz, Michael (1986), 'Ṣāfīs Šahrangīz. Ein persisches Maṯnawī über die schönen Berufsleute von Istanbul', *AS/EA*, 40: 2, 133–45.

Grotzfeld, Heinz (1970), *Das Bad im arabisch-islamischen Mittelalter. Eine kulturgeschichtliche Studie*, Wiesbaden: Harrassowitz Verlag.

Gulchīn Maᶜānī, Aḥmad (1380/2001), *Shahr-āshūb dar shiᶜr-i Fārsī*, 2nd ed., Tehran: Rivāyat.

al-Ḥaymī al-Kawkabānī, Shihāb al-Dīn Aḥmad b. Muḥammad (1986), *Ḥadāʾiq al-nammām fī l-kalām ᶜalā mā yataᶜallaq bi-l-ḥammām*, ᶜAbd Allāh Muḥammad al-Ḥibshī (ed.), Beirut: Dār at-Tanwīr.

al-Ḥillī, Ṣafī ad-Dīn ᶜAbd al-ᶜAzīz b. Sarāyā (2000), *Dīwān*, Muḥammad Ḥuwwar (ed.), 3 vols, Beirut: al-Muʾassasah al-ᶜArabiyyah li-d-Dirāsāt wa-n-nashr.

—— *Dīwān* (2016), Muhammad Maẓlūm (ed.), 2 vols, Beirut: Manshūrāt al-Jamal.

Hirschler, Konrad (2012), *The Written Word in the Medieval Arabic Lands: a Social and Cultural History of Reading Practices*, Edinburgh: Edinburgh University Press.

Ibn Baṭṭūṭah (1997), *Riḥlat Ibn Baṭṭūṭah al-musammā Tuḥfat an-nuẓẓār fī gharāʾib al-amṣār wa-ᶜajāʾib al-asfār*, ᶜAbd al-Hādī al-Tāzī (ed.) 5 vols, Rabat: Akādīmiyyat al-Mamlakah al-Maghribiyyah.

Khayyāṭah, Ḥasan Aḥmad (ed.) (2009), *Mawsūᶜat al-mawāwīl al-Ḥalabiyya*, Aleppo: Dār al-Qalam al-ᶜArabī.

Kuru, Selim (1999), "Review of W. G. Andrews, N. Black, and M. Kalpaklı, *Ottoman Lyric Poetry*," in *Turkish Studies Association Bulletin*, 23: 1 (Spring), 9–81.

Lane, Edward William (1863–93), *An Arabic-English Lexicon*, 8 vols, supp. Stanley Lane Poole, London: Williams and Norgate.

Lyons, Malcolm C. (2012), *The Man of Wiles in Popular Arabic Literature: A Study of a Medieval Arab Hero*, Edinburgh: Edinburgh University Press.

Ibn Makānis, Fakhr al-Dīn (1997), *Muḥāwara bayn ahl al-ḥiraf*, Amīnah Muḥammad Jamāl ad-Dīn (ed.), Cairo: Dār al-Hidāya.

—— Ibid. (Gotha MS orient, A 2310, digitized MS available at http://archive.thulb.uni-jena.de/ufb/receive/ufb_cbu_00005683 (accessed 10 November 2017).

Ibn Qalāqis (2001), *Dīwān*, Sihām Furayḥ (ed.), Cairo: al-Majlis al-Aᶜlā li-th-Thaqāfah.

Al-Mihzamī, Abū Hiffān ᶜAbd Allāh b. Aḥmad (2011), *Akhbār Abī Nuwās*, Faraj al-Ḥiwār (ed.), Beirut, Baghdad, Freiburg: Manshūrāt al-Jamal.

Al-Musawi, Muhsin J. (2015), *The Medieval Islamic Republic of Letters, Arabic Knowledge Construction*, South Bend IN: University of Notre Dame Press.

Partridge, Eric (1968), *Shakespeare's Bawdy: a literary & pscyhological essay and a comprehensive glossary*, London: Routledge & Kegan Paul.

Al-Qāsimī, Muḥammad Saʿīd (1960; repr. 1988), *Qāmūs aṣ-ṣināʿāt ash-Shāmiyyah*, Ẓāfir al-Qāsimī (ed.), 2 vols, Paris: Mouton; Damascus: Dār Ṭalās.

Aṣ-Ṣafadī, Ṣalāḥ ad-Dīn Khalīl b. Aybak, *al-Ḥusn aṣ-ṣarīḥ fi miʾat malīḥ (Pure Beauty: On One Hundred Handsome Lads)*, Princeton MS Garrett Yahuda 935.

—— ibid. (2003), Aḥmad Fawzī al-Hayb (ed.), Damascus: Dār Saʿd ad-Dīn.

Roud, S. and Bishop, J. (eds) (2014), *The New Penguin Book of English Folk Songs*, London: Penguin.

Schick, Irvin Cemil (2004), "Representation of Gender and Sexuality in Ottoman and Turkish Erotic Literature," *Turkish Studies Association*, 28, 1–104.

Semerdjian, Elyse (2013), "Naked Anxiety: Bathhouses, Nudity, and the *Dhimmī Woman* in 18th-century Aleppo," *IJMES*, 45: 4, 651–76.

—— (2015), "Sexing the *Hammam*: Gender Crossings in the Ottoman Bathhouse," in Gul Ozyegin (ed.), *Gender and Sexuality in Muslim Cultures*, Farnham: Ashgate.

Sharma, Sunil (2000), *Persian Poetry at the Indian Frontier: Masʿûd Saʿd Salmân of Lahore*, Delhi: Permanent Black.

Al-Shirbīnī, Yūsuf (2005–13, 3 vols; repr. 2016, 2 vols), *Kitāb Hazz al-quḥūf bi-sharḥ qaṣīd Abī Shādūf* (*Brains Confounded by the Ode of Abū Shādūf Expounded*), Humphrey Davies (ed. and trans.), Leuven: Peeters; (repr.) Ser. Library of Arabic Literature, New York NY: New York University Press.

Stilt, Kristen (2012), *Islamic Law in Action, Authority, Discretion, and Everyday Experiences in Mamluk Egypt*, Oxford: Oxford University Press.

Talib, Adam (2012), "Pseudo-Ṭaʿālibī's *Book of Youths*," *Arabica*, 59: 6, 599–649.

Tuğcu, Emine (2011), "Bursa şehrengizlerinde güzellerin mekânları: bahçe, hamam ve çarşı," *Journal of Turkish Studies*, 35, 275–84.

ʿUbayd-i Zākānī (1999), *Kullīyāt-i ʿUbayd-i Zākānī*, Muḥammad-Jaʿfar Maḥjūb (ed.), New York NY: Bibliotheca Persica.

Vanita, Ruth (2012), *Gender, Sex, and the City: Urdu Rekhtī Poetry in India, 1780–1870*, New Delhi: Orient Blackswan.

Zipoli, Riccardo (2015), *Irreverent Persia, Invective, satirical and burlesque poetry from the origins to the Timurid period (10th to 15th centuries)*, Leiden: Leiden University Press.

9

Between Utopia and Dystopia in Marrakech

Gretchen Head

"What other age are you dreaming of, what other land?"
(*Mundus Alter Idem*, Bishop Joseph Hall, 1607)

Introduction

Shortly after Ibn al-Muwaqqit published *al-Riḥla al-Marrākushiyya, aw, Mirʾāt al-masāwiʾ al-waqtiyya* (Travels in Marrakech, or, a Mirror of Momentary Evils) in 1930,[1] a firestorm of controversy erupted. Three of Marrakech's most important judges joined forces with the heads of the city's main Sufi orders and filed a complaint against al-Muwaqqit with the city's Pasha, who immediately took the matter to the king. The king unexpectedly responded by saying, "Whoever is attacked by the pen can only respond by the pen" (al-Muwaqqit 2000: 12). The dispute was then relegated to the world of print. Nevertheless, the text had undoubtedly struck a nerve. The merciless critique to which al-Muwaqqit had subjected so many in the book's pages, especially the sheikhs of the Sufi brotherhoods, was largely responsible. But in addition to this, the text's method of writing the urban space of Marrakech was something wholly new, and it held the potential to disrupt the fundamental sense of orientation intimately held by most of Marrakech's residents at the time, an orientation tied to their individual identities and collective histories. It is this aspect of al-Muwaqqit's writing that will be the concern of this chapter.

Muḥammad bin Muḥammad bin ʿAbd Allāh al-Muwaqqit (d. 1999) – more generally known as Ibn al-Muwaqqit – authored more than eighty titles. He lived during a time characterized by the rising tension between a number of binary oppositions: tradition vs. modernization, development vs. preservation, nationalist activism vs. support of colonialism, orthodox Islam or Salafism vs. the traditional Sufi orders (Jallāb 1994: 10). His work is infused with the existential turmoil of these conflicts, his own positions shifting radically through the course of his life. Born in 1894,[2] he grew up in Marrakech's old city near the Ibn Yūsuf mosque (see Ben Youssef mosque, Figure 9.1[3]). Arguably Marrakech's oldest and most important mosque, it was here that his father, Muḥammad bin ᶜAbd Allāh al-Muwaqqit, served as resident timekeeper. A notable scholar himself, he taught his son his vocation from an early age. The young al-Muwaqqit was deeply affected by the environment in which he was raised; his immediate surroundings not only comprised the mosque and its attached school, but also the nearby Qurʾānic school, among Morocco's largest and attended by the majority of Marrakech's scholars, and the *zāwiya* of Būᶜamrū with its steady stream of disciples and initiates (Jallāb 1994: 9). This is the geography that is the topic of both *Al-Saᶜāda al-abadīyya fī al-taᶜrīf bi-mashāhīr al-ḥadra al-Marrākushiyya* (Eternal Happiness in the Identification of Marrakech's Notables) published as a lithograph in Fez in 1918 and *al-Riḥla al-Marrākushiyya*, which he published more than a decade later by sending the manuscript to a press in Cairo (Jallāb 1994: 13). The visions of Marrakech constructed in each of these texts, however, could not be more different. In the former, al-Muwaqqit writes Marrakech in a localized model of the ideal city, or *al-madīna al-fāḍila,* while the latter edges towards dystopia, with Marrakech imagined as a paradigmatic example of the corrupt city, or *al-madīna al-fāsida.* To the extent that contemporary critics of Arabic literature are familiar with Ibn al-Muwaqqit, interest in his work has been primarily focused on *al-Riḥla al-Marrākushiyya,* often because of its clear relationship to Muḥammad al-Muwayliḥī's *Ḥadīth ᶜĪsā ibn Hishām, aw fatra min al-zaman.*[4] What gets lost in a discussion of this text in isolation is its role as the dystopian inverse of the image of Marrakech charted by al-Muwaqqit in his earlier writings. The range of implications of the author's acute disillusionment with the city as its encounter with modernity deepened found in *al-Riḥla al-Marrākushiyya* only comes into full focus when read against *al-Saᶜāda al-abadiyya.*

Al-Saᶜāda al-Abadiyya: The Virtuous City

The idea of *al-madīna al-fāḍila* in the Arabic tradition is most commonly associated with Abū Naṣr al-Fārābī's (d. 950 CE) use of the term in his *Mabādiʾ ārāʾ ahl al-madīna al-fāḍila* (Principles of the Opinions of the People of the

Virtuous City), where, following the thought of Plato and Aristotle, he considers the criteria for an ethical society through a vision of the ideal city. The term, however, can be used more broadly to describe the concerns of a number of classical modes of writing about the city with utopian impulses. Though al-Fārābī himself was decidedly against mystical practice as irreconcilable with reason, in the Maghreb it was Sufi writing that developed the most popular means of representing the ideal city (al-Fārābī 1985: 15). Hagiographical anthologies commonly known as *rijāl* compilations were a central literary genre from the twelfth century onwards, and they constructed their own version of *al-madīna al-fāḍila* in spirit if not in name. Muḥammad ibn Qāsim al-Tamīmī's (d. 1207–8 CE) *Al-Kitāb al-mustafād fī manāqib al-ᶜubbād bi-madīnat Fās wa mā yalīhā min al-bilād* (The Book of Benefits on the Virtues of the Devout of Fez and its Environs) is widely considered to be the founding book of the hagiographical tradition in the Maghreb. Al-Tamīmī's *mustafād* was followed by the now more famous *Kitāb al-Tashawwuf ilā rijāl al-taṣawwuf* (The Book of Revelation on the Men of Mysticism) by Abū Yaᶜqūb al-Ṭadilī, completed in 1220 CE. Both books organize their content spatially, with the *Mustafād* focused on Fez and *al-Tashawwuf* on Marrakech. The rhetorical staging of the city in these Moroccan *rijāl* compilations bears some resemblance to earlier Christian figurations of the city of God (*civitas Dei*), whose origins can be traced to the writings of Saint Augustine (Cornell 1998: 98). Though in contrast to Augustine's city of God found exclusively in heaven, the *rijāl* featured in the compilations are, in keeping with the norms of sacred biography in Arabic, portrayed as living exemplars who reaffirm the values of Muḥammad's original community in Medina (99). These texts therefore constitute the living city as a sacred space, yet also one highly localized as each text is concerned with the discursive establishment of the discrete identity of an individual Maghrebi city.

In Praise of the City

Al-Saᶜāda al-abadiyya is divided into three parts: an introduction, the body (*maqṣid*), and a conclusion that shifts attention to al-Muwaqqit's sheikh at the time, the *Quṭb* Fatḥ Allāh al-Banānī (d. 1934). The core of the text is a long elucidation of the holy figures buried within the city ordered by Marrakech's seven patron saints; through these biographies and anecdotes, the text covers every gate and quarter of the medina: "In its explication of [the city's] *awliyāʾ*,[5] the *maqṣid* is arranged according to the *sabᶜat rijāl* (seven saints), gate by gate, inside and out, quarter by quarter" (al-Muwaqqit

2002: 46). As a *rijāl* compilation, the book is generically similar to the biographical dictionaries associated with specific places, texts Franz Rosenthal considered "theological local historiographies" (1968: 151). It is fitting, then, that al-Muwaqqit begins with an exposition on the benefits of historiography before moving on to a brief dynastic history of Marrakech from its founding in 454 AH (1062 CE) to the current ʿAlawite period.[6] This is followed by a section entitled, "As for the Description of the City of Marrakech" (*wa-ammā waṣf al-ḥaḍra al-Marrākushiyya*), where Marrakech's many virtues are extolled in rhymed prose of al-Muwaqqit's own composition. In keeping with the volume's theme, the city's relationship with religious piety is emphasized: "It is a city that has been a home of jurisprudence (*fiqh*), knowledge (*ʿilm*), righteousness (*ṣalāḥ*), religion (*dīn*), government (*wilāya*), and mystery (*sirr*) since its founding" (al-Muwaqqit 2002: 53). Before the topographical introduction that describes Marrakech's many mosques, minarets, and *madāris* (religious schools), as well as its natural attributes, al-Muwaqqit includes a selection of verses from well-known panegyrics, each of which are carefully chosen to craft an image of Marrakech that brings specific qualities to the forefront. Some verses establish Marrakech's general religious legitimacy, others its superiority to competing Moroccan cities, even those with greater claims to religious prestige, while others support al-Muwaqqit's own intimate ties to the city.

Much like Andalusian cities, Moroccan cities have not historically been able to claim the geopolitical or cosmological centrality of urban centers like Baghdad, Mecca, or Jerusalem (Antrim 2012: 40–1). As a result, poetic verses praising Maghrebi cities would often seek to rhetorically establish their connections to both the canonical literature of the Islamic tradition and its geographical centers. In this spirit, al-Muwaqqit includes an excerpt from a long praise poem by the sixteenth-century Marrakech-born poet Qāsim ibn Aḥmad al-Ḥalafāwī (d. 1591 CE):

وقد علا يوسف في الحسن حتى علت / بالسر مراكش الحمراء بالعبر
بيداء محمرة الاسوار مخضرة الاقطار / معدومة الانظار للفكر
ليس لها بعد مكة وطيبتها / مثل وشبهتها بمنتهى نظر
كفاها من شرف ما فيها من عارف / لله معتبر بالله منتصر
عديمة المثل لاضد لها ابدا / من حسن اتقانها مفروغة الصور

Yūsuf, surpassed in beauty just as / by a mystery, Marrakech excelled in its model
A wilderness of red walls and green lands / without equal in one's mind

After Mecca and Medina, it has no parallel / or equivalent for those with insightful discernment
It has more than its share of honor in the divine sages / who are reliant on God
It has no parallel or opposite / because of its perfection, it is unimaginable
(al-Muwaqqit 2002: 54)

The opening simile that links Marrakech to the Prophet Yūsuf, the Qur'ānic ideal of beauty frequently referenced in the classical poetic tradition, compensates for its comparatively late eleventh-century founding. If Marrakech could not claim to be a long-standing site of pilgrimage attested by scripture or the capital of one of the great caliphates, the poet could nevertheless propose an analogical aesthetic equivalence with a sublime Qur'ānic archetype. This religious legitimacy is strengthened by the assertion that Marrakech is second in importance only to Mecca and Medina, bypassing not only capitals like Baghdad, but Jerusalem as well, a status justified in the verses by the sheer number of holy men who have resided there ("It has more than its share of honor in the divine sages / who are reliant on God").

Marrakech's competition was not limited to the far-away centers of the Islamic world, a number of other Moroccan cities possessed equal or greater status (Fez, Meknes, Salé, Tetouan, to name a few). Aware of this, al-Muwaqqit includes a section of the well-known poet Muḥammad ibn Idrīs al-ᶜAmrāwī al-Zammūrī's (d. 1847 CE) *qaṣīda* written in praise of Sultan ᶜAbd al-Raḥmān (r. 1822–59). Al-ᶜAmrāwī was one of the most distinguished literary figures of nineteenth-century Morocco and was born in Fez, a city whose claim to the country's seat of religious authority is hard to contest. It is home to the al-Qarawiyyīn mosque and university inaugurated in 859 CE, a full two hundred years before Marrakech was founded. Nevertheless, in these lines that resemble a *mufākhara* (boasting match) between the two cities, the poet prefers Marrakech:

فان تفخر بفاس فإن فخري / بمراكش على الدنيا كفاني
بلاد أسست للمُلك قدما / وفاقت في الجوار وفي المكان

[And] if you boast of Fez, I would boast of / Marrakech over this world is enough for me
A town founded to rule since ancient times / it is superior in its proximity and location
(al-Muwaqqit 2002: 53)

In another couplet, in this case unattributed, the tone shifts to the type of poetry found in *ḥanīn ilā l-awṭān* (longing for the homeland) anthologies:

أحن إلى الحمراء في كل ساعة / حنين مشوق للعناق وللضم
وماذاك إلا أن جسمي رضيعها / ولا بد من شوق الرضيع إلى الأم

> I long for the Red City every moment / the longing of a lover for an embrace
> This is only because my body is its infant / and an infant always longs for its mother
>
> (al-Muwaqqit 2002: 54)

The verses recall a recurring sentiment widespread in classical Arabic literature. Even al-Jāḥiẓ (d. 868–9 CE) considered the longing for one's homeland to have the same sanctity as the longing for one's parents (al-Qadi 1999: 8). In the lines above, the city of Marrakech – often called *al-Ḥamrā*ʾ, or "the Red" for its rose-colored walls – is the homeland, and the anonymous poet's ties are accentuated through one of the central tropes used to demonstrate fidelity to an author's primary site of belonging. Throughout the Arabic poetic corpus, an author's place of origin is frequently personified as a mother who gives life and sustenance to her child. In the anthologies of al-Jāḥiẓ, Ibn Marzubān (d. tenth century CE) and Ibrāhīm ibn Muḥammad al-Bayhaqī (d. 1169–70 CE),[7] for example, the homeland is described as "the country (*balad*) that suckled you with its water;" "the birthplace (*masqaṭ al-ra*ʾ*s*) and site (*maḥall*) of suckling;" and "the country (*balad*) that gave you the milk you suckled" respectively (Antrim 2012: 17). Here al-Muwaqqit's identity as author merges with the anonymous poet he cites, as intimately entwined with his native city as the maternal relationship the lines describe.

Sufi Hagiography as Hierotopical Project

The sections discussed above are a preamble. When we think about the function of *al-Sa*ᶜ*āda al-abadiyya* as a whole, and the genre of Moroccan *rijāl* compilations in general, we can consider them hierotopical projects – to borrow a term created by Alexei Lidov – meaning, texts that not only work to sanctify the urban space but also to simultaneously create the city's "imageability" for those for who live there. Derived from the two Greek roots *hieros* (sacred) and *topos* (place, space, notion), hierotopy is a complement to Mircea Eliade's explanation of the role of hierophany in the creation of sacred spaces, the "irruption of the sacred that results in detaching a territory from the surrounding cosmic milieu and making it qualitatively different" (Lidov 2006: 32;

Eliade 1959: 26). While a hierophany implies the sacred itself as an actor, a form of divine intervention or communication, the hierotopic project shifts our attention to the human creativity behind the formation of sacred spaces. Hierotopies memorialize the hierophany, or the mystical appearance of the sacred. Although discussions of hierotopic spaces generally address the actually made spaces of religious worship – the architectural forms, aspects of the way a space is experienced such as lighting, fragrance, etc. – Lidov acknowledges that the literary text has a role to play as well, citing Peter Brown's coining of the term chorotope to denote a particular hierotopical modeling of a space through textual description (Lidov 2012: 83–5). An extension of Mikhail Bakhtin's chronotope – a concept that speaks to how temporal and spatial structures work in tandem to create specific genres of narrative – Brown uses the word to describe the imaginative geography he found in Byzantine hagiographical literature, where topographical descriptions of sacred landscapes follow a symbolic logic of their own. The accurate representation of distance is of no importance, for example, and the presentation of landscape is instead molded by strong imaginative patterns rooted in the Byzantine ascetic tradition (P. Brown 2006: 123). These patterns allowed the texts to memorialize a new site as holy by creating an analogical connection with Christianity's canonical sacred places; Anatolia could be scripted in such a way as to render it equivalent to Jerusalem, despite the difference in topography.

Along similar lines, even though Morocco's *rijāl* compilations are in many ways akin to other genres within the Arabic tradition that are focused on the city – *faḍāʾil* treatises,[8] *tārīkh al-mudun* (city histories), *rithāʾ al-mudun* (city elegies), *ṭabaqāt* (prosopography or biographical collections), *madḥ al-mudun* (city panegyrics) – they are, at the same time, primarily invested in constituting the cities they describe as a particular type of sanctified space. In these texts, the city is mapped through the saints' lives narrated within, establishing a clear semiotic relationship between the intimate mystical connection the saint held with God – the hierophany so to speak – and the city as a whole, whose gates, alleys, and architecture are discursively linked together by the memorializations of these instances of the sacred. This is how the city is made legible to the readers of these texts, the symbolic pattern through which the city is perceived, what the urban planner Kevin Lynch calls the "imageability" of a city. Lynch proposes a model of how city-dwellers use visual points of reference to create conceptual maps that they then call upon to understand and navigate their urban landscapes, an idea Fredric Jameson notably borrowed to generate his theory of cognitive mapping (Jameson

1991: 51). The imageability of a city is an internalized image connected to the "dynamics of practice," to the meaning given to the various sites and landmarks that the residents encounter during their daily routines (B. Brown 2005: 741). City-dwellers are only properly oriented in their environments when objects "have some meaning for the observer, whether practical or emotional" (Lynch 1960: 8). The external environment should have markers with resonances that are personal and collective, contemporary and historical; "the landmarks that most successfully orient the city dweller are allegorical objects, with multiple levels of significance" (B. Brown 2005: 741).

A City of *Sabᶜat Rijāl:* The Seven Saints of Marrakech

The image of the city as Lynch conceives it is born of a person's essential need for identity and structure in the world around them (Lynch 2005: 10). It is something that develops in a two-way process between the observing city dweller and the observed environment, and Lynch proposes that "it is possible to strengthen the image ... by symbolic devices ... [to] provide the viewer with a symbolic diagram of how the world fits together: a map or a set of written instructions". As long as reality can be imaginatively matched to the diagram, it can provide "a clue to the relatedness of things" (11). *Al-Saᶜāda al-abadiyya* provides precisely this type of map to Marrakech's urban spaces by taking the city's *sabᶜat rijāl* – referred to in English as the seven saints – as its organizing principle. Historically, the city has been renowned for the great number of *awliyāʾ* buried in its cemeteries, the source of the adage, "Marrakech, Tomb of the Saints" (*Marrākush turbat al-awliyāʾ*) (de Castries 1924: 260). It was only in the seventeenth century, however, that Marrakech was officially designated the city of *sabᶜat rijāl* by Sultan Ismāᶜīl (r. 1672–1727), widely considered the founder of the modern state. The idea itself was not new in Morocco; a regionally-bound group of seven saints near Marrakech to whom a pilgrimage would carry special significance already existed in a slightly different form. By the time the Almoravids were in power in the eleventh century, the Maṣmūda Berbers of Regrāga had a tradition that told of seven *awliyāʾ* who had been Berber companions of the Prophet and were said to have introduced Islam to Morocco before the Arab armies of ᶜUqba ibn Nāfī and Mūsā ibn Nuṣayr arrived (Cornell 1998: 50).[9] When Ismāᶜīl instituted the pilgrimage to the seven *awliyāʾ* of Marrakech, it was primarily to replace the pre-existing pilgrimage to these seven saints of Regrāga (de Castries 1924: 260). The sultan assigned the task of choosing the most important of Marrakech's holy men to Abū ᶜAlī al-Ḥasan al-Yūsī (1631–91), the age's pre-eminent scholar, whose close and complicated relationship with the sultan is as famous as the many works of *adab* he produced.[10] In the beginning of *al-Saᶜāda al-abadiyya*'s main section, al-Muwaqqit includes the poem, simply entitled "al-ᶜAyniyya" (poem rhyming in the letter *ᶜayn*), in which al-Yūsī introduced the men who were to be Marrakech's patron saints:[11]

بمراكش لاحت نجوم طوالع / جبال رواس بل سيوف قواطع
فمنهم أبو يعقوب ذو الغار يوسف / اليه تشير بالأكف الأصابع
ونجل أبي عمران عياض الذي / إلى عمله في الكون تصغى المسامع
وبحر أبي العباس ليس يخوضه / سواء كريم لا يزال يمانع
ونجل سليمان الجزولي فضله / شهير ومن يدعو اليه يسارع
وتباعهم بحر الكرامة والهدى / وسيدنا الغزواني نوره ساطع
أبا القاسم السهيلي دأبا أضف لهم / إمام التقى والعلم بحره واسع
فزرهم على الرتيب في كل حاجة / يسهلها المولى وعنك يدافع

"Al-ᶜAyniyya"
In Marrakech, rising stars glimmered / imposing mountains, or rather sharp swords
They are, Abū Yaᶜqūb Yūsuf, the man of the cave / to whom hands point with full fingers
Bin Abū ᶜAmrān ᶜIyāḍ / to whose work all the ears in the universe listen carefully
The great Abū al-ᶜAbāss, into whose sea of knowledge no one would plunge / except the most stubborn and honorable
Bin Sulaymān al-Jazūlī, whose virtue / is celebrated and who rushes to the call of those who invoke him
Then comes Tabbāᶜa, a sea of generosity and rightful guidance / and our Master al-Ghazwānī, whose light is always brilliant
Add immediately to them, Abū al-Qāsim al-Suhaylī / who is a master of knowledge and piety
Visit them in order for everything you need / God will make it easy for you and protect you (al-Muwaqqit 2002: 54)

Al-Yūsī's composition of "'al-ᶜAyniyya" did more than simply designate the seven *awliyāᵓ* to be visited, it established a ritual topography in Marrakech's old city. The poem concludes with an imperative, "Visit them in order," a phrase that functions as an explicit performative utterance in J. L. Austin's sense of the term.[12] Taken together, the verses comprise an act of cartography that transformed Marrakech's medina into a site of pilgrimage with a route that covers most of its area and contains the majority of the old city's spaces within it. Figure 9.1, a map of Marrakech's walled medina, shows the pilgrim's itinerary through the tombs of the *awliyā*ᵓ, numbered 1 through 7. The *ziyāra*, or pilgrimage, should begin in the south-east of the medina near Bāb Aghmat and the tomb of Abū Yaᶜqūb Yūsuf (more commonly known as Sidi Youssef Ben Ali). From there, the itinerary goes north to the tomb of Qādī ᶜIyāḍ ibn Mūsā (Qadi Ayyad) near Bāb Aylen, then north-west to the tomb of Sīdī Abū al-ᶜAbāss (Sidi Bel Abbas) before proceeding south-west to pass by Bāb Taghzout en route to the tomb of Muḥammad ibn Sulaymān al-Jazūlī (Sidi Suleiman Al Jazuli). The pilgrim should then walk south to the tomb of Sīdī ᶜAbd al-ᶜAzīz Tabbāᶜa (Sidi Abdel Aziz), continuing in the same direction to the tomb of Sīdī ᶜAbd Allāh al-Ghazwānī (Sidi Abdullah Ghazouani, also known as Mouley el Ksour), then finally to the far south-west and the tomb of Abū al-Qāsim al-Suhaylī (Imam Abderahim Souhaili), situated in a cemetery just outside the city's walls. This is the geography mirrored by *al-Saᶜāda al-abadiyya* as a whole, which begins at Bāb Aghmat before moving on to Bāb Aylen, Bāb Debbagh, Bāb el Khemis, the *zāwiyah* of Sīdī Abū al-ᶜAbāss, al-Jazūlī 's tomb etc.

In *Les historiens des Chorfa*, Évariste Lévi-Provençal essentially dismisses al-Muwaqqit's text as a pastiche of Muḥammad al-Kattānī's similar but earlier work on Fez, *Salwat al-anfās wa-muḥādathat al-akyās bi-man al-ᶜulamā*ᵓ *wa-l-ṣulaḥā*ᵓ *bi fās* published in lithograph in 1897 (Lévi-Provençal 1922: 385). Al-Kattānī's book was both extremely well-received and widely imitated, proving the continuing popularity of the genre through the end of the nineteenth and the first half of the twentieth centuries.[13] Despite the resemblances between the two texts, Lévi-Provençal's assessment misses the significance of the role works like al-Kattānī's and al-Muwaqqit's played at the time in constituting the imageability of individual Maghrebi cities. Lynch's thoughts on how city images work were inspired by Florence and the organizing power of the Duomo, the city's main cathedral – a testament to the continuing orienting work of Christianity within the everyday life of Florence's urban environment. In the same vein, Marrakech's most religiously meaningful sites, including the many small tombs of locally known Sufi sheikhs, *zawāyā,* and *madāris,* are the markers that organize the environment, the pattern that allows for navigation of the urban space. They are also an intrinsic part of the collective memory that ties the individual to the place. In *al-Saᶜādah al-abadiyya*, al-Muwaqqit both participates in the tradition that has historically served to construct this image of Marrakech – an image itself inaugurated

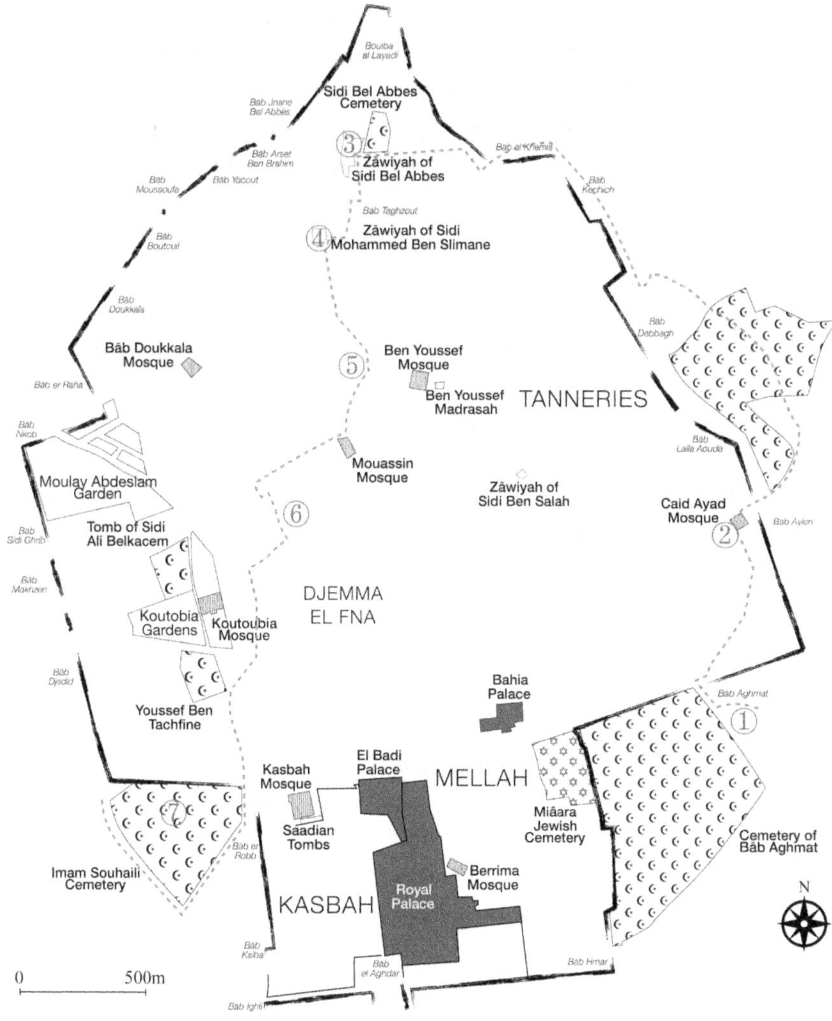

ITINERARY OF THE *ZIYĀRAH* (PILGRIMAGE)

1. **Abū Yaᶜqūb Yūsuf** (Sidi Youssef Ben Ali)
2. **Qādī ᶜIyāḍ ibn Mūsā** (Qadi Ayyad)
3. **Sīdī Abū al-ᶜAbāss** (Sidi Bel Abbas)
4. **Muḥammad ibn Sulaymān al-Jazūlī** (Sidi Suleiman Al Jazuli)
5. **Sīdī ᶜAbd al-ᶜAzīz Tabbāᶜa** (Sidi Abdel Aziz)
6. **Sīdī ᶜAbd Allāh al-Ghazwānī** (Sidi Abdullah Ghazouani)
7. **Abū al-Qāsim al-Suhaylī** (Imam Abderahim Souhaili)

Figure 9.1 The Marrakech Medina. The names of the *sabᶜat rijāl* (seven saints) are listed, their names given in both standard Arabic transliteration and their more common Latinized spellings. Other proper names are given in the Anglicized French transliteration generally found on English maps of Marrakech.

with a poem – and provides his readers with an aid to increase their own understanding of the city in which they live, a means of orientation.

Beyond this, if we remember Peter Brown's observations about the symbolic logic of Byzantine hagiographical literature and its reliance on the imaginative geographical patterns of the ascetic tradition mentioned earlier, we can see that *al-Saᶜāda al-abadiyya* performs another function as well. The text provides an allegorical map, or more precisely, a "precartographic diagram" that charts a circumambulation of the city symbolically analogous to the *ḥajj* in Mecca (Jameson 1991: 51–2; de Castries 1924: 280). With its multiple levels of signification, it is a vision of the urban space that offers al-Muwaqqit and his contemporaries no cognitive resistance; following Lynch's theory, it is an ideal image of the city with affective value at once contemporary and historical, collective and personal. This is especially true for the author himself. Under Bāb Aghmat, for example, al-Muwaqqit writes the members of his immediate family into the cityscape. His father – who in the language of Sufi discourse he describes as a well-known pious friend of God (*walīy ṣāliḥ shahīr*) – has an entry that runs nearly seven full pages, while his paternal grandmother, Khadīja bint al-Mubārik al-Tādilī, is distinguished by her righteousness, memorization of the Qur'ān, and habit of secluding herself in prayer, qualities that frequently led supplicants to seek her out (al-Muwaqqit 2002: 93–9; 104).[14] Marrakech's spaces are thereby personalized, made al-Muwaqqit's own, allowing for a representation of the city in which the author is fundamentally linked to his urban environment, much like the image found in the anonymous verses cited earlier ("I long for the Red City every moment / the longing of a lover for an embrace / This is only because my body is its infant / and an infant always longs for its mother").

Al-Riḥla al-Marrākushiyya: an Anti-utopian Satire

In 1930, twelve years after the appearance of *al-Saᶜāda al-abadiyya,* al-Muwaqqit published his second book directly concerned with Marrakech's urban spaces. The work is, in fact, the first part of a kind of trilogy, though it has come to be more well-known than the two volumes that followed it (Faure 1952: 191). *Al-Riḥla al-Marrākushiyya,* along with the more explicitly allegorical *Aṣḥab al-Safīna* (1935), and *al-Riḥla al-ukhrawiyya, aw, al-Maqāla al-bāhira fī kashf al-ghiṭāʾ ᶜan asrār al-ākhira* (1946) together show al-Muwaqqit's growing disillusionment with modernity and his increasingly dark dystopian vision. The underlying conceit of *al-Riḥla al-Marrākushiyya* is that al-Muwaqqit – a fictionalized version of the author is the initial narrator[15] – is in search of what is essentially *al-madīna al-fāḍila*:

> قد شغفت منذ زمان باختبار البلاد والخلق، رغبة في اللحاق بالطائفة التي لا تزال قائمة على الحق، فلم أزل أبحث عن ذلك، وأرتكب كل صعب في التوصل لتلك المسالك، وأنتقل من بلد إلى بلد، وأتقلب في أطوار السفر من سرور إلى نكد، أجوب أرضا بعد أرض، بين رفع وخفض، وترحال وحط، وضيق وبسط، وطال بي السير وحصل الضجر، وفتر العزم وسئمت الحركة. فجلست أنتظر الفرج من موارد التعسير، وأنفس كرب المسير، وصرت أفكر في هذا الدهر وعجائبه، وما ناب أهله من نوائبه، وقلت يا ترى هل أجد صاحبا يكون عونا لي على هذا المرغب ....

> I've always loved to explore different countries and their people hoping to come upon a group still living piously. I continue to search for this. I endure every hardship to find the path [that will lead me there]. I've wandered from country to country and throughout my journey vacillated between joy and misfortune. I've traveled through land after land, through peaks and valleys, setting off and coming back, through good and bad. I traveled for so long that discontent set in, my resolve cooled and I wearied of moving. So, I sat waiting for relief from the sources of hardship and to dispel the anxiety of the journey when I began to think about this age and its marvels (*ᶜajāʾib*) and the calamities that have befallen its people. I said to myself, "I wonder if I could find a friend to help me in what I desire …"(al-Muwaqqit 2000: 57)

Almost immediately after voicing this thought, a sheikh well-versed in the religious sciences named ᶜAbd al-Hādī appears amidst a cloud of dust like an ᶜafrīt in *The Thousand and One Nights*. The two then continue with al-Muwaqqit's quest to no avail: "We would spend a few days in some land or other; the listener would be shocked (*yastaghrib*) by the news we could relate" (al-Muwaqqit 2000: 59).[16] Though the places they visit may have beautiful sites within them, the people are inevitably corrupt. When a third companion by the name of ᶜAbd al-Bāsiṭ, a native of Marrakech, joins them, the text embarks upon the critique that is its central goal. Despite the fictionality of the narrative's frame, it is less a precursor to the novel than it is a classic example of anti-utopian satirical writing of the sort initiated by Bishop John Hall's *Mundus Alter et Ideim* (*Another World and Yet the Same*) in seventeenth-century England.[17] Like Hall's satire and Thomas More's iconic *Utopia, al-Riḥla al-Marrākushiyya* is not concerned with plot or story-telling but is constructed as a dialogue between various narrators as they move through Marrakech's different spaces. And in the same vein as these early-modern European utopias, al-Muwaqqit's text is hybrid, "integrating the 'literary' and 'political' into a polygeneric and polymodal literary genre" that ultimately aims to "recognize, mobilize and transform" (Pohl 2010: 51). Its objective is tangible political and social reform.

In direct contrast to the vision of the city created by *al-Saᶜāda al-abadiyya,* here Marrakech is fundamentally dissolute and immoral. Yet the idea of Marrakech as *al-madīnah al-fāḍilah* is not completely absent from the text. When the narrator and ᶜAbd al-Hādī first meet ᶜAbd al-Bāsiṭ, they ask him to describe his native land[18] (al-Muwaqqit 2000: 61). He begins with a three-page speech praising Marrakech in a rhetoric similar to that of *al-Saᶜāda al-abadiyya.* The city retains its connection to jurisprudence, the religious sciences, and piety, and remains the most important city in the Maghreb, a place with unparalleled natural attributes (61).[19] But, ᶜAbd al-Bāsiṭ continues, vice (*radhāʾil*) and depravity have taken hold of its population (63). His point is quickly illustrated in a chapter titled "*dahshatunā ᶜind dukhūl Marrākush*" (Our Astonishment upon Entering Marrakech), in which the three try to enter the walled city via Bāb Nkob (see Figure 9.1), the gate leading to the medina through Moulay Abdeslam garden. Soldiers in European-style uniforms demand identification documents, something of which neither the narrator nor ᶜAbd al-Hādī have ever heard. Though they plead that they are harmlessly searching for a place that remains on the right path (*aḥwāluhā mustaqīma*), the soldiers terrorize and curse them.[20] Only once their native guide ᶜAbd al-Bāsiṭ explains that they need to offer the soldiers a bribe are they allowed to enter, the soldiers immediately deferring to the trio while exclaiming, in another nod to *The Thousand and One Nights,* "*samᶜan wa-ṭāᶜatan*" (I hear and obey) (65). The corruption of the encounter is clear, but the more subtle, underlying reference to the *Nights* in the passage, and the references to the *Nights* throughout the text in its entirety, merit some attention.

ᶜAjab as Affect

ᶜAjāʾib (marvels), *yastaghrib* (to be shocked), *dahsha* (surprise) – these examples of a vocabulary of astonishment are embedded within the passages of *al-Riḥla al-Marrākushiyya* quoted above. In his study of the way this emotion works in *The Thousand and One Nights,* Roy Mottahedeh cites ᶜAbd al-Qāhir al-Jurjānī's (d. 1078 CE) definition: "the change of the *nafs* [spirit or soul] through something the cause of which is unknown and goes out of the ordinary" (Mottahedeh 1997: 30). In *The Thousand and One Nights*, this quality of being out of the ordinary produces an emotion akin to suspense. It is how Shahrazad continues to save her own life, through Shahrayār's desire to know more, a feeling of anticipation shared by the reader as story after story produces something astonishing and promises something still more astonishing to come (Mottahedeh 1997: 32). In the story cycle's internal narratives, characters inevitably compete to tell the most amazing story, often saving their own lives or the lives of others in the process. The astonishment in the *Nights* is rarely negative. In *al-Riḥla al-Marrākushiyya*, the emotion of *ᶜajab* is no less important. The multiple narrators' observations of the *ᶜajāᵓib*, or marvels, of the age form the primary subject of their discussions as they wander around the city. Walking to the Ben Youssef mosque (see Figure 9.1) near where the actual al-Muwaqqit was born, Shaykh ᶜAbd al-Bāsiṭ says, "By God, yā Mulay, if I told you about what happens in this country every day and night, you would hear something astonishing (*al-ᶜajab*) (al-Muwaqqit 2000: 151). He describes some of Marrakech's new *ᶜajāᵓib* and *gharāᵓib*: "Its cafés have filled up and its mosques emptied, its youth have become Westernized and its women put themselves on display, its water has receded and its evil flooded" (al-Muwaqqit 2000: 223).[21]

ᶜAbd al-Raḥīm Mawdin has pointed out the spatial dimension of al-Muwaqqit's critique; the vices with which he imagines Marrakech to now be riddled are tied to the places in which they are practiced: the cafés, theaters, bars, gambling houses, the modern schools that contribute to the decline in the traditional fields of knowledge (Mawdin 2006: 124–5). Even Marrakech's public spaces are marred by degeneracy as the city's streets have become overrun with prostitutes, something also counted among the *ᶜajāᵓib* (al-Muwaqqit 2000: 151). Unlike the *ᶜajab*, or astonishment, of the *Nights* that alternately leads to consolation or suspense, the *ᶜajab* that these phenomena evoke is connected to al-Muwaqqit's urban disorientation. If the city in *al-Saᶜāda al-abadiyya* is chiefly characterized by the fundamental sense of orientation it offers the reader, the city in *al-Riḥla al-Marrākushiyya* is defined by its cognitive estrangement. All of the *ᶜajāᵓib* and *gharāᵓib* that the narrators observe as they traverse the streets of Marrakech show the breakdown of the city's imageability. It is the same geography covered by *al-Saᶜāda al-abadiyya*, but it has become illegible at best and colored by a palpable sense of fear at worst (the verb used to describe the soldiers' behavior toward the three narrators seeking to enter the city is *arᶜabūnā*, "they terrified us"). The city's patterns of continuity are lost, its basic image disrupted, a patent illustration of Lynch's observation, "let the mishap of disorientation once occur, and the sense of anxiety and even terror that accompanies it reveals to us how closely it is linked to our sense of balance and well-being" (Lynch 1960: 4).

By Way of Conclusion

Shortly after the narrator and ᶜAbd al-Hādī meet ᶜAbd al-Bāsiṭ, their guide to Marrakech, he proclaims, not without some pride, "It is the Cairo of Morocco" (al-Muwaqqit 2000: 61). They later come across another interlocutor, Shaykh ᶜAbd al-Ṣamad from Egypt, who tells them, "Yā Sīdī, if you could see the state of our Egypt today, how reality has been turned upside down, you would see something amazing (*al-ᶜajab*) (143).[22] Then, in the style of *The Thousand and One Nights* again, ᶜAbd al-Bāsiṭ and Shaykh ᶜAbd al-Ṣamad compete in their recountings of various *ᶜajāʾib,* each trying to prove that their respective city is indeed the most astonishing, but in the negative sense used throughout the text. This is a significant difference in comparative mode. In *al-Saᶜāda al-abadiyya,* it is Baghdad, Mecca, and Fez that carry analogical weight; in *al-Riḥla al-Marrākushiyya* this notably shifts to Cairo. The influence of contemporary Egyptian literature is clear enough in al-Muwaqqit's adaptation of the structure used by al-Muwayliḥī in *Ḥadīth ᶜĪsā ibn Hishām,* a text he had read along with Muḥammad Ḥāfiẓ Ibrāhīm's *Layālī Saṭīḥ* (Faure 1952: 175). But the most important transformation to occur in al-Muwaqqit's work in the years between *al-Saᶜāda al-abadiyya* and *al-Riḥla al-Marrākushiyya* has less to do with the importation of this innovation in form in and of itself and more to do with the particular meaning attached to this form in al-Muwaqqit's hands. *Al-Riḥla al-Marrākushiyya* marks a specific type of disruption in Moroccan literature, with consequences both for local genres and for imaginings of the city.

Al-Muwaqqit's reading in literature from the East was not limited to satirical fictions; he had also come across the writings of Muḥammad ᶜAbduh and his disciple Muḥammad Rashīd Riḍā, and was convinced by their project of religious reform (Faure 1952: 169). This included the rejection of Sufism, which both ᶜAbduh and Riḍā considered "a weakness to society" and "a danger to religion" (Hourani 2001: 226, 232). For al-Muwaqqit, a turning-away from Sufi practice necessarily meant a repudiation of most of the sites memorialized in *al-Saᶜāda al-abadiyya:* the tombs of the *sabᶜat rijāl,* the countless burial sites of lesser known Sufi sheikhs, and the numerous *zawāyā* throughout the city. It is only by the cessation of all visits to the *awliyāʾ* that the Islamic world will return to its former glory, he states, singling out four of the *sabᶜat rijāl* by name, al-Jazūlī, al-Ghazwānī, Tabbāᶜa, and al-Suhaylī (al-Muwaqqit 2000: 321). This new image of the city void of these sites meant the imaginative destruction of most of the landmarks that had provided him with a sense of orientation in Marrakech since childhood, objects that had resonated with al-Muwaqqit personally, historically, and allegorically. At the same time, his embrace of a new way to write the city along the lines of al-Muwayliḥī came with his abandonment of the *rijāl* tradition, that distinctly Maghrebi type of hagiography that had been used to create symbolic guides to individual Moroccan cities since the twelfth century. His vision of Marrakech as *al-madīna al-fāsida* in *al-Riḥla al-Marrākushiyya* is not only the result of growing European influence; the text is equally a renunciation of a religious practice distinctly Moroccan in character, the very thing that constitutes the city as sacred in his earlier work. The *madīna fāḍila* for which the narrator searches is one that had never existed in Marrakech in actual fact. It is based upon a model exported by the literature coming from the East. The shifting locations of al-Muwaqqit's printing houses – *al-Saᶜāda al-abadiyya*'s in Fez and *al-Riḥla al-Marrākushiyya's* in Cairo – are symbolic of a larger literary question. As the city becomes a site of disillusionment and disorientation for the writer and the older genres no longer hold, we can ask if the cause is its encounter with Europe or its encounter with Cairo.

Notes

1. It is not certain whether *al-Riḥla al-Marrākushiyya* was published in 1930, as it is listed in the Arab Union catalog, or 1933, the date given by both Adolphe Faure and ᶜAbd al-Raḥīm Mawdin. In either case, it was published in lithograph by Muṣṭafā al-Bābī al-Ḥalabī's press in Cairo.
2. Ḥasan Jallāb has speculated that al-Muwaqqit was likely born in 1880 rather than 1894 based on the publication of his first book in 1911, a year in which his father also died and al-Muwaqqit became responsible for timekeeping at the Ben Youssef mosque (al-Muwaqqit 2002: 9). ᶜAbd al-Raḥīm Mawdin lists al-Muwaqqit's birth year as 1882 (2006: 119).
3. I would like to thank Christian Go, who so kindly created the map for this chapter.
4. See, for example, Allen (2011); Gonzalo (2006). In Arabic, see Mawdin (2006: 119–28). Though Mawdin does not engage with al-Muwaqqit's earlier work, he does also explore his apocalyptic final text, *al-Riḥla al-ukhrawiyya, aw, al-Maqāla al-bāhira fī kashf al-ghiṭāʾ ᶜan asrār al-ākhira* (2006: 129–42).

5. The term *awliyāʾ* (s. *walīy*) refers to *awliyāʾ Allāh*, or the friends of God. In Sufism, these holy men are thought to offer protection or intercession as God's deputies or vice-regents, in a sense. The term is popularly translated as "saint," which will be used here, though the word should not be understood to carry the same connotations of sainthood as in the Christian tradition.
6. The ᶜAlawites have been the ruling dynasty since the seventeenth century and remain in power.
7. See al-Jāḥiẓ's *al-Ḥanīn ilā l-awṭān*; Ibn Marzubān's *kitāb al-Ḥanīn ilā l-awṭān*; al-Bayhaqī's *al-Maḥāsin wa-al-masāwī* (Merits and Faults). Full references cited in Antrim (2012: 17, 151).
8. These are defined by Zayde Antrim as treatises that praise a city, "which resemble *adab* anthologies by bringing together quotations, poetry, and anecdotes from a variety of sources" and which, "sometimes exhibit a pious orientation by favoring material from the Qur'ān and Ḥadīth," (2012: 33).
9. An anonymous poem preserving their names makes this claim explicitly:

زيارة أهل الله من اعظم الذخر / وكنز فلاح في القيامة والحشر
فقدم بأقصى الغرب سبع أجلة / لهم رتب عليا على أهل ذا القطر
بصحبة خير الخلق خصوا وقدموا / بمغربنا طرا على كل ذى قدر

Visiting the people of God is among the greatest sources of salvation / and a treasure of bliss for the Day of Resurrection and Judgement
Seven of the most honorable came to the furthest West / who were of a higher station than the people of that country
As companions of the most moral and noble [the Prophet] / they were distinguished in our Maghreb above the best of men (de Castries 1924: 256)

10. For a detailed discussion of the literary consequences of al-Yūsī's relationship with Ismāᶜīl, see Head (2016: 231–59).
11. The criteria that al-Yūsī used in his selection of *awliyāʾ* from the hundreds buried in Marrakech is unclear; the seven men of his choosing have little in common beyond their place of burial and their Arab rather than Berber lineage. This in itself was an important factor. Ismāᶜīl had won a struggle for power with competing Berber tribes and the institution of the pilgrimage to Marrakech's seven saints was a clear political move to replace the seven Berber saints of Regrāga with seven Arab saints who were to be visited instead.
12. For Austin words do not just *say* things, but also *do* things. His emphasis is on language as a social process and all linguistic utterances "must be understood in

relation to the sociohistorical context of their production and reception" (Petrey 1990: 3). In this case, the poem was intended to create this new pilgrimage route, endowing Marrakech with a distinct religious status.

13. See al-Kattānī (2004).
14. لها من الصلاح مكانة عالية، ومرتبة سنية، أعطيت التصرف والاطلاع على الوقائع، كاملة الفرار من الناس ولا تجدها إلا ذاكرة أو مصلية على النبي صلى الله عليه وسلم أو تالية لكتاب الله لأنها كانت تحفظ من القرآن العظيم سبعة أحزاب من سورة الرحمن إلى الفاتحة.
15. Despite the fictional turn taken by the text's frame, al-Muwaqqit names himself as narrator:

> فيقول العبد الفقير الى الله محمد بن محمد بن عبد الله الموقت بالحضرة المراكشية وقته...:قد شغفت..

16. فنزلنا بعض الأيام قطرا من الأقطار، يستغرب السامع ما نحكيه عنه من الأخبار
17. A literary chronicler of the seventeenth century described the book as follows:

> A satire against the corrupt manners of the present age; in which, while he assigns separate stations to the several vices, and distinguishes the nations inhabiting them, and the places themselves, by names ingeniously compounded and feigned, suitably to the nature of every thing, he, in my opinion, founds a Poneropolis (a City of the Wicked), which will no less divert the readers, than inflame their minds with the love of virtue. (Hall 1839: x)

18. فأخبرنا عن حال أرضك
19. هي مدينة لم تزل من حيث أسست دار فقه وعلم وصلاح، وهي قاعدة بلاد المغرب وقطرها ومركزها وقطبها...جمعت بين عذوبة الماء، اعتدال الهواء وطيب التربة، وحسن الثمرة، وسعة المحرث، وعظيم بركته.
20. تكلموا بأشياء من السبّ لا تقال، وأرعبونا حتى كادت آمالنا أن تكون مرفوضة...
21. وأيّ شيء أحكيه لك في عادات المدينة، عمرت قهواتها، وفرغت مساجدها، وتفرنجت شبانها، وتبرجت نساؤها، غاض ماؤها، وفاض شرّها.
22. فالتفت الشيخ عبد الصمد إلى الشيخ عبد الهادي: وقال له يا سيدي لو رأيت حال قطرنا المصري اليوم كيف انقلبت حقيقته لرأيت العجب.

Works Cited

Allen, Roger (2011), "Rewriting Literary History: The Case of Moroccan Fiction in Arabic," *The Journal of North African Studies*, vol. 16: 3, 311–24.

Antrim, Zayde (2012), *Routes & Realms: The Power of Place in the Early Islamic World*, Oxford: Oxford University Press.

Austin, J. L. (1975), *How to Do Things with Words*, Boston MA: Harvard University Press.

Brown, Bill (2005), "The Dark Wood of Postmodernity (Space, Faith, Allegory)," *PMLA* 120: 3 (May), 734–50.

Brown, Peter (2006), "Chorotope: Theodore of Sykeon and His Sacred Language," in A. Lidov (ed.), *Hierotopy: Creation of Sacred Spaces in Byzantium and Medieval Russia*, Moscow: Progress-tradition, 117–25.

De Castries, Henri (1924), "Les Sept Patrons de Marrakech," *Hesperis*, vol. 4, 245–304.

Cornell, Vincent J. (1998), *Realm of the Saint: Power and Authority in Moroccan Sufism*, Austin TX: University of Texas Press.

Eliade, Mircea (1959), *The Sacred and the Profane: The Nature of Religion*, trans. William R. Trask, New York NY: Harcourt.

Al-Fārābī, Abū Naṣr (1985), *On the Perfect State (Mabādiʾ ārāʾ ahl al-madīna al-fāḍila)* (Introduction), trans. Richard Walzer, Oxford: Oxford University Press, 1–19.

Faure, Adolphe (1952), "Un réformateur marocain: Muḥammad b, Muḥammad b. ᶜAbd Allāh al-Muwaqqit al-Marrākušī," *Hesperis*, tomo XXXIX (primer y segundo trimestre), 165–95.

Gonzalo, Parrilla Fernández (2006), *La literatura marroquí contemporánea: la novela y la crítica literaria*, Cuenca: Ediciones de la Universidad de Casilla-La Mancha, 284–8.

Hall, Joseph (1839), *The Works of Joseph Hall D.D. (Successively Bishop of Exeter and Norwich with Some Account of his Life and Sufferings, Written by Himself)*, vol. XII, Oxford: D. A. Talboys.

Head, Gretchen (2016), "Space, Identity, and Exile in Seventeenth-Century Morocco: The Case of Abū ᶜAlī al-Ḥasan al-Yūsī," *Journal of Arabic Literature*, vol. 47, no. 3/3, 231–59.

Hourani, Albert (2001), *Arabic Thought in the Liberal Age, 1798–1939*, Cambridge: Cambridge University Press.

Jallāb, Ḥasan (1994), *al-Ḥaraka al-Ṣūfiyya bi-Marrākush: Ẓāhirat sabᶜat rijāl*, Marrākush.

Jameson, Fredric (1991), *Postmodernism, or, the Cultural Logic of Late Capitalism*, Durham NC: Duke University Press.

Al-Kattānī, Muḥammad bin Jaᶜfar (2004), *Salwat al-anfās wa muḥādathat al-akyās bi man al-ᶜulamāʾ wa al-ṣulaḥāʾ bi fās*, ᶜAbd Allāh al-Kattānī *et al.* (eds), Casablanca: Dār al-Thaqāfah.

Lévi-Provençal, Évariste (1922), *Les historiens des Chorfa: essai sur la littérature historique et biographique au Maroc du 16e au 22e siècle*, Paris: Emile Larose.

Lidov, Alexei (2006), "Hierotopy: The Creation of Sacred Spaces as a Form of Creativity and Subject of Cultural History," in A. Lidov (ed.), *Hierotopy: Creation of Sacred Spaces in Byzantium and Medieval Russia*, Moscow: "Progress-tradition", 32–58.

——— (2012), "Creating the Sacred Space: Hierotopy as a New Field of Cultural History," *Spazi i percorsi sacri*, 61–90.

Lynch, Kevin (1960), *The Image of the City*, Cambridge MA: MIT Press.

Mawdin, ᶜAbd al-Raḥīm (2006), *al-Riḥla fī al-adab al-Maghribī: al-naṣṣ, al-nawᶜ, al-siyāq*, al-Dār al-Bayḍāᵓ: Afrīqiyā al-Sharq.

Mottahedeh, Roy (1997), "*ᶜAjāᵓib* in *The Thousand and One Nights*," in *The Thousand and One Nights in Arabic Literature and Society*, Richard G. Hovannisian and Georges Sabagh (eds), Cambridge: Cambridge University Press, 29–39.

Al-Muwaqqit, Muḥammad bin Muḥammad bin ᶜAbd Allāh (2000), *al-Riḥla al-Marrākushiyya, aw, Mirᵓāt al-masāwiᵓ al-waqtiyya wa-yusammā ayḍan al-Sayf al-maslūl ᶜalā al-muᶜriḍ ᶜan sunnat al-Rasūl*, Dr. Aḥmad al-Shuqayrī al-Dīnī (ed.), Dār Bayḍāᵓ: Matbaᵓah al-Najah.

——— (2002), *Al-Saᶜāda al-abadīyya fī al-taᶜrīf bi-mashāhīr al-ḥaḍra al-Marrākushiyya*, Ḥasan Jallāb (ed.), Marrākush.

Petrey, Sandy (1990), *Speech Acts and Literary Theory*, New York NY and London: Routledge.

Pohl, Nicole (2010), "Utopianism after More: the Renaissance and Enlightenment," in Gregory Claeys (ed.), *The Cambridge Companion to Utopian Literature*, Cambridge: Cambridge University Press, 51–78.

Al-Qadi, Wadad (1999), "Expressions of Alienation in Early Arabic Literature," in Angelika Neuwirth, Briget Embaló, Sebastian Günther, and Maher Jarrar (eds), *Myths, Historical Archetypes, and Symbolic Figures in Arabic Literature: Towards a New Hermeneutic Approach*, Beirut: In Kommission bei Franz Steiner Verlag Stuttgart, 3–31.

Rosenthal, Franz (1968), *A History of Muslim Historiography*, Leiden: E. J. Brill.

10

Revolutionary Cityscapes: Yūsuf Idrīs and the National Imaginary

Yasmine Ramadan

Introduction

In the 1956 introduction to Yūsuf Idrīs' novel *Qiṣṣat ḥubb* (A Love Story), Ṭāhā Ḥusayn praises the young writer but adds that the author's use of colloquial denigrates his work. Ḥusayn ends his introduction with the hope that Idrīs will strive to present the voices of his characters in Arabic *fuṣḥā* (standard Arabic) in his upcoming works.[1] "I want to become an artist even though I write in the language of the street" was Idrīs' response to Ḥusayn, explaining that he did not see a contradiction between art and the use of colloquial Arabic.[2] Indeed Idrīs' innovation lay largely in his move away from the literary production of his predecessors, of the giants such as Ṭāhā Ḥusayn, who had dominated the landscape. In creating a linguistic and geographical map of Cairo, Idrīs departs from the rural novel that marked the canonical literary production of the *nahḍa* (renaissance) period of the late nineteenth and early twentieth centuries. Instead he places the urban metropolis front and center in his literary exploration of a transformative moment in Egypt's history. His work invites crucial questions about the role of literature in times of revolution and its capacity to interrogate and expand official nationalist discourse.

This chapter focuses upon *Qiṣṣat ḥubb,* Idrīs' first novel and a strongly anti-colonial work, published four years after the July Revolution of 1952, which ended British colonial rule in Egypt.[3] Although Idrīs is known first and foremost for his short stories and plays, it is this early novel which opens up the question of the national. I employ recent scholarship that has drawn attention to the spatial turn in the humanities and social sciences, drawing on the work of Franco Moretti in particular, to reveal the complexity of Idrīs' nationalist vision, through a reading of the different spaces constructed in the novel. It is Moretti's contention that a "literary geography" in the sense of "a study of space in literature" or of "literature in space" can inform our reading of literary texts in crucial ways.[4] Moretti's "study of space in literature" frames the current analysis, illuminating the geographic imaginary at the heart of Idrīs' first novel. Such a focus on the spatial alerts us to the process of mapping undertaken by Idrīs, while also revealing the connection between the geographic and the linguistic, and providing an analytical framework for the intersection between the two. Significant studies in the field of Arabic literature, like those of Samia Mehrez, and Mara Naaman, amongst others, foreground the importance of the urban in Egyptian literature specifically.[5] As Mehrez argues, in literary texts "the city emerges as an actor with real agency that embodies and structures social power as well as political, economic, and symbolic processes. As the writers come to represent the city in literature, they, in turn, become architects of its history whose literary works reconstruct and re-map the city."[6] In doing so, writers produce the city as symbol but also as material reality, as physical space that is inhabited and experienced by its dwellers in multifarious ways.

Indeed, in Idrīs' work Cairo is cast in a metaphorical role, representing the nation writ large, but perhaps more importantly, it is also "mapped" and represented in all its complexity and difference; the Cairo of the center and the periphery; of the upper and lower classes; of the communities of migrants drawn to the capital from all over Egypt. Idrīs then provides a geographical map of the city. Moreover, with the geographic is a concern for the linguistic, and the novel captures the intersection of the two. Although the text is written in *fuṣḥā* (standard Arabic), dialogue is written in *ᶜāmmiyya* (colloquial Egyptian).[7] It is not one colloquial but many; the speech of the multitude of people across the social, regional, and economic spectra that populate the enclaves of the capital.[8] He also grapples with the limitations of national identity, and the possibilities of social equality, at a time when the question of Egyptian identity is at the front and center of the postcolonial nation building project of Gamal ᶜAbd al-Nasser. As such Idrīs both breaks with the canonical literary production that preceded him, and offers a critique of the regime's representations of the nation by way of a more complicated notion of national identity. *Qiṣṣat ḥubb* insists upon an expanded idea of nationalist identity, and the inclusion of a multitude of Egyptians within the vision of a postcolonial Egypt. By mapping the physical contours of Cairo, and utilizing the multiplicity of colloquial registers in the dialogue of his novel, Idrīs expands the conceptualization of Egyptian identity, presenting his idea of a classless society as the answer to social inequality, inextricably linked to the question of national independence.

Yūsuf Idrīs and the Legacies of the *nahḍa*

Yūsuf Idrīs (1927–91) is part of a generation of writers that made the city of Cairo come alive in the literary imagination. Alongside Muḥammad al-Muwayliḥī (1858–1930), Najīb Maḥfūẓ (1911–2006) and Yaḥyā Ḥaqqī (1905–92), Idrīs put the capital city on the literary map. To understand the significance of Idrīs' contribution is to understand his rejection of the legacies of the *nahḍa*, against which he positioned himself, even in his earliest works. Throughout the *nahḍa* (1850–1930), debates raged around the best path to modernity.[9] This was largely connected to aesthetic questions, and the struggle against British rule was accompanied by "a struggle to liberate the Egyptian sensibility from the chains of social convention and blind imitation of what was now seen as an aging and decrepit literary canon."[10] The novel was understood to be a primary means by which the Egyptian citizen could imagine and construct his/her identity, in ways that recall Benedict Anderson's seminal work on the relationship between nationalism and the novel.[11]

The Egyptian countryside was at the heart of both the debates and the literary production of the period; Egyptian giants Ṭāhā Ḥusayn (1889–1973), Tawfīq al-Ḥakīm (1898–1987), Maḥmūd Taymūr (1894–1973) and Muḥammad Ḥusayn Haykal (1888–1956) are a case in point.[12] Their novels were tied to the goal of social reform, centered primarily on the countryside, and yet exhibited a clear ambiguity; the harmony of the Egyptian countryside is accompanied by "the urban reformist's pointed distaste for rural life."[13] The destitution of the rural population is a result, according to Haykal, not "of poverty, but rather of ignorance and fear."[14] Haykal's 1913 novel *Zaynab*, considered among the early examples of the Arabic novel, is a telling case. A rural novel, like many of the works of the period, *Zaynab* tells the story of a young peasant girl – Zaynab of the title – and the three suitors who pursue her. The tragedies and hardships that befall the characters of the novel are seen largely to be the result of archaic social customs in desperate need of reform, customs that stifle love and destroy the individual.[15] Haykal's narrative presents an idealized peasant who embodies the national character of the

Egyptian, and who has become "used to that state of eternal bondage in which they lived their lives and submitted to it without complaint or misgiving."[16] The romanticized vision of rural life, in which peasants "regard the results of their work with shining eyes while the proprietor alone gathered the fruits of their labor" disregards the problems of class and socioeconomic injustice.[17]

Idrīs' turn to the city of Cairo is telling, both as a rejection of the reformist rhetoric of the *nahḍa* period and its connection to the rural, and an expansion of nationalist understanding.[18] His works do not merely shift the focus, employing an urban instead of rural metaphor for the nation, but rather connect the rural and the urban, and suggest that revolutionary change can only be realized through social and economic justice for the rural and urban poor in Egypt. That *Qiṣṣat ḥubb* is a city novel is also a reflection of the growing importance of the capital throughout the early twentieth century, and in the imagination of a postcolonial Egypt, particularly under the regime of ᶜAbd al-Nasser (1956–70). It was, after all, during the decades of ᶜAbd al-Nasser's rule that Cairo was cast as the symbol of the modern, cultural, and industrial power of Egypt.[19]

Expanding the National: Mapping Cairo

The idea that literary production played a role in the creation and perpetuation of national identity remained pervasive throughout the *nahḍa* and well into the twentieth century, providing a useful point of departure when examining *Qiṣṣat ḥubb*. The events of the novel take place in January and February 1952, six months before the Free Officers' Revolution that overthrew King Farouk, bringing British rule in Egypt to an end. While British troops had withdrawn from much of Egypt, after the signing of the Anglo-Egyptian treaty in 1936 they continued to occupy the Suez Canal Zone, and it is there, as well as in the capital city, that much of the anti-colonial activity captured so vividly in Idrīs' novel was taking place. As an ardent nationalist and outspoken socialist, Idrīs draws upon his own experience in recreating the unstable situation of post-war Egypt. He was a great supporter of the 1952 Revolution, and founded the first magazine *Al-Taḥrīr* (Liberation) published by the army in September of that same year.[20] The novel centers on Ḥamza, the committed young activist battling to establish a secret armed force to fight against British rule, and follows his efforts to avoid imprisonment and establish a resistance movement in a time of increasing police surveillance and suppression of anti-colonial activities. Through his revolutionary activity Ḥamza meets Fawziyya, a young woman equally committed to the fight for national independence. The couple is forced to question the possibility of love in a time of national struggle, when everything is to be sacrificed for the greater cause.

Within the novel Cairo comes to embody the idea of nationhood.[21] *Qiṣṣat ḥubb* dramatizes the historic burning of Cairo on 26 January 1952, following an attack by British troops on the Ismalia police headquarters. The day, which came to be known as "Black Saturday," witnessed the burning of large parts of the city by crowds angry at the British forces; restaurants, stores, movie theaters, and the Cairo Opera House were all destroyed. The Egyptian army was finally able to re-establish order, but the antagonism of the people continued to brew, eventually prompting the overthrow of the government (and the removal of British troops) in July of that year.[22] That the upheaval occurred in the capital was itself significant, with demonstrations, protests, and even violence and looting taking place within the urban environment; the attack in the canal city of Ismalia produced fierce reverberations in Cairo.

This event, in which the protagonist finds himself at the very start of the novel, epitomizes the exact moment of dislocation: "the incandescent fires, the charred timbers, shops with doors ripped out and contents smashed, all parts of the Cairo he loved hemorrhaging ruins and rubble as its trembling buildings pondered their destiny. The signs pointed to a black future."[23] The apocalyptic image captures the destruction wrought upon the city – and Egypt in general – by the colonial powers.[24] The upheaval is inscribed in the history of the buildings, in the very materiality of the city. Cairo, at once city and nation in the text, becomes the beloved, whose demise is mourned by Ḥamza. This conflation is further solidified through Ḥamza's relationship with Fawziyya, whose love is part and parcel of the nationalist struggle; "I love Egypt in you" Ḥamza declares to Fawziyya. "I love the Nile that's in your blood, I love the whiteness of ripe cotton in your face."[25] There is no doubt an important critique to be made of the gendered nationalism at work in Idrīs' novel, in which the female body, as nation, is the site upon which the fight for sovereignty is played out (Ḥamza's conquest of Fawziyya immediately precedes the resurgence of the resistance movement).[26] Yet it should be noted that Idrīs does write a complex female character; Fawziyya occupies a significant position within the revolutionary struggle, aiding Ḥamza as his equal. She also plays a dynamic role in their romantic and sexual relationship, initiating physical intimacy with Ḥamza herself. While Idrīs may here be drawing on metaphors of woman as nation that hark back to *Zaynab* and the literary discourse of the *nahḍa* (the "white cotton" of Fawziyya's face is just one example) he nonetheless presents an active female character with noticeably more agency than her predecessors. We do not, however, follow Fawziyya's movements around Cairo. This mapping is reserved only for the male protagonist. The "love story" of the title thus encapsulates the love of Ḥamza and Fawziyya and also their love of the nascent Egyptian nation amidst the anti-colonial struggle. And yet, the novel resists being read only as a nationalist allegory.

Idrīs' Cairo is not merely symbolic, but rather a city teeming with difference and conflict, a pulsing capital with diverse neighborhoods and residents. *Qiṣṣat ḥubb* does not paint a picture that focuses on one part of the city to the exclusion of others. The opening paragraph of the novel, which presents Ḥamza on the tram between Shubrā al-Balad and Cairo, begins the process of mapping that takes place throughout the novel. There is continual interaction between the heart of Cairo and its suburbs, between it and the villages in Egypt, not so much to insist on the dominance of the capital, but rather to present the possibilities of community that exist:

> The tram terminal in Shubra al-Balad is more than just the beginning of a tramline. It is a pivot of constant interplay between Cairo and its suburbs, between the city and the many factories scattered around it. You see village folk here coming to the capital, awestruck by the city, breathless at the drone of the great bustle and the new world. You see sullen workers in the bustle too, resentful of the city but unable to escape it.[27]

The tram recurs as a symbol of mobility and connection, but also as the way Ḥamza follows the political events taking place in the city; he learns of the burning of Cairo by overhearing conversations on the tram. The training camp, the heart of the revolutionary organization towards which Ḥamza is headed at the start of the novel, is located between Cairo and Shubrā al-Balad, at once outside the city while simultaneously serving as a link beween it and the outskirts.

Throughout the work, movement is traced through the different areas of Cairo: the reader follows Ḥamza as he moves from Shubrā al-Balad, to Bāb al-Khalq, from ᶜAtaba to Duqqī. These locations not only represent different geographic spaces, but are markers of particular social and economic environments. It is here that a return to Moretti's theoretical contribution is instructive; the study of "space in literature," of the literary geography of the novel, reveals the complexity of Idrīs' national vision. Cairo here is a multi-faceted city, a collection of different economic and social spheres. In reading nineteenth-century novels, Moretti claims that London is "not really a city: it's a class."[28] What is so striking in Idrīs' novel is the insistence on representing the many classes of Cairene society and the spaces they inhabit.

In bringing together various parts of the city Idrīs engages in a different project than that of other writers of the period. As Sabry Hafez argues, until the 1990s most novelists concentrated upon either "old Cairo," located in the east of the city, or the newer areas of downtown, Garden City, and Zamalek.[29] Idrīs brings these areas together, revealing the constant interplay between them:

> Cairo's streets were day, its lanes dawn, its alleyways jet black night. The many districts – Shubra, ᶜAbdīn, Sayyida Zaynab, Old Cairo, al-Azhar, Tulun, Fuad Street, Darb al-Ahmar … prodigious bank buildings resting solidly like pyramids of the modern age – the National, the Misr, the Crédit Lyonnais, the Arab Nation, the Bank of the Colonies and Overseas; Europeans, Turks, Greeks, people of every faith and color; garbage collectors, hawkers, and beggars.[30]

This process of mapping, and the importance of movement and mobility, recalls Naaman's exploration of walking, per Michel De Certeau, particularly in Raḍwā ᶜĀshūr's novel *Qiṭᶜa min Urubba* (A Piece of Europe). Naaman argues that for De Certeau (and ᶜĀshūr) it is "the act of walking – of using the street – that symbolizes a form of pedestrian enunciation."[31] More importantly for my argument here, Naaman reads ᶜĀshūr's mapping of downtown Cairo as a form of imaginative and political space-making that recovers the space of the capital from the legacy of the colonial enterprise; "ᶜĀshūr reclaims this district and these streets as a unique space of converging social forces where the colonial project served to perpetuate the staging of Western modernity in the downtown and where the nationalist movement then set about to interrupt this project in an effort to reclaim these spaces, in the name of an independent, soon to be socially modernized Egypt."[32]

While Idrīs' project extends beyond downtown Cairo, he too is involved in a form of literary mapping that brings together the spaces of the capital and the country at large in an attempt to reimagine, reclaim, and retrieve the nation within the context of the postcolonial, Egyptian national enterprise. Idrīs' mapping is also significant when compared to projects undertaken by other writers of the period. For example, Najīb Maḥfūẓ and Yaḥyā Ḥaqqī both represent the popular areas of Cairo, the alleys and districts of "old" Cairo, the Islamic neighborhoods of the capital. In Maḥfūẓ's *Zuqāq al-Midaq* (Midaq Alley, 1947) it is the *ḥāra* (alley) of the old city that is the primary focus. The breadth of spatial movement in Idrīs' work sets him apart from writers such as Maḥfūẓ; it is a type of movement also prevalent in his other works. In *Qāᶜ al-Madīna* (The Dregs of the City, 1964), for example, ᶜAbd Allāh, the protagonist of the novel, takes a journey from his home in the richer neighborhood of Cairo to the poor area behind *al-Azhar*, in Islamic Cairo. Idrīs' mapping also documents the transformation of the city during this period, and the changing constitution of its inhabitants; the longer passage quoted earlier focuses on the cosmopolitan composition of Cairo increasingly threatened at the time of the writing of this novel. The "Europeans, Turks, Greeks, people of every faith and color" would begin leaving the capital, and the country at large, in post-revolutionary Egypt, as a result of both the increasing animosity towards the foreign communities in the post-revolutionary context, and the Arab nationalist agenda propagated by ᶜAbd al-Nasser's regime. The novel records a moment of changing diversity in the city; while the cosmopolitanism of earlier decades is coming to an end, Idrīs brings a different diversity to our attention, that of the different social and economic classes that inhabit the city, the migrants from across the country; from the villages of the Delta; from the coastal towns of the north; from the worker communities on the outskirts of the city, who all make the capital their home.

Al-shaᶜb (the people) are central both to Idrīs' narrative and to the struggle beyond national liberation; the coming together of diverse groups in the space of the city is connected to possibilities of socialist transformation. In reply to an accusation that once the British have left Egypt Ḥamza will have no concern for "the people," he replies, "it's not a question of the British, it's a question of us, of our lives, of our future for at least the next hundred years, until we lead a 'life of luxury' as you say."[33] In this sense Idrīs is very much in line with the intellectuals who emerged in the 1940s and rejected the political and economic liberalism of the previous generation of *nahḍāwī* intellectuals.[34] He is also in line with support for ᶜAbd al-Nasser's program of state socialism, instituted throughout the 1950s and 1960s, that included projects of land reclamation, nationalization, and redistribution of wealth.[35] It was perhaps because of such political and economic programs that Idrīs repeatedly stressed that despite his growing disillusionment with the regime, he never doubted the importance of the July Revolution. His decision not to write about his imprisonment in August 1954 for criticizing ᶜAbd al-Nasser's negotiations surrounding the future of the British Canal Zone base was built on the desire not to "taint the core of the Revolution."[36] For him it was important always to remember that "the people had taken an enthusiastic stand for the Revolution in 1952, 1953, and [only] with the start of 1954 did the Revolution start striking at the national forces," causing supporters such as Idrīs to question the strategies of the regime.[37] Idrīs thus occupied a tenuous position vis-à-vis ᶜAbd al-Nasser's regime; he both supported the Revolution and the July regime's core tenets and also found himself under attack for voicing his critique. He was among many writers and intellectuals (particularly leftists and communists) targeted by the regime; arrests began as early as 1954 and would continue in varying waves throughout the following decade.[38] A decade later however, Idrīs' view remained unchanged (though his critique became much more poignant in his literary works).

Idrīs' depiction of space allows him to use the geographic as a means of representing the possibilities of socialist reform. These possibilities are poignantly captured in the description of the *ᶜizab* (workers' camps or settlements) where Ḥamza's parents live.[39] Such camps, despite poverty and hardship, emerge as idealized sites of community whose inhabitants are absolutely equal, even in their misery, and whose behavior is worthy of emulation. Significantly, it is the peripheral spaces outside the city limits that are of central importance in the novel, suggesting possibilities of justice and equality:

> The rail camps that were the pasture of his childhood and boyhood, the camps that the rail authority set up between stations for workers repairing the tracks. The closed sealed community of workers. People faced life together. Secrets were the property of all; poverty was fairly distributed among all. Eggs were the currency among the women, hand rolled cigarettes among the men, but real money had to change hands between the men and women or else.[40]

This passage encapsulates Idrīs' socialist vision but is still attentive to the existing problems of the community described. The *ᶜizab* are liminal spaces, communities that are established for the workers repairing the railway tracks. The position of the camps is illuminated when read in light of what Michel Foucault calls "heterotopic spaces," "counter-sites, a kind of effectively enacted utopia in which the real sites, all the other real sites that can be found within the culture, are simultaneously represented, contested, and inverted."[41] Here Idrīs confronts the reader with the communities as the site of tension between the ideal and the real; the possibilities and realities of socialist reform; the periphery and the center. This description of the camps is also a moment in this realist novel, in which reality is exceeded in some way, to suggest other, more ideal possibilities of community. That the community is set up "between stations" suggests an emphasis upon mobility and movement, evocative of the tram and taxi motifs used at different moments in Ḥamza's travels. They are paradoxically "closed sealed communities" shut off from the external world, keeping outsiders at bay. Here too Foucault's claim that heterotopias always "presuppose a system of opening and closing that both isolates them and makes them penetrable" is noteworthy; the communities in question are hermetic, but nevertheless connected to the rest of the city.[42]

In *Qiṣṣat ḥubb*, however, Idrīs extends this socialist vision beyond the isolated examples of the *ᶜizab* or the factory, to encompass the larger urban context. The process of mapping the city does not only point to the complexity of national identity and the diversity of its inhabitants but also allows for a negotiation of class structure. Ḥamza's movement, through both geographic and social spaces, cannot be seen as separate from considerations of class dynamics. This is exemplified in the changing location of Ḥamza's hiding place. When he is first pursued by the police, after the burning of Cairo, he retreats to his friend Bidīr's apartment in Duqqī. This location is the very symbol of the upper class and Ḥamza describes his discomfort with this situation, stating that even the word "*al-shaᶜb*" (the people) sounded strange on his lips, having no place among the chandeliers, carpets, and ornate furniture.[43] As the struggle continues, however, Ḥamza must seek another hiding place and retreats to the graveyards of Bāb al-Wazīr, "the strange heterotopia of the cemetery," the home of the lower classes, where he is given shelter by the old man Abū Dūma.[44] Ḥamza withdraws underground, into the cemetery's chambers, where he is able to hide from the police. Here too is a liminal space, this time one that occupies the threshold between life and death, and one that reaffirms the connection between the various social and economic areas of the city.

Abū Dūma, a rural migrant to Cairo, who saves Ḥamza from arrest and provides him with shelter, is crucial to the success of the anti-colonial struggle. He also mirrors the author's own biography: Idrīs, a native of the Delta village of Al-Bayrūm, migrated to Cairo only as a university student. The connections between the rural and the urban, both through people and place, signals another important shift; in a turn away from the *nahḍa* ideology that posited the countryside as representative of the "new" Egyptian nation, Idrīs gestures to the ongoing interplay, connection, and negotiation between two places that had been traditionally represented as existing in conflict but that come to be viewed in terms of "shared notions of oppression and resistance."[45] *Qiṣṣat ḥubb* ends with a scene that solidifies these ideas. In the final pages of the novel, Ḥamza runs through the streets of Cairo, to escape the police, ultimately immersing himself in a crowd of people. With this scene, as with so many throughout the novel, the success of national independence is dependent upon multiple Egyptians, rich, poor, rural, and urban, coming together in the various spaces of the city.

Colloquial Egyptian and National Identity

The spaces constructed by Idrīs within the novel are not limited to the geographical, the physical or the social. Rather he reimagines the national, as represented by the urban, by considering questions of language, and by charting the intersection between the physical/geographic and the linguistic. Thus, Idrīs' literary geography brings together spatial and linguistic mapping. This is related to the importance Idrīs placed upon the role of the artist as an agent of change, and his decision to write dialogue in colloquial Arabic is in keeping with the stark realism and socialist preoccupation that characterizes much of his work in the 1950s.[46]

The exchange with Ṭāhā Ḥusayn cited at the start of the chapter was part of a larger discussion surrounding the use of *ᶜāmmiyya* (colloquial) in Egyptian literature that had appeared during the *nahḍa.* The late nineteenth century saw the emergence of writers such as ᶜAbd Allāh al-Nadīm (1854–95), Yaᶜqūb Ṣannūᶜ (1839–1912) and Bayram al-Tunisī (1893–1961), who composed work in the colloquial.[47] The debate about whether colloquial was a valid literary language, and its role in the creation of a "national" literature specifically, had been fiercely raging for decades; for example in the 1920s Egyptian writer, journalist, and reformer Salāma Mūsā advocated the use of colloquial in literary expression as a "modern mode of expression" provided that this use be "conducted chastely."[48] Maḥmūd Taymūr, the renowned short story writer, also supported this direction, but later renounced his position with regard to the colloquial, insisting that a cohesive "literary Arabic" should be used throughout the text.[49] This matter was further complicated by the colonial context; the use of colloquial Egyptian had been championed by the British in Egypt and was thus seen as a divisive tool, in opposition to the Egyptian national project, and indeed the Arab nationalist project writ large. As Reem Bassiouny explains, "the British aimed at weakening SA [Standard Arabic] by promoting the vernacular … For the British, the diglossic situation was inhibiting and difficult to understand. Thus Britain tried hard to raise the status of the colloquial at the expense of SA," through administrative and educational policies.[50] And yet ᶜAbd al-Nasser himself, the "father" of the Arab nationalist movement in the 1950s and 1960s, gave all his speeches in colloquial, not in *fuṣḥā*. The success of pan-Arabism at this time, then, was not antithetical to the continued existence and even celebration of the multitude of colloquials of the Arab world. In her study of Egyptian colloquial poetry from the same period, Noha Radwan argues that "modern Egyptian colloquial poetry was the outcome of a historical moment when, at the height of the Cairo-centered pan-Arabist movement, it was possible to reconcile colloquial Egyptian literary expression with pan-Arabist ideology."[51] This is certainly the case with Idrīs, who while not exploring pan-Arab nationalism explicitly in this novel, can hardly be seen as dismissing its importance. Though more importantly, Idrīs' use of the colloquial shows both his socialist orientation and an attempt to present the multiplicity of voices within the urban imaginary, representing an attempt to widen the category of national identity or at least to question its formulation in official discourse.[52] It is not that Idrīs does not include language in his concept of national identity but rather that he raises the question of "which Arabic" is, or should be, given precedence. Idrīs' use of the colloquial is striking in comparison to his contemporaries; Maḥfūẓ for example, while famous for his creation of a "third language" that used words found in both *fuṣḥā* and colloquial, particularly in his dialogue, "bridg[ing] the gap between the two registers in his style by adopting structures and vocabulary common to both," nevertheless remained largely averse to the use of actual colloquial in literature.[53]

In *Qiṣṣat ḥubb*, however, there is an attempt to question this single, monolithic language: the characters' speech serves to situate and differentiate them both geographically and socially within the larger national context. In fact one of the first characters Ḥamza encounters is Ḥasan, whose accent identifies him as coming from the northern coast of Egypt. Phrases like "شي ... نعملولك شي" (Tea. We'll make you some tea) quite quickly differentiate his Arabic as that of someone from the North Coast, possibly the city of Alexandria or its surroundings.[54] The first phrase "شي ... نعملولك شي" uses the distinctly colloquial feature of Arabic which combines "a whole sentence into one phonological word"; here "نعملولك " is used to mean "we will make for you."[55] It also uses the "Maghrebi form of the first persons of the imperfect," (نعملولك) a form which David Wilmsen identifies as a key feature of the dialect of Bihira, (north-west) Minufiyya and (north) Giza.[56] Furthermore, Ḥasan uses the contracted version "شي" which marks him as coming from the city of Alexandria or its surrounding area. Other examples include "إن حنعملو معسكر تدريب" (That we are going to make a training camp).[57] The difference in class and rank between the two men is also conveyed in Ḥasan's insistence on always referring to Ḥamza as " أستاذ حمزة" (Mr Ḥamza).

By contrast Ḥamza's speech more closely resembles the Cairene vernacular. In explaining to his friend Bidīr, his commitment to the struggle he says:

> 'ما هو طبعاً لازم تكون موش فاهم ...أنت راجل ليك حياتك الخاصة ... وبيتك الخاص و عملك الخاص .. أنا ماليش حياة خاصة ..أنا واضع نفسي و حياتي في خدمة الشعب ..إذا إستدعت الحاجة إني 'أهرب أهرب.. أسجن أسجن..أموت'
>
> Well, of course you wouldn't understand. You're a man with your own life, your own home, your own work. I don't have a life of my own. I've put myself and my life in the service of the people. If necessity dictates I run, I run.[58]

Furthermore, Ḥamza comes to be identified with his oft-repeated rhetorical phrase "فاهمني إزاي" (know what I mean) which suggests his constant desire to connect with his interlocutor.[59] Fawziyya's speech too underscores her educated, middle-class urban, background. Her response to Ḥamza's declaration of love is as follows:

> 'متتكلم بصراحة أكثر..متقول يا أخي انك بتحبني و تنتهي و إنك عايزني أحبك ..مش هي دي المشكلة؟! مش هي دي الحكاية اللي اجتمعنا علشنها؟! احنا ورانا إيه غير كده ... لا كفاح ولا يحزنون ... فضينا للحب'
>
> Why don't you just come out with it? Why don't you just say you love me and be done, and say you want me to love you too? Isn't that the "issue"? Isn't that what we're here to discuss? What else do we have to worry about? No cause, or anything like that! We have nothing better to do than fall in love![60]

The end of Fawziyya's statement draws on the well-known colloquial Egyptian phrase "لا ... ولا يحزنون" to mean "neither … nor anything at all."[61]

While Ḥamza's father was a factory worker, we are told that Sayyid, a friend of Ḥamza's who helps in the resistance movement, once a *fellāḥ* (peasant), has become a factory worker in the city, but has not achieved the education or mobility of the former. In telling Ḥamza of his transition from farming to factory work he says 'يا ما تعلمت من يوم ما سبت الفلاحة .. كنت مرابع .. باشتغل عند واحد بأردبين دره في السنة' (I've learned a lot since I left the land. I was a farmhand. I worked for a man for two ardabbs of corn a year)[62] and in chastising Ḥamza:

> 'كل أما بشوف واحد متعلم زيك و سايب عيشة لوكس و جاي يناهد ويانا احنا اللي الواحد
> بتطلع روحه علبال ما يطلع اللقمة أبقى عايز أقوم على أولاد الكلب أخنقهم واحد واحد'

> Every time I see an educated man like you leaving a life of luxury to come and struggle with us, people who have a tough time just finding something to eat, I want to attack the bastards and strangle them one by one.[63]

Sayyid's use of the insult "أولاد الكلب" and the colloquial phrase "عيشة لوكس"are just two examples that serve to separate his language from that of Ḥamza's.

This differentiation in language is also clear in the speech of Bidīr, a member of the upper class, whose dialogue is exaggerated and frivolous. He peppers his speech with both French and English words, using expressions such as "au revoir," "pardon," and "hello" in a way that distinguishes him from the other characters. This is contrasted with Abū Dūma, who also draws on English phrases, but his register of Arabic and his "misuse" of English immediately identify him with the lower classes. In relaying a story about his interaction with English soldiers (who he goes on to kill) Abū Dūma says 'جرج (جورج) جرج.. وانت زجزج جرج بري كود وانت .. بري كودز جزج كويس كتير' (Gorg, Gorg … and you same – same Gorg, bery kood and you berry kood, kwayyis kitiir.)[64] And so it is that Idrīs is able to present a linguistic map of the city that contains a multiplicity of colloquials, suggesting a more nuanced, diverse, and complicated notion of Egyptian national identity through a representation of the urban space.

Conclusion

"*Anā waṭanī, Anā waṭanī*" (I'm a nationalist. I'm a nationalist) yells Ḥamza as he runs from the police in the closing pages of the novel, hiding in the crowd to escape his pursuers.[65] And with this scene, as with so many throughout the novel, the success of national independence is dependent upon multiple Egyptians; those that inhabit the richest and poorest areas of the capital; those from the city; and those from the countryside, in a struggle that brings together the diversity of Egypt in the urban landscape.

Qiṣṣat ḥubb, a novel that has garnered less critical attention in Idrīs' oeuvre, suggests that Idrīs, though largely supportive of the 1952 Revolution, and of ᶜAbd al-Nasser, struggled with the definition of a postcolonial national identity. In providing a geographical and linguistic map of Cairo that departs significantly both from the works of his *nahḍāwī* predecessors, and also from many of his contemporaries, Idrīs' early novel offers a significant contribution to the discussion of post-Revolutionary Egypt. Written at a time when Idrīs still championed the possibilities of revolution, *Qiṣṣat ḥubb* suggests the urgency of an expansive and expanded understanding of national identity that draws upon urban diversity, and an independence that includes social and economic justice. It is by providing a geographic and linguistic map of the city of Cairo, and by exploring the intersection between the material, the symbolic, and the linguistic, that Idrīs is able to bring these questions to the fore. To enter into the Cairo of *Qiṣṣat ḥubb* is to encounter its myriad inhabitants, who occupy a wide range of very different spaces, and hail from different parts of Egypt. It is this diversity and complexity that Idrīs insists be included in post-revolutionary Egypt.

Notes

1. Ṭāhā Ḥusayn, quoted in Kurpershoek (1981: 114–15). This is similar to other views expressed by Ḥusayn regarding the "proper" form of Arabic to be taught in schools and used in literary production. For his wider discussion see Ḥusayn (1993).
2. Yūsuf Idrīs, quoted in Kurpershoek (1981: 115).
3. *Qiṣṣat ḥubb* is Idrīs' first novel, and his second work, published after his first collection of short stories, *Arkhaṣ layālī* (The Cheapest Nights, 1956). The title, *Qiṣṣat ḥubb,* appears in the English translation as *City of Love and Ashes.*
4. Moretti (1998: 3).
5. Mehrez (2001); Naaman (2011).
6. Mehrez (2001: 5–6).
7. The distinction here is between *fuṣḥā* (standard Arabic) and the different forms of *ᶜāmmiyya* (colloquial). The diglossic nature of Arabic means that there is a standard language acquired largely through formal education, and used in official contexts across the Arab world, and different vernaculars learnt and used in everyday interactions. Idrīs uses *fuṣḥā* for the text of his novel, and Egyptian colloquial for his characters' dialogue. He is careful to represent the different colloquials found in Egypt; that of Cairo, the Delta, and the North Coast, which often also differ in phonology, morphology and syntax. These differences are almost impossible to render in English and thus are unfortunately lost in the translation. For more on this distinction see Bassiouney (2009) and Zack (2001: 193–219).
8. Idrīs was by no means the first to employ colloquial in his dialogue; writers such as Muḥammad Ḥusayn Haykal and Maḥmūd Ṭāhir Ḥaqqī had done this decades earlier. However, Idrīs' range of colloquial and attention to regional and social distinctions is remarkable.

9. The relationship between fiction and the formation of the Egyptian nation was fundamental within national and literary debates. Writers such as Ṭāhā Ḥusayn, Tawfīq al-Ḥakīm, Maḥmūd Taymūr, and Muḥammad Ḥusayn Haykal were concerned with the reformation of the Egyptian national character, understood largely in terms of social practice, education, and intellectual renewal, and as the necessary antecedent for the achievement of national independence. They also, by and large, championed economic liberalism. For an excellent discussion of this period see Selim (2004: 1–91).
10. Selim (2004: 75).
11. Anderson (1991).
12. For more on the rural novel see Selim (2004).
13. Selim (2004: 84).
14. Muḥammad Ḥusayn Haykal, quoted in Selim (2004: 84).
15. Haykal's heroine tells us as much prior to her death, attacking her mother for her acceptance of social conventions, and labeling arranged marriages a crime. Haykal (1989: 211).
16. Haykal (1989: 8).
17. Ibid.
18. Idrīs did of course also write some rural works, most notably *Al-Ḥarām* (The Sin, 1959).
19. During the 1950s and 1960s the capital became the symbol of a modern, liberated Egypt. Tahrir Square, with its looming *Mugammaᶜ* building, came to symbolize ᶜAbd al-Nasser's socialist, Arab nationalist project. This was accompanied by the nationalization of businesses, banks, and factories that all contributed to the image of the industrialized capital. This period also witnessed a boom in migrants from other parts of the country who came to the capital in search of economic opportunities. Idrīs' choice to foreground the city of Cairo as a symbol of modernity is in accord with the regime's position. However, at times Idrīs' literary work and political activities nevertheless placed him in opposition to the regime.
20. As a student in Cairo Idrīs participated in the political movement in the lead-up to the 1952 revolution, and was imprisoned twice (in 1949 and 1951) for his involvement. See Allen (1993: 1) and Fawzī (1991: 11).
21. The novel's title was rendered as *City of Love and Ashes* by R. Neil Hewison (1999) in his English text, perhaps to avoid the connotations of the English term "love story," which is in fact the more accurate translation from the Arabic. This also foregrounds the capital in clear ways.
22. R. Neil Hewison "Translator's Note," in Yūsuf Idrīs, *City of Love and Ashes* (1999: v–vii). See also Reynolds (2012: 1). As Reynolds explains "Encouraging

guerrilla fighting in the canal zone seemed to deflect, at least initially, popular anger from the internal contradictions of Egyptian politics and society."

23. Idrīs (1999: 15). I cite from the English translation of the novel unless otherwise noted.
24. The novel lays the blame for the destruction of the capital at the feet of the colonial powers. It is not the urban Egyptian crowds that are attacked for the burning and looting, but the British forces whose presence and violence instigated the attacks. For an excellent discussion of the events of the Cairo Fire within the context of the colonial period, see Reynolds (2012).
25. Idrīs (1999: 92).
26. See Baron (2005); Ahmed (1992: 125–208). For more on Idrīs' female characters see Mikhail (1992).
27. Idrīs (1999: 3).
28. Moretti (1998: 79).
29. Hafez (2001: 189).
30. Idrīs (1999: 113–14).
31. Naaman (2011: 55). In the case of Idrīs' novel, the reader does not follow the protagonist's steps with quite the same precision. Ḥamza is less of a Cairene flâneur and more of a revolutionary fighter whose movement is always in service to the national cause. His ability to traverse vast and diverse spaces is significant precisely because it brings together different communities in the anti-colonial struggle.
32. Ibid.: 58.
33. Idrīs (1999: 149).
34. Selim (2004: 130–4).
35. Historians and economists differ in their analysis of ʿAbd al-Nasser's policies and their success. John Waterbury for example uses the term "state capitalism" to describe the Nasserist project. See Waterbury (1983).
36. Fawzī (1991: 65).
37. Ibid.
38. See Gordon (1992); Jacquemond (2008).
39. We are told that Ḥamza spent his childhood in the *ʿizab* in *al-Dirisah*, and moved to Alexandria for university. It is not clear from the text whether this area is the one close to Port Said, Alexandria, or Ismailia.
40. Idrīs (1999: 24).
41. Foucault (1986: 24).
42. Ibid.: 26.
43. Idrīs (1999: 23–4).

44. Foucault (1986: 25).
45. Selim (2004: 182). This is clear in his later short story *The Leader of Men* in which Sultan, the protagonist, himself from humble rural origins, points to the way that change, though undertaken in the city, must rely on its connections to the rural.
46. Kurpershoek (1981: 120).
47. For more on the colloquial in poetry in particular see Radwan (2012: 5). This work offers an important and much-needed examination of the modernist poetic movement at this time and the place of colloquial poetry within in it.
48. Mūsā (1961: 126).
49. Maḥmūd Taymūr, quoted in Hafez (1993: 189). See also Brugman (1984: 254–9).
50. Bassiouney (2009: 237).
51. Radwan (2012: 5). Perhaps this also suggests the limits of Arab nationalism and the possibility that this reconciliation occurs in Egypt as a sort of center, but not elsewhere.
52. In identifying the multiplicity of "Arabics" Idrīs raises interesting questions regarding the official discourse put forward by Gamal ᶜAbd al-Nasser among others, who saw language as the basis of Egyptian and Arab national identity. See ᶜAbd al-Nasser (1955: 88–94).
53. El-Enany (1992: 188).
54. Idrīs (2010: 5–6; 1999: 5). For my discussion of the different registers of Arabic I cite the text from the Arabic original, followed by the English translation in parentheses. This is in the hope of conveying the differences and distinctions in the language, a difference that is lost in the English translation. Hewison notes this loss in the introduction to his translation. See Hewison, "Translator's Note," *City of Love and Ashes* (1999: vi).
55. Greis (2000: 25).
56. Wilmsen (n. d.).
57. Idrīs (2010: 6; 1999: 5).
58. Idrīs (2010: 29; 1999: 23).
59. Idrīs (2010: 11; 1999: 8).
60. Idrīs (2010: 105; 1999: 78–9).
61. Badawi and Hinds (1986), s.v. حزن. This phrase originates from the Qurᵓān, *Ṣūrat Yūnis*, Aya 62.
62. Idrīs (2010: 193; 1999: 147).
63. Idrīs (2010: 194; 1999: 148).
64. Idrīs (2010: 166; 1999: 128).
65. Idrīs (2010: 212; 1999: 163).

Works Cited

ᶜAbd al-Nasser, Gamal (1955), *Egypt's Liberation: The Philosophy of the Revolution*, Washington DC: Public Affairs Press.

Ahmed, Leila (1992), *Women and Gender in Islam: Historical Roots of a Modern Debate*, New Haven CT: Yale University Press, 125–208.

Allen, Roger (1993), "A Biographical Sketch," in Roger Allen (ed.), *Critical Perspectives on Yūsuf Idrīs*, Boulder CO: Three Continents Press, 1–5.

Anderson, Benedict (1991), *Imagined Communities: Reflections on the Origin and Spread of Nationalism*, New York NY: Verso.

Badawi, El Said and Martin Hinds (1986), *A Dictionary of Egyptian Arabic*, Beirut: Librairie du Liban.

Baron, Beth (2005), *Egypt as Woman: Nationalism, Gender, and Politics*, Berkeley CA: University of California Press.

Bassiouney, Reem (2009), *Arabic Sociolinguistics: Topics in Diglossia, Gender, Identity and Politics*, Washington DC: Georgetown University Press.

Brugman, J. (1984), *An Introduction to the History of Modern Arabic Literature in Egypt*, Leiden: E. J. Brill.

El-Enany, Rasheed (1992), "Mahfouz: A Great Novel and a Wanting Translation," *Third World Quarterly*, vol. 13, no.1: 187–9.

Fawzī, Maḥmūd (1991), *Yūsuf Idrīs: ᶜAlā fawhat burkān,* Cairo: al-Dār al-Miṣriyya al-Lubnāniyya.

Foucault, Michel (1986), "Of Other Spaces," trans. Jay Miskowiec, *Diacritics*, vol. 16, no. 1 (Spring), 22–7.

Gordon, Joel (1992), *Nasser's Blessed Movement: Egypt's Free Officers and the July Revolution*, New York NY and Oxford: Oxford University Press.

Greis, Naguib (2000), *Aspects of Modern Egyptian Arabic: Its Structure, Humor, Proverbs, Metaphors, Euphemisms and Common Expressions*, College Park MD: ERIC Clearinghouse.

Hafez, Sabry (1993), *The Genesis of Arabic Narrative Discourse*, London: Saqi Books.

—— (2001), "*Jamāliyyāt al-riwāya al-jadīda: al-qatīᶜa al-maᶜrifiyya wa-al-nazᶜa al-mudadda li-l-ghinaʾiyya,*" *Alif: Journal of Comparative Poetics* 21, 184–246.

Haykal, Muḥammad Ḥusayn (1989), *Zaynab*, trans. John Mohammed Grinsted, London: Darf.

Hewison, R. Neil (1999), "Translator's Note," in Yūsuf Idrīs, *City of Love and Ashes*, Cairo: American University in Cairo Press, v–vii.

Ḥusayn, Ṭāhā (1993), *Mustaqbal al-thaqāfa fī Miṣr*, Cairo: al-Hayʾa al-Miṣriyya al-ᶜĀmma lil-Kitāb.

Idrīs, Yūsuf (1999), *City of Love and Ashes*, trans. R. Neil Hewison, Cairo: American University in Cairo Press.

—— (2010), *Qiṣṣat ḥubb*, 2nd ed.,Cairo: Nahḍit Miṣr lil-ṭibāᶜa wa-al-nashr wa-al-tawzīᶜ.

Jacquemond, Richard (2008), *Conscience of the Nation: Writers, State, and Society in Modern Egypt*, trans. David Tresilian, Cairo: American University in Cairo Press.

Kurpershoek, P. M. (1981), *The Short Stories of Yūsuf Idrīs*, Leiden: E. J. Brill.

Mehrez, Samia (2001), *The Literary Life of Cairo: One Hundred Years in the Heart of the City*, Cairo: American University in Cairo Press.

Mikhail, Mona (1992), *Studies in the Short Fiction of Mahfouz and Idris*, New York NY: New York University Press.

Moretti, Franco (1998), *Atlas of the European Novel, 1800–1900*, New York NY: Verso.

Mūsā, Salāma (1961), *The Education of Salāma Mūsā*, trans. L. O. Schuman, Leiden: E. J. Brill.

Naaman, Mara (2011), *Urban Space in Contemporary Egyptian Literature: Portraits of Cairo*, New York NY: Palgrave Macmillan.

Radwan, Noha (2012), *Egyptian Colloquial Poetry in the Modern Arabic Canon: New Readings of Shiᶜr al-ᶜAmmiyya*, New York NY: Palgrave Macmillan.

Reynolds, Nancy Y. (2012), *A City Consumed: Urban Commerce, the Cairo Fire, and the Politics of Decolonization in Egypt*, Stanford CA: Stanford University Press.

Selim, Samah (2004), *The Novel and the Rural Imaginary in Egypt, 1880–1985*, New York NY and London: Routledge Curzon.

Waterbury, John (1983), *The Egypt of Nasser and Sadat: The Political Economy of Two Regimes*, Princeton NJ: Princeton University Press,

Wilmsen, David (n. d.) "Egypt," *Encyclopedia of Arabic Language and Linguistics*, Lutz Edzard and Rudolf de Jong (eds), Brill Online, http://referenceworks.brillonline.com/browse/encyclopedia-of-arabic-language-and-linguistics (accessed 11 June 2016).

Zack, Elisabeth (2001), "The Use of Colloquial Arabic in Prose Literature: 'Laban il-ᶜAṣfūr' by Yūsuf al-Qāᶜid," *Quaderni di Studi Arabi* 9: 193–219.

11

Lost Cities, Vanished Worlds: Configurations of Urban Autobiographical Identity in the Arabic Literature of the 1980s

Valerie Anishchenkova

An amazing city
In a state of dream and hallucination:
History remembers her poems by heart.
Ṣādiq al-Ṣāʾigh

Over the course of the twentieth century, cities have increasingly become privileged sites of identity production in both its collective and individual forms. This is a global phenomenon, where metropolises in different parts of the world – from Mexico City to London, from Tokyo to New York, from Cairo to Berlin – are posed as producers of dominant culture, social norms, ideologies, and political discourses. Whereas the interdisciplinary field of urban studies has grown exponentially, the Arab city – noting the caution that should be exercised when engaging the term to avoid its further Orientalization, as several studies have effectively pointed out (Aldous 2013, Elsheshtawy 2008) – remains a largely unexplored territory, especially regarding the interdependency of Arab urban space and contemporary Arab identities – national, private, social, gendered, and others.

Arab urban space is simultaneously an agent of transformation and its object – it is a site of revolution and political upheaval, of rapidly changing landscapes, of social movements, and of wartime destruction. It is also a powerful cultural force that continues to inform literary and cinematic masterpieces, such as Najīb Maḥfūẓ's *Zuqāq al-Midaqq*, Yūsuf Shāhīn's Alexandrian trilogy, Ilyās Khūrī's *Al-Wujūh al-Bayḍā*, ʿAbd al-Raḥmān Munīf's *Mudun al-Milḥ*, and many others. Moreover, an Arab metropolis has the potential to generate an intense sense of belonging – so intense that it may override other identity affiliations. If "the labyrinthine spaces of the modern city have been construed as the sources of modern anxiety, from revolution and epidemic to phobia and alienation," the close ties between the urban space and the psyche of its residents should be particularly visible in Arab metropolises, taking into consideration their turbulent histories (Vidler 1992: ix). Indeed, "it is within urban space that the social imaginary of a culture and its orders of civilization manifest themselves most clearly and where the culturally repressed and excluded resurfaces" (Rosenthal 2011: 3).

Thus, the exploration of the intersection of the Arab city – a powerful site of identity production and identity politics – and Arab autobiographical writing – a literary form particularly preoccupied with self-representation – offers compelling possibilities. This chapter proposes to consider urban autobiographical writing as a distinct genre within Arab representational discourse. Since "an understanding of individuality and identity within the modern city translate[s] into a better understanding of how environment imposes itself on both our bodies and our interactions with place, space and time" (Arnold 2014), a close examination of Arab urban autobiography can potentially reveal some new and yet to be explored aspects of contemporary Arab selfhood, especially given the important role metropolises, "caught between a variety of worlds, ideologies, and struggles" (Elsheshtawy 2008: 4), play in shaping of various aspects of modern Arab life.

This chapter will consider the following three autobiographical novels as case studies: Idwār al-Kharrāṭ's *Turābuhā Zaᶜfarān: Nuṣūṣ Iskandarānīya /City of Saffron: Alexandrian Texts*[1] (1986), ᶜĀlīya Mamdūḥ's *Ḥabbāt al-Naftālīn/ Mothballs* (1986), and Ḥamza al-Būqarī's *Saqīfat al-Ṣafā /The Sheltered Quarter* (1983).What makes these autobiographical texts urban is the intricate multidimensional connection between the autobiographical subjects and their cities. "I experience myself in the city, and the city exists through my embodied experience. The city and my body supplement and define each other. I dwell in the city and the city dwells in me" – the architect Juhani Pallasmaa has poetically said about the unbreakable bond between the urban subject and their city (Pallasmaa 1996: 43). Like Pallasmaa's declaration, and as their autobiographical narratives illustrate, al-Kharrāṭ's, Mamdūḥ's and al-Būqarī's relationships with Alexandria, Baghdad, and Mecca, respectively, are the foundation for the making of their personal selfhood articulated through these texts. The story of the city is the story of the self, and vice versa.

My choice to focus on texts written in the 1980s is based on the specificities of this historical moment and the crucial role it played in the evolution of Arab urban culture. The second half of the twentieth century witnessed particularly rapid and profound transformations to Arab urban centers, and by the 1980s the changes to the cityscape and its social fabric had settled in and brought about a nostalgia for the bygone albeit not so distant era. Unsurprisingly, all three texts have complex negotiations of memory and space at the center of their autobiographical discourse. The spatial, social, and cultural metamorphoses of Alexandria, Baghdad, and Mecca and their impact on individual and collective identities of the cities' inhabitants during this period should not be underestimated, as they laid the foundation for Arab urbanism of the twenty-first century – with its city-based nationalism, continuous rupturing and reshaping of socio-cultural discourses, spatial and cultural confrontations between the "old city" and the "new city," but also powerful social movements, vibrant cultural life, and postcolonial economic development.

The 1980s: Cities under Erasure, Identities in Question

Ḥamza al-Būqarī's, ᶜĀlīya Mamdūḥ's and Idwār al-Kharrāṭ's native cities could not be more different. Their respective positions as the holiest Muslim metropolis, the legendary Abbasid capital, and the cosmopolitan jewel of the Mediterranean highlight the incredible diversity of Arab urban histories, landscapes, and sociocultural compositions. As might be expected, literary configurations of these cities offer a great range of narrative styles, voices, and languages. Al-Būqarī's linear first-person *Bildungsroman* stands in sharp contrast to both Mamdūḥ's polyphonic and colorful storytelling and al-Kharrāṭ's collection of psychedelic hallucinations – some scripted as memories, others as dreams. However, while acknowledging the undisputable diversity, we should also consider the important commonalities between these urban centers, especially since we are approaching them through the highly personal accounts of these authors. As Yasser Elsheshtawy points out in his discussion of contemporary urban developments in the Arab world, "Cities are repositories of memories. Their spaces are inscribed with meaning by their users, thus common elements/themes emerge defying artificiality and imposed binary distinctions" (Elsheshtawy 2008: 10). Indeed, if we look deeper into al-Būqarī's, Mamdūḥ's and al-Kharrāṭ's narratives, we find some shared mechanisms of identity-making: namely, a deeply nostalgic relationship with the urban space and a highly complex network of public and private identities that inform the construction of autobiographical subjectivities.

These unifying themes are likely related to the profound spatial and cultural transformations that Mecca, Baghdad and Alexandria have all gone through in the decades leading to the 1980s.

An important Arabian urban center since ancient times, with the advent of Islam Mecca's religious and ideological position gained unique importance even among the world's greatest metropolises. Yet only a few decades ago, Mecca was not nearly as significant an economic center or massive pilgrimage destination as it would later become as a result of Saudi Arabia's rapidly developing oil economy and the ever decreasing cost of travel. As evidenced by photographs and documentary footage, as recently as the mid-twentieth century – the time when Ḥamza al-Būqarī's story takes place – Mecca continued to retain its ancient character, with low-built buildings, narrow streets, and small neighborhoods. Since then the face of the city has drastically changed, and not only in a physical sense, in which old neighborhoods have been erased and new steel-and-glass Western-style buildings erected in their place, but also socioculturally, as the city metamorphosed from a spiritual capital into a capitalist metropolis. Many architects and sociologists have highlighted the problem of the urban destruction of Mecca facilitated by the growth of tourism for the Ḥajj and ᶜUmra, something the Saudi authorities have handled poorly in their allowance of large increases in construction quotas. The urban designer ᶜAbd al-Ḥalīm Jabr has pointed to the irreversible nature of this gentrification project which, he states, "occurred before they had a plan for a proactive, protected form of development for Mecca. They have tried to place strict controls for quotas now, but the damage is already done" (Saadi 2014). In recent years, a stunning visual marker of capitalist Westernization of the city has been erected in the form of Abrāj al-Bayt Towers, overlooking the Grand Mosque: "the new 485-metre-high Mecca clocktower … [bears] a remarkable resemblance to Big Ben, were it not for the gold crescent and Arabic calligraphy adorning it, and represents a new era for Mecca, symbolizing the dizzying vision and growth of the religious tourism industry in Saudi Arabia" (Butt 2010). Many critics of the commercialization/commodification project go so far as to compare the transformed Mecca to Las Vegas and Manhattan, dubbing it Mecca-ttan.

Baghdad, too, has seen a series of deep changes to its architectural and social spaces in the second half of the last century. The July 14 Revolution witnessed an incredible surge in the nationalization of its cityscape. The establishment of the first Iraqi school of architecture in 1959 and the mushrooming of monuments that served as architectural symbols of the new regime forever changed the face of the Caliph's City. Among the typical examples of such monuments are the bas-relief of Liberty on Tahrir Square and the monument to the Unknown Soldier on Firdaus Square (Pieri 2008: 34). The Baᶜathist regime in Iraq facilitated further spatial metamorphoses: "the public environment became one of composite, even schizophrenic symbolism, inspired by 'European' styles of sculpture and by Soviet-style rhetoric, but also by a kitsch reintegration of the Iraqi past as well as global Arab icons" (ibid: 35). Ṣaddām Ḥusayn's rise to power in 1979 further "transformed the capital into a gigantic building yard, the showcase of Saddam's power" which resulted in significant disruptions to the city's skyline where high-rise buildings stood "in total discrepancy with the surrounding horizontal build work" (ibid: 35). Baghdad's social composition had undergone equally drastic transformations: the exodus of the Jewish community, rural–urban migrations, and the emergence of new social classes after the revolution created new social spaces that were very different from those described in ᶜĀlīya Mamdūḥ's book.

Alexandria went through similarly substantial changes informed by Egypt's rapidly changing ideological agendas after World War II. Famous for its cosmopolitan character, this busy and culturally diverse Mediterranean port city experienced large demographic shifts during the course of a few decades. The Arab–Israeli wars and the Suez War of 1956 catalyzed massive immigrations of Alexandrian Jews and foreign residents. Many communities, especially the Armenians and the Greeks, were affected by the Nasserist socialist legislation and left the city en masse in the 1960s: "they left because their businesses and assets were sequestrated; or because they felt that their Egyptianized children had no future in a nationalist Egypt" (Mabro 2004: 253). As the new national narrative saw Alexandria's cosmopolitanism as "equated with the excesses of the bad old days of foreign domination," the city's architectural character endured visible changes while it "was transformed from cosmopolis to regional capital" (Starr 2009: 32). Streets were renamed, neighborhoods reshuffled, statues of former rulers removed and new monuments erected. For example, Khedive Ismail's statue was recycled into the tomb of the Unknown Naval Soldier, visually representing a new articulation of nationalism, in which "the tomb … privileges military memorialization over civilian memory – patriotism over pluralism" (ibid: 32). In short, the Alexandria of the late 1970s to early 1980s was a city transformed in both its visual and its sociocultural composition.

For an urban subject, such substantial rapid changes in physical, visual and cultural aspects of the metropolis are likely to cause a sense of displacement, generating an identity crisis. This is precisely what Ḥamza al-Būqarī, ᶜĀlīya Mamdūḥ and Idwār al-Kharrāṭ articulate in their texts – a narrative representation of an urban identity crisis. Their autobiographical novels are narrative spaces formed upon the intersections of memory, nostalgia, and the need to define and solidify a sense of selfhood against the chaos of metamorphosing cityscapes. These narrative spaces attempt to re-create the city of the author's youth, although the end-result is in no way a replica of the past but a completely new construct: a phantom of the imagination; a product of remembrance and the simultaneous negotiation of the contemporary surrounding environment; a nostalgia for the past and a coping mechanism for the present.

Nostalgia, Memory, and City Space

In his discussion of Dublin's urban renewal and the rise of urban memoir, Andrew Kincaid highlights the ways in which the production of memory confronts the city's changing landscape: "Memoirs … can be both critical and reaffirming of the present. Inasmuch as they remember a city of an earlier time, particularly in a nostalgic way, they may lodge a protest about the current wave of 'creative destruction' taking place in the capital" (Kincaid 2005: 18). The simultaneous nostalgia for the past and a confrontation with the present are also true for al-Būqarī's, Mamdūḥ's and al-Kharrāṭ's narratives. Published in the early to mid-1980s, their autobiographical novels epitomize a transformative historical moment shared by their respective cities. It is likely more than a coincidence that Ḥamza al-Būqarī published his *Saqīfat al-Ṣafā* just a few years after the infamous Siege of Masjid al-Haram of 1979 – a bloody and highly symbolic revolt against the Westernization of the Holy City which critics saw as a betrayal of its spirituality. ᶜĀlīyah Mamdūḥ wrote *Ḥabbāt al-Naftālīn* while in Morocco, immediately after leaving Baghdad – a capital that had been drained by the Iran–Iraq war (1980–8). In the case of Idwār al-Kharrāṭ's Alexandria, the late 1970s completed the nationalization of the city and continued to methodically erase its cosmopolitanism. Combined with the increasing activity of Islamic groups, these political and socioeconomic conditions created a favorable environment for the growth of the sectarian violence which began in the 1980s, becoming a major societal problem through the 1990s. Al-Kharrāṭ, a Copt himself, may have been particularly sensitive towards the calamitous changes inflicted upon his community and beloved city. *Turābuhā Zaᶜfarān*, filled with nostalgic sadness, is an ode to a city that has vanished forever.

"Privileged places of social interaction, and yet too vast to be imagined in their entirety, cities are probably the most dense and complex reservoirs of memorative signs,[2] and thus key nodes in the geography of nostalgia" (Dora 2006: 212). Indeed, Arab cities are immense containers of generations of human memory, both in its individual and its collective forms. Not only have these cities gone through transformations dictated by internal economic, technological, and social shifts, they were also violently reshaped by the colonial powers (often more than one) and endless military conflicts: "plague-stricken and bombed, moved and refounded, expanded and contracted, cities have been subjected to all the vicissitudes of real objects in the world" (ibid). Albeit highly diverse, Mamdūḥ's, al-Kharrāṭ's, and al-Būqarī's autobiographical narratives share a common ground, where the authors attempt to resurrect the identity of the childhood city. Here, nostalgia is related to both space and time, in Svetlana Boym's understanding of the term as "a longing for a place, but it's actually a yearning for a different time – the time of our childhood … The nostalgic desires to turn history into private or collective mythology, to revisit time like space, refusing to surrender to the irreversibility of time that plagues the human condition" (Boym 2007: 8). Their stories resemble therapeutic writing: to heal one's inner self, the author must reconcile with the loss by actively engaging memory. Idwār al-Kharrāṭ captures the pain of this process well, equally shared by all three writers:

> The compassion and divine sadness that infused the streets of my childhood in Gheit el Einab, with its anxieties and dreams, where are they now? Can I ever resurrect those distant paradises of promise, gates open onto their vineyards, and closed to me forever and ever? … Memory, the force of it, stabs the heart. (al-Kharrat 1997: 187)[3]

The historical transformation of the urban landscape highlights the intricate relationship between urban identities and city geographies. It is precisely this relationship that stands front and center in all three texts, where the juxtaposition of the "before" and the "now" of the authors' urban realities clearly prioritizes the former and paints it as a defining marker of narrative autobiographical identity. Urban memory has a distinct physical aspect: the city – a massive human artifact – is permeated with various objects–reminders, or Starobinski's "memorative signs," that jog one's memory at every step:

> An old song, a street name, a decaying building, a broken shutter are all fragments of the past that strike our senses and "revive in our imagination all

> our former life and all the associated images with which it is connected" … Whether consciously or unconsciously, physicality and memory, urban geography and history, memorative sign and nostalgia intertwine in complex urban "topologies of memory." (Dora 2006: 212)

All three novels contain material spatial markers that connect their narrative spaces to concrete locations. Al-Būqarī's Mecca is not an amorphous sacred site, but a very real city where legend and history are intertwined with the physicality of streets, alleys, buildings and mosques, as seen through the eyes of al-Būqarī's adolescent alter ego Muhaisin. The Holy Mosque is where he takes Arabic grammar classes and prays for the dead (Bogary 1991: 33). The Kaaba is where he searches for inner calm after a disappointment at a new job (71). The Ajyād Gate is where his mischievous childhood friend Sufyan steals a bag of sandals from the cobbler (36). Muhaisin's storytelling "normalizes" the place that is sacred to every Muslim and makes it familiar and homely. At the same time, the reader discovers numerous less-known spaces that reveal the autobiographical narrator's intimate knowledge of the city: the Misfala quarter where his beloved teacher lives (39), the Amir alley, whose inhabitants appreciate ᶜAmm al-Ashmūnī's infamous pastries (69), the ᶜUtaybiyya quarter where local women gather for the Qays festival (93), and so on. Al-Būqarī's text is full of references to specific locations. On the one hand, these memorative signs tie the narrative autobiographical identity to the Mecca of Muhaisin's and the author's youth. On the other hand, they attempt to capture the fleeting image of the bygone Mecca and document its unofficial history. For example, this is how al-Būqarī describes the Abū Righāl Alley where the local boys used to fight: "None of us knew the origin of its name or whether it was in some way associated with the infamous Abū Righāl, and failing to attract the attention of local historians, its history died out, just as the history of all alleys and byways of Mecca have" (29).[4]

ᶜĀlīya Mamdūḥ's novel, too, contains numerous indications of particular places in Baghdad described by her adolescent autobiographical narrator Huda. Once again, we see the systematic domestication of sacred and historically significant spaces, such as the Ruṣāfa side (the legendary abode of Hārūn al-Rashīd) or the Abū Ḥanīfa mosque which Huda, Mamdūḥ's autobiographical narrator, sees as nothing more than a simple memory from her childhood: "The Abū Ḥanīfa Mosque was the mosque of my first quarrel, and my first temptation to play under the tall lotus tree" (Mamdouh 2006a: 103).[5] There are also places that hold significance only to Huda, her family, and friends. These include the colorful neighborhood of al-Aᶜẓamiyya, the "quiet at dawn" Great Imam Street, the public bath in the Safina district, the "broad and clean" Rashīd Street, and many others.

Similarly, al-Kharrāṭ's narrative, while offering dream-like and often fantastical storytelling, is remarkably particular when it comes to depicting Alexandrian urban space. Al-Kharrāṭ's young alter ego Mikhail invites the reader to join him on a journey through the Alexandria of al-Kharrāṭ's youth, where every turn is punctuated with specific spatial markers, such as in the following scene:

> I found *haret* el-Qadi el-Fadil immediately beyond the ruins of a house hit by an Italian rocket the previous year ... When I turned down the long alley I felt more at ease. The blue street-lamps were spaced widely apart, the house-doors open and darkened, as if they were never closed ... I walked down the street, trying to read the numbers of the houses. I passed a bar with a narrow door and one word written above it in English, bar. A round red lamp flashed on and off above it. (al-Kharrat 1989: 95)

This almost obsessive attention to spatial detail emphasizes the interconnectedness of the urban autobiographical subject and space in all three texts, where the retrospective identity-making seems only possible when attached to concrete locations within the city – always meticulously documented from memory.

Beyond this, specific types of locations are central to the making of the narrative urban space and to the configuration of urban autobiographical identity. One such location is the rooftops – an important visual marker of a cityscape, "an oasis of quiet or an island in the air, the urban rooftop has invited diverse utopian visions," both in literature and visual art (Yablon 2011: 14). Holding both architectural and social importance in Mecca and Baghdad of the mid-twentieth century, the rooftop (*al-saṭḥ*) is an important space in both *Saqīfat al-Ṣafā* and *Ḥabbāt al-Naftālīn*. Al-Būqarī's Meccan rooftops are places of serenity and self-reflection, where Muhaisin goes to breathe fresh air and find internal peace: "I considered those moments and hours I spent on the roof of our house to be the most poetic of my life, nearly all of them having been spent peacefully in the company of the brilliant stars in the quiet of the night" (Bogary 1991: 59). And further: "She [mother] ... led me to the rooftop so that I might get a breath of fresh air, as she expressed it, all the while repeating prayers" (71). Indeed, as Gaston Bachelard points out in his *The Poetics of the City*, "up near the roof all our thoughts are clear"

(Bachelard 1964: 18). In *Ḥabbāt al-Naftālīn*, too, rooftops are places of silence and solitude – Huda's only opportunity to be one on one with herself, away from her abusive father and the rest of the family: "You stood on the roof; there was … only the sky" (Mamdouh 2006a: 54). In contrast, the roof in *Turābuhā Zaᶜfarān* is a source of danger: "the light was faint in the room on the roof, and where in that place there was a kind of secrecy and tension" (al-Kharrat 1989: 53). It is a site of violence that is usually associated with an urban space, where young boys are lacking a continuous protective surveillance of the family. As Mikhail's friend Gabir recalls the abuse he suffered from older boys on the roof, Mikhail runs away from the trap: "I felt that I was in a trap and that something dangerous and frightening and furtive was going on around me. I said: 'I must go now – it's a long way to our house' and I rushed down the stairs" (ibid). Such a diametrical difference of how the roof as a symbolic place is treated in al-Būqarī and Mamdūḥ on the one hand, and al-Kharrāṭ on the other, is a good example of the clashing contrasts that are at the essence of both the urban spaces and the subjectivities that dwell in them.

The close connection between urban space and identity is evident even on a structural level in the three texts, where the narrative framework resembles the physical and social spaces of its corresponding cities. *Saqīfat al-Ṣafā* displays a certain narrative circularity reminiscent of the circumambulation of the Kaᶜba, only in al-Būqarī's case the story seems to rotate around death. It begins with the deaths of Muhaisin's father and uncle, returning later to the theme of death in Muhaisin's obsession with funerals, and finally ending with the mother's succumbing to cancer. Significantly, the last scene also connects the mother's passing with the birth of Muhaisin's son, highlighting the circularity of death and life: "Life and death follow each other, but no one knows which was the first – night or day" (Bogary 1991: 107). Mamdūḥ's clashing narrative voices – she uses first-, second- and third-person narration intermittently throughout the text – point to the densely populated polyphonic social spaces of her city, especially those representing Baghdadi women. The author often reinforces the feminine dimension of Baghdadi urban space by connecting female physicality with the physicality of the architecture. For example, the first pages of *Ḥabbāt* talk about women as if they were buildings: "Women: souls painted with fire, bodies over which the open air passes making them radiant, over which the salts of the sea pass, making them blaze, at whom fear fires its incomparable rays" (Mamdouh 2006a: 8). Whereas al-Kharrāṭ's sporadic nonlinear narrative resembles Alexandria's fragmented cosmopolitan social network. Additionally, the novel's alternations between the real and the imaginative evoke "a wavelike movement characteristic of Alexandria, a city essentially located by the sea" (Awadalla 1991: 226).

Language is yet another important tool of nostalgic remembering employed in the three novels. For instance, the authors utilize colloquialisms representing the unique dialects of their cities, further binding the autobiographical subjects to very concrete locations. In the case of *Saqīfat al-Ṣafā*, in addition to distinctly Meccan terminology and dialectisms, the text contains numerous expressions typically used by Meccan elders – expressions that were no longer in circulation at the time in which Ḥamza al-Būqarī composed *Saqīfat al-Ṣafā*. Thus, al-Būqarī's reimagining of the pre-oil Mecca is reinforced by reconstructing the city's language from the 1940s. Elizabeth Fernea, who oversaw the novel's translation project into English, pointed out the many linguistic challenges surrounding the text:

> When we were preparing the novel, we came across many words and references which needed explanation. Only Saudis could help in this respect. However, there were many words which only Meccans could understand, and even then, there were a few others which only Meccans from the older generation could remember. (Bogary 1991: xi–xii)

Similarly, F. A. Haidar notes the difficulties facing ᶜĀlīyah Mamdūḥ's translator who must accommodate the linguistic reverberations of her surroundings: "her innovative use of Arabic can be problematic for any translator, especially as she deals with an environment that is unknown to her translators and social concepts that are totally different from theirs" (Mamdouh 2006a: 212). Meanwhile, Idwār al-Kharrāṭ produced a linguistic mélange that imitates his native city: "the language of the book itself, like Alexandria the city, incorporates several levels: the classical languages, infiltrated with everyday colloquial speech medium as well as purely Alexandrian dialects which are pasted in with Mediterranean terminology used by Alexandrians at that period" (Awadalla 1991: 224). Therefore, language is an important participant in articulating nostalgia for an earlier chronotope.[6] The crucial bond between autobiographical subjects and their respective cities is further reinforced using these linguistic nuances intended to transport the reader into a bygone version of that space.

Public and Private Spaces, Individual and Collective Identities

The intricate connection between urban space and autobiographical selfhood is especially important when considering the relationship between different aspects of identity. The metropolis often facilitates the urban dweller's conflict between their private and public/performative identities. The city space is where one's individuality is emphasized, yet it cannot escape clusters of collective identities; the multiplicity of communal roles prescribed to urban subjects by their families, neighbors, friends, coworkers, and passersby, are contrasted with an urge to formulate a highly individualized and unique identity. Furthermore, the perpetual clashing of public and private spaces typical of the urban environment contributes to the autobiographical subjects' uneasy liaison between their public and private selves. Henri Lefebvre's theory of space discusses the overlapping nature of representational spaces: "*Social spaces interpenetrate one another and/or superimpose themselves upon one another*. They are not *things*, which have mutually limiting boundaries and which collide because of their contours or as a result of inertia" (Lefebvre 1991: 86–7). This implies an unavoidable and continuous clashing of shared and enclosed spaces within any given metropolis. These tensions between public and private spaces are at the core of al-Kharrāṭ's, Mamdūḥ's and al-Būqarī's autobiographical stories.

"Auntie Asma's frequent alternations between the window and the corridor were to ensure that no one who disapproved of such unorthodox religious practices would hear the *muzahhid*'s melodious voice" – this scene from *Saqīfat al-Ṣafā* is a perfect illustration of the contrasting dichotomy of public and private spaces and identities in al-Būqarī's Mecca (Bogary 1990: 18). Among the cities under discussion, Mecca is the urban center where the clash between "indoor" and "outdoor" social locations is most striking, a result of the strictly imposed divisions between male and female spaces. In fact, the social performance of women's identities occurs almost exclusively within the confinement of private spaces. This is how Muhaisin describes his childhood friend Jameela's disappearance from the public space: "I had not seen her for a considerable period of time, since she was five or six years old. After that she had begun to wear the veil and effectively vanished" (Bogary 1991: 80). If the public Mecca is the "center proper" of the Muslim world and the location of the most important Islamic ritual, the private Mecca is where magic, sorcery and dream-reading take place. This private Mecca is ruled by women and constructs a subversive, even rebellious (in its own way) space that offers a counter narrative to the hegemonic male culture of the city. Muhaisin's mother and Auntie Asma represent this side of Mecca, with their magical stories about jinns, amulet wearing, and ceremonial chanting: "Later on, coming of age, I was to ask God forgiveness for the many unorthodox religious practices I had followed while under the guidance of my mother and Auntie Asma" (18).

Social roles are also clearly divided into public and private. For instance, Muhaisin's mother forbade him to go to his teacher's house in the evening: after the evening prayer, the proper place to stay was at one's designated home, within the social circle of the family. The autobiographical narrator's "student persona" belonged to the daytime, whereas after sunset the family took ownership of his social identity and his mandated social task was to be his mother's only son:

> She [mother] discouraged me from staying at any house other than our own, Auntie Asma's, or those of our immediate neighbors. In those days it was considered a late hour for a child of my age to be out after evening prayer, a tradition maintained by those of our generation who were accustomed to the nighttime being for the family and daytime for the outside world. (Bogary 1991: 39)

Moreover, unfamiliar private spaces that belonged to others were not to be trusted: "mother's daily refrain [was]: 'Take care you don't drink anything from the hand of a stranger. Don't eat in other people's houses. Don't go in. Don't come out. Don't'" (41). The uniqueness of Meccan spaces where, for various cultural, religious, and ideological reasons, the physical and social separation between the communal and the intimate is more prominent than in most other Arab metropolises, facilitates the autobiographical subject's awareness of his identity's split into public and private.

The gendered division between public and private spaces of Baghdad resembles Mecca's: "When the men went to coffeehouses, women left to go to a gathering in someone's house and to streets further away" (Mamdouh 2006a: 107). But if al-Būqarī situates his autobiographical self within the male space, ᶜĀlīya Mamdūḥ's Baghdad belongs to the women. They are sensual, unafraid to flaunt their sexuality behind closed doors, strong and self-sufficient. Some even have lesbian relationships. The strongest of them, Huda's paternal grandmother, rules the house and is undoubtedly the owner of this space. Although the women in the novel are abused by men who also strictly regulate the women's movement through public places and their public performative identities, the women nevertheless exert authority over their private spaces and establish its complete autonomy from the outer man's world. The house where the grandmother's sisters live without any male members of the family epitomizes a woman's paradise: "We called this the house of dreams. We wore our finest clothes when we went there" (11). And then of course there are public baths, where women create their own world, free of various societal restrictions imposed by men: "There were no partitions in Iraqi baths, the borders were open, and the one language in which everyone conversed was physical touch" (24). Mamdūḥ's autobiographical subject does not have access to unrestricted public spaces outside of her school as does al-Būqarī's Muhaisin, but this does not stop her from taking on the active social role of a neighborhood rebel and family anarchist. Not only is she fearless in front of her father, she preys on him in retaliation for his forcing her mother out of the house. She skips school when she wants to. She fights with boys. She blatantly chooses her childhood friend Mahmoud to be "her man." Despite the autobiographical subject's inability to move through public spaces, the potent private space of Baghdadi women allows her to formulate a powerful public persona: "There [in the women's bath] I made my first discoveries and won my first arguments, and shouted 'No, no' among the long 'Yeses' you heard from everyone else. Once there you were given the bloody title of Huda, a flaming fire" (24).

Unlike al-Būqarī's and Mamdūḥ's, al-Kharrāṭ's identity-making narrative completely internalizes his urban space and, therefore, offers an interesting example of blurred public and private spaces. *Turābuhā Zaᶜfarān* is reminiscent of Italo Calvino's hallucinatory reading of a city:

> With cities, it is as with dreams: everything imaginable can be dreamed, but even the most unexpected dream is a rebus that conceals a desire or, its reverse, a fear. Cities, like dreams, are made of desires and fears, even if the thread of their discourse is secret, their rules are absurd, their perspectives deceitful, and everything conceals something else. (Calvino 1974: 44)

The author seamlessly combines the concrete description of a public place, such as the Muhammad Ali cinema on Fuᵓad street, with a dream-like sequence, where Shahrazad from *The Thousand and One Nights* pulls up in a shiny Packard automobile in front of that same cinema (Kharrat 1989: 62). In a similarly fantastical episode, a mermaid figure suddenly appears in the middle of a thoroughly realistic description of the Mediterranean (46). Although rooted in Alexandrian urban realities, *Turābuhā*'s narrative spaces are articulated through the creative imagination, resembling the way in which a young child would likely remember things. Everything is not what it seems; these spaces are shifty and un-fixed, they are intersections of the real and the imaginary. Al-Kharrāṭ constructs a hybrid of public and private, a collage of social spaces that despite their clashing differences are seamlessly connected by the "everlasting, eternal, in the face of our extinction" sea (105). The autobiographical narrator and his reader effortlessly move between these spaces, just like the Alexandrian tram that "both divides and brings together the various parts of poor and rich Alexandria" (Awadalla 1991: 224).

City-based Nationalisms?

Idwār al-Kharrāṭ's, ᶜĀlīyah Mamdūḥ's and Ḥamza al-Būqarī's autobiographical renderings of urban space shed light on the role these cities and their modern-era metamorphoses play in the formation of contemporary Arab selfhood. This, in turn, points to the existence of city-based nationalism – an interesting but often-overlooked layer in the intricate structure of Arab identity discourses, although not dissimilar from other urban nationalisms: New York, Beijing, London, Hong-Kong, Berlin, Mexico City, to name just a few. This discourse implies that big cities and their various features – architecture, social fabric, cultural trends – can serve as the dominating force in framing the subjectivities of their inhabitants. Further investigations of urban autobiographical writing in Arabic, rapidly growing into a distinct genre especially in light of ongoing violent destructions and the radical redesigns of numerous cities in the region, would expose the complex relationship between Arab urbanism and Arab identity. As ᶜĀlīyah Mamdūḥ points out, "To create is to arrange and reinvent the cities and countries that we have left behind, and it's a good thing to have confrontations between ourselves and our native land, without hostility or usurpation … I listen, I taste and I smell how the city recreates its movements, how I free myself from its ties of holiness and its despotic authority" (Mamdouh 2000: 56).

Notes

1. A more accurate translation of the title is "her [the city's] sands/soil are saffron."
2. The term coined by Jean Starobinski in "The Idea of Nostalgia" (1966).
3. Here and further I quote from Frances Liardet's translation of al-Kharrat's work into English, titled *City of Saffron* (1989).
4. Here and further I quote from the English translation of *Saqīfat al-Ṣafā* by Olive Kenny and Jeremy Reed, which appeared under the title *The Sheltered Quarter: A Tale of a Boyhood in Mecca* (1991).
5. Here and further I quote from the English translation of *Ḥabbāt al-Naftālīn* by Peter Theroux: *Naphtalene: A Novel of Baghdad* (2006a).
6. I am using Mikhail Bakhtin's concept of chronotope, "the intrinsic connectedness of temporal and spatial relationships" (1981).

Works Cited

Aldous, G. (2013), "The Islamic city critique: revising the narrative", *Journal of the Economic and Social History of the Orient* 56, 471–93.

Arnold, W. (2014), "Urban spaces and architecturally defined identity in Nathaniel West's *Miss Lonelyhearts*," *European Journal of American Studies*, 9(2). Retrieved from http://ejas.revues.org/10345.

Al-Būqarī, H. (1983), *Saqīfat al-Ṣafā*, Riyadh: Manshūrat Dār al-Rifā[c] ī.

Awadalla, M. (1991), "The wedding of imagination and reality in al-Kharrāṭ's Alexandria: *The City of Saffron*", in H. Gindi (ed.), *Images of Egypt in Twentieth Century Literature*, Cairo: University of Cairo, 221–30.

Bachelard, G. (1964) [1994], *The Poetics of the City*, with M. Jolas (trans.) and John R. Stilgoe, Boston MA: Beacon Press.

Bakhtin, M. M. (1981). "Forms of time and of the chronotope in the novel: notes toward a historical poetics," in Michael Holquist (ed.), *The Dialogic Imagination: Four Essays*, Caryl Emerson and Michael Holquist (trans.), Austin TX: University of Texas Press, 84–258.

Barthes, R. (1997), "Semiology and the urban", in N. Leach (ed.), *Rethinking Architecture: A Reader in Cultural Theory*, New York NY: Routledge, 166–72.

Bogary, H. (1991), *The Sheltered Quarter: A Tale of a Boyhood in Mecca*, trans. Olive Kenny and Jeremy Reed, Austin TX: Center for Middle Eastern Studies, University of Texas at Austin.

Boym, S. (2007), "Nostalgia and its discontents," *Hedgehog Review*, 9 (2), 7–18.

Butt, R. (2010), "Mecca makeover: how the Hajj has become big business for Saudi Arabia," in *The Guardian* (10 November). Retrieved from https://www.theguardian.com/world/2010/nov/14/mecca-hajj-saudi-arabia (accessed 30 January 2015)

Calvino, I. (1974), *Invisible Cities*, New York NY: Harcourt Brace Jovanovich.

Dora, V. D. (2006), "The rhetoric of nostalgia: postcolonial Alexandria between uncanny memories and global geographies," *Cultural Geographies*, 13 (2), 207–38.

Elsheshtawy, Y. (2008), *The Evolving Arab City: Tradition, Modernity and Urban Development*, New York NY and Abingdon: Routledge.

Al-Kharrāṭ, I. (1986), *Turābuhā Za[c]farān: Nuṣūṣ Iskandarānīyah*, Cairo: Dar al-Mustaqbal al- [c]Arabī.

Kharrat, I. (1989), *City of Saffron*, trans. Frances Liardet, London: Quartet.

—— (1997), "My city, sacred and untamed," in R. Ilbert, I. Yannakakis and J. Hassoun (eds), *Alexandria 1860–1960: The Brief Life of Cosmopolitan Community*, Alexandria: Harpocrates Publishing, 179–87.

Kincaid, A. (2005), "Memory and the city: urban renewal and literary memoirs in contemporary Dublin," in *College Literature*, 32 (2), 16–42.

Lefebvre, H. (1991), *The Production of Space*, Malden MA and Oxford: Blackwell Publishing.

Mabro, R. (2004), "Alexandria 1860–1960: the cosmopolitan identity," in A. Hirst and M. S. Silk (eds), *Alexandria, Real and Imagined*, Farnham: Ashgate, 247–62.

Mamdūḥ, A. (1986), *Ḥabbāt al-Naftālīn*, Cairo: al-Hayʾa al-Miṣriyya al-ʿĀmma li-l-Kitāb.

Mamdouh, A. (2000), "Interview with Aliya Mamduh," in G. F. Parrilla and A. van Beugen (eds), *Remembering for Tomorrow*, Madrid: European Cultural Foundation, 55–8.

____ (2002), "An Interview with Alia Mamdouh: in conversation with Mona Chollet," in *The Handstand*. Retrieved from http://www.thehandstand.org/archive/august2002/articles/alia.htm (accessed 5 June 2015).

—— (2006a), *Naphtalene: A Novel of Baghdad*, trans. Peter Theroux, New York NY: Feminist Press at the City University of New York.

—— (2006b), "Untitled," in *New Literary History*, 37 (1), 57–64.

Neill, W. J. V. (2004), *Urban Planning and Cultural Identity*, Abingdon: Routledge.

Nowaihi, M. (1994), "Memory and imagination in Idwār al-Kharrāṭ's *Turābuha Zaʿfarān*," *Journal of Arabic Literature*, 25 (1), 34–57.

Pallasmaa, J. (1996), *The Eyes of the Skin: Architecture and the Senses*, Chichester: Wiley.

Pieri, C. (2008), "Modernity and its posts in constructing an Arab capital: Baghdad's urban space and architecture," in *Middle East Studies Association Bulletin*, 42 1/2, 32–9.

Pike, B. (1996), "The city as image," in R. T. LeGates and F. Stout (eds), *The City Reader*, Abingdon: Routledge, 243–9.

Rosenthal, C. (2011), *New York and Toronto Novels after Postmodernism: Explorations of the Urban*, Rochester NY: Camden House.

Saadi, Y. (2014), "Mecca's changing face: rejuvenation or destruction?" in *Al-Akhbar Online*. Retrieved from http://english.al-akhbar.com/node/18888 (accessed on 15 August 2015).

Starobinski, J. (1966), "The idea of nostalgia," *Diogenes*, 54, 81–103.

Starr, D. (2009), *Remembering Cosmopolitan Egypt: Literature, Culture, and Empire*, New York NY and Abingdon: Routledge.

Vidler, A. (1992), *The Architectural Uncanny: Essays in the Modern Unhomely*, Cambridge MA: MIT Press.

Yablon, N. (2011), "John Sloan and 'the roof life of the metropolis'," *American Art*, 25 (2) 14–17.

12

The Sufis of Baghdad: A Topographical Index of the City

Boutheina Khaldi

The renewed interest in Sufism in Baghdad within the last two decades should direct our attention not only to the contemporary Iraqi scene, but also to Abbasid Baghdad itself (762–1258) as the milieu where Sufi masters practiced an everyday life in Michel de Certeau's sense of the term. This chapter will focus on three modern texts that look back at the intersection of Sufism and Baghdad's urban landscape when the city was the recognized leader of the Islamic world. Azīz al-Sayyid Jāsim's *Mutaṣawwifat Baghdād* (The Sufis of Baghdad) appeared in 1990[1] and Hādī al-ᶜAlawī's *Madārāt Ṣūfiyya* (Sufi Orbits) in 1997.[2] Both Jāsim and al-ᶜAlawī were prominent neo-Marxists who later turned to Sufism; the former was executed by Ṣaddām Ḥusayn in April 1991 and the latter died in exile in Syria in 1998. The third text, introduced by the well-known Iraqi historian and distinguished authority on the Abbasid economy ᶜAbd al-ᶜAzīz al-Dūrī (d. 2010), is ᶜUmar al-Tall's comprehensive study, *Mutaṣwwifat Baghdād fī al-Qarn al-Sādis al-Hijrī/al-Thānī ᶜAshar al-Mīlādī: Dirāsa Tārīkhiyya* (The Sufis of Baghdad in the Sixth Century AH/ Twelfth Century: A Historical Study), which will serve as a complement to Jāsim's and al-ᶜAlawī's works.[3] Al-Tall's study is helpful in understanding the "production of space" in this context, to borrow Lefebvre's phrase, whereby Sufis appropriated a "differentiated space"[4] for opposition and dissent.[5]

The question all three texts raise is that of why twentieth-century Iraqi writers would feel compelled to turn to an interrogation of Sufi practice in Abbasid Baghdad. These studies should not be read as an anomalous historical engagement on the part of their authors, rather there is an urgency within the pages of these texts to recall old Baghdad, to save it from erasure and oblivion. Although there is no direct reference to present-day Baghdad, a sense of mourning and loss permeates these works. While the Baghdad of the Sufi masters enjoyed cultural and architectural glory, the perceptive eye of the figures described in these volumes was more discerning. We find that they often critique those in power, standing up for the common people. By addressing the Sufi itineraries of everyday life in Abbasid Baghdad as they are portrayed by twentieth-century Iraqi intellectuals, their interactions with the rest of society, and the fundamental role they played in maintaining social justice in the city's spaces, this chapter will ultimately suggest that the nostalgia of modern authors for this epoch provides a pointed comment on the present.

Why Baghdad?

The affluence and opulence of Baghdad distinguished it from other Iraqi urban centers like Baṣra and Kūfa, but this was not the only reason Sufis were attracted to the city. In his study, al-Tall emphasizes the circularity of Baghdad,[6] something that could have carried conscious or unconscious resonances for Sufi practitioners as their rituals were often associated with this form. In *Madārāt Ṣūfiyya*, Al-ᶜAlawī points out that the whirling of dervishes and the idea of *ṭawāf* (circumambulation) can be seen as more than a preparatory step for *fanāᵓ* (physical self-annihilation). There are other associations that bring geography and circumambulation together, placing them in tandem with the Qurᵓānic presentation of the planetary system and the endless circular motion of the sun. Al-ᶜAlawī cites the grand Sufi master Abū Yazīd al-Bistāmī (d. 874), who has been quoted as saying, in al-Sahlajī's transmission, that he was "circumambulating around the Kaᶜbah in search for Him, when I saw the Kaᶜbah revolving around me."[7] He adds: "Al -Bistāmī meant the centrality of the perfect man to the universe."[8] This sublimation initiates an elevation of signs that situates Baghdad in a grid that avowedly partakes of both the physical and the spiritual. It also endows its topoi with another meaning that turns the sign into an icon and the icon into an ascent to the beyond.

Its shape is not the only thing that connects Baghdad to the sacred, as al-Khatīb al-Baghdādī (d. 1071) reports in his *Tārīkh Baghdād*:

> Once the ascetic Aḥmad Ibn Abbās left Baghdad running away from what he deemed rampant corruption, a pious man stopped him, telling him:

> 'come back and don't worry. Baghdad has the tombs of four pious men who shield her against all misfortune: al-Imām Ibn Ḥanbal, Maᶜrūf al-Karkhī, Bishr al-Ḥāfī, and Manṣūr Ibn ᶜAmmār.'[9]

Along the same lines, it was reported that:

> the ascetic Ibn Mujāhid al-Maqarrī said: "I saw Abū ᶜAmr Ibn al-ᶜAlāᵓ, the philologist and transmitter of the Prophetic tradition, in my dream. I asked him: 'what did God do to you?' He replied: 'Don't ask me what God did to me. Whoever lives and dies in Baghdad following the *Sunna* (Prophetic Tradition) and *Jamāᶜa* is being transferred from one paradise to another.'"[10]

We can see in these quotes the growing association between heaven and Baghdad that was, in part, based on its large number of important shrines. Many of these Sufi shrines have since become prominent itineraries for visitation, prayer, and vows, defining the urban space of the city. The shrine of the Sufi master Maᶜrūf al-Karkhī (d. 815), for example, would grow into a large and privileged cemetery; whereas al-Kāẓimiyya, an area that takes its name from the shrines of Imam Mūsa b. Jaᶜfar and his family, is now a large and distinguished district in Baghdad. The above are representative of a number of narratives and anecdotes that speak to the association between Sufis and space presenting Baghdad as a sacred center.

Another anecdote reads as follows: "Someone said: I wanted once to leave Baghdad for another place but I saw in my dream someone saying: 'Do you want to move from a place that has ten thousand saints?' So I decided to stay."[11] These narratives should not be taken at face value, rather they draw upon a set of beliefs and practices that endear the place to many. Indeed, the Abbasids labored to build their legitimacy in association with a tradition where icons and cities were loaded with a multitude of religious and cultural connotations.[12] Although aiming at a different analysis based on al-Khaṭīb al-Baghdādī's history of the city, Zayde Antrim's idea of the "foundation narrative" is relevant here, as these shrines and associated practices create a consortium of beliefs that has proved hard to question, even under a secular government like that of Ṣaddām Ḥusayn and its campaign against popular beliefs and practices that stretch back to the time of the Buyids.[13] Despite the renaming of streets and districts under secular rule, the old street names, with their references to Sufi saints and the blessings of which they are suggestive, have remained current among the city's inhabitants.

A Community Connected to Baghdad's Everyday Spaces

In *Mutaṣawwifat Baghdād* and *Madārāt Ṣūfiyya*, Jāsim and al- ᶜAlawī respectively take the Sufi masters' involvement in everyday life as both a topography and an index of their social and political engagement. To Jāsim and al-ᶜAlawī, everyday life is rooted in writings on space. De Certeau argues that: "everyday practices, 'ways of operating' or doing things, no longer appear as merely the obscure background of social activity."[14] Space and everyday practice assume an integral relationship whereby the one reflects upon the other. The three texts under consideration here debunk the binary distinction between bucolic and urban space that tacitly implies the shunning of the city, with its police apparatus and formal administration, in favor of the pastoral.[15] Even the choice of the books' titles deliberately undermines the common pragmatic structuration of Sufism along theological parameters that presumably corresponds to a divide between a normative Islamic theology and deviant (and hence free) practices. This divide gained significance in the seventeenth and eighteenth centuries, for as Anne-Marie Schimmel notes, concurring with A. J. Arberry, it was then that Sufism was associated pejoratively with the "seller of patched frocks."[16] Jāsim, al-ᶜAlawī, and al-Tall dispute such categorizations as only one aspect of the complex history of Sufism. Like any urban phenomenon, and particularly in the case of the Sufis of Baghdad, there were always instances of departure from dominating social practices that brought about condemnation or serious charges of heresy.[17]

What moves to the forefront in these three works is the image of an urban environment where Sufis, non-Sufis, and institutions constitute the life of the city in the heyday of its cultural and economic growth. While agency-oriented, i.e. propelled and perpetuated by the presence and practices of the Sufi masters, these works give the city a voice of its own. Thus the cultural topography of Baghdad emanates not only from daily transaction, but also from the legacy and reputation of the Sufi masters who have left an abiding impact on the makeup of the cultural identity of the urban space. The result is a two-fold transaction of production and consumption. The Sufi as a businessman or craftsman is at the same time a consumer. Sufi practice in Baghdad opens up a "schemata of action"[18] whereby Sufis as such, and other consumers and producers, sustain a long-time transaction, a model that participates in the composition of culture.[19] In other words, though different in many respects, Sufis were not wayward outliers in a dynamic city life from which they were alienated, rather they were an intrinsic part of the urban space.

In some ways, the veneration shown to Sufi masters can be better traced to the centrality of their tombs and shrines in the urban center. Taken as an embodiment of faith and piety, these shrines became integral to the city. In the city, they have been emblematically associated with the power to survive misfortune. Rather than being driven to the outskirts as symbols of death, as was the case with cemeteries in Western cities as Michel Foucault has analyzed in his discussion of heterotopias ("Of Other Places"), the centrality of these shrines and tombs reflect, in Jāsim's reading, the distinctive character of Baghdad, which is, perhaps, like Cairo and Damascus, derived from a heterogeneity of space. Foucault's reading demonstrates the historical shift in the way that cemeteries have been viewed, from an extension of the sacred to their desacrilization and transformation into a site of illness and death. As a result, he argues, the European city renounced the belief in the immorality of the soul: "The cemeteries then came to constitute, no longer the sacred and immortal heart of the city, but the other city, where each family possesses its dark resting place."[20] Foucault's insights into the break-up of temporal, spatial, and cultural norms that reflect on the position of the cemetery inside or outside a city center help to demonstrate how Sufis and saints conversely brought into Baghdad a strong faith in resurrection, the soul's immortality, and hence the sanctity of the cemetery.

The original core of Baghdad was round and was encircled by shrines (see Figure 12.1).[21] They were built to its left and western sides, cemeteries such as the Quraysh, Bāb al-Shām, and Bāb al-Tibn, on the trench close to the fief of Umm Ja[c]far, and the cemeteries of Bāb al-Kunās, near Burātha Mosque, al-Shunayziyya (where the shrine of Sarī al-Saqṭī is located), and that of Ma[c]rūf al-Karkhī on the Kharkh side.[22] Although mosques were generally at the center of an individual quarter, populated areas with their own mosques and markets would be built around shrines. In other words, they do not neatly fit into Foucault's theorization of heterotopic or liminal spaces, since they generated an active and thriving life around them while simultaneously serving as a sanctified space. They transformed into lucrative and vibrant economic and social centers, as was the case in other parts of the Islamic world. Though writing about a different context, we can apply Rudolf Arnheim's *The Power of the Center: A Study of Composition in the Visual Arts.*[23] Although these districts have the spatial prototype of the village, they emerge as central to the urban and spiritual routes that run across Baghdad: "when a system is free to spread its energy in space," argues Arnheim, "it sends out its vectors evenly all around, like the rays emanating from a source of light. The

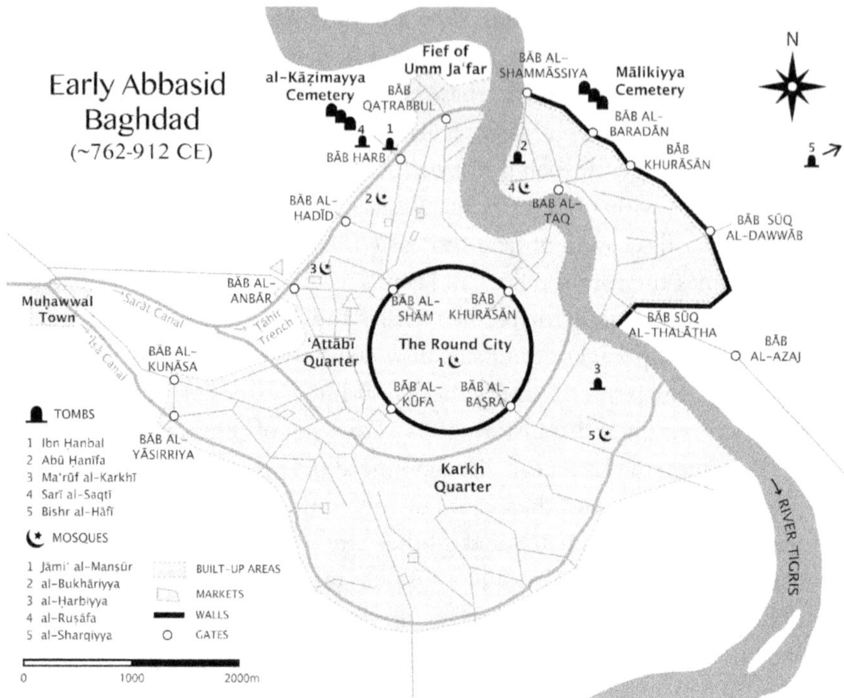

Figure 12.1 The Round City of Baghdad.

resulting … pattern is the prototype of *centric composition*."[24] In Jāsim's book, and in the other two texts as well, we find a view of the cityscape that is wider, more heterogeneous, and topographically richer than what we generally see in a non-Islamic metropolis. Baghdad topoi are not the deserted abodes and forsaken campsites of the classical poetic tradition; they are rather embued with life and multilayered levels of significance that stem from the dynamic exchange between Sufis, the city's inhabitants, and the urban space.

These associations between place, belief, and tradition figure prominently in *Mutaṣawwifat Baghdād*. Theorists of urban space suggest that the associations attached to old or emerging practices are conducive to behavioral patterns and responses. De Certeau for one takes into account, "readers' practices, practices related to urban spaces, utilizations of everyday rituals, re-uses and functions of the memory through the 'authorities' that make possible (or permit) everyday practices, etc."[25] Everyday life in Baghdad involved Sufis and their communities in a sanctified structure of belief, a structure that necessarily undermined officialdom. For instance, the Sufi Abū al-Ḥusayn al-Nūrī (d. 907–8), "the commander of hearts" (*amīr al-qulūb*) and "the moon of the Sufis" (*qamar al-Ṣūfiyya*), worked as *muḥtasib* (market inspector) in the reign of the caliph al-Muᶜtaḍid (r. 892–902). He supervised the banks of the River Tigris and used to stroll outside into the suburban areas and forests surrounding Baghdad to monitor prices and regulate weights and public morals, something that provoked officials like Aḥmad Ghulām Khalīl, in one case, to charge him with heresy in 885.[26]

True to Baghdad's name as the abode of peace and the center of the Islamic world (*madīnat al-salām or dār al-Islām wa-l-salām*), the city exerted a strong centripetal pull. It attracted many, the *ᶜulamāᵓ* and tradesmen among them. Magnetic, gravitational, and seductive, it was often called by the alias "*Ṣayyāda taṣīdu al-rijāl*" (a seductive woman who seduces men).[27] A great center of learning, the Mecca for many Sufis who sought knowledge and an *entrepôt* of international trade, Baghdad was known for its moderation, openness, and pluralism as indicated in its political, intellectual, and religious diversity.[28] Whether masters or disciples, Sufis found in Baghdad freedom of religious practice.[29] The confederation of Sufis in the city in the late eighth century and early ninth century was so prominent that it generated manuals, compendiums, and biographical dictionaries.[30] Knowledge and Sufism would seem to have grown in tandem with Baghdad's growth as an Islamic center, something manifest in the large number of Sufi orders that flourished within it, and though they are referred to as a collective entity here, each had its distinctive characteristics and practices. Some of the most important orders at the time were al-Saqṭiyya, the followers of Sarī al-Saqṭī; al-Junaydiyya, the followers of Qāsim al-Junayd; al-Kharziyya, the followers of Saᶜīd al-Kharrāz; al-Nūriyya, the followers of Abū al-Ḥusayn al-Nūrī; al-Muḥāsibiyya, the followers of al-Ḥārith Ibn Asad al-Muḥāsibī; and al-Ḥallājiyya, the followers of al-Ḥusayn bin Manṣūr al-Ḥallāj.

Promoting Virtue

The concentration of Sufi masters and their tombs in Baghdad did not, however, mean that the city was free from corruption, immorality, and debauchery. It is on record that Baghdad had a strong police apparatus because of the vice it harbored. Sufi registers and itineraries have left us an index of this life and the Sufi practices employed to curb vice and criminality. It was reported for instance that there was once at Bāb al-Ṭāq a man holding a knife against a woman's throat, threatening to kill her and anybody else who dared to come nearby. The notable Sufi Bishr al-Ḥāfī (d. 841) ignored the threat and approached the man, who then dropped his knife and let the woman go. When asked what made the criminal respond in that way, Bishr al-Ḥāfī replied: "I told him God is watching you." The criminal fainted and subsequently suffered from a fever that led to his death a week after the incident.[31] This anecdote, and many others, reminds us of what de Certeau calls "ways of operating," whereby dispersed groups develop "makeshift creativity" when caught up in the nets of discipline."[32] The Sufi, Bishr al-Ḥāfī in this case, offers his own model of justice and serves as an instrument of law enforcement and also, ultimately, of divine retribution, a counter to the official authorities of the state.

Located in urban sites with bustling spaces, Sufis often interfered to put an end to injustice, moral transgression, and the misuse of power. These practices generated transactions that took the shape of a confrontation whereby a Sufi master would act upon the scene as an adversary in the fight against corruption. Furthermore, as Sufis would generally choose professions in trade and the artisan crafts, their work included engagement with everyday life where sites of transaction would grow into differentiated spaces of protest against corruption and the misuse of power.[33] This phenomenon was particularly conspicuous during the Seljūk period (1055–1194) in Baghdad. When the Seljūks enforced laws on inhabitants compelling them to take part in festivities and indulge in wine-drinking and debauchery, the Sufis stood up against them. The ascetic Ibn al-Kawwāz (d. 543 AH), for example, threatened Sultan Masᶜūd that he would incite the people in the mosques to revolt.[34] Al-Shaykh ᶜAbd al-Qādir al-Jīlānī (d. 1166), the traditional founder of the Qādiriyya Sufi order, had the power of Baghdad's populace behind him, enabling him to defy caliphs and sultans. Aware of the powerful influence ᶜAbd al-Qādir al-Jīlānī exercised over the people, the caliph tried to win him over by lavishing him with gifts. ᶜAbd al-Qādir al-Jīlānī, however, refused to accept them and reprimanded him for squandering the people's money.[35] ᶜAbd al-Qādir al-Jīlānī's residence in Bāb al-Azaj, later named Bāb al-Shaykh, has become an index of revolt and protest in Iraqi memory ever since. It played a crucial role, for example, in the fight against British occupation and the rise of political consciousness that accompanied the struggle for independence, as al-ᶜAlawī indicates.[36] It likewise figures prominently in both the noted Iraqi writer Fuʾād al-Takarlī's novel *al-Rajᶜ al-Baᶜīd* (1980) (*The Long Way Back*, 2007)[37] and the Iraqi poet ᶜAbd al-Wahhāb al-Bayātī's poem, "Kitāba ᶜalā Qabr al-Sayyāb" (Writing on al-Sayyāb's Tomb).[38]

The stand taken against Sufis by influential officials like Aḥmad Ghulām Khalīl, and the viziers Abū al-Faḍl Ibn al-Furāt and Ḥāmid Ibn ᶜAbbās in the reign of the caliph al-Muqtadir Billāh (r. 907–32), shows how Sufis displayed a "field of power," to borrow Pierre Bourdieu's phrase in relation to the language and symbolic power associated with space.[39] They were capable not only of influencing individuals and communities, but also of reaching out to the social fringes.[40] Rather than being a group of recluses and solitary individuals, Sufis were very much involved in everyday life. They were craftsmen and professionals, as their nicknames indicate: al-Sarrāj (saddler), al-Kharrāz (pearl-piercer), al-Ḥaddād (blacksmith), al-Warrāq (papermaker), al-Qawārīrī (bottle maker), al-Nassāj (weaver), to mention but a few.[41] While there were exceptions, like Al-Ḥārith al-Muḥāsibī (d. 857), who first dedicated himself to fighting corruption, debauchery, and materialism, calling for a life of moderation in thought and behavior,[42] only to then choose a hermetic life devoted to the love of God, there were Sufi masters on the other side of the spectrum. Sarī al-Saqṭī (d. 867), the uncle and mentor of Abū al-Qāsim al-Junayd (d. 910), the "undisputed master of the Sufis of Baghdad," went so far as to participate in war expeditions.[43] He also used the street as a site for public preaching and teaching against corruption and exploitation. Al-Saqṭī undermined the colossal body of jurists who had built around themselves a highly complex corpus of writing beyond the reach of common people. In other words, al-Saqṭī brought knowledge – and Sufi thought in particular – close to the populace.[44] Baghdad as such turned into a pinnacle of learning where knowledge was produced and disseminated through the mediation of these Sufi masters, a point which Louis Massignon's review of al-Ḥallāj's (d. 922) itinerary substantiates:

> With the return from his last pilgrimage to Mecca, the features of Ḥallāj that are already so original are silhouetted in full light on the stage of events, at the center of public life, among elites and throngs both, in Baghdad, that immense, complex and subtle city.[45]

Using their thorough knowledge of history and employing their neo-Marxist methodology while negotiating their own turn to Sufism, Jāsim and al-ᶜAlawī perceive the Baghdad of the Sufis not only as a "subtle city," but as an interstitial space, a space which in Jennifer Anna Gosetti-Ferencei's reading was "constituted by striking negotiations of the relation between different positions within experience."[46] While many Sufis were craftsmen and professionals, their renunciation of this world without a claim to the hereafter involves a series of poetic expressions that re-draw the divides between the abstract and the concrete. In the developing Sufi lexicon, binary distinctions between heaven and hell, good and evil, collapse. Instead, the inner self becomes the testing ground, and hence the domain of an essential struggle, in constant search for another expression that outsiders would call cryptic. The so-called cryptic style of al-Junayd and al-Muḥāsibī was only the voicing of that innermost struggle. Abū Bakr al-Karrāz (d. *ca.* 899), who was also a disciple of al-Saqṭī, had already resorted to allusions and symbols rather than common expressions to convey an intimate spiritual experience in an enormous urban complex. By this time a Sufi lexicon had already begun to establish itself, especially in the sayings of the grand Sufi Abū al-Ḥusayn al-Nūrī, "the forerunner for later poets."[47] The turn to the esoteric and symbolic is important to our reading of a city that had for its urban planning names of places that refer to the routes taken by travelers, like Bāb al-Ṭaq and Bāb al-Shām. In the Sufi lexicon, abstract terminology is prevalent while concrete terms assume other semantic connotations. Jāsim includes a number of examples without overlooking the ascetic turn that makes a prominent figure like Abū Hāshim al-Zāhid (d. *ca.* 767) rely on spatial images to convey his prioritization of the hereafter when he says: "If the world was only castles and gardens and the hereafter only huts, I would choose the latter because of its permanence and not the former because of its ephemerality."[48]

In their search for a negotiated space with respect to Sufi masters, their orders, and disciples, historians and critics tend to divide them along ascetic, moderate, and Sunnī lines. Such classification overlooks the fact that Sufi masters were able to transcend bodily limitations in search of a primordial covenant. The Sufis' moment of transcendence is part of a larger one that does not fit any of the existing schema found in postmodern theories of space. Transcending limits, Sufis provide possible alternatives for our reading of space. Perhaps what has been applied to the criticism of the novel, and specifically narratives of a third space, a wedge that "holds two extremes together,"[49] may apply to Sufi navigation. The Sufi experience cannot be compartmentalized; the Sufi practitioner can move beyond space while anchored in space. Thus, he can be a shopkeeper or a blacksmith while reaching a state of transcendence at the same time, a space where there is another reality, a truth beyond spatial pragmatics.

Social Space: Markets and Mosques

Jāsim argues that the Sufis shunned "*al-kathāfa al-māddiyya*" (dense materiality)[50] without abandoning social life. Hence he associates Baghdad's urban expansion with the growth of business, wealth, and also impoverished suburbs. This urban space generates more vice than virtue. Bishr al-Ḥāfī gives us an excellent example of this two-sided struggle not only against corruption, but also against the soul prone to evil:

> I was once a ringleader. One day when I was walking, I found a piece of paper on the road which I lifted, finding in it "In the Name of God the Beneficent, the Merciful." I wiped it and put it in my pocket. I had only two dirhams. So I went to the perfume vendor and bought with them a perfume made of musk and ambergris with which I rubbed the piece of paper. When I slept that night, I saw in my dream someone saying to me: "You Bishr al-Ḥāfī, you have lifted our name from the road and perfumed it. Verily I will perfume your name in this world and the hereafter."[51]

I have chosen al-Ḥāfī, not only because he was renowned for his asceticism and renunciation of material life, but also because the two stages in his life – the first as a ringleader of thieves and criminals, the second as a Sufi master – betray the complexity of Baghdad's urban space at this time.[52] What distinguishes al-Ḥāfī is his unique way of traversing the city markets and alleys barefoot. When turning to Sufism, al-Ḥāfī asked a shoemaker to repair his sandals. The shoemaker reproached him for leading an extravagant life. Al-Ḥāfī decided to never wear sandals again and to be subsequently barefoot, hence the epithet "al-Ḥāfī" (barefoot). The bottom of his feet turned black after a long period of living as a wanderer, vagabond, and traverser of markets.[53]

In Sufi itineraries, there are urban spaces and borders. The border signifies an exceptional practice that departs from a mainstream urban life. In al-Tall's comprehensive historical review, the frontier as a geographical borderline functions as a double bind; it is a war front against infidels which an early ascetic Sufi saint like Ibrāhīm Ibn Adham (d. 777), the son of the king of Balkh, Sarī al-Saqṭī, and Ḥātam al-Aṣam (d. 851) would defend, and a point of departure towards the center of Baghdad where a different war against corruption begins.[54] In their peregrinations, the Sufi wanderer and ascetic could compete with any urbanite or geographer. Combined with a renunciation of material life, al-Ḥāfī was a model of asceticism and piety that won him the admiration of many, among whom was the prominent conservative jurist Aḥmad Ibn Ḥanbal (d. 855).[55] Al-Ḥāfī used to frequent the Flour Market to check on its prices, for the price of flour would indicate how well a society – its economy and administrative system – was running. Deception was rampant, and deceitful practices meant going astray from the Islamic path,[56] the primary factor behind al-Ḥāfī's concern. Around the time of the following anecdote, prices soared, especially under the "monopolizing deals of the vizier Ḥāmid Ibn al-ᶜAbbās and his associates in speculation."[57] The story goes that, "[o]ne day al-Ḥāfī asked the flour merchant about the price of flour. The merchant replied: 'Be happy Abū Naṣr. It is less than yesterday.' Al-Ḥāfī thanked God and said: 'If you are worried about the rise in prices, remember death because it makes you forget about it.'"[58] The anecdote provides a clear illustration of the concern Sufis often showed for the general livelihood of Baghdad's people. What also emerges in this exchange is the dialogue between a Sufi master and a place, a city of variegated audiences and functional spaces. As vizier and a tax farmer, al-ᶜAbbās was notorious as he "insanely intended to have the rate of wheat raised to 55 dinar … This meant starvation, and rebellion broke out and prevailed."[59] As it was in many places, flour was a staple in Baghdad. Officials like al-ᶜAbbās, known for compiling a case against al-Ḥallāj, monopolized the market and were behind the persecution of many Sufis. We can consider here why the urban economy in old Baghdad has attracted the attention of twentieth-century intellectuals like Jāsim, al-ᶜAlawī, and al-Tall. The focus on societal, economic, and political issues may very well reflect on post-1980 Baghdad, its staggering currency, weakened infrastructure, and impoverished communities. The Sufi master is shown as the representative of the downtrodden and the unprivileged, a figure with undeniably modern relevance.

Along the dividing lines that are often applied in studies of Sufism, the reader may confuse the "wanderer" with "the recluse" or find them incompatible. There were Sufis who chose solitude but there were others who were known for their engagement in public life. The Sufi is often a wanderer par excellence whose peripetatic life leads him to engage in social and political issues.[60] Hence the involvement of many Sufis in issues pertaining to the ethics of commanding right and forbidding wrong. Both Jāsim and al-ᶜAlawī focus on the interaction between a lucrative center of business and culture and the role of the Sufi as a corrective and counterbalance to excessive materiality. Sufi masters were understandably against itinerant mendicancy or social withdrawal and estrangement.[61]As Ahmet Karamustafa argues in another context, many Sufis "planted themselves firmly into the social fabric of Baghdad, although they occupied the 'grey areas' on many social fronts."[62] Echoing Jāsim in *Mutaṣawwifat Baghdād,* he explains:

> In this, their rootedness within urban society, they resembled the majority of the scholars, the *ᶜulamāʾ*, who occupied the social center of major towns

> in Islamic polities of the time. In brief, the Ṣūfiyya, like scholars of discursive knowledge, took shape at the very heart of ᶜAbbāsid urban culture in Baghdad, and put forward their claim to be central players on the main stage in the unfolding drama of authority in urban Muslim communities.[63]

To compare Sufis with "the majority of the *ᶜulamāʾ*" can be misleading, however. Many theologians and scholars were not as devoted as Sufi masters to the renunciation of worldliness. Maᶜrūf al-Karkhī (d. 815), for instance, was known for his noble character and decency. He was an ascetic worshipper who renounced earthly pleasures in an age where the frantic search for sexual opportunity and the participation in the explosive growth of the white slave trade had become the norm.[64] His renunciation of earthly pleasures, however, did not deter him from being socially engaged, an engagement that brought him closer to common people, professionals, and craftsmen, and made him among the most sought-after of the Sufis.[65] Al-Ḥallāj's career shows us another relatively well-documented case that collapses the variegated sites which we usually associate with urban space. It is known that he joined the populace with a readiness to converse with the elite, the educated society. According to *Akhbār al-Ḥallāj*, his itinerary of public preaching in markets, mosques, notables' libraries, *warrāqīns*' (scribes and copyists) homes, and distinguished assemblies (*majālis*) made him a well-known public figure who was even received by notable women and visited in his private mosque and home.[66]

The itinerary provided in *Akhbār* is vital to the understanding of the topography of Baghdad. Sūq al-Qaṭīᶜah (fief of Umm Jaᶜfar) is particularly important. Al-Ḥallāj's house was built east of the center of the round city in a suburb called Bāb al-Shām, where the fief of Umm Jaᶜfar (i.e. Zubaydah) was located. Sūq al-Qaṭīᶜah was the place where al-Ḥallāj was reported to preach quite often. According to Aḥmad Ibn Fāris: "I saw al-Ḥallāj in the Sūq al-Qaṭīᶜah, standing before the entrance to the mosque." After ending his sermon in tears, "the people of the sūq began to weep with him."[67] While preaching, he used to move at times in the aforementioned *sūq*, until, according to Ibn Fāris, he "came to a halt before the entrance to the ᶜAttāb mosque, and he began to utter his words, some of which were intelligible, though the rest escaped us."[68] The ᶜAttāb Mosque, mentioned in al-Jāhiẓ's *Kitāb al-Ḥayawān* and which al-Ḥallāj used to attend,[69] was situated in the ᶜAttābī district that was populated by cloth and textile laborers. Sūq Qaṭīᶜat al-Rabīᶜ was known as a working district not strictly divided between Shiᶜites and Hanbalites.[70]

Al-Ḥallāj's attendance of specific assemblies is no less significant for the Sufi cartography of the city.[71] In his *masjid* (part of his house east of the round city, located in the suburb of Bāb al-Shām), he preached the following, according to ᶜAbd al-Karīm Ibn ᶜAbd al-Wāḥid:

> If out of my heart a single atom were thrown into the mountains of the earth, they would begin to melt! And if I were, myself, on the day of Resurrection, thrown into Hell, the infernal fire would be burned up; and if I entered Paradise, the dwellings of Paradise would crumble![72]

In this quote we can see the peculiarity that de Certeau refers to as "spatial syntax."[73] While Sufis used space to interrogate its materiality, they left behind a rich legacy, a map of practice that has proved resilient. The spatial syntax which Jāsim and al-ᶜAlawī trace in *Mutaṣawwifat Baghdād* and *Madārāt Ṣūfiyya* respectively led Louis Massignon to draw a map of al-Ḥallāj's itinerary.[74] The significance of this map to our reading is as important as it is to the narrative itself. In regard to fiction, Franco Moretti has argued that "maps bring to light the *internal* logic of narrative: the semiotic domain around which a plot coalesces and self-organizes."[75] Sufi itineraries are maps where social engagement works in tandem with Sufi teaching.

Al-Saqṭī took knowledge to the streets to disseminate social equality and expose social ills and exploitation.[76] Jāsim shows how this commitment entailed participation in social and intellectual life, and fighting narrow-minded theologians, corrupt governors, and scholars who held a monopoly over culture to sustain their own views and enforce their way of thinking onto others.[77] Thus to him, the only justification for knowledge is its use and value to people, those with whom he used to interact and meet in the streets of Baghdad. Jāsim quotes al-Saqṭī in this regard: "A wise man was asked: 'when does an erudite man do badly?' He replied: 'When he becomes known by his domes and his books are widespread but he becomes upset if somebody criticizes his work.'"[78] Of course Al-Kharkhī, al-Saqṭī, and al-Ḥallāj, to mention but a few, did not confine their dissemination of knowledge to the street per se. Mosques, libraries, and cemeteries were also a locus of their cultural activity.

As mentioned earlier, al -Nūrī, as *muḥtasib* under the caliph al-Muᶜtaḍid, was responsible for the supervision of the banks of the River Tigris, and would frequently stroll in the areas surrounding the city, monitoring prices and regulating weights and public morals. Al-Ghazālī relates the following anecdote: "Al-Nūrī went down to a drinking place near the river, known as the drinking place of the local merchants, where he saw a boat loaded with thirty containers in which were written in tar 'benevolence.' He read and disapproved of it … breaking all except one," which he left as the caliph's own share, which would be the *muḥtasib*'s message to him.[79] Al-Nūrī, whom al-Ghazālī quotes throughout his *ḥisba* treatise, told the caliph why he dared to break the jugs even though he knew they belonged to him: "the corruption of citizens is due to the corruption of rulers, the corruption of rulers is due to the corruption of the scholars, and the corruption of the scholars is due to love of wealth and fame."[80] When the caliph asked him who commissioned him with *ḥisba,* he responded: "The same one who entrusted you with rulership entrusted me with *ḥisba,* O Commander of the Faithful."[81] As noted earlier, al-Nūrī suffered for his straightforwardness and moral struggle against vice, and was once apprehended along with other Sufis who were accused by Aḥmad Ghulām Khalīl of heresy. He presented himself to the caliph and assumed full responsibility for what he had done. The caliph was so touched by his honesty that he pardoned him and those with whom he was apprehended, to the chagrin of his vizier.[82]

Both Jāsim and al-ᶜAlawī draw a number of parameters that define and cut across social, economic, and political space. Urban space gains its validity and conspicuity through the impact of these parameters on its structures, including that of feeling, in Raymond Williams' sense of the term.[83] Sufi masters are dialectically preoccupied with the sacred and quotidian.[84] This combined undertaking necessarily negates the binary distinctions between these two poles as it situates Sufis in an intersectional space of great cogency in a vibrant and heterogeneous urban center like Baghdad. To account for the interrelatedness between the sacred and the quotidian, we can once again turn to Foucault: "We live inside a set of relations that delineates sites which are irreducible to one another and absolutely not superimposable on one another."[85] Foucault addresses heterotopias in general, but in an Islamic context where Sufism holds sway, this interrelatedness is conspicuous. This resistance to reductive reasoning and analysis stems from the nature of Sufism itself that operates in real and virtual spaces. The Sufi use of the pulpit, for instance, needs to be differentiated from its common use in the Islamic congregational prayer where it is used to address the community whenever there is the need to do so. Sufism rarely succumbs to regulations and rules set by the state or the ruler. Hence the Sufi pulpit, even when belonging to a mosque recognizably attached to the state, functions as a unifier with a base in piety and affection. The Islamic city takes the pulpit as a forum of which Sufi masters often made use to address their community. A well-known narrative quoted by Jāsim relates to the first producer of a specific Sufi terminology, Ibrāhīm al-Ṣadafī al-Baghdādī (d. 883), who fell from the pulpit while preaching, affected as he was by ecstasy and rapture (*wajd*), to then die a few days later.[86] The instance brings to light variegated Sufi practices, their preaching, devotion, intoxication with divine love, and presence in the institutional spaces of the city. Each Sufi itinerary ends up as an index of the topographical and cultural sites of a space. Rather than being limited to individual practices, Sufism was able to provide answers to philosophical questions: it was not confined to the escapades of some individuals and the circles of Sufi masters and their disciples. It became part of everyday life, present in mosques, markets, private gatherings, devotional circles, and the city streets. Rather than something that existed in stark opposition to reigning societal norms, as a movement, Jāsim argues, Sufism stressed conformity with Islamic law,[87] a point which the celebrated historian al-Dūrī observes as well: "Some Sufi masters were teachers or judges, a significant turn that meant that Sufism was integral to society, unseparated from it."[88]

Sufi Transactions

The Sufis of Baghdad belonged to the urbanite middle and upper-classes. Jāsim, al-ᶜAlawī and al-Tall trace this urbanity in their dealings, practices, and speeches.[89] Before converting to the Sufi path, Abū Bakr al-Shiblī (d. 946) was a chamberlain in the caliphate palace.[90] Al-Junayd was a silk merchant.[91] Al-Nūrī was an artisan.[92] Al-Ḥallāj was a cotton carder. Al-Saqṭī was a shopkeeper.[93] Work was their means to helping the poor and the needy.[94]

> One day al-Saqṭī was doing business when al-Kharkhī asked him to help clothe an orphan, which he did. Al-Kharkhī was pleased and told him: "May God make you hate this world and relieve you of what you own." Al-Saqṭī commented: "I left the shop with nothing more hateful to me than this world thanks to al-Kharkhī's blessings."[95]

On the other hand, the acclaimed leader of the Sufi school of Baghdad, al-Junayd, did not stop working. He perceived it as a way to strengthen belief and consolidate worship. More connected to urban and middle-class concerns, he disapproved of some Sufis' lax approach to the idea of earning a living. To him, as to a number of Sufi masters, there is no disparity between Sufi practice and family or economic activity, perhaps part of the reason that he is considered "the pivot in the history of early Sufism"[96] and why "representatives of divergent mystical schools refer to him as their master."[97] Al-Junayd used to open his shop on a daily basis, attending to his business without overlooking his prayers. Al-Salamī said: "my grandfather Ismā^cīl Ibn Najīd said: 'Every day al-Junayd used to come to the market to open his shop. He used to drop the curtain and pray forty times.'"[98]

Al-Ḥallāj is another example, who, as Massignon notes, took up his profession as a cotton carder whenever he needed to earn a living.[99] Al-Nūrī was an artisan. He rarely let others, even his family, notice his devotional piety. Every day on his way to work as a shopkeeper, while fasting, he used to distribute whatever food he had as alms, which was usually bread. Then he would go to the mosque and pray till shortly before midday. Only then would he open his shop. His family would think that he ate at the market, and people of the market would think that he ate at home. He maintained this routine for twenty years in his early life,[100] offering another exemplary practice in the heart of a business center. As noted by scholars, his proclivity for "ascetic hunger" appears to have stayed with him throughout his life.[101] Baghdad's urban space is much larger than its business and administrative components, however.[102] Some Sufis often attended houses of entertainment and assemblies where well-known male and female singers allowed them to experience ecstatic states inspired by the music (*ṭarab*) within. *Ṭarab*, as Michael Frishkopf defines it, is "an emotional resonance among participants, powerful enough to create *wiḥdat al-shuᶜūr* (unity of feeling). It is an *insijām* (harmony) and *tabaddul al-shuᶜūr* (exchange of feeling) among participants, or even the 'melting' (*dhawb*) of individual identities into one."[103] Baghdad provided a great variety of these houses of entertainment and assemblies. Thus Abū al-Fatḥ al-Ṣūfī (d. 1234) would attend an assembly where a specific slave singer used to sing a verse by ᶜAbd al-Ṣamad Ibn al-Muᶜazzal: "Your wished for face is our proof when people bring proofs."[104] The metaphorical dimension of "face" and "proof" here connect the Sufi with the beauty of the Divine, leading to the experience of ecstatic union. What the Sufi hears and understands may not elicit the same response in the rest of the audience. No less a Sufi master than al-Shiblī was known to fall into an ecstatic state upon listening to Ibn Tūmar's singing. Others experienced the same upon listening to the recitation of the Qurᵓān by Abū Bahlūl al-Kūfī.[105]

This variegated space of markets, taverns, assemblies, and houses of entertainment provides us with an index to Baghdad's heterogeneity: a city that accommodated all types of Sufis opens itself to a reading of its interior, which I read as interstitial, allowing for the pleasurable metamorphoses into a state of ecstasy that takes the Sufi to the infinite. So great was the attachment to city life that it generated queries and elicited responses that grew into treatises:

> It was said in *Ḥilyat al-Awliyāʾ* that Junayd said: "Al-Ḥārith al-Muḥāsibī used to come to our house and say: 'Come out for a stroll with me.' I would say to him: 'And let you take me away from my seclusion and security to the streets, the realm of evil and lustful sights!' He would say: 'Come out with me and don't be scared!' So I would go out with him. The street used to be empty of everything – we do not see anything to dislike! And whenever I came across Muḥāsibī, in the place where he would sit, he would say to me, 'Ask me something!' I would tell him, 'I do not have a single question to ask you!' He would say, 'Ask me about anything that comes to your mind!' Questions would then rain down upon me and I would ask him about them. He would answer them for me on the spot and then go to his house and put them into writing."[106]

To conclude, the cityscape, as perceived through Sufi sites like shrines, resonates with feelings of mourning and latent protest that permeate current writings on the Sufis of Baghdad. Sufi shrines, along with other sites like mosques and markets, present a cartography of Abbasid Baghdad as read and engaged with in Sufis' everyday practice. The fact that these sites continue to carry the names of the Sufi masters in popular memory despite the sites' renaming can be read as an act of social and political resistance. The "sustained popular memory of sites bearing the names of Baghdad Sufi masters relegates renaming to naught."[107] Thus memory functions as a scriptorium and register of Sufism as it progresses from early esotericism to its mature form, something that can be considered a "massive education in a tradition of protest."[108] In sum, recent interest in the Sufis of Baghdad reflects the unease that modern Arab intellectuals feel with respect to the transformation of the city's space to conform to the politics of the modern nation state and its ideological apparatus. In the hands of these intellectuals, Sufi itineraries serve as a kind of oblique criticism while simultaneously providing a topography of the city that resonates in the popular imaginary with both the piety and protest of its past Sufi masters.

Notes

1. Jāsim (1990). For more on Jāsim's Sufism, see Driss (2004: 71–87).
2. Al-ᶜAlawī (1997).
3. Al-Tall (2009).
4. Lefebvre (1991: 52).
5. Al-ᶜAlawī (1997: 34).
6. Al-Tall (2009: 50).
7. Unless otherwise stated, all translations from Arabic sources are mine.
8. Ibid.: 21–7; al-ᶜAlawī (1997: 57).
9. Cited in Jāsim (1990: 37).
10. Cited in Jāsim (1990: 33); al-Baghdādī (1417 AH: 1: 70).
11. Cited in Jāsim (1990: 33); al-Baghdādī (1417 AH: 1: 71).
12. Al-Baghdādī (1417 AH: 1: 74–75).
13. Antrim (2012: 55–60).
14. de Certeau (1984: xi).
15. On binarism, see for example Watenpaugh (2005: 535–65).
16. Schimmel (2011: 21); and Arberry (1950: 121–2).
17. For a brief discussion on how some Sufis were persecuted in their times, see Schimmel (2011: 60, 68). On practices shunned by traditionalists, see Karamustafa (2015: 101–2, 107–10).
18. de Certeau (1984: xi).
19. Ibid.: xii.
20. Foucault (1986: 6).
21. I would like to thank Ernest Tan Sze Shen for creating the map of Baghdad that accompanies this chapter.
22. Lassner (1970: 173); Massignon (1982: 1: 284–5).
23. Arnheim (1988). Cited in Moretti (2005: 24).
24. Ibid.: 39.
25. de Certeau (1984: 4).
26. See Schimmel (2011: 60, 84).
27. Jāsim (1990: 33); al-Baghdādī (1417 AH: 1: 71).
28. Jāsim (1990: 36).
29. See Karamustafa (2015: 103–4).
30. Al-Tall (2009: 326–43).
31. Al-Mināwī (1999: 1: 564–5).
32. de Certeau (1984: xiv–xv).
33. Al-ᶜAlawī (1997: 40).

34. Cited in al-Tall (2009: 31–3).
35. Al-ᶜAlawī (1997: 35).
36. Ibid.: 35–6.
37. Al-Takarlī (1980).
38. Al-Musawi (2006: 148).
39. Bourdieu (1996).
40. See Karamustafa (2015).
41. Al-Tall (2009: 52).
42. Jāsim (1990: 116).
43. Ibid.: 129–30.
44. Ibid.
45. Massignon (1982: 1: 224).
46. Gosetti-Ferencei (2007: 302).
47. Schimmel (2011: 61); Arberry (1950: 74–83).
48. Jāsim (1990: 60).
49. Moretti (1998: 116).
50. Jāsim (1990: 48).
51. Ibid.: 75–6.
52. Conversion to Sufism was not unique to Bishr al-Ḥāfī. Al-Tall cites many converts. See al-Tall (2009: 55).
53. For more on the change of his life, see al-Mināwī (1999: 1: 557–8).
54. Al-Tall, *Mutaṣwwifat Baghdād fī al-Qarn al-Sādis al-Hijrī,* 53.
55. Jāsim (1990: 85).
56. Ibid.: 81.
57. Massignon (1982: 1: 234–5).
58. Cited in Jāsim (1990: 82).
59. Massignon (1982: 263).
60. Al-ᶜAlawī (1997: 41).
61. Ibid.: 24.
62. Ibid.
63. Ibid.
64. Jāsim (1990: 72).
65. Al-ᶜAlawī (1997: 35); al-Tall (1990: 84).
66. Massignon (1957) lists his preaching by place: visits to notables (nos. 39, 40, 42); preaching in the market (nos. 10, 36, 38, 45, 52); mosques (nos. 5, 11, 43, 46, 50); at home (nos. 7, 42–4, 51, 73). See also Massignon (1982: 1: 226).
67. Cited in Massignon (1957: no. 36; 1982: 1: 285).
68. Massignon (1982: 1: 284).

69. Al-Jāhiẓ (2008: 3:439).
70. Ibid.: 283.
71. Massignon (1957: no. 39). Cited in Massignon (1982: 1: 287).
72. Massignon (1957: nos. 11, 16); Massignon (1982: 1: 288)
73. de Certeau (1984: 115).
74. Massignon (1982: 1: 266–94).
75. Moretti (1998: 5).
76. Al-ᶜAlawī (1997: 36).
77. Jāsim(1990: 126).
78.Ibid. See also al-ᶜAlawī (1997: 36).
79. Al-Ghazālī (2000: 188–9).
80. Ibid.
81. Ibid.
82. Ibid; for more, see Schimmel (2011: 60).
83. The term was first used by Raymond Williams in his *Preface to Film* (with Michael Orrom, 1954), developed in *The Long Revolution* (1961), and extended and elaborated throughout his work, in particular *Marxism and Literature* (1977). Williams first used this concept to characterize the lived experience of the quality of life at a particular time and place. It is, he argued, "as firm and definite as 'structure' suggests, yet it operates in the most delicate and least tangible part of our activities." Later he describes structures of feeling as "social experiences in solution." Thus a "structure of feeling" is the Culture of a particular historical moment, though in developing the concept, Williams wished to avoid idealist notions of a "spirit of the age." The industrial novel of the 1840s would be one example of the structure of feeling which emerged in middle-class consciousness out of the development of industrial capitalism. See Bourne Taylor (1997).
84. Al-ᶜAlawī (1997: 37–40).
85. Foucault (1986: 3).
86. Jāsim (1990: 51).
87. Ibid.: 153. See also Melchert (1996: 66–70).
88. Al-Tall (2009: 10–11).
89. Jāsim (1990: 48); al-ᶜAlawī (1997: 40); al-Tall (2009: 206).
90. Jāsim (1990: 48); Karamustafa (2007: 23).
91. Karamustafa (2007: 163).
92. Al-ᶜAlawī (1997: 40).
93. Ibid.: 119.
94. Al-Tall (2009: 304–10).

95. Jāsim (1990: 120).
96. Schimmel (2011: 57).
97. Ibid.
98. Cited in Jāsim (1990: 165).
99. Massignon (1982: 1: 281).
100. Jāsim (1990: 44).
101. Karamustafa (2007: 11).
102. On Baghdad's commercial life, see Lassner (1970: 173).
103. Frishkopf (2001: 15).
104. Jāsim (1990: 47).
105. Ibid.: 48.
106. Cited in ibid.: 103.
107. Al-Tall (2009: 84).
108. Al-ᶜAlawī (1997: 35).

Works Cited

Al-ᶜAlawī, Hādī (1997), *Madārāt Ṣūfiyya*, Damascus: Dār al-Madā lil Thaqāfa wal-Nashr.

Antrim, Zayde (2012), *Routes and Realms: The Power of Place in the Early Islamic World*, Oxford: Oxford University Press.

Arberry, A. J. (1950), *Sufism: An Account of the Mystics of Islam*, New York NY: Dover Publications, Inc.

Arnheim, Rudolf (1988), *The Power of the Center: A Study of Composition in the Visual Arts*, Berkeley CA: University of California Press.

Al-Baghdādī, al-Khatīb (1417 AH), *Tārīkh Baghdād*, Muṣṭafā ᶜAbdul Qādir ᶜAṭā (ed.), Beirut: Dār al-Kutub al-ᶜIlmiyya.

Bourdieu, Pierre (1996), *The State Nobility: Elite Schools in the Field of Power*, trans. Lauretta C. Clough, Stanford CA: Stanford University Press.

Bourne Taylor, Jenny (1997), *Dictionary of Cultural and Critical Theory*, Michael Payne (ed.), Malden MA and Oxford: Wiley-Blackwell, Blackwell Reference Online http://www.blackwellreference.com/public/book?id=g9780631207535_9780631207535 (accessed 14 November 2017).

De Certeau, Michel (1984), *The Practice of Everyday Life*, trans. Steven F. Rendall, Berkeley CA: University of California Press.

Driss, Hager Ben (2004), "The Unholy Trinity: Sex and Mysticism in Azīz al-Sayyid Jāsim's Narratives," *Journal of Arabic Literature* 35. 1: 71–87.

Foucault, Michel (1986), "Of Other Spaces: Utopias and Heterotopias," trans. Jay Miskowiec, *Diacritics* 16. 1: 22–7.

Frishkopf, Michael (2001), "Tarab in the Mystic Sufi Chant of Egypt," in S. Zuhur (ed.), *Colors of Enchantment: Visual and Performing Arts of the Middle East*, Cairo: American University in Cairo Press.

Al-Ghazālī, Abū Ḥāmid (2000), "Treatise on Ḥisbah from *Iḥyā*ᵓ *ᶜUlūm al-Dīn*," in ᶜAbd al-Raḥmān Naṣr al-Shayrazī, *Nihāyat al-Rutba fī Ṭalab al-Ḥisba*, trans. Ronald Paul Buckley, Oxford: Oxford University Press, 188–9.

Gosetti-Ferencei, Jennifer Anna (2007), "Interstitial Space in Rilke's Short Prose Works," *The German Quarterly* 80.3 (Summer): 302–24.

Al-Jāhiẓ, Abū ᶜUthmān ᶜAmr Ibn Baḥr (2008), *Kitāb al-Ḥayawān*, Īmān al-Shaykh Muḥammad and ᶜAzīz al-Shaykh Muḥammad (eds), Beirut: Dār al-Kitāb al-ᶜArabī.

Jāsim, Azīz al-Sayyid (1990), *Mutaṣawwifat Baghdād*, Beirut: al-Markaz al-Thaqāfī al-ᶜArabī.

Karamustafa, Ahmet (2007), *Sufism: The Formative Period*, Berkeley CA: University of California Press.

—— (2015), "Antinomian Sufis," in Lloyd Ridgeon (ed.), *The Cambridge Companion to Sufism*, Cambridge: Cambridge University Press, 101–24.

Lassner, Jacob (1970), *The Topography of Baghdad in the Early Middle Ages: Text and Studies*, Detroit MI: Wayne University Press.

Lefebvre, Henri (1991), "The Production of Space," trans. Donald Nicholson-Smith, Oxford: Wiley-Blackwell.

Massignon, Louis (1957), *Akhbār al-Hallāj: Recueil d'Oraisons et d'Exhortations du Martyr Mystique de l'Islam Husayn Ibn Manṣūr Ḥalāj*, Paris: Vrin.

—— (1982), *The Passion of al-Hallāj: Mystic and Martyr of Islam*, trans. Herbert Mason, Princeton NJ: Princeton University Press.

Melchert, Christopher (1996), "The Transition from Asceticism to Mysticism in the Middle of the Ninth Century CE," *Studia Islamica*, 83: 66–70.

Al-Mināwī, Zayn al-Ḍīn Muḥammad ᶜAbd al-Raᵓūf (1999), *Ṭabaqāt al-Ṣūfiyya: Al-Kawākib al-Dhuriyya fī Tarājim al-Sāda al-Ṣūfiyya*, Muḥammad Adīb al-Jādir (ed.), Beirut: Dār Ṣādir.

Moretti, Franco (1998), *Atlas of the European Novel: 1800–1900*, London and New York NY: Verso.

—— (2005), *Graphs, Maps, Trees*, London and New York NY: Verso.

Al-Musawi, Muhsin (2006), *Arabic Poetry: Trajectories of Modernity and Tradition*, New York NY: Routledge.

Schimmel, Annemarie (2011), *Mystical Dimensions of Islam*, Chapel Hill: University of North Carolina Press.

Al-Takarlī, Fuᵓād (1980), *al-Rajᶜ al-Baᶜīd*, Beirut: Dār Ibn Rushd.

Al-Tall, ᶜUmar Salīm Abd al-Qādir (2009), *Mutaṣwwifat Baghdād fi-l-Qarn al-Sādis al-Hijrī/al-Thānī ᶜAshar al-Mīlādī: Dirāsa Tārīkhiyya* (The Sufis of Baghdad in Sixth Century AH/Twelfth Century: A Historical Study), Ammān: Dār al-Ma᾿mūn lil Nashr wal Tawzīᶜ.

Watenpaugh, Heghnar Zeitlian (2005), "Deviant Dervishes: Space, Gender, and the Construction of Antinomian Piety in Ottoman Aleppo," *International Journal of Middle East Studies* 37.4 (Nov.): 535–65.

13

Baṣrayātha: Self-portrait as a City

William Maynard Hutchins

> In my head there is a map of the city: each street, house, coffee shop, date palm, river, oar, and sail to the south, along with the familiar faces of my friends.[1]

Premise and Method

Baṣrayātha, the celebrated contemporary Iraqi author Muḥammad Khuḍayyir's memoir as a cityscape, is a unique way of writing both the Arab city and a self-portrait. Since demonstrating a work's uniqueness is a fool's errand or a lifetime task, this chapter will instead attempt a meditative interpretation of *Baṣrayātha* by providing a careful analysis of the text through the mirror of Khuḍayyir's extensive literary criticism and other works of fiction.

Introduction

Khuḍayyir in *Baṣrayātha* instructs the reader cryptically that: "Before Baṣra, there was Baṣrayātha."[2] In other words, the city's model existed before the real city. In this work Khuḍayyir merges narrator and city, style and content, drawing on an eclectic group of inspirations, both medieval and modern, Middle Eastern and European. Thus he creates the literary equivalent of a secret spice blend[3] including: a Neo-Cubist collage style, a mixture of narrative and discursive sections, an emphasis on the storyteller who creates and preserves a city, the use of vintage photographs as part of the text rather than illustrations for it, the author's self-conscious construction of a model city – which by reference to Foucault he terms a heterotopia – rather than a narrative that uses a protagonist or a family to personify a city or a country, and the way in which the model city he creates crosses over into his other works. Each element of *Baṣrayātha* has mirrored or prefigured – as if in a cut-glass *muqarnas* (a squinch composed of many little squinches) – other Arabic-language novels, but Khuḍayyir's precise combination is unlikely to be paralleled or to have been paralleled. Fabio Caiani and Catherine Cobham refer, for example, to his Arabic prose style as "one of the most original to appear in the last few decades ..."[4]

Baṣrayātha as Model and Collage

In *Baṣrayātha*, Khuḍayyir constructs a model of his native city: Baṣra, Iraq, from a collage of fragments from a memoir. Each of us, consciously or not, forms a mental map of the community in which she lives, and this contains streets, stores, and restaurants but also events like the puppet parade on the Fourth of July and people like the young autistic man who once laughed in arpeggios while splashing water into the air at the county swimming pool. *Baṣrayātha* draws on accounts of Baṣra's history through the centuries, including those of other storytellers. Childhood memories, folklore, local history, and traditional storytelling all inspire this work, as do Foucault and Plato.

Baṣrayātha is, then, a collage of dream and story fragments, and in *al-Ḥikāya al-Jadīda* ("The New Story"), a collection of his essays of literary criticism, Khuḍayyir writes:

> In my latest stories I have received from somewhere, from a time of invisible inspiration, a collection of voices that finally evolve into visible images ... In the beginning I did not possess – before I planned the story – any clear sequence of actual, visual scenes or synchronization with a tangible, real experience that would help shape events the person receiving the inspiration could compare with a previous source. I received parts of incoherent images and sounds like wind whistling musically through the reeds of the marshlands or into perforated metal posts planted in the desert to mark the route for caravans. The sounds came before the images, and this is what I call "presentiments of the vision," since no path yet existed to a full portrayal of an event, characters, or plot.[5]

In a book-length work of fiction, *Kurrāsat Kānūn* ("January Sketchbook") Khuḍayyir explains his approach to writing further:

> I choose the decisive moment when I am united with all the faces I depict and write. I have chosen my moment, and I am here and there, in the writing and outside of it ...[6]

In the chapter of *Baṣrayātha* called "First Exploration," the young narrator explores Baṣra with friends, with whom he merges, and discovers Baṣrayātha. In "The Ḥammam of Happiness," a section of the chapter "Friday's Gifts," Khuḍayyir's narrator recounts that, after passing through the various chambers of the public bath: "our bodies unite into a single naked form that sinks into the large basin ..."[7] Later, in "Moons and String Instruments," Khuḍayyir as a character in his book walks through Baṣra and hears a war-damaged electric pole whistle in the night wind and comments: "That was when musical light posts entered the desert of Baṣrayātha."[8]

While writing *Baṣrayātha*, Khuḍayyir used stories from Baṣrans of various centuries and incorporated "found" stories (comparable to found or ready-made objects in the visual arts – like Marcel Duchamp's urinal and bicycle wheel). In an interview included in *al-Ḥikāya al-Jadīda*, he explains that this was more than a technique or strategy:

> Many individuals ... intervene in the construction of my story ... My father, mother, brothers, friends, children, pupils, and characters visit in broad daylight. They all demand their legacy. This includes the banquet of the cemeteries, the desert of goodness, and "The Castle of al-Sarūjī" ... which are inherited by traveling, peace-loving, joyful storytellers – living and dead – who are helpful and encouraging. I believe that we are not free to write [merely] what we want.[9]

Khuḍayyir's interaction with his city is transmitted in both narrative and discursive passages (like the four prefaces or "Points of Entry")[10] as the author and city in effect create each other. Chapters like "First Exploration" are composed of words strung like semi-precious stones on a necklace. Khuḍayyir wrote in the preface for his short story collection entitled *Ruʾyat Kharīf* ("Autumn Vision"): "There is no harm now ... in admitting the 'affective cloak' [*jubba wijdaniyya*] and the stylistic intensity [*shidda uslubiyya*] that clothe my stories."[11]

When *Baṣrayātha*'s translator asked Khuḍayyir about a string of words in "The Ḥammam of Happiness," he replied that the words italicized below were chosen to create a mood rather than to describe items found in a bathhouse in Baṣra:

> I descend to the warm changing room – *oleander flowers, cotton boll, and stick cinnamon* – and proceed to the benches ... spread with waist wraps and wet towels.[12]

Khuḍayyir has invoked Picasso's Cubism to help explain his approach to writing and recounted a familiar story told by Gertrude Stein about Picasso. After she endured eighty sittings for her portrait, Picasso painted out her face and left Paris for Spain. Then, without seeing her again, he completed the portrait.[13] Stein wrote presciently, "The rose period ended with my portrait …"[14] Khuḍayyir has referred to Picasso's portrait of Gertrude Stein as a Cubist work that foreshadowed his writing style in which disparate images gathered from memory are reassembled with a verisimilitude not based on a one-to-one correlation between physical reality and the model of it.

Referring to Dora Maar's photographs of the stages through which Picasso's painting *Guernica* progressed, Khuḍayyir writes in *Kurrāsat Kānūn* that the sketches for it, "portrayed the stages of entry into the labyrinth of the dream in which the minotaur (the man/bull) was imprisoned, and then the exit from it as misshapen body parts and amputated limbs."[15]

Picasso himself explained:

> In the old days pictures went forward toward completion by stages … A picture used to be a sum of additions. In my case a picture is a sum of destructions. I do a picture – then I destroy it. In the end, though, nothing is lost; the red I took away from one place turns up somewhere else.[16]

Khuḍayyir, too, mentions destruction and construction when discussing model cities in *al- Ḥikāya al-Jadīda*:

> An adequate amount of consideration of previous utopias for types of imaginary cities in our era will goad a contemporary author to persist in attempts at destruction and construction …[17]

He explains his approach further (if somewhat murkily) in *Kurrāsat Kānūn*:

> The only hope for these sketches is sharing in a communal exhibition of hidden dreams and approaching the minotaur's archives – a symbol shared by the subterranean labyrinths of the ancient world as well as by the new world's aircraft carriers, which navigate the high seas."[18]

In *al-Sard wa-l-Kitāb* ("The Narrative and the Book"), a work of literary criticism, Khuḍayyir writes that paintings by Henri Rousseau and David Siqueiros and sculptures by Giacometti influenced the composition of his short story "A Scream" but admitted it was difficult for him to reconstruct how.[19] Khuḍayyir is arguably one of the better-informed members of his generation of Arab authors with regard to the plastic arts. The cover of *Kurrāsat Kānūn* features reproductions of *Guernica*, Goya's *The Sleep of Reason Produces Monsters*, and a depiction by Henry Moore of people sleeping underground in London during World War II. Judged by its cover, this book was intended as a protest against war and violence. Its cover art – like *Baṣrayātha*'s vintage photographs – is surely an integral part of the book.[20] When the quality of the photographs in the Arabic text was not adequate for reproduction in the English translation, Khuḍayyir selected a new set of vintage images to form part of the completed collage that is *Baṣrayātha*.

Despite all his talk about Picasso's Cubism, the actual works Khuḍayyir mentions (*Gertrude Stein*, 1905–6, *Les Desmoiselles d'Avignon*, 1907, and *Guernica*, 1937) either preceded or followed Picasso's signature Cubist works.[21] Khuḍayyir's comments suggest that *Baṣrayātha* represents an art form more like collage than stereotypical prismatic Cubism. Picasso's collage approach to the painting of *Guernica* and Khuḍayyir's collage style of writing in *Baṣrayātha* differ from the Dada-era collage poems or the cut-ups of Brion Gysin and William Burroughs, because Picasso and Khuḍayyir dismembered and recombined their own designs and dreams. From 1935 to 1959, though, Picasso did write verbal poetry suggestive of downloads from consciousness. Jerome Rothenberg, who translated some of these works, wrote that their "intensities and densities come into the poetry before … they inform the paintings."[22]

As a collage of stories mixed with discursive insights, *Baṣrayātha* is a book that al-Jāḥiẓ (d. 868 CE), Baṣra's greatest Arabic stylist, might welcome as a descendant of his *adab*, which could be described as edifying essays larded with poems and anecdotes.[23] Al-Jāḥiẓ drew a few of his anecdotes from his personal experiences. His *Kitāb al-Bukhalāʾ* (The Book of Misers) offers a good precedent for *Baṣrayātha*, because it consists of a series of portraits of stingy men in Baṣra (and some other communities), but lacks the feeling of collage found in either his own epistles (*Rasāʾil*) or *Baṣrayātha*.[24] In "Before I Was Born, If I Truly Was Born," the second "Point of Entry to Baṣrayātha," Khuḍayyir imagines al-Jāḥiẓ in Baṣrayātha, before there was a Baṣra, rubbing shoulders with someone resembling Khuḍayyir. That alter ego "lived the book before me."[25] He also wrote: "If not for his book 'The Misers,' al-Jāḥiẓ would not have existed."[26] Khuḍayyir clearly belongs to a rich succession of Baṣra authors, medieval and modern.

In *al-Sard wa-l-Kitāb*, though, Khuḍayyir refers not to *adab* or to al-Jāḥiẓ but to *iqtibās* – which can refer to the use of an unacknowledged quote from the Qurʾān – as in Abū Ḥayyān al-Tawḥīdī's book *al-Muqābasāt*.[27] *Iqtibās* in this instance, according to Khuḍayyir, however, is a term comparable to *tanāṣṣ* or intertextuality. Yet in an essay entitled "Akthar min Tanāṣṣ" ("More Than Intertextuality"), Khuḍayyir mentions not the Qur'ān or al-Jāḥiẓ but Umberto Eco's chapter "The Novel as Cosmological Event" in his *Postscript to* The Name of the Rose,[28] where Eco refers to a river as "an intertextual space."[29] Baṣrayātha (or *Baṣrayātha*?) is surely another such intertextual space.

The Qur'ān itself was revealed to the Prophet Muḥammad in segments that were eventually reassembled and recorded in the best possible order – but not in the order in which they were revealed. In Sūra 17, verse 106, for example, God says that He revealed the Qur'ān in stages. For pious Muslims, the Holy Qur'ān established the standard for Arabic literature; perhaps it is not only an example of a religious (or divine) literary collage but an inspiration for instances of intertextuality like those in works by al-Jāḥiẓ, al-Tawḥīdī, and Khuḍayyir.

Finally – one more point about collage – in an elegant and lengthy tribute to the twentieth-century Baghdad author ᶜAbd al-Malik Nūrī, Khuḍayyir describes Nūrī, as:

> The maestro of this approach, that of free association, which distributes fragmented voices and interconnected chatter and then traces tattoos on crumbling bodies.[30]

This quote suggests another (Iraqi) stream leading to the river of collage, and his metaphor of a tattoo also suggests superimposed tattoos of influence – a collage of tattoos.

The Storyteller

Khuḍayyir has emphasized the need he feels to encourage younger generations of Baṣrans to continue telling the story of Baṣra. No city is bigger than its story or even exists without a story, and a city's residents have a duty to keep their hometown's stories fresh by retelling them.[31] In a lengthy review of *Baṣrayātha*, Shakit Mustafa mentions the paradox that although Khuḍayyir portrays himself as a simple storyteller, "accidentally thrown into the business of salvaging stories … " he is also clearly an author with "a shameless desire to perfect his craft."[32] Each observer is potentially a storyteller described in this way by Khuḍayyir in *al-Ḥikāya al-Jadīda*:

> The storyteller's memory need be no larger than an apothecary's shop, where the scents of herbs, seeds, and oils mix together … [His] hands reach

for numerous boxes – [and he] distinguishes between their familiar scents to select the container he needs.[33]

Khuḍayyir seems to allude to a storyteller's secret spice blend here. In *Baṣrayātha*'s chapter "Abū al-Khaṣīb: Story Road" Khuḍayyir invites readers to:

> Imagine with me a man whose job is collecting stories. What road would he take? What would he ride? Who would he be?
>
> I knew … the last man … who held this profession.[34]

Then, later, Khuḍayyir repeats advice from that storyteller:

> Stroke the void, drink silence, and breathe to your last gasp. Then close your eyes and allow things to settle into the furrows of your memory … the story will come to you and unfold like a mute flower …"[35]

Here the fictional storyteller echoes Khuḍayyir's own collage approach to writing.

According to Khuḍayyir, a successful vision emerges in "disordered images" – think collages – but he states in *al-Ḥikāya al-Jadīda*:

> It is not the goal of a visionary storyteller … to convince the reader of real occurrences or to narrate the life of characters. His goal is, rather, to confirm the reality of the formation of a visual image from unseen associations …[36]

The reference here to a visual image is a telling hint of a collage and of the influence of the visual arts on Khuḍayyir's works.

In *Baṣrayātha*, when the governor searches for the storyteller after the devastating plague of 1831, he is told that the man had been mistaken for a thief and killed. Then he, sensibly or even necessarily, demands that a new storyteller be found.[37] In "al-Zubayr: The Camel's Eye," in addition to the storyteller, Khuḍayyir introduces the word-weaver: "One sand dune asks another 'Where is the word-weaver?'"[38] His words lead people "with language's plaited ropes …"[39] This word-weaver appears with or is himself a figure the Baṣran scholar Nadeen Odeh refers to in her thesis on the English translation of *Baṣrayātha* as a "jester."

In *al-Ḥikāya al-Jadīda*, Khuḍayyir writes that the house of fiction has many windows, and that the observer at each window is assured "an impression distinct from every other."[40] With specific reference to short stories, he writes in an essay called "al-Ruʾya al-Marʾiyya" (The Visible Vision") that also appears in *al-Ḥikāya al-Jadīda*:

> The short story is content with a brief view from a small window of a few transitory characters … They come from one place and go someplace else. Through this small aperture we can see only details or parts of the big scene of external reality. Great events may occur outside, but for us – even though we hear only echoes and see only glints and hints of them – they strike our souls like a thunderbolt stronger and brighter than any pyrotechnics from great matters and mighty events lumped together. When, occasionally, this small window is blocked, the outside still remains a primary source of our concepts, expectations, impressions, and memories.[41]

In *al-Ḥikāya al-Jadīda* as well Khuḍayyir quotes approvingly – from Edgar Allan Poe's second review of Hawthorne's *Twice-told Tales* – Poe's praise for a writer who thinks first of the effect he desires and only "then invents such incidents … as may best aid him in establishing this preconceived effect."[42] Khuḍayyir liked Poe's emphasis on "the unity of effect or impression …"[43] and states that a storyteller should unite himself with his style and his style with his subject as quickly as possible.[44] One way for a storyteller to unite style and subject would be to follow Khuḍayyir and make his memoir a tribute to his hometown.

Baṣrayātha as Heterotopia

Philip Glass writes in his memoir that he realized early in his career:

> Music was no longer a metaphor for the real world somewhere out there. It was becoming the opposite. The "out there" stuff was the metaphor and the real part was, and is to this day, the music. Night trains can make these things happen.[45]

Night trains appear in *Baṣrayātha*[46] (and are themselves heterotopias), but the salient point here is that a metaphor or model can, depending on a person's perspective, become the reality, while reality is the metaphor or model.

In "Utopias and Heterotopias," the third of the "Four Points of Entry to Baṣrayātha," Khuḍayyir makes it clear that while model cities like Baṣrayātha are inspired by existing cities, they have also served as models for cities, at least since the time of Plato's *Republic*.[47] In an essay entitled "Madīnat al-Ruʾya" (City of the Vision) in *al-Ḥikāya al-Jadīda*, Khuḍayyir surveys literary utopias and dystopias and begins:

> An issue that preoccupied writers and philosophers in the early history of thought was the organization of the good life in a model city ... In a world threatened by depletion of food supplies, environmental pollution, and general destruction, the ancient dream of a happy utopia is subject to an alarming, nightmare perversion ...[48]

He concedes:

> It must be admitted that the famous utopias of the past were a lofty product of a lofty intellect and that each of them was a gift to mankind from Prometheus. Just as he failed in his struggle with the gods of Olympus, the utopia has failed in its struggle with the lords of the machine. When the utopia wished to idolize the age of the machine, the industrial revolution swept it away.[49]

Thus, *Baṣrayātha* is a continuation both of a series of utopias beginning with Plato's *Republic* and of dystopias including Orwell's *1984*.[50]

Although Plato's *Republic* is a utopia, most readers today find more than a few dystopian aspects in it. Similarly, as a model for Baṣra, Baṣrayātha is a utopia, but as a memoir of life in Baṣra, it is partly a dystopia. In "I Should Erase and Draw," a section of the final chapter "Morning Airs and Nocturnes: A War Diary," Khuḍayyir chronicles the devastation he and two friends found on an automobile excursion during the Iran–Iraq War as well as their hopes for the future:

> Each of us was concocting his own stew: what he would erase and draw ... He should sweep up all the shattered glass and install a new façade ... We should erase a city and build a paradise.[51]

According to Khuḍayyir:

> Here in the Islamic East, there has been no project for a terrestrial utopia since *al-Madīna al-Fāḍila* with which al-Fārābī wished to update Plato's *Republic.*

A new initiative:

> Will push us farther toward the common springs of the human vision in a region that has many names ... a region hanging between nowhere and a real place.[52]

Khuḍayyir already considered Baṣrayātha to be a mirror for Baṣra before he read an essay on heterotopias by Michel Foucault. That essay offered him an alternative way of articulating what he was doing.[53] Foucault writes:

> The mirror is, after all, a utopia, since it is a place without place … But it is also a heterotopia in so far as the mirror does really exist … The mirror functions as a heterotopia in the respect that it renders this place that I occupy at the moment when I look at myself in the looking glass at once absolutely real, connected with all the space that surrounds it, and absolutely unreal, since, in order to be perceived it has to pass through this virtual point, which is over there.[54]

Foucault's use of a mirror to illustrate the meaning of "heterotopia" also illustrates one of this essay's themes: that Baṣrayātha mirrors both Baṣra and Khuḍayyir.

According to Foucault, primitive societies had what he termed crisis heterotopias, which were reserved for "adolescents, menstruating women, pregnant women, the elderly, etc."[55] As societies developed, these were eventually replaced by "heterotopias of deviation" reserved "for individuals whose behavior is deviant in relation to the required mean …" As a society progresses through its history, its heterotopian/mirror spaces change their function in interesting ways.[56]

In "Utopias and Heterotopias," the third of the "Four Points of Entry to Baṣrayātha," Khuḍayyir offers a detailed summary of Foucault's discussion of the various types of heterotopias and concludes with the ship, which in Khuḍayyir's model world is also "the train … a mobile city." Ships and trains are, according to Khuḍayyir, "a great storehouse for the imagination and a way to travel toward cities lacking any real existence except as mirrors of real places."[57] In *Baṣrayātha*'s seventh chapter, a train's coach demonstrates "the validity of the notion that every Iraqi has the potential to become a storyteller …"[58] The river is also a heterotopia – "a mobile prisoner that welcomes its season, breaks its fetters, and guides its ships …"[59] It is also, as in the quotation from Eco cited earlier, an intertextual space. The desert as portrayed in "Al-Zubayr: The Camel's Eye" is a heterotopia, and the Iran–Iraq War in "Morning Airs and Nocturnes: A War Diary" is one too.[60] "Garden, river, desert, and railway stations are happy, miniature worlds" when observed in the mirror of a heterotopia or when they serve as one.[61] Are they not also happy miniature collages?

Cemeteries surely are heterotopias, and the subtitle for "Umm al-Burūm," *Baṣrayātha*'s third chapter, is "Banquet in a Cemetery." "Al-Zubayr: The

Camel's Eye," the sixth chapter, ends with another cemetery and the cobbler to the dead:

> Anyone who quickly traverses the souk in the dark of the night will see a slender thread of light stealing from cracks in the panels of the closed door, because the cobbler's spirit is busy making another pair of sandals, since in order to enter their world the dead need red leather footwear, handcrafted by a cobbler from al-Zubayr.[62]

Foucault also points out that "Heterotopias are most often linked to slices of time … heterochronisms." He adds: "The heterotopia begins to function fully when people find themselves in a sort of absolute break with their traditional time …"[63]

Baṣrayātha's eighth chapter, "Friday's Gifts," which is clearly a collage, celebrates a heterotopia in time, a heterochronism, because the Muslim Sabbath acts as a mirror for weekday life by, for example, providing trips to the cinema and the public bathhouse.[64] Khuḍayyir comments: "For an author, every day is Friday."[65] The city restaurant where a rural visitor dines on Friday "seems even larger on account of the mirrors, in which the villager observes his companions …"[66] The last phrase echoes Foucault's explanation of a heterotopia.

Khuḍayyir distinguishes between "unrealized utopias" and real constructions built according to utopian ideals. According to him, the former are inevitably "truer."[67] Foucault did not write extensively about the heterotopia, but the concept has caught on, especially among urban planners. Of course, Lewis Carroll went through this looking glass long before Foucault or Khuḍayyir did. Arguably he found a heterotopia or a dystopia there.

Baṣrayātha beyond *Baṣrayātha*

Like some literary characters – say Romeo and Juliet – Baṣrayātha has enjoyed an active life beyond the covers of *Baṣrayātha.* Baṣrayāthan (as opposed to the Baṣran) elements are evident in Khuḍayyir's quasi-novel *Kurrāsat Kānūn* ("January Sketchbook"), and Baṣrayātha is the setting for his short-story collection *Ruʾyat Kharīf* ("Autumn Vision"). The latter work's two-page preface, dated 1994, states that all its stories:

> reinforce each other and share a single vision … that has been nourished … by a single subject that is based in Baṣrayātha … in its times of war and of peace.[68]

In fact all the stories in *Ruʾyat Kharīf* are Baṣrayātha stories. The first question on the roster in "Ṣaḥīfat al-Tasāʾulāt" ("Roster of Questions") is:

> If the ascending road is the descending road, if the outbound road is also the inbound road, in which direction does Baṣrayātha lie?[69]

"Al- Ḥukamāʾ al-Thalātha" ("The Three Sages") offers a longer version of the story told about the important Baṣran poet Badr Shākir al-Sayyāb in "Umm al-Burūm: Banquet in a Cemetery" in *Baṣrayātha*.[70]

Oddly enough, some of the short stories about Baṣrayātha are more dystopian than *Baṣrayātha*. The opening paragraph of "Dama, Dami, Damu" explains, for example, the way the city's three genders play three potentially lethal Baṣrayāthan board games:

> Dama is the game of silence, a game of mute dialogue. I learned to play Dama when I was in prison. I believe that every Baṣrayāthan of the first gender has perfected this game. The second gender, on the other hand, is infatuated with the game Dami. Only Baṣrayāthans of the third gender have mastered the game Damu. Just a few of all of these citizens play all three games perfectly. Such scattered masters combine a skill at concealing their genders with their artistic play.[71]

Bored with being limited to two genders? Move to Baṣrayātha, where there are three.

In *Fī Darajat 45 Miʾawī* ("At 45 Degrees Centigrade"), another collection of Khuḍayyir's short stories, there is a fuller account of the historic 1831 plague mentioned earlier that occurred in both Baṣra and Baṣrayātha in Khuḍayyir's story "Iḥtiḍār al-Rassām" ("The Painter's Death").[72]

Al-Ḥikāya al-Jadīda ends with a 1992 interview,[73] in which Khuḍayyir – after admitting that his quest "may be a wild-goose chase … and the exposition a fantasy" – refers to Baṣrayātha by name and hypothesizes that there might be "six, seven, or ten" more stories about it.[74] Khuḍayyir also refers to "the storyteller considered as a single character in all the stories" and predicts:

> The repeated voyage will take branching ways with improvised techniques, and interconnected stories … Each new printing of the stories will constitute an argument for the truth of the journey to the City of the Vision.[75]

Khuḍayyir's essay "Dhākirat al-ᶜAṭṭār" ("The Apothecary's Memory"), also in *al-Ḥikāyā al-Jadīda*, includes a paragraph that could fit unaltered into *Baṣrayātha*:

> Let us contemplate the scenes embedded in the consciousness of the story writer:
>
> A dirt road between two mud brick walls twisting through the inner reaches of a date plantation; a heavily shaded narrow creek overgrown by plants and grasses; the aged watchman's shack there; the trunk of a venerable tree deeply scarred by ropes from repeated moorings of boats; night-long drumming in an otherwise unremarkable corner of the city; a shoemaker who sews his last pair of sandals, which he will put on to rise to the heavens; a coppersmith who is oblivious to time and taps diligently on the throat of a container or a large cauldron; the apothecary's shop crowded with dust-laden containers ... as a blend of herbs, seeds, and oils scent the air.[76]

Several dots are connected: the storyteller, the collage technique, and the theme of a heterotopia.

Ḥasan Naṣr: An Exception whose Works Prove the Rule

Two possible exceptions to this chapter's claim that Khuḍayyir's formula in *Baṣrayātha* has no clear major rivals are *Dār al-Bāsha* (1998, *Return to Dar al-Basha*, 2006) and *Sijillāt Raʾs al-Dīk* (2001, Cockhead's Files) – both by the contemporary Tunisian author Ḥasan Naṣr. In the first work the author lyrically and vividly describes the coevolution of the protagonist and the Medīna of Tunis. In the second, he creates an imaginary world reminiscent of Tunisia – using the literary conceit of files spewed out by a crashing computer. Although I know of no direct link between these two authors, Naṣr has arguably written texts with a spice blend comparable to Khuḍayyir's.[77]

Naṣr's *Return to Dar al-Basha* is a set of stories of about Murtaḍa's painful childhood framed by an account of the protagonist as an adult finding his way back to his childhood home in the Medīna of Tunis after an absence of decades. The text's narration shifts (as does the Qurʾān) from third to first and to second person[78] as his protagonist, the narrator, and occasionally the reader merge.[79] The author enters this autobiographical story as a character, much as Khuḍayyir does in *Baṣrayātha*. Vignettes simultaneously depict the hero and the old city of Tunis – just as Khuḍayyir portrays himself by portraying Baṣra in *Baṣrayātha*. The farther Murtaḍa penetrates into the Medīna of Tunis, the deeper he digs into painful childhood memories.

Eventually his shattered ego is reflected by (or precipitates) a nightmarish earthquake that is followed by an idyllic ending. Murtaḍa, though, is an identifiable individual with a family and a back story, unlike Khuḍayyir's protagonist in *Baṣrayātha*, and does not merge with his peers as the narrator does in Khuḍayyir's novel. Finally, in contrast to *Baṣrayātha,* the novel has a plot that proceeds to a climax.

Naṣr's other text, *Sijillāt Ra'ˀs al-Dīk*, contains a science-fiction frame story that then has its own frame story, which may remind the reader of *The Thousand and One Nights* or even Roald Dahl's *James and the Giant Peach*. Most of the book consists of narratives allegedly derived from Mr. Cockhead's security agency's computer files, tales that are also vignettes of Tunisian life. The frame story's conclusion – found in the book's final chapter ("*Suqūṭ al-Ḥikāya*" or "The Tale's Downfall") – assures the reader that the stories narrated "do not contain a single truth." The author, with post-modernist bravado, announces the overthrow of the traditional story and the arrival of a prismatic narrative style: "Since the basis of storytelling is orderly arrangement, its downfall implies the rout of that order and of arrangement altogether."[80] When Khuḍayyir, for his part, announces "the new story," perhaps he and Naṣr were setting off on parallel journeys. In his "new story," however, Khuḍayyir seeks the simplicity of the ancient tale and emphasizes "enjoyment, imagination, and the invention of a new world."[81]

Baṣrayātha could be understood, like *Sijillāt Raˀs al-Dīk*, to be in part, a selection of files from the archives of an imaginary city where Khuḍayyir's archivist is the storyteller. There is certainly a hint of the heterotopia or dystopia in these novels by Ḥasan Naṣr, who is arguably a miniaturist at heart and most at home with the short story. Khuḍayyir has also primarily written short stories and once listed his only novel as *Kurrāsat Kānūn*, although in an email to *Baṣrayātha*'s translator, he wrote that it may be considered a novel as well.

"The short story," Khuḍayyir writes, "is the genre most appropriate for focusing a vision in a spontaneous moment."[82] He also defines the short story as: "a simple exposition (*burhān basīṭ*) of a truthful emotion (*infiᶜāl ṣādiq*)."[83] In his essay "Barāhīn Basīṭa" ("Simple Expositions") in *al-Ḥikāya al-Jadīda* Khuḍayyir writes that the short story loses its simplicity when its constituent elements are overemphasized:

> This simplicity reminds us of surprise autumn visions – a quivering paper that moist winds waft over the shore of reality or a dream, an inkling that illuminates the imagination and fills it with brilliant light, a message that

> throbs with mysterious symbols that have descended from the language of the first man.[84]

Both Khuḍayyir and Naṣr, moreover, occasionally tiptoe along the delirious line between coherence and incoherence. Here is Khuḍayyir:

> I rocked back and forth on a thin thread of wakefulness stretched between mulberry trees ... beneath setting suns and flying mirrors ... From tiny windows between the fronds, the features of a radiant, childish face appeared, bowing and smiling.[85]

And here is Ḥasan Naṣr in *Return to Dar al-Basha*:

> As you enter the Dār al-Bāsha neighbourhood, you discover the special aroma it derives from perfumes that waft in every direction ... As you advance down its covered streets ... you linger, contemplating spaces washed by rainbow colors and the soft light that steals through gaps between the fingers of the district's hands: peeking from the eyes of windows ... slipping through the cracks of doors left ajar and over rooftops.[86]

Finally, recent works by both authors – Naṣr's *Kāʾināt Mujannaḥa* (2010, Winged Creatures) and Khuḍayyir's *Ḥadāʾiq al-Wujūh (Aqniᶜa wa-Ḥikāyāt)* (2008, Gardens of Faces [Masks and Tales]) – start from original (or eccentric) presuppositions. Jawhar Nājī, a denture-maker in Naṣr's book, imagines the lives of the unseen patients, based on their dentures, in a series of vignettes. In Khuḍayyir's work, his character, the Gardener, nurtures a series of literary gardens like "The Face as a Youth."[87] These include gardens dedicated to Rabindranath Tagore, Jorge Luis Borges, Gabriel Garcia Marquez, Gibran Khalil Gibran, and Abū al-ᶜAlāʾ al-Maᶜarrī.[88] These are obviously all authors Khuḍayyir admires. Tagore's first place on the list is significant because Khuḍayyir, in his previously mentioned tribute to ᶜAbd al-Malik Nūrī, writes:

> Your tattoo is clearly inscribed beside the Indian tattoo that Tagore pricked deep into my narrative flesh – a serpent that dances and transmigrates endlessly.[89]

All the same, *Baṣrayātha* and *Return to Dār al-Bāsha* differ in significant ways. Dār al-Bāsha is not a model of Tunis and has not spilled beyond its novel's pages. Khuḍayyir has published many essays that comment directly on his own fiction. Naṣr's novels blur reality and fantasy but are not a collage of narrative and discursive passage. *Return to Dar al-Basha* has a plot and does not, for example, incorporate vintage photographs of Tunis. Some of Naṣr's short stories are arguably fantasies, because they would be too politically sensitive in a realist narrative, but Khuḍayyir has many other reasons for his indirections; escaping the censors does not seem to have been a primary motivation for him, even though Ikram Masmoudi lists *Baṣrayātha* among Iraqi novels in which authors resorted to self-censorship with the use of "myth and a symbolic language ..."[90]

Conclusion

Baṣrayātha is not a typical set of reminiscences about life in Baṣra or a typical memoir. It is a series of story-laden essays about the city during its coevolution with its inhabitants, some of whom were immigrants who had "mastered the Indians' secret of mixing spices."[91] *Baṣrayātha* leapfrogs between centuries without following the fortunes of any particular character or family. It is an extended prose poem that recounts and celebrates the city through its stories. Even the work's discursive passages have a cumulative aesthetic effect. *Baṣrayātha* is predictably packed with information about physical, literary, and folkloric versions of Baṣra, but Muḥammad Khuḍayyir made his model city a vehicle for a more universal message and a self-portrait.

Although related to the *adab* literature of medieval Iraq, *Baṣrayātha* is arguably a Neo-Cubist literary collage, where slices of life fall into place as remembered, dreamt, or visualized by the storyteller. It is also properly described as a heterotopia that creates a new space for Baṣra while existing, like a mirror, inside Baṣra. By adding many different condiments, Khuḍayyir, in *Baṣrayātha*, arguably creates a secret combination that allows *Baṣrayātha* to mirror many other works of contemporary Arabic literature in specific respects, while standing apart as an idiosyncratic masterpiece.

Postscript

Fabio Caiani and Catherine Cobham have, in *The Iraqi Novel: Key Writers, Key Texts*, demonstrated Khuḍayyir's admiration for ᶜAbd al-Malik Nūrī and translated a memorable paragraph from Khuḍayyir's amazing tribute to him. They have also suggested pairing Muḥammad Khuḍayyir with Mahdī ᶜĪsā al-Ṣaqr and *Baṣrayātha* with al-Ṣaqr's work *al-Maqāma al-Baṣriyya al-ᶜAṣriyya* of 2005.[92] Consideration of these excellent points will need to wait for another essay, possibly by a different critic.

Notes

1. Khuḍayyir 2007: 143.
2. Ibid.: 5.
3. The notion of a writer's spice blend comes from Amir Tag Elsir, *Telepathy* (2015: 14).
4. Caiani and Cobham (2013: 244–5).
5. Khuḍayyir (1995: 93–4). Unless otherwise attributed, all English translations in this essay are by the essay's author.
6. Khuḍayyir (2004: 22).
7. Khuḍayyir (2007: 134).
8. Ibid. (153).
9. Khuḍayyir (1995a: 104).
10. In the Verso Books edition of the English translation, these prefaces were placed by the publisher at the end of the book. Khuḍayyir (2008a).
11. Khuḍayyir (1995: 10).
12. Khuḍayyir (2007: 133), emphasis added.
13. Gertrude Stein, *Picasso* (1984: 8).
14. Ibid. (21).
15. Khuḍayyir (2004: 21).
16. Pablo Picasso as quoted in Ashton (1988: 38).
17. Khuḍayyir (1995a: 84).
18. Khuḍayyir (2004: 21).
19. Khuḍayyir (2010: 69).
20. New vintage images were provided by the author for the English translation, because the publisher could not procure copies of the originals that met their technical specifications.
21. Khuḍayyir (2004: 21–2).
22. Rothenberg and Joris in Picasso (2004: vii, xi).
23. For an extensive discussion of *adab* see al-Musawi (2015: 176 ff).
24. Al-Jāḥiẓ (1999).
25. Khuḍayyir, (2007: 5). (The Verso Books (2008a) edition put the first section, "Four Points of Entry to Baṣrayātha," at the end, thus changing the page numbers, to page 170 in this case.)
26. Ibid.
27. Khuḍayyir (2010: 79): "The purpose of the author in it was to write a prose work that combined storytelling, witty remarks, and polemic discussion in the framework … of *al-iqtibās* … We entertain no doubts now about Abū Ḥayyān's

eloquent and artistic prose ... but it offers only an approximate framing of the work of intertextuality (*al-tanāṣṣ*) ..."

28. Khuḍayyir (2010: 82) and Eco (1984: 23).
29. Eco (1984: 24).
30. Khuḍayyir, (2012).
31. Khuḍayyir (2007: 4).
32. Mustafa (2002).
33. Khuḍayyir (1995a: 25–6).
34. Khuḍayyir (2007: 67).
35. Ibid.: 70.
36. Khuḍayyir (1995a: 94).
37. Khuḍayyir (2007: 38).
38. Ibid.: 100.
39. Ibid.: 101.
40. Khuḍayyir (1995a: 95–6).
41. Ibid.: 27.
42. Poe (1965: xi, 108); Khuḍayyir, "Barāhīn Basīṭa," (1995a: 50).
43. Poe (1965: 106); Khuḍayyir (1995a: 49, 97).
44. Khuḍayyir (1995a: 28).
45. Glass (2015: 22).
46. Khuḍayyir (2007: 123).
47. Ibid.: 7.
48. Khuḍayyir (1995a: 71).
49. Ibid.: 84.
50. Ibid.: 71.
51. Khuḍayyir (2007: 150).
52. Khuḍayyir (1995a: 84).
53. Khuḍayyir (2007: 8). See also: Foucault (n. d.).
54. Foucault (2008), 17.
55. Ibid.: 18.
56. Ibid.: 17.
57. Khuḍayyir (2007: 10).
58. Ibid.: 121.
59. Ibid.: 51.
60. Ibid.: 11.
61. Ibid.: 11.
62. Ibid.: 107.
63. Foucault (2008: 20).

64. Khuḍayyir (2007: 125 ff).
65. Ibid.: 128.
66. Ibid.: 130.
67. Khuḍayyir (1995a: 81).
68. Khuḍayyir (1995b: 9).
69. Ibid.: 99.
70. Ibid.: 21 ff.
71. Ibid.: 61.
72. Khuḍayyir (1978 and 2006: 79 ff). French translation in Khodayyir (2000: 108 ff).
73. Khuḍayyir (1995a: 101): "Writing is a Costume Party," interview conducted by Riyadh Ibrahim.
74. Ibid.: 103.
75. Khuḍayyir (1995a: 103).
76. Ibid.: 25.
77. Luay Hamza Abbas has been suggested as one possible Baṣran exception: http://www.banipal.co.uk/selections/53/93/luay-hamza-abbas/ and http://www.banipal.co.uk/selections/53/93/luay-hamza-abbas/.
78. William Hutchins, "Introduction," (2006: xi).
79. Ibid.: xiii.
80. Naṣr (2001: 90).
81. Khuḍayyir, "Dhākirat al-ᶜAttār," (1995a: 30).
82. Khuḍayyir (1995a: 98).
83. Ibid.
84. Ibid.: 45.
85. Khuḍayyir (2007: 70).
86. Naṣr (2006: 3).
87. Khuḍayyir (2008b: 29–31).
88. Ibid.: 206.
89. Khuḍayyir (2012).
90. Masmoudi (2015: 13–14).
91. Khuḍayyir (2007: 130).
92. Caiani and Cobham (2013: 245–6).

Works Cited

Ashton, Dore (1988), *Picasso on Art: A Selection of Views*, New York NY: Da Capo Press.

Caiani, Fabio and Catherine Cobham (2013), *The Iraqi Novel: Key Writers, Key Texts*, Edinburgh: Edinburgh University Press.

Eco, Umberto (1984), *Postscript to* The Name of the Rose, trans. William Weaver, San Diego CA, New York NY, London: Harcourt Brace Jovanovich.

Elsir, Amir Tag (2015), *Telepathy*, trans. William Hutchins, Doha: Bloomsbury Qatar Foundation Publishing.

Foucault, Michel (2008), "Of other spaces (1967)," trans. Lieven De Cauter and Michiel Dehaene, in Michiel Dehaene and Lieven De Cauter (eds), *Heterotopia and the City: Public space in a postcivil society*, London and New York NY: Routledge.

—— (n. d.), "Of Other Spaces (1967), Heterotopias," online at http://foucault.info/doc/documents/heterotopia/foucault-heterotopia-en-html.

Glass, Philip (2015), *Words Without Music: A Memoir*, New York NY and London: Liveright Publishing Company/W. W. Norton & Company.

Hutchins, William (2006), "Introduction," in Ḥasan Naṣr, *Return to Dar al-Basha*, trans. William Hutchins, Syracuse NY: Syracuse University Press, xi–xvi.

Al-Jāḥiẓ (1999), *Avarice and the Avaricious*, trans. Jim Colville, London and New York NY: Kegan Paul International.

Khodayyir, Mohammad (2000), *Le Royaume Noir*, French translation by Guy Rocheblave and Kadhim Jihad, Arles: Actes Sud; Sindbad.

Khuḍayyir, Muḥammad (1978 and 2006), *Fī Darajat 45 Miʾawī*, Baghdad: Wizarat al-Thaqāfa 1978, and Köln: Al-Kamel Verlag 2006.

—— (1995a), *al-Ḥikāya al-Jadīda: Naqd Adabī*, Amman: Dar Azmina.

—— (1995b), *Ruʾyat Kharīf*, Amman: Dar Azmina.

—— (2004), *Kurrāsat Kānūn*, Amman: Dar Azmina.

—— (2007), *Baṣrayātha: Portrait of a City*, trans. William M. Hutchins, Cairo and New York NY: American University in Cairo Press.

—— (2008a), *Baṣrayātha: The Story of a City*, trans. William M. Hutchins, London and New York NY: Verso Books.

—— (2008b), *Ḥadāʾiq al-Wujūh (Aqniʿa wa-Ḥikāyāt)*, Damascus: al-Madā Publishing Company.

—— (2010), *al-Sard wa-l-Kitāb*, Dubai: Kitāb Dubay al-Thaqāfiyya.

—— (2012), "Al-Washm al-Baghdādī, ilā ʿAbd al-Mālik Nūrī," *Kuttāb al-ʿIrāq: Minbar al-Kātib al-ʿIrāqī* (8 June), http://www.iraqiwriters.com/inp/view.asp?ID=3116 (accessed 10 November 2017).

Masmoudi, Ikram (2015), *War and Occupation in Iraqi Fiction*, Edinburgh: Edinburgh University Press.

al-Musawi, Muhsin J. (2015), *The Medieval Islamic Republic of Letters*, Notre Dame IN: University of Notre Dame Press.

Mustafa, Shakit (2002), "Genre Negotiations: Review of Muḥammad Khuḍayyir, *Baṣrayātha: Ṣūrat Madīna*. Baghdad: Manshūrāt al-Amad, 1993," *Edebiyat: Journal of Middle Eastern Literatures*, vol. 13, issue 1.

Naṣr, Ḥasan (2001), *Sijillāt Raʾs al- Dīk*, Tunis: Siras li-l-Nashr.

—— (2006), *Return to Dar al-Basha*, trans. William Hutchins, Syracuse NY: Syracuse University Press.

Poe, Edgar Allan (1965), "Twice-Told Tales," *Graham's Magazine*, May 1842, in James A. Harrison (ed.), *The Complete Works of Edgar Allan Poe*, New York NY: AMS Press, Inc.

Rothenberg, Jerome with Pierre Joris (2004), "Pre-Face," in Pablo Picasso, *The Burial of the Count of Orgaz & Other Poems*, Jerome Rothenberg and Pierre Joris (eds), Cambridge MA: Exact Change.

Stein, Gertrude (1984), *Picasso*, New York NY: Dover Publications, Inc.

14

Of Cities and Canons in an Age of Comparative Consumption

Hanadi Al-Samman

In *Warrāq al-ḥubb* (2008; Eng. *Writing Love: A Syrian Novel*, 2012),[1] Khalīl Ṣuwayliḥ evokes the ever-present authorial angst of Harold Bloom's "anxiety of influence," which he redeploys within the context of a troubled postcolonial, local and global politics of representation, translation, and comparative consumption. Ṣuwayliḥ is the 2009 recipient of the Naguib Mahfouz Medal for Literature, and in this avant-garde novel he articulates a complicated set of anxieties and fears that paralyze the creativity of the author, threatening to consign his literature to the ghettoes of translated world literature; it is an unease so severe that it ultimately halts the beginning of his narrative. The text's male narrator alerts the reader to the act of writing, sharing his anxiety with his interlocutors and thereby producing a novel within a novel that mocks the very process of writing the literary genre to which it belongs. Of particular importance to this chapter is the way in which what I call the authorial mapping of a novel intersects with the spatial mapping of the old city of Damascus. As the author/narrator retraces lost love manuscripts in the streets of the city, he underlines the resemblance between "writing a novel and building homes brick by brick" (Ṣuwayliḥ 2008: 19). He further admits the following to his readers, "I have to break the laws of the novel, and to move comfortably amongst chronology and characters as if I were back in my parents' house in the village where [discordant rooms] coexist in marvelous architectural form" (Ṣuwayliḥ 2008: 59).

This intersection between the literary and the urban is unique in the text as the writer equates his ability to write with that of constructing a house grounded in a strong local foundation. But his writing endeavor proves to be anything but "comfortable." Indeed, the self-reflective design of the novel calls attention to the art of writing, and chronicles several attempts of aborted narrative beginnings by the narrator who searches unsuccessfully for an introduction to his book, anchored in the local tradition of premodern Arabic manuscripts. However, the narrator's constant allusions to the masterpieces of the Western canon throughout the narrative demonstrate that he is haunted by the influence of their celebrated, if domineering, narrative models. Yet the ghosts that haunt the narrative are not all of the literary kind; for real ghosts materialize in the person of security police agents and the State's censors forever ready to arrest and erase any counter-narratives from the public domain. In this oppressive atmosphere, literature and love are doomed to perish. The novel articulates the difficulty of writing about love in an environment riddled with local constraints of censorship and the political coercion of contemporary Syria, but also with the terror of Western literary and military dominance over Arab lands.

The Haunted City

From the onset the narrator's relationship, or lack thereof, to space is vital to his ability to create his masterpiece. His city, Damascus, functions as a coveted space that simultaneously inspires and terrorizes him. Central to Ṣuwayliḥ's plot in *Writing Love* is the narrator's search for the missing medieval manuscripts of a forlorn Iraqi lover in the city of Damascus. At the request of his beloved, the Damascene Yasminzade, the lover traveled the earth to find the books that best expressed romantic passion in order to copy them into a single masterful love manuscript to present to her. At the end of his travels, he returns with thousands of sentimental manuscripts collected from different parts of the ancient world. Paralyzed and unable to deliver the manuscripts to his beloved as promised, he dies at the entrance of the city. It is reported, at a later time, that the manuscripts were lost during the time of Tamerlane's invasion of Damascus in the fourteenth century, only to resurface later at the library of a nameless "orientalist" in Europe at the end of the nineteenth century. Nothing remains from this rich traditional literary heritage but the one copy of Ibn Ḥazm's *The Ring of the Dove*, claims Ṣuwayliḥ's narrator (Ṣuwayliḥ 2008: 8–9).

To find the essence of love, the ancient lover had to traverse numerous cities, compiling and contrasting discordant perceptions of the nature of love in a manner that appreciates rather than appropriates all of its varied local and global articulations. However, the legacy of the manuscript's loss haunts the narrative and is, in turn, indicative of the disappearance of love in Arab culture, the loss of the narrator's authorial confidence, and the lack of access to his city. Hence, his quest for the best opening to the novel is tied to the topography of Damascus itself. Not surprisingly, we see him roaming the streets restlessly, documenting, in this process, the name of each street and its historical significance. For example, he searches for a copy of *The Ring of the Dove* in the renowned Ẓāhirīyya library, visits the Umayyad Mosque and the Buzūrrīyah spice market for the sights and smells of the organic, old city. He often traverses al-Abyadh bridge, al-Ḥijāz train station, al-Umayyad square in search of the lost connections between space, history, and people. In *The Production of Space*, Henri Lefebvre contends that space is produced by social relations that it also reproduces, mediates and transforms.[2] In *Writing Love*, the narrator's ability to gain spatial control of the streets of Damascus is tied to the social relations he cultivates with his surroundings, and is inextricably linked to his mastery of his narrative craft. Even his capacity to fare well in his romantic relationships is tied to his skill in exploring the streets as he walks with his girlfriend. In this capacity, he conjures the image of the *flâneur*, the figure of the leisurely urban stroller developed by Baudelaire and later disseminated in the works of Walter Benjamin and Michel de Certeau (Benjamin 1985, de Certeau 1984). The *flâneur* establishes walking as a primarily masculine urban act, capable of retrieving the lost history of the city. According to Nedra Reynolds, the "spatial practices of walking as writing, writing as walking" transform the city into text; the text into a city, thereby reaffirming once more the intertwining of the literary with the urban (Reynolds 2004: 70).

Indeed, the narrator/writer firmly believes that strolling in the Damascene streets will unlock his writing block. Finally, he declares, "I found the key to my novel," he asserts, "all the previous keys I have tried encountered rusty locks and impenetrable doors" (Ṣuwayliḥ 2008: 33). However, his freedom to remap the cartography of both city and text is limited because his mobility is restricted by the secret police (*mukhābarāt*) of the Syrian regime and its checkpoints. Damascene public spaces become contested and indicative of a present absent, of a lack to be filled, reconfigured through contingent and pre-determined social relations and silencing practices.[3] For example, the narrator is harassed by the police as he walks in Nizār Qabbānī Street, named after the Arab world's most renowned contemporary love poet (1923–98), in a failed attempt to invoke his spirit. After this encounter, the jasmine flowers in the narrator's hands, which are symbols of Damascus' essence and Qabbānī's poems, are crushed as love is figuratively replaced by war and the blood of all Syrians (52). Invoking Qabbānī's name is significant because even though he is celebrated for his love poems, the political poems of his later period are often occulted in Syrian cultural circles, erased by the regime exactly as original texts are scraped in a palimpsest. Qabbānī was also absented from the spatial and cultural scenes of Syria until he returned in a casket after his death in exile in London in 1998. It was only after he had been forever silenced that Ḥāfiz al-Assad's government, at the time, decided to honor him by giving a street his name. Qabbānī's return represents a haunting of the erased political text, as the street that carries his name becomes a beacon celebrating his revolutionary spirit. Though on the surface people are only allowed to circulate his love poems, his political poems were, and continue to be, circulated in secret among Arab citizens, particularly after the onset of the Arab Spring and the Syrian Revolution in March 2011. The novel advances the idea that limiting the writer's mobility in Qabbānī's street, in fact in all of Damascus, as is the case in authoritarian regimes, prevents him from freedom of speech and writing as well. It is significant that common writing blocks are described in terms of spatial traffic signs such as, "Stop, do not enter," "treacherous turn, slow down" in order to establish a symbiotic relationship between the city/the novel, and walking/writing (Ṣuwayliḥ 2008: 58).

Fear is cast as a hindrance to the launch of the narrator's prologue. It is manifested in several nightmares where the narrator's pen becomes suddenly dry, signifying his literary impotence (92, 101). In a state where Emergency Law has not been lifted since 1963, fear reigns supreme. It is revealed in the form of the prevalence of the secret police surveillance, the dominance of local censors, and the general oppression of the authoritarian state. Nizār Qabbānī articulated the state of siege experienced by the Syrian citizen in his poem "Taqrīr sirrī jiddan min bilād Qamᶜistān" (Top- Secret Report from the Country of Smotherland) by stating that he is, "A citizen who can't go out / for a drink on the town, / so nervous that the State Police / – who knows? – might jump up / from the Darkest places / at the bottom of his cup."[4] Similarly, in "The Tattoo" Qabbānī's contemporary, Muḥammad al-Māghūṭ, documents the paralyzing effects of what Mohja Kahf calls the motif of the "violent knock at the door."[5] He asserts, "Whenever a knock resounds / whenever a curtain moves / I cover my papers with my hand / like a prostitute covers herself during a raid."[6] This state of constant surveillance leads citizens to internalize their panopticon-like existence where, as

Zakarīyyā Tāmir's short story "Tigers on the Tenth Day" suggests, they become as trained tigers who no longer need cages because "the tiger became a citizen and the cage a city."[7] The silencing of these Syrian authors, and others such as Ulfat al-Idlibī (1912–2007), ᶜAbd al-Salām al-ᶜUjaylī (1918–2006), Ḥannā Mīna (b. 1924), Saᶜd Allāh Wannūs (1941–97), Muḥammad al-Māghūṭ (1934–2006), Zakariyyā Tāmir (b. 1931), casts the urban space of Damascus, under the Baᶜth party rule, as a cage. To escape this prison-like environment, authors adopt specific literary genres and stratagems unique to Syrian literature in order to combat the ongoing state of martial law and the ever-present censorship.[8]

The ghosts of oppression continue to follow Ṣuwayliḥ's narrator. Later at home, he is terrified upon hearing the sound of violent knocking at his door. The narrator's two fears, the literary and the political, often collide in one literary image, as is evident in the following pronouncement:

> I could not recognize this ghost in the dark hallway. Certainly it was not the ghost of Hamlet's father, nor the ghost of Mitᶜeb al-Hathal in *Cities of Salt*.[9] My terror increased as I simultaneously started preparing a defense; proving my innocence against any charge pertaining to the State's security. (Ṣuwayliḥ 2008: 53)

It is significant that the ghosts the narrator mentions at his moment of anxiety, laced with the fear of arrest, are those related to treason and the illegal ascension to power. Hamlet's father's ghost in Shakespeare's *Hamlet*, and Mitᶜeb al-Hathāl's ghost in Abdelraḥman Munīf's *Cities of Salt* are reminders of the plunder of the throne of Denmark and that of the environment of the Arab Gulf for the sake of oil excavation and capitalism. These events are what we read on the surface of Ṣuwayliḥ's text; however, what remains unsaid and erased from the palimpsest/the text is the plunder of power in Syria by Assad's dynasty since 1971. The contaminants of fear and anxiety erase beauty and serenity by scraping love, exactly as in a palimpsest's text, and replacing it with violence, with terror. Ultimately a novel about love cannot be written in the violent environment of a city terrorized by the grip of a ruthless dictator, and so a second attempt at writing the novel's prologue is aborted as well (34; 39–40).

Ṣuwayliḥ's unique contribution in this novel is in expanding the traditional literary zone of "anxiety of influence" so as to encompass the anxieties generated through constant subjugation to the State's security apparatus – one capable of exacting unspeakable atrocities against its own citizens as we are currently witnessing in the unfortunate events of the Syrian Revolution (2011–present) and the ensuing civil war. *Writing Love*'s narrator recalls an incident when after the Israeli invasion of Beirut in the summer of 1982, a group of intellectuals and political singers gathered in "Palestine's camp" district, an area inhabited by 1,967 Palestinian refugees and members of Damascus' working classes, to discuss the humiliating defeat. Suddenly, the secret police raids the place, doling out humiliating slaps to those arrested and the political singer (Ṣuwayliḥ 2008: 55).[10] Lamenting these dismal humanitarian conditions, the narrator states, "If our miserable rulers, police, and security officers were to read novels, they would not have displayed so much superficiality and brutality. For even Shahrayār himself, who used to deflower and kill a virgin every night, could not resist the power of Shahrazād's stories, and had to postpone her execution indefinitely" (31). Ṣuwayliḥ realizes that the redemptive essence of storytelling is forever locked in an existential struggle with the forces of violence and tyranny. The secret agents mentioned above are called *shabbīḥa* in the Syrian dialect, a derivative of *shabaḥ* (ghost), an epithet indicative of their role in terrorizing people, and of the dark cars they drive and notably use to arrest citizens. This metonymy contributes to Ṣuwayliḥ's seamless blending of the double haunting experienced by the narrator from the ghosts of local and global literary luminaries, and from the shadows of intelligence agents lurking in the dark alleys of his city, Damascus. In turn, the city itself becomes at once a cage and a hostage to these tyrannical powers.

In his praise of *Writing Love*, Egyptian critic and member of the Naguib Mahfouz award committee Jābir ᶜUṣfūr states that "the novel critiques the Arab's reality sharply, and depicts a series of catastrophes which results in love's demise. In this novel, reality suffocates both the novel and love. Consequently, I see that we are living in a world that kills creativity and smothers love."[11] Another member of the committee; Jordanian critic Fakhrī Ṣāliḥ, concurs and adds,

> [Ṣuwayliḥ] is a master at infusing his narrative with intertexuality. At once, his novel invokes and mocks love. It is an intelligent game of intertextuality that sheds light on love, narrative genre, and the act of writing in an attempt to clarify the meaning of living in tumultuous times haunted by the fear of persecution and the government's pressing control in this unfortunate part of the world. (Shaᶜīr 2009)

Indeed, a return to the Arabic narrative archives of *The Thousand and One Nights*, the *maqāmāt*, the epistolary genre, the *ḥakawātī* character, and popular folktales is a mechanism to combat this fear, and to find comfort in tradition. Ṣuwayliḥ is quick to remind the reader that the very act of bridging the past with the present stands in defiance of the "whole world [which] wants to destroy memory, but [the narrator] want[s] to resurrect and reconstruct it" (Ṣuwayliḥ 2008: 126). Resurrecting the memory of the erased heritage texts of the palimpsest, of a peaceful Damascus – one characterized by a robust, uncensored literary scene, and ruled by the coexistence of all of its minorities, by love instead of the controlling grip of the domineering Baᶜath ideology – is paramount to saving its citizens from the Assad regime's ongoing terror.

The Palimpsest and the City

The narrator's fear of the security apparatus is not the only hindrance to his writing. Other anxieties emerge, manifesting in his fear of not measuring up to literary Western and classical Arab predecessors. The narrator's search for the missing manuscripts of a forlorn lover in the old quarters of Damascus is meant to herald a return to the roots of the city's heritage, and to defy forces of local oppression and global dominance. His angst emerges out of his desire for a narrative design worthy of consideration for a Nobel prize. This anxiety clearly demonstrates the extent of the canonical Western masterpieces' influence over the aspiring contemporary Arab writer. It is important to note, though, that the narrator's discomfort does not arise from an inferiority complex, nor from a lack of Arabic masterpieces, but rather from his awareness, as Pascale Casanova outlined in *The World Republic of Letters*, of the competitive nature of the global literary system and of his aspiration to be part of it.[12] He is likewise frustrated by the erasure of some aspects of Arabic literary history that he vows to reclaim. Initially, he decides to follow the style of the traditional *ḥakawātī* (storyteller) in fashioning his story after the legendary *sīrahs* or sagas of a heroic Arab past, such as *Sīrat ᶜAntar, Sīrat al-Malik al-Ẓāhir Baybars, Sīrat Abī Zayd al-Hilālī* (Ṣuwayliḥ 2008: 7). To this extent, he decides to introduce his theme with the story of the premodern Iraqi lover. However, after his failure in finding the lost manuscripts and love within the caged walls of the city, he resorts to other stratagems, intent on fashioning his opening after Arab and Western texts alike.

The void created by the disappearance of the legendary love manuscripts bears an uncanny resemblance to the idea of the palimpsest. The metaphor of the palimpsest, as first defined by Thomas de Quincy and elaborated on by Sarah Dillon, is extremely useful in explaining the conflicting relationship between Arabic and Western sources vying for presence in Ṣuwayliḥ's novel. Palimpsests are parchments where original texts were erased to make room for new, unrelated texts. The practice was common in the Middle Ages (seventh to fifteenth centuries) due to the scarcity and exorbitant cost of paper. Though the old texts seemed to be erased, they would often reappear in subsequent centuries when the iron in their ink reacted with the oxygen in the air, producing a reddish-brown oxide. The red color is symbolic of the violence committed upon the original text in scraping and erasing its traces. According to Sarah Dillon, "a palimpsest is thus a surface phenomenon where, in an illusion of layered depth, otherwise unrelated texts are involved and entangled, intricately interwoven, interrupting and inhabiting each other" (Dillon 2007: 29). When traces of the old texts spectrally reappear, they make for an incestuous relationship between these pre-existing words and the new, unrelated texts. This forced cohabitation is considered, to use Gérard Genette's phrasing, "palimpsestuous" – a term that integrates the meaning of "incestuous" with that of the palimpsest (Genette 1997). In this context, the dilemma of Ṣuwayliḥ's narrator is his inability to find the traces of the original love manuscript and Arabic sources. Faced with this loss, he has no recourse but to simultaneously pursue this traditional Arabic literary trace that has been erased, and to seek inspiration from the Western canonized tradition. He consults luminary writers such as Ovid, Shakespeare, Honoré de Balzac, Fyodor Dostoevsky, Gabriel García Márquez, Mikhail Bakhtin, Italo Calvino, Milan Kundera, Isabel Allende and others. The voices of these writers and their respective plot designs converge in his head along with key medieval Arab classical writers such as Ibn Ḥazm, al-Jāḥiẓ, al-Ghazālī, al-Tījānī, al-Ṭīfāshī, and al-Nafzāwī. Repeatedly, the narrator confesses his agonizing writer's block to the reader with this enigmatic question, "Damn, how could one write a novel?" (Ṣuwayliḥ 2008: 19). He decides to divide his text into three chapters on Love, Separation, and Death. Yet upon contemplating the choice of his narrative style, he is "struck by an acute vertigo." Frustrated, he declares, "I could not decide amongst the multitude of narrative techniques: Gabriel García Márquez's devices, Italo Calvino's recommendations, Milan Kundera's madness, Jorge Luis Borges' delirium, *The Thousand and One Nights*' erotic suspense, Honoré de Balzac's realism, Emile Zola's naturalism, or the style of al-Hamadhānī's *maqāmāt*. This confusion has struck me with an acute vertigo" (24). Not surprisingly, the narrator finds no easy answers to resolving the question of the lost heritage of Arabic writings or how it could be revived so as to ward off the influence of dominant Western narrative models. In the end, his repeated attempts to reconcile Arabic and Western literary role models create a palimpsestuous text – a multi-layered novel that fails to even launch its own beginning.

While the narrator is obsessed with the project of writing "the novel of all novels," of finding the "key" to unlocking his manuscript, of discovering a unique prologue and design for his novel about love, separation, and death, his postmodern and postcolonial condition haunts him with a sense of persistent paralysis (6, 20). Repeatedly, he experiences a Bloomian "anxiety of influence" and is acutely aware of his temporal and geographic disadvantages in the contemporary "world republic of letters": both as a belated author (having arrived at the literary scene with all the masterpieces already written) and as an Arab author (with limited access to print, the need for the recognition of Western-influenced literary awards, and subsequent translations to popular world languages so as to achieve globalism and a wide readership). His project of bridging Western and Eastern cultures in one literary work – represented in his search for the Andalusian Ibn Ḥazm's manuscript, composed in a location where these cultures were historically bridged in Muslim Spain – has failed. Commenting on the status of Arab writers, Egyptian literary scholar Samia Mehrez has outlined a set of challenges, ranging from the state's co-optation of some authors to the rebuke and censorship of others. This situation forces writers to "accede to the international republic of letters" and to "face a double bind, both unable to maneuver freely within the local cultural field because of the influence of the state on the cultural establishment and locked out – 'underrepresented' and often 'misrepresented' – in the global literary field."[13]

In this sense, the narrator is afflicted by a number of different types of violence: the violence of accepted Western literary models, something he sees as analogous to the violence committed by the erasure of original Arabic literary predecessors, and by the violence of the US war machine on the Arab population. He proclaims that "his reason for wanting to write a novel, one that summarizes all the previously written novels of the last thirty years, is perhaps to eliminate the smell of the dirty war that America waged on the [Iraqi] poor and hungry people in its audacious pursuit for world domination, and to erase the Other's specificities" (Ṣuwayliḥ 2008: 6). In both cases, he feels that this Western hegemony spills over to include not only the affected geographical locations, but also Arabic literature since "erasing the Other's unique attributes" is one of the sacrifices local literatures have to make in order to conform to Western standards of readability and global appeal.

The novel's own intertextual engagement with previously canonized Western masterpieces clearly demonstrates the level of anxiety and difficulty associated with the attempt to reconcile the palimpsestuous coexistence of traditional Arabic narrative modes with Western ones, thereby merging the Arab subaltern with the global human. On the one hand, the narrator's angst demonstrates the need of contemporary Arabic literature to escape the postcolonial ghetto of nationally centered and politically committed literature, and the pressure of worldwide globalism. On the other hand, it is a reminder that in the Arab writer's quest to utilize a spot within the ranks of the humanities, s/he must never forget, as Gayatri Spivak aptly reminds us, to define "who slips into the place of the 'human' of 'humanism' at the end of the day?"[14] The answer to such a question might lead the writer back to the limitations of ethnic and postcolonial compartmentalization. Indeed, this intertextual game leads the author to think that s/he is an "imposter," pretending to be an "authentic" author while catering to a global, imagined idea of an exotic "orient." On this point the narrator elaborates, "I have a long list of imposters who suddenly became renowned novelists and poets. In book festivals, they confidently sign their new books and translation contracts assured that foreign translators are even more ignorant than some local publishers. Thus, they are taken by the Orient's charm and wonder – a prominent feature in the novels of these authors, or rather 'imposters'" (Ṣuwayliḥ 2008: 42). In "Teaching for the Times," Spivak comments on the tension resulting from the disharmonious representation of both ethnicity and identity politics in "ethnic" literature:

> I think the literature of ethnicity writes itself between *ethnos* – a writer writing for her own people (whatever that means) without deliberated self-identification as such – and *ethnikos*, the pejoratively defined other reversing the charge, (de)anthropologizing herself by separating herself into a staged identity. The literature of ethnicity in this second sense thus carries, paradoxically, the writer's signature as divided against itself.[15]

Similarly, Spivak is also suspicious of the term "globalization" since it "is the imposition of the same system of exchange everywhere" (Spivak 2003: 72). Instead, she suggests a different critical mindset to be employed particularly by practitioners of comparative literature studies, one that involves invoking the image of the planet and not the globe. She explains her point thus:

> If we imagine ourselves as planetary subjects rather than global agents, planetary creatures rather than global entities, alterity remains underived from us; it is not our dialectical negation, it contains us as much as it flings us away. And thus to think of it is already to transgress … what is above

> and beyond our own reach is not continuous with us as it is not, indeed, specifically discontinuous. (Spivak 2003: 73)

One can certainly read Ṣuwayliḥ's *Writing Love* as the contemporary Arab writer's attempt to simultaneously escape "global savagery," and the violence of the "postcolonial nightmare." It is a desperate endeavour to resurrect the erased Arabic heritage from the palimpsest and to engage the subalternity of traditional *adab* (belles-lettres) literature with the canonized Western classics in a "planetary" discussion. Take, for example, Ṣuwayliḥ's attempt to engage the eighteenth-century writer of erotic literature Muḥammad ibn Aḥmad al-Tījānī (1735–1815) with the twentieth-century theorist Mikhail Bakhtin (1895–1975) in a planetary discussion based on the former's ideas of intertextuality, and the latter's polyphony and dialogism. For al-Tījānī, "life as a whole is built on intertextuality;" events are repeated in the same mechanism, however, our perception of them differs distinctly each time, while Bahktin claims via our narrator that "there are no virgin words. All words are haunted with the others' voices" (Ṣuwayliḥ 2008: 118). Indeed, the "geology of writing," the narrator proclaims, is built on intertextuality or, "as Roland Barthes claims, it relies on stacking a 'layer upon layer' of writing" (119). The narrator's excavation into the literary archives unearths a rich tradition of intertextual writing that rivals any of the discoveries of contemporary theorists like "Roland Barthes, Umberto Eco and Julia Kristeva" (119).

Arabic Literature and the Global City

In its search for love that precedes the oppressive apparatus of the modern state, Ṣuwayliḥ's *Writing Love* engages with premodern Arabic erotic literature. Al-Jāḥiẓ, al-Tījānī, al-Nafzāwī, to name but a few, make regular appearances in the body of the novel, and the narrator's desperate search for three lost erotic manuscripts cements the primacy of the body in his text (Ṣuwayliḥ 2008: 64–5). At times, he attempts to switch his attention to Sufi ideals and spiritual love instead, but shortly thereafter abandons this project declaring "first and foremost, my destiny is tied to the knowledge of the body" (100). Ṣuwayliḥ intertwines the human body with the personified body of the city of Damascus, whereby a search for one represents a longing for the other. Henri Lefebvre has argued that old cities possess an organic spatiality that is closer to "the intelligence of the body."[16] He "talks of a time, long before the inauguration of either 'historical' or modern, 'abstract' spatialities, when the body's relationship to space had 'an immediacy which would subsequently degenerate and be lost'."[17] For him, "the politics of space are inseparable from the history of the body and from the history of space."[18] Meaning, knowledge of the body is central to our awareness and mastery of space. Similarly, in Ṣuwayliḥ's text, the reclamation of the primacy of the body in Arab erotic manuscripts signals a desire to recover the spatialities of the city which, in Lefebvre's words, have been subject to "decorporealization" by the brutality of the state. According to Lefebvre, masculine violence engenders this "phallic brutality" which "does not remain abstract, for it is the brutality of political power, of the means of constraint: police, army, bureaucracy."[19] All of these corrosive measures create a violent abstract space, devoid of organic spatiality, intimacy, and love. Hence reclaiming Damascus' old city as a spatialized form of resistance by walking in its streets is akin to caressing the lover's body, just as important as retrieving the lost manuscripts of Arab erotica.

In the same vein, the recovery of a forgotten terminology of desire highlights the narrator's agency and skill as a writer. Exhibiting his linguistic and cultural mastery, he even quotes a passage of al-Jāḥiẓ in defense of the proper use of Arabic words in reference to genitals and love-making (61–2). Moreover, he articulates the centrality of the body in the recounting of the intimate details of his escapades with three different women throughout the novel (111). It is noteworthy in this context that another Syrian novella – in this case written by a woman – Salwā al-Naᶜīmī's *Burhān al-ᶜAsal* (2007; Eng. *The Proof of the Honey*, 2009),[20] also engages with the work of al-Jāḥiẓ and premodern erotic texts in the same manner. Yet unlike al-Naᶜīmī's novella, which was critiqued and celebrated simultaneously for delving into explicit erotic material, Ṣuwayliḥ's engagement with erotic literature has gone unnoticed in Arabic literary circles. Most of the critics reference *Writing Love*'s use of intertextuality as "an intelligent narrative scheme," but none take notice of the erotic premodern references (Shᶜīr 2009). Ṣuwayliḥ's masculine gender and his avoidance of the explicit use of sexual terminology has undoubtedly added to this critical oversight. By the same token, al-Naᶜīmī's use of explicit sexual vocabulary and her feminine gender identity were the prime reasons for the banning of her novella in most Arab countries, its wide readership, and its multiple translations in the West. Some of the challenges faced by contemporary Arabic translated literature is the sensationalism which accompanies its consumption in Western markets, particularly when its female author "uncovers" taboo subjects. However, when the same subjects are addressed by Arab male writers, there is a systematic neglect in critical coverage and celebration. Subsequently, three issues come to the fore: where the authors who deal with traditional texts reside, their gender, and their access to translation. Whether authors exercise their archival retrieval projects from inside or outside the Arab world may have a tremendous bearing on the success, or lack thereof, of their reclamation of tradition. Both al-Naᶜīmī and Ṣuwayliḥ set out to resurrect "the spirits of the ancestors,"[21] to jumpstart the memory of both the erotic past and a peaceful city before the advent of tyranny, and to position their works beyond outdated models of feminist and postcolonial agendas. However, the consumption rules of the Western publishing world insist on placing al-Naᶜīmī's novella in the fixed categories of the "veil," "confessional," and "exotic" narratives by and about Arab women, despite its author's utter denunciation of these labels. It is peculiar that the translation of *Writing Love* (2012) did not command the impressive sales figures that al-Naᶜimi's well-positioned novella achieved in most of its eighteen multi-lingual translated versions, despite the fact that Ṣuwayliḥ tackled the same erotic subject matter.[22]

Describing the challenges of contemporary Arab authors, Ṣuwayliḥ's Naguib Mahfouz award acceptance speech decries globalization, postmodern hybrid texts, and Western hegemony:

> ... at this moment of *global savagery* the writer finds himself a prisoner of hegemonic narrative and visual scenes that blind him with their technical glitter, leading him to write a fragmented and hybrid text, a mish-mash of indigenous foundational sources, borrowed ones stamped with the glamor of dominant Western literary conventions, and media propagation of a *modern language* register that lacks *authentic depth*.[23]

Ṣuwayliḥ's words highlight the contemporary Arab writer's recent predicament in the "world republic of letters" which he locates in the author's forced need to alter his traditional, "authentic" language in two distinct ways. One to avoid local censorship, and another to acquiesce to the hegemony of global literary molds in order to render the artistic work more translatable and palatable to Western taste. The Arabic writer is forced to replace his traditional language with "modern" registers, to succumb to the "global savagery" of Western narrative modes that eventually lead to the adulteration of the Arabic text, to the cutting-off of its roots and of its connectedness with its heritage. This dilemma is a new phenomenon related to the advent of modernity and colonialism in the Arab world directly related to the spatial disconnection of Arab states from each other and to their partitioning by colonial borders.

For example, Ṣuwayliḥ's narrator laments the intentional destruction of the historic railroad (built by the Ottoman Sultan ʿAbd al-Ḥamīd II in 1908) that connected Istanbul and Damascus to the Red Sea and the Ḥijāz region (modern-day Saudi Arabia). The railroad was targeted twice: first by the British forces during World War I, and second by the Haganah Jewish militias in 1946 (Ṣuwayliḥ 2008: 39). Consequently, the severance of the railroad changed the literary and geographical maps of the whole Arab world and prevented the citizens of Arab cities from connecting with one another exactly in the same fashion that the security checkpoints of modern, authoritarian states dismember the streets in cities, thereby assimilating violence into their geography and destroying citizens' accessibility to each other and to the organic city.

During the Golden Age of Islamic conquest, classical Arabic literature had no cause to worry about the modern need to be translated and recognized by Western readers and critics. As the Moroccan critic Abdelfattah Kilito reminds us in *Thou Shalt Not Speak My Language*, ancient Arabic culture translated from Greek, Latin, Persian, and Hindi into Arabic; but never had to concern itself with the translatability of its own literature into any other languages. The Arab's political and cultural dominance at that time fostered a secure literature that benefited from the philosophical knowledge of others, but was not required to alter its own linguistic and literary registers to satisfy a foreign mold. In fact, most of these premodern texts guarded themselves against translation, which al-Jāḥiẓ saw as "antagonistic," inflicting *ḍaym* (injury) on the translated language.[24] For that reason, al-Ḥarīrī's "linguistic dexterity" in his *maqāmāt* can be viewed as a shield protecting his text "from the tyranny of another tongue," as if declaring to the world "no one can possibly translate me." As a result, Kilito asserts, "his *maqāmāt* cannot be imagined in any language but Arabic and are impossible to translate. This is not only the case with al-Ḥarīrī's *maqāmāt*, but also with many ancient texts" (Kilito 2008, 18).

Towards the middle of the nineteenth century, however, the rules of the political and literary games changed and the Arabs who were now colonized by French, British, and Italian forces found that they needed to interact with their colonizer using the latter's own linguistic and literary tools. With this came the bitter discovery, as the Lebanese writer Aḥmad Fāris al-Shidyāq (1804–87) remarks, "that Arabic literature is untranslatable, and that on the whole it matters only to Arabs" (Kilito 2008, 18). "Since that time," Kilito contends, "the Arab writer, whether consciously or not, takes translation into account, that is translation as comparison, evaluation, transformation of one literature into another … we read an Arabic text while thinking about the possibility of transferring it into a European language with texts from French, English, or Italian in mind" (19). The extent of this double contamination, in Kilito's opinion, is not restricted to Arabists or Orientalists who insist on misreading Arabic literature through judging it by Western standards. In my estimation, in the twenty-first century this contamination has spread from the realm of reading to the realm of Arabic text production, whereby Arab readers "read the ancients with reference to European literature," and Arab writers approximate the latter in order to "increase many times over" the "marketability," the "popularity" and the translatability of their literature (20).[25] Furthermore, contemporary Arabic literature suffers from the forced submission of its literary corpus to Western-produced theoretical tools, even when the specificity of its own local and literary production calls for the application of Arabic theories and modes of criticism. Arab scholars who inhabit Western academic circles have often been forced to rely heavily on Western criticism in order to publish in academic journals. The present writer and chapter are no exception to this rule, thereby proving the paradoxical nature of this unbalanced relationship. This is a state of comparative consumption – a state where Arabic texts supply the body of research and Western-based literary theorists the scalpels; thereby highlighting the dismembering, destructive effect of this mode of investigation. Ṣuwayliḥ's narrator attempts to rectify this imbalance by relying equally on both the Western and Arabic canons in order to engage the two fields in a fruitful dialogue, however, the reality of the market privileges the Western canon instead.

In her analysis of the Western reception of Nawāl al-Saᶜdāwī's fictional works, Amal Amireh exposes "the imbalance of power relations between Western-based intellectuals and their Arab-based counterparts." Quoting W. J. Mitchell, she underscores the deficiency of a literary criticism binary in which the third world is expected "to supply primary texts but that criticism of these texts is more aptly done in the first world."[26] Commenting on the new role of world literature studies in an age of globalization, David Damrosch is equally critical of what he calls the "postcanonical," "hypercanonical" world literature age, where "literary theory has come to fill the void left by the previous Western canonical masterpieces." It is often the case, he argues convincingly, that "we rely on Butler, Foucault, Said, and Spivak to provide the common basis for conversations formerly underwritten by a common fund of knowledge of Shakespeare, Wordsworth, Proust, and

Joyce."[27] Any Arabic text or researcher who is reluctant to engage in this forced "postcanonical" theoretical discussion is doomed to dwell forever in the academic ghettoes of ethnic and area studies. Hence the Arabic text, culture, and city are thrust into a forced globalization process leading to their estrangement from their authentic milieu. These illegitimate, violent encounters between Eastern and Western texts create works that inhabit each other in an incestuous manner, thereby creating what Sarah Dillon calls, a "palimpsestuous intimacy" – a forbidden intimacy with barren outcomes (Dillon 2007: 36).

Writing Love's mastery resides in revealing the painful process of this forced conversation, its double contamination, and comparative consumption. With great poignancy, the novel excels at reproducing the disorienting effects of this cultural encounter through the process of confused narrative structure, dense intertextuality, and aborted beginnings. The narrator's paralysis and his failure in launching the prologue of his narrative displays the level of difficulty in writing from militarized cities, in engaging traditional Arabic literature in a conversation with its Western counterparts, and also the narrator's anxiety in having to betray the locale of the organic city or risk being ghettoized by the consuming global. Amidst this journey, Damascus emerges as the enigmatic city where past and present, love and violence, local and global forces converge and collide in contentious encounters and a dizzying maze.

Notes

1. The novel was first published in Syria in 2002, and then reprinted in Egypt in 2008 as Khalīl Ṣuwayliḥ, *Warrāq al-ḥubb*, translated into English by Alexa Firat as *Writing Love: A Syrian Novel* (2012). All translations of this text are my own. Further citations are bracketed in text.
2. See Lefebvre (1991).
3. The 1963 Emergency Law in Syria prohibits assembly of citizens, gives the State's agents absolute power to haphazardly arrest people, and exacts strict censorship rules on all media and publication outlets. A loosening of the assembly and censorship rules briefly occurred from 17 July 2000 (the date Bashār al-Assad came to power) to 17 February 2001 in what is known as the Damascus Spring. However, this proved to be a fleeting lull, since most of the ninety-nine Syrian intellectuals who were the initial signatories of "*bayān 99* (Manifesto of the 99)," a document that demanded the lifting of the emergency law, the release of political prisoners, and more freedoms to citizens, were summarily arrested. Subsequently, the intellectual salons' "*muntadayāt thaqāfiyyah*" numbers

dropped from seventy to two, and the government security apparatus tightened its grip on citizens with increased ferociousness.

4. Quoted in Kahf (2001: 232).
5. Ibid.: 232.
6. Ibid.: 232.
7. Ibid.: 234.
8. For more on the genres used by Syrian authors to avoid censorship, see al-Samman (2006).
9. Mitᶜeb al-Hathāl was a character who stood up for the voice of desert authenticity and tribal tradition amidst the oil-motivated Western expansion into Saudi Arabia and other Gulf states in Abdelraḥman Munīf's *Cities of Salt* (1989).
10. I have discussed the significance of the "slap" as a visual and literary metaphor for the regime's oppression and torture of Syrian citizens in the context of Syrian cinema in my article, "Syria, Cinema of. The Suspended Utterances of Syrian Cinema" (2016).
11. Shᶜīr (2009).
12. See Casanova (2005).
13. Quoted in Naaman (2010: 451).
14. Spivak (2003: 26).
15. Quoted in Spivak (2003: 83).
16. Lefebvre (1991: 229).
17. Ibid.: 110–11.
18. Quoted in Gregory (1997: 216, 219, 227).
19. Lefebvre (1991: 287).
20. Al-Naᶜīmī (2007), translated into English by Carol Perkins as *The Proof of the Honey* (2009).
21. "Riwāyat Warrāq al-Ḥubb Tafūzu bi-Jāʾiza," *al-Jirān* (15 December 2009).
22. For more on *The Proof of the Honey*'s erotic context and its Arabic and Western reception, see Al-Samman, "Remapping Arab Narrative and Sexual Desire" (2012).
23. Quoted in Petkova (2009). Emphasis mine. Further citations in text.
24. Kilito (2008: 23).
25. Kilito references the following information related to him by an Egyptian professor who states that "some Arab novelists write while thinking of their potential translators and endeavour to facilitate their task, for example by avoiding expressions and allusions which may not carry into another language. The distant goal, in this case, is not writing a novel and publishing it in Arabic, but publishing it in translation. Thus in its composition, the novel looks to its transfer into English or French; it is written literally for those two languages" (19).

26. Amireh (2000: 239).
27. Damrosch (2006: 44).

Works Cited

Abdelrahman, Munif (1989), *Cities of Salt*, New York: Vintage.

Amireh, Amal (2000), "Framing Nawal El Saadawi: Arab Feminism in a Transnational World," *Signs* 26.1, 215–49.

Benjamin, Walter (1985), "Central Park," *New German Critique*, 32–58, 34.

Casanova, Pascale (2005), *The World Republic of Letters*, trans. M. B. DeBevoise, Cambridge MA: Harvard University Press.

Damrosch, David (2006), "World Literature in a Postcanonical, Hypercanonical Age," in Haun Saussy (ed.), *Comparative Literature in an Age of Globalization*, Baltimore MD: The Johns Hopkins University Press.

De Certeau, Michel (1984), *The Practice of Everyday Life*, trans. Steven Rendall, Berkeley CA: University of California Press.

De Quincey, Thomas (1845) "The Palimpsest of the Human Brain," in Patrick Madden (ed.), *Quotidiana*, 1 Dec. 2006: http://essays.quotidiana.org/dequicet/palimpsest_of_the_human_brain/ (accessed 25 May 2016).

Dillon, Sarah (2007) "Palimpsesting: Reading and Writing Lives in H.D.'s 'Murex: War and Postwar London (Circa AD 1916–1926)'," *Critical Survey*. 19.1, 29–39.

Genette, Gérard (1997), *Palimpsests: Literature in the Second Degree*, trans. Channa Newman and Claude Doubinsky, Lincoln NE: University of Nebraska Press.

Gregory, Derek (1997), "Lacan and Geography: The Production of Space Revisited," in Georges Benko and Ulf Strohmeyer (eds), *Space and Social Theory: Interpreting Modernity and Postmodernity*, Malden MA and Oxford: Blackwell Publishers, 203–31.

Kahf, Mohja (2001), "The Silences of Contemporary Syrian Literature," *World Literature Today*, 75: 2, 225–36.

Kilito, Abdelfattah (2008), *Thou Shalt Not Speak My Language*, trans. Waïl Hassan, Syracuse NY: Syracuse University Press.

Lefebvre, Henri (1991), *The Production of Space*, trans. David Nicholson-Smith, Oxford: Basil Blackwell.

Munif, Abdelrahman (1989), *Cities of Salt*, New York: Vintage.

Naaman, Mara (2010), "Disciplinary Divergences: Problematizing the Field of Arabic Literature," *Comparative Literature Studies*, 47.4, 446–71.

Al-Naᶜīmī, Salwā (2007), *Burhān al-ᶜAsal*, Beirut: Riyāḍ al-Rayyis lil-Kutub wa-l-Nashr.

Al-Neimi, Salwa (2009), *The Proof of the Honey*, trans. Carol Perkins, New York: Europa Editions.

Petkova, Mariya (2009), "Syrian Writer Wins Naguib Mahfouz Medal for Literature," *Daily News Egypt* (14 December): http:// www.thedailynewsegypt.com/article.aspx?ArticleID=26438 (accessed 23 June 2017).

Reynolds, Nedra (2004), *Geographies of Writing: Inhabiting Places and Encountering Difference*, Carbondale IL: Southern Illinois University Press.

"Riwāyat Warrāq al-Ḥubb Tafūzu bi-Jāʾiza," *al-Jirān* (15 December 2009): http://aljeeran.net/cultrue/3511.html (accessed 9 January 2010).

Al-Samman, Hanadi (2006), "Contemporary Syrian Literature: An Introduction," in Words Without Borders (ed.), *Literature from the "Axis of Evil": Writing from Iran, Iraq, North Korea, and Other Enemy Nations*, New York: The New Press, 175–8.

—— (2012), "Remapping Arab Narrative and Sexual Desire in Salwā al-Naʿīmī's *Burhān al-ʿAsal* (*The Proof of the Honey*)," *Journal of Arabic Literature* 43.1, 1–20.

—— (2016), "Syria, Cinema of. The Suspended Utterances of Syrian Cinema," in *Oxford Islamic Studies Online. Oxford Islamic Studies Online*: http://www.oxfordislamicstudies.com/article/opr/t343/e0236 (accessed 13 April 2017).

Shʿīr, Muḥammad (2009), "Khalīl Ṣuwayliḥ: "Aqdār al-Ḥā ris al-ʿAzal," *Al-Akhbār* (15 December): http://www.jehat.com/Jehaat/ar/Mahrajanat/Jawaez/15–12–095.htm (accessed 28 June 2012).

Spivak, Gayatri Chakravorty (2003), *Death of a Discipline*, New York NY: Columbia University Press.

Ṣuwayliḥ, Khalīl (2008), *Warrāq al-ḥubb*, Cairo: Dār al-Shorūq.

Sweileh, Khalil (2012), *Writing Love: A Syrian Novel*, trans. Alexa Firat, Cairo: American University in Cairo Press.

15

Everyday Writing in an Extraordinary City

Ghenwa Hayek

Beirut is a city that has often been described in the superlative mode. During its cosmopolitan heyday in the 1960s and 1970s, Beirut was fêted for its legendary openness to the new, its adaptability, and its absorption of all sorts of cultural, social, and political change. When civil war broke out in 1975, Beirut and Lebanon quickly became a metaphor for the consequences of excess, and the death of a certain way of life.[1] This dynamic of excess on both ends of the scale can perhaps be most quickly summarized in Etel Adnan's enduring image of a city that "was heedless to the point of folly. She gathered the manners and customs, the flaws and vengeance, the guilt and debauchery of the whole world into her own belly. Now she has thrown it all up, and that vomit fills all her spaces" (Adnan 2011: 20). In poetry, the city was elegized and mourned; as Elise Salem put it, "poets … competed to lament the tragedy of Beirut …, the new symbol of the Arab tragedy" (Salem 2003: 137). In prose, the civil war era became most strongly associated with the rise of the experimental, fragmented urban novel. The end of the civil war in 1990, and the ushering in of a new era of *hudū᾽ nisbī* – relative calm – brought with it new modes of writing about the city, exemplified in the work of authors like Hoda Barakat or Rashid Daᶜif, whose post-war novels feature characters who often struggle with issues of sexuality, family, and mental illness. As many critics have pointed out, these novels also all perform a similar trope of commemoration in which the destroyed center of Beirut plays a central role.[2]

Since Beirut and its literary imaginings have been so intertwined for so long, one of the questions this chapter asks is: If the violent crises and events of the 1970s and 1980s produced a tormented, fragmented literary prose that has been celebrated as an innovative way of processing and reproducing the tragedies of the civil war, and the 1990s brought forth, or continued to develop, a literature that Ken Seigneurie has characterized as an "elegiac humanism"[3] – a literature of lament and mourning for a lost Beirut grounded in the *wuqūf ᶜalā al-aṭlāl* mode of classical Arabic poetry – then how can we characterize the prose of this decade, which attempts to contend with the realities of the post-war city?

Of course, there are several answers to this question, and several literary and cultural experiments have emerged in Lebanon since the end of the civil war. As Felix Lang points out in his study of the field of Lebanese fiction, *The Lebanese Post-Civil War Novel*, there continues to be a steady stream of contemporary Lebanese fiction by authors in multiple generations in Lebanon and its diaspora that explores the histories, memories and legacies of the Lebanese civil war. But there have also been literary and cultural attempts to address other issues. One such example is the historical fiction written by Rabee Jaber, Alexandre Najjar, and others (Jaber has also dabbled in science fiction); another could be the recent surge of comic books and graphic novels about life in Beirut, published in such venues as the trilingual journal *Samandal*, but also online, such as Mazen Kerbaj's *Kerblog*, and in print, such as Zeina Abirached's *Un Jeu D'Hirondelles* (*A Game for Swallows*) and *Je Me Souviens* (*I Remember Beirut*). In *Beirut, Imagining the City*, I have explored these millennial texts and the work they perform in articulating a new generation of writers' literary and social concerns.

During moments of social change, such as a post-conflict, uneasily-at-peace Lebanon, different expressive modes emerge; some endure, others do not. Nevertheless, as markers of a particular moment in time, these textual artifacts are significant for what they reveal – and sometimes conceal – of that moment, what Raymond Williams describes as "structures of feelings," the nebulous emergent concerns of a given place at a given moment, which can inform new modes and genres of representation.[4] Just as they look towards new modes of narrative representation, emergent modes also always engage in a critical reflection upon, and sometimes critique of, other, older narrative forms. In Lebanese fiction, which has been dominated by tropes of war at home and in the diaspora, one emergent genre that deserves attention is what I am calling "everyday fiction," a kind of writing typified by its deliberate attempt to distance itself from both the civil war and – more significantly for this chapter – its literary tropes and discourses through a deepened engagement with the present and with ordinary life in Beirut.[5] Published in the aftermath of the assassinations of Rafiq Hariri and other political figures since 2005, the 2006 war, and the outbreak of sectarian conflict in Beirut and beyond (2008–), this fiction, in addition to the two novels that will be discussed in this chapter, includes novels like Hilal Chouman's *Nāpolītānā* and *Līmbo Bayrūt* (*Beirut Limbo*), as well as Sahar Mandour's *Ḥubb Bayrūtī* (*Beiruti Love*). Together, the novels operating within this genre produce conceptions of "a contemporary moment from within that moment," focusing on the day-to-day lives of middle-class urban youth in present-day Beirut, and self-consciously marking a clear distinction from Lebanon's literary past (Berlant 2011: 4).

In what follows, I will focus on the latter, specifically, on the ways in which Sahar Mandour's 2011 novel *32* and Alexandra Chreiteh's debut 2009 novel *Dāyman Coca-Cola*, (*Always Coca-Cola*) use parody to deconstruct some of the most dominant cultural modes of representing Beirut and Lebanon.[6] Written by two young female authors, the novels turn a wry eye to the everyday lives of young, college-educated, urban women living in Beirut, relentlessly and humorously problematizing stereotypes of Lebanese women and men.[7] Mandour's is a self-reflective metafictional tale of a young woman attempting to write what she describes as "an everyday story, like the stories of the everyday that we live through"/ *qiṣṣa ᶜādiyya, ka qiṣaṣ al-ayyām al-ᶜādiyya al-latī naᶜīshuhā* (2011: 88), the Arabic demonstrating a clear parallelism in its use of the adjective *ᶜādiyya* to describe both text and "days;" in other words, ordinary life. In this sentence, the author's desire for ordinariness is made explicit, as is the link between narrative and everyday life. As the first-person narrator and her friends spend their days in Beirut, the issue of how one is to write a story about the everyday in Beirut, and the forms that this novel should take, rise to the forefront, as the aspiring storyteller and her friends participate in discussions about how one is to start such a story, the modes of telling these tales, and how to end a novel about everyday life in Beirut. In other words, *32* performs the struggle of writing about the contemporary city, a task made all the more difficult by the novel's awareness – and rejection – of the ways in which Beirut and Lebanon have been represented in the (local) literary and (global) popular tradition. "I don't like to feel melancholic about ruins/*aṭlāl* that I stand in front of side-by-side with millions of others," Sahar Mandour's first-person narrator claims, deliberately distancing herself from the elegiac formula for apprehending Beirut and Lebanon, and concomitantly marking a new place for her literary project (106).

In a similarly humorous, though less overtly metafictionally self-aware vein,[8] *Always Coca-Cola* is told from the naive and slightly histrionic perspective of Abeer Ward, a young university student. The novel recounts incidents from Abeer and her friends' lives; it focuses in particular on her often-resentful relationship with her friends Yana, a Romanian model who moved to Beirut with her Lebanese (now ex-)husband, and Yasmine, a Lebanese-German friend. Through overplaying Abeer's naivety – her overwrought reactions to such matters as seeing a young couple make out, or her parents seeing her on the back of a motorcycle – *Always Coca-Cola* becomes a wry satire of a particular social class in Lebanon, one of liberal means but conservative demeanor. But, as several critics have also pointed out, the novel embeds within it a critique of how Beirut has been (mis)read by Orientalist and Orientalizing discourses that insist on seeing the city in one way while it is something else.[9] For example, in one episode, Abeer gloats that Yana cannot understand – literally – the writing on the wall in Hamra, where someone has defaced a sign that originally said "rooms for rent" to now read "whores for rent." This, and other passages that mock Orientalizing – and self-Orientalizing – ways of representing Lebanon, highlights one of the ways that self-awareness works in the text.

While issues of class, gender and violence in these novels are important ones that should be (and, in Chreiteh's case, are) addressed elsewhere, in this chapter, the focus will be on the literary argument that these novels are making, how these young authors use a parodic humor to engage with their literary and cultural predecessors, and, the manner in which Beirut and Lebanon have been represented in local and global discourses. I will follow the opposition that Linda Hutcheon draws between satire and parody, in which she defines the former as "moral and social in its focus and ameliorative in its intention," while limiting the target of the latter to what she calls "coded discourses", without of course suggesting that there cannot be intersections between both (Hutcheon 2000: 17–18).[10] I am interested in the potential of the parodic form to simultaneously critique older traditions – in this case specifically, traditions of writing and other forms of cultural representation – and its potential to create new ones (Waugh 1984: 77). What is at stake in such parodic representations, I believe, is an attempt to wrest representations of Beirut out of the myriad and multiple forms the superlative mode takes, from the melancholic to the exotic, thereby creating a space for these new writers within it. As they deal with their literary legacies, cultural burdens, and everyday challenges with humor, young Beiruti writers like Mandour and Chreiteh try to inscribe a place for themselves and their peers within the cityscape and within the literary landscape of Lebanese letters.

Writing against Local Legacies of Loss

As Ken Seigneurie and others have demonstrated, the prevailing tone of writing about Beirut for many years has been a nostalgic, lamentful one; it is this tone, identified with an older generation, that *32* and *Always Coca-Cola* parody. One recent example of the elegiac, superlatively melancholic and nostalgic mode of writing about Beirut by a generation that lived through the civil war can be found in an article written for the inaugural issue of the cultural journal *Bidāyāt*, where Elias Khoury laments the 'Lebanese winter' at the outset of 2011, during the so-called Arab Spring, calling out especially, writers and artists:

> The legend of Beirut was formed by a long history of writing, suffering, and the insistence on the primacy of freedom of expression as an entry point to freedom of society [...] But the legend is being destroyed (*tataḥaṭṭam*) today, as the Arab Spring ... becomes a long Beiruti winter. (Khoury 2012: 29)

In the piece, Khoury bemoans the current state of Lebanese politics, before writing that "it is hard to accept this cultural, political and moral apathy (*khumūl*) that can only be explained by the disappointment following the independence intifada taken over by sectarian forces," adding that, "the image of Beirut's cultural and moral collapse is awful, and invokes fear and worry, since it threatens to fold the page over a long legacy of Lebanese culture," and concluding that, "misery (*al-buʾs*) is not our fate, comrades. Challenging misery and confronting it is the last sign of life that Beirut awaits before it erases its image in the mirror of death" (31). Khoury's mournful lament for the city and all that it symbolizes evokes several strong political and aesthetic associations; of art and suffering, of art and freedom,[11] of Beirut as a laboratory for creative and cultural innovation, as his piece builds to its concluding sentence, quoted above, regarding the mirror of death and the final collapse of Beirut's legend.[12] Even as he extols hopefulness, Khoury's language is redolent with mournfulness.

Chreiteh's novel rises to Khoury's challenge of confronting misery with humor on both the satiric and parodic levels. While the novel's satiric potential has been recognized, its parodic qualities have been less scrutinized.[13] In

Always Coca-Cola, parody becomes a tactic of defiance, operating against the mournful and old-fashioned, and a way by which a younger generation finds its distinctive voice, particularly in a post-war context. For example, Khoury's vocabulary of collapse finds a parodic literary echo when the protagonist, Abeer, describes her father lamenting that an old pop song from his past has been re-released:

> He was remembering those halcyon times, the years of his youth and glory, which coincided, at least in part, with the years of Sabah's youth and artistic glory. He sighed again and said, "Back then who would have expected that so much magnificence would simply fall apart, as if it were nothing, just to become some debris tossed back and forth in the winds of time?" (Hartman 2012 trans.: loc. 454)
>
> (*man kāna fī dhālika l-waqt yatawwaqaᶜu anna kulla dhālika al-majd sawfa-yanhāru hākadhā wa bi-kulli basāṭatin li-yabqā ḥuṭāman tataqādhafuhu riyāḥu l-zaman!*) (Chreiteh 2009: 41)

The language used to describe the father's relationship to Sabah's pop song is one marked by melancholy and sadness, as well as with something of the elegiac mode of the lament for the past. The father sighs, and reminisces about his glorious youthful days – *ayyama ṣibāhi wa majdihi* (41) – before lamenting their loss. The words associate youth with glory, and tinge the paragraph with nostalgia before giving way to words like *yanhār*, to collapse, and *ḥuṭāman*, debris – a noun that derives from the same root *ḥ/ṭ/m* as the verb *taḥaṭṭama*, which Khoury uses in the preceding excerpt above – with their intimations of physical destruction of property, that evokes and mimics the language often used to describe the destruction of the city during the civil war. Furthermore, the present – to the father – can only be experienced as a bad copy of an authentic past, a sentiment that also echoes the language used to critique the controversial reconstruction of downtown Beirut in the 1990s. Samira Aghacy reads this encounter as a moment of mutual generational misunderstanding on the characters' parts; this is true, but the novel is also making a literary point (Aghacy 2015: 118). By casting this florid, excessively nostalgic language usually used to lament the city in the context of a lament over a pop song, the novel, which has already cast the father as a rather absurd figure, thus defamiliarizes it, highlighting its overuse and the triteness of the form.

Just as *Always Coca-Cola* parodies the superlatively nostalgic mode of the Beirut elegy, *32* also uses parody to undermine another superlatively nostalgic mode: that of rural pastoral writing. Initially, the passage jars the reader, since it is a departure in style and form from the rest of the novel, yet it is written in the same first-person narrative voice. This confusion emerges as a deliberate tactic once the paragraph is completed:

> I sit under the tall tree with the branches spread out like birds everywhere, listening to history whispering stories into my ear, many stories, about me, and my grandfather, and my distant village. History tells me about this tree that my grandfather planted the day he bought the land. In its roots he saw his life forming, and his memories expanding, and his lineage growing. This pine tree was born before us. It grows with us to tell us about our days, although we no longer spend enough time in our village to be truly connected to it, but we are connected to it, and to this tree that held a story each time my grandfather watered it. Stories about my grandfather and grandmother. Stories about myself, this child who …
>
> AAAAAAAAA this novel is going to kill me! (Mandour 2011: 114)

The nine *alif maddas* that make up the scream of *32*'s real narrator serve not only to alert the reader to the fact that they have not been reading the young protagonist's narrative voice, but also, in its exaggerated use of the verb "to kill," serve to underscore the implied metaphorical violence of this kind of generic pastoral writing, with its trite evocations of nature, familial history, and its over-worn metaphor of the tree rooted in the soil of the village. Significantly, *32*'s narrator cannot get beyond page 8 of this novel, and almost immediately afterwards, launches into a long discussion of the difficulty of securing an apartment in Ras Beirut in the present. In other words, the passage marks the narrator's difference from everything that the passage represents, namely, the older, rural pastoral form of writing about Lebanon.[14] Thus, both novels use gentle parody to draw attention to – and highlight their difference from – older traditions of writing.

Photoshopping Glamour onto Beirut

While the novels gently parody local forms of representing the city and the country, they aim a more acerbic critique at global ones that emerge both from the popular media and from academic discourses that insist on framing Beirut as an exotic, extraordinary site, emphasizing notions of trauma and violence and/or decadent excess. Particularly in the Western press, even when not discussing its violent past and amnesiac present, Beirut is often referred to as an extraordinary city, and Lebanon as an extraordinary country. A cursory online search of UK- and US-based English-language newspapers draws up such metaphors as "former Paris of the Middle East," "Athens on speed," "life after the apocalypse," but also "2009's most glamorous tourist destination," "a former war zone reborn as a nightlife hot spot," and a personal favorite, "the Provincetown of the Middle East."[15] Since 2006, descriptions of the city in the foreign and foreign-language media oscillate between the two poles of Beirut's extremes: the 15-year civil war and the 'glamorous' and 'glitzy' reconstruction of the city center. Of course, as Jennifer Robinson points out in *Ordinary Cities*, there is a reason why some cities – mostly those of the third-world – are singled out as extraordinary or different; by doing so, Robinson argues 'ordinary' Western cities are privileged as exemplary spaces where ordinary people have ordinary experiences, while fetishizing or Otherizing the experiences and narratives of other urban dwellers (Robinson 2006: 2). Media representations of Beirut are no different, often privileging the exceptional and impressionistic over the ordinary.

As Nadine Sinno and Samira Aghacy point out in their work on Chreiteh's novel, *Always Coca-Cola* is as attentive to patterns and modes of globalized consumption in Lebanon with its references to Coca-Cola, Always and Starbucks as it is to the ways that Lebanon and Beirut are themselves represented and consumed in the global marketplace. The novel calls attention to the ways that these global brands interfere in the landscape and in people's bodies – Abeer has a birthmark shaped like a Coca-Cola bottle, lives under the shadow of a Coca-Cola billboard, and is raped by the general manager of the Coca-Cola plant in Lebanon, for example. But, the novel points most of its acerbic humor to the specific manner that the global audience has of seeing Lebanon, the legacy of decades of Western (mis) representation. It is most present in Abeer's life through her friend Yana, a Romanian woman who came to Lebanon in search of the Orientalist fantasy on which she was raised, borrowed from translated books and Hollywood movies; a figure that Sinno calls "a contemporary caricature of the 18th-century and 19th-century Orientalist travelers and scholars" (Sinno 2015: 131). Many of the novel's funniest depictions of Yana are of her shock at finding out that Beirut is just like any other place, and not like the "deserts, palm trees, and mirages" that she had been certain were there – not only that, but try as she might to assimilate, Yana cannot, even being allergic to that most Lebanese of dishes, *tabbouleh* (Chreiteh 2012: loc. 118). While Yana quickly burns her literary books about the exotic East in a fit of despair, even her non-fictional texts, like her travel guide, lie to her. The novel matter-of-factly conveys that the reality of Beirut turns out to be that "the soft, golden sand pictured in her travel guide was actually covered with the glass of broken bottles and used needles" (Chreiteh 2012: loc. 124). Embedded into the depiction of Yana's innocence is also an inside joke about what Lebanon and Beirut are really like for those in the know that emphasizes through exaggeration this community of "insiders;" those who, in Aghacy's felicitous phrase, "speak Beirut" (Aghacy 2015: 119).[16] Within the novel, Yana's constant disappointment by the reality of living in Beirut and dealing with Lebanese individuals becomes a way for the author and her reader to share a laugh at the expense of the exoticizing foreigner and her body of cultural texts that do not prepare her for everyday life in the city or within the culture.[17]

It is not only globalized signifiers like Coca-Cola or Westernized beauty standards that circulate, re-circulate, and are consumed in *Always Coca-Cola*'s Beirut. While mocking cultural appropriations and Orientalist modes of producing Beirut and Lebanon, the novel also underlines the ways in which these are then re-absorbed into the local culture, and the latter's uncomfortable relationship with these products. At one point in the narrative, Abeer visits a set where Yana is filming a video clip. The novel gleefully points out that the director had to modify the video in post-production because the reality did not comply with his desires. So, the fountain that gushes water in the video, whose owners insist does not work originally emits "a sticky brown-colored liquid," and the house's windows can't be filmed "because the glass was broken in a number of places and the gaps were covered by plastic bags, stuck onto the glass with Scotch tape" (Chreiteh 2012: loc. 1120). Despite the obvious flaws of the house, Abeer goes on to add that she feels proud when she thinks that:

> Today this house appears on German, French, English and American television screens where people, sitting in the living rooms of their houses on the other side of the globe, daydream about a world that looks like paradise … (Chreiteh 2012: loc. 1124)

As the novel thus satirizes Western modes of representing Beirut and Lebanon, it also suggests the uncomfortable position of the Lebanese themselves as consumers and propagators of these discourses; Abeer's uneasy confession of pride in this photoshopped version of Lebanon becomes itself part of *Always Coca-Cola*'s self-aware commentary on processes of textual and visual representation and appropriation/re-appropriation.

Writing Disaster, Writing Everyday

Uncritical Western representations of Beirut as a glitzy, glamorous party capital are mocked in *Always Coca-Cola*, whereas *32* turns its attention to the other side of the Western representational coin: the focus on Beirut and Lebanon as a gritty warzone constantly suffering through trauma and violence. Because of *32*'s metafictional narrative, concerns about representation are made explicit throughout the novel in conversations about writing the novel of everyday life that the book's author/narrator is undertaking. These concerns operate on two distinct, yet interrelated imaginaries: the representation of Lebanon and Beirut by outsiders and emigrant Lebanese, as well as the representation by locals to a regional and global audience. Together, they suggest that Mandour is seeking a way to move beyond representations of Lebanon that focus on narratives of trauma and violence while acknowledging the presence of violence as a part of life in contemporary Beirut.

For example, in a scene set in the moments immediately following a car bomb, the narrator and her friends run into an old friend of theirs who now lives abroad. The young man, playfully described as a "civil engineer, and a civil society activist," insists on filming the site, making the narrator wonder whether, since he has spent a lot of time abroad, "and has gotten used to seeing the news from here through a camera lens, in a dramatic context that ends with a televised discussion … does he hold a camera to be able to see the scene 'live,' like he has gotten used to [*iᶜtāda*]?" (Mandour 2011: 57). The use of the verb *iᶜtāda*, to become accustomed to, echoes back while contrasting with the *ᶜādīyy*, the normal/everyday, that the protagonist and her friends are living. It highlights the disjuncture between those capable of experiencing and processing an event live with those who are only capable of apprehending it through the lens of the camera. In the text, the cameraman is clearly unwelcome, and when he turns his lens on a woman waiting for news of her son, bears the brunt of harsh criticism: "his face shows an expression like he understands my consternation … but the image must be transmitted through YouTube and Facebook" (58).[18] Importantly, the novel stresses how the local mode of apprehending tragedy is not speculative, but rather based on community and empathy; the narrator and her friends comfort the woman who has lost her son, then make their way along Hamra Street, eat ice-cream and try to distract and comfort each other. The novel underscores that the event must be apprehended and processed, but then filed away, instead of becoming the focal point of the narrative action, the only slice of Beirut life available and broadcast. In this manner, it marks its difference from the emigrant who can only see the tragic event as a discrete spectacle that must be shared with a global audience.

In *32*, however, it is not only the media that sees Beirut through the lens of narrative trauma; this is also part of the literary and cultural heritage of Lebanese fiction and its critical reception that the novel parodies.[19] Recent, particularly Western, academic discourses that focus on Beirut and Lebanese literature have tended to focus on issues of exceptional violence, trauma, memory – or the lack of it, extending beyond the war to the post-war era.[20] As one recent editorial argues, Lebanon and Beirut evoke:

> Landscapes and cityscapes wounded by bullets and shelling [that] form the backdrop to massacres, executions, torture, to primal crimes of rape and castration. Encoding representations of the effects of this violence, formed by a universal loss of power in the Arendtian sense, forms the bedrock of writing the disaster of Beirut and Lebanon. (Launchbury *et al.* 2014: 458)

The language of this paragraph and the rest of the editorial continue to frame Beirut and Lebanon as a "disaster" whose traumatized inhabitants and cultural producers are struggling to make sense of the war-scarred, amnesiac landscape. Launchbury *et al.* describe Beirut as an "unimaginable cityscape," and argue that it can only be properly understood through a framework of the post-traumatic (457). This work is certainly valuable and necessary; yet the point that *32* attempts to make is that, through a focus on trauma and violence, such narrow readings also end up obscuring other forms and genres of writing about the city and country.[21] It alienates an everyday local experience by privileging a certain lens through which the city is written, read, and understood.

Since *32* is intensely preoccupied with the question of representation, especially with how one is to set about writing the story of being young in contemporary Lebanon, the novel makes its point about trauma through a discussion about the writing, and reading, of fiction. Just as in the earlier literary reference to rural novels, at first, the reader is unsettled because the transition from the protagonist's first-person narrative voice and the other first-person narrative voice is left deliberately ambiguous. By allowing this slippage in narrative voice, it is as if *32* is trying on these characters. Yet these first person, predominantly male, narrative voices of the older traditions of Lebanese writing do not quite fit the young narrator, and are eventually discarded. In the first example, the first-person voice belonged to a rural, pastoral tradition. However, in this second incident, the voice belongs to a torture victim who is a veteran of the civil war. Though ultimately *32* rejects both with characteristic good humor, initially, the effect is disconcerting. The narrative lurches from what has hitherto been a humorous and light series of mundane adventures between friends in private and public spaces into a surrealist episode that involves torture and the attempted extraction of the first-person narrator's name, to which the torture victim gives several options borrowed from a wide swathe of popular cultural references, from the British '80s popstar Samantha Fox to the Egyptian film star Faten Hamama. The scene is reminiscent of Elias Khoury's 2008 novel *Yālo*, in which a young man is tortured by the police in post-war Lebanon and forced to confess his serial sexual crimes.

Yet, unlike *Yālo*, *32* has an embedded reader in the shape of the narrator's good friend Zumurrod, who abruptly interrupts her/our reading of the torture scene. The narrator, puffed up with pride, and misinterpreting Zumurrod 's interruption for confusion – in other words, her inability to read properly – condescendingly responds:

> That man, Zumurrod, is society. Or Lebanon. I summed the place up in the body of a man who beats us up whenever he feels like it. Despite this, we find …
>
> She interrupts me angrily, "Oof, I got it, and I didn't want to believe it. What's wrong with you? Why don't you write what we're living?" (Mandour 2011: 153)

The conversation continues to heat up, with the narrator angrily asking Zumurrod, "maybe you want the story to end with all of us leaping on a beach, as the depth and innocent joy of living in the third world sparkles in our eyes?" (153). The rejoinder is framed as a sharp contrast between "authentic" traumatic narratives and the "feel-good" local narratives targeted at a Western audience, but by juxtaposing them in this argument, it reveals that the narrator has limited herself to these two modes of thinking and writing about Lebanon in a manner targeted to a foreign readership that reads either for trauma or for redemption. Yet, as the conversation continues, the narrator's reader inserts herself and her demands into the text. Continuing the exchange and refusing to pander to the writer, Zumurrod snaps back:

> Maybe we can just go on living our lives, as they are, and nothing happens. What do you think about nothing happening? Would you be upset if nothing happened [*lā yaḥṣul shayʾan*]? Is it not enough if we stayed as we were,

> advancing in age and in experience, and dying in the end, each in her own way? Does Lebanon have to beat you up and do you have to change your name to David Charles Samhon?[22] (Mandour 2011: 154)

This exchange between reader and author summarizes while parodying several modes of representing Lebanon-as-trauma, from the violent torturer that has held its citizens hostage to the feel-good narrative of triumph over adversity that the narrator ascribes to third-world forms of self-representation, before proceeding to reject them all through Zumurrod's irritated comments. Zumurrod dismisses the narrator-author's condescending explanation; her problem as a reader is not that she does not understand the analogy, it is that she rejects its drama and its violence. Similarly, she also rejects the narrator's sarcastic offer of a happy ending, which itself mocks more saccharine feel-good narratives targeted to a Western audience. What the local reader wants, *32* seems to suggest, are texts that tell stories in which the characters "can just go on living their lives," since, as Zumurrod explains in an intervention she stages with the narrator-author's other friends: "I liked the idea of you writing our everyday life, because the novels that I read usually talk about exceptional things. I wanted to read about the everyday/normal [*al-ᶜādīyy*] because it is … normal *[ᶜādīyy]*! And I wanted to find 'us' in the story" (122); the others all agree.

32's sensitivity to issues of self-representation as well as representations by others also embeds a self-critique into the novel, one that has to do with the complicity of the writer in what gets published about Lebanon. As in the case above, this critique extends both outwards towards the global (Western) reading public, but also regionally to the Arabic-language reading public. When the narrator protests that she cannot write her friends' everyday stories because they would not be published "in an Arab world filled with the forbidden," the others dismiss this as an excuse (122). Although their lives may be scandalous, Zumurrod points out, they are hardly as scandalous as content that does get published; within the story, these female characters refuse to become stereotypes of any kind; they insist on their ordinariness in an environment that insists on perceiving them as extraordinary (122).

Both novels use parody for its potential to highlight and deconstruct dominant narratives about Beirut, but also for its potential to create community. As Andreas Pflitsch points out in his discussion of postmodern literature in the Arab context, while elements of postmodernism such as its emphasis on parody and language have been taken up by Arab authors, literature's potential for political intervention and sociopolitical commentary has not been left behind (quoted in Kappert 2010: 27). By marking their distinction from their literary past through such devices as parody, and deliberately drawing the melancholic lament and tragic, event-focused modes of writing the city into question, Chreiteh and Mandour force their readers to engage with their novels on their own terms; significantly, this creates a sense of shared community. After all, in order to work, parody (like satire) depends on a shared understanding between writer, text, and reader. Through humor, these texts engage their audience in a shared community, as they mediate in the rhythms and occasional struggles of everyday life for a certain group of young people in contemporary Beirut while self-reflexively posing questions about *how* – and often, how *not* – one can work, live, and write about the city.

The Desire for the Ordinary

> Shwikar (serious): OK, what are you writing?
>
> (I think, then I answer soberly): I'm writing our story, those of us who are living in Beirut today, and are 30.
>
> Zumurrod: 32
>
> Everyone laughs, and I laugh along with them (Mandour 2011: 90)

Humor is an often-overlooked mode in which individuals participate in collective forms of making meaning. Through its stage direction-like language, the quote above emphasizes the transition between individual seriousness and collective mirth; the author and her friends can laugh together at Zumurrod's intervention. The author takes on her role of writing about being thirty in Beirut with gravitas and soberness; Zumurrod's joke lightens the mood and moves the discussion away from its former seriousness. The conversation emphasizes the author's desire to tell an everyday story, but the text makes sure that she doesn't take her role as generational spokeswoman too seriously.

However, the incident also gestures to a possible pitfall of jokes, namely, their deflective potential. By making her joke, and pushing the conversation out of the realm of the serious, Zumurrod essentially shuts down the discussion of what the narrator's project of writing everyday life may look like. Through this, the text delineates the limits of humor as a productive tool of critique; yet, perhaps that is the point. Humor certainly operates in these novels to critique restrictive representations of Beirut and Lebanon, but it is also used to articulate the ordinary, everyday concerns of their young protagonists. In

32 and *Always Coca-Cola*, humor is the tactic through which the everyday is articulated and a new literary community is formed, but there are many other tactics of the everyday whose exploration needs to be undertaken.

Developing this point further is beyond the scope of this chapter, but it is worth noting that the disciplinary study of everyday life emerged from a postwar moment, and there is a recent move to think about the ordinary and what it might mean in societies that have experienced or undergone violence.[23] In postwar France, "a period during which the return ... to everydayness, in a word, was on everyone's mind," theorists like Henri Lefebvre and Michel De Certeau posited the everyday as a site and space of resistance against overwhelming social forces, particularly the state (Schilling 2003: 25). In the movement and manner in which individuals practiced and thought about everyday things, from walking in the city to eating, Lefebvre and De Certeau saw what De Certeau described as "tactics," manners in which the socially weak were able to assert their right to belong.[24] In this chapter I have highlighted merely one, among many, tactics of the literary production of everyday life in postwar Lebanon. Sarcasm, humor and a focus on the ordinary are not apathetic, apolitical gestures of the weak; rather, they are formal tactics used to assert a presence *in* and a difference *from*.[25]

The two novels I discuss here are highly aware of the tensions between representations of the extraordinary and the desire for the ordinary, although they struggle more with articulating the latter than exposing the former. Yet, their critique of other modes of imagining Beirut and Lebanon allows us to start thinking about what may be missed when we read Lebanese literature exclusively through the lens of trauma and violence, or through a defeatist nostalgia for a long-gone revolutionary past. The more complex question of exploring this desire for the ordinary, and its different modes of being articulated in fiction, remains open. What is clear, however, is that in the postwar Lebanese context, this clamor for ordinariness has deeper political significations. A desire for ordinariness, as Tobias Kelly points out is always "rooted in concrete social relationships;" moreover, "the search for the ordinary," whether in occupied Palestine or in post-war Lebanon, is a residually optimistic sense of how things ought to be, "shot through with a residual hope that it still may be possible, but a fear that it might not" (Kelly 2008: 366). Despite the stresses and anxieties of being young in Lebanon – or, perhaps, because of them, these young writers insist on their right to participate in the cultural conversation about being a part of the city and its cultural and literary heritage, even if all they want to tell are stories of the *ᶜādīyy*.

Notes

1. The scope of this piece means that I do not have time to discuss in depth these various transformations. For a political and social history of Beirut, see Kassir (2011). For a cultural and literary history of the transformation of the city, see Salem (2003) and Hayek (2014).
2. See Hayek (2014) and Seigneurie (2011).
3. Seigneurie (2011: 20–7).
4. See Williams (1977), "Dominant, Residual and Emergent" and "Structures of Feeling" 121–40.
5. For more on the tropes of war and memory in Lebanese fiction, see Lang (2016).
6. In what follows, I will use my own translations of *32*, and Michelle Hartman's English language translation of *Always Coca-Cola.* Moreover, I use the definition of parody outlined by Linda Hutcheon (2000) in *A Theory of Parody*: "a form of repetition with ironic critical distance" (xii).
7. For example, see Sinno (2015) on Chreiteh's re-casting of the lost virginity/family honor narrative, 128–9.
8. Although, by definition, Hutcheon points out, the parodic form is self-aware.
9. See Sinno and Aghacy's *Writing Beirut* (2015).
10. In fact, Hutcheon points out, writing by women often uses parody for satirical purposes (44).
11. Ken Seigneurie has studied Khoury's work in the context of a literature of commitment; for more, see *Crisis and Memory* (2003).
12. For more on the trope of urbicide in Beirut, see Fregonese (2009), "The Urbicide of Beirut?".
13. See Mubayi (2012), Sinno (2015) and Aghacy (2015) for discussions of satire in *Always Coca-Cola.*
14. This has been described by Hanssen (2005) and Stone (2007) as "mountain Romanticism."
15. These quotes are taken from searches on the following websites: http://www.theguardian.com/travel/beirut and http://www.nytimes.com/travel/guides/middle-east/lebanon/beirut/overview.html (both accessed on 5 July 2015).
16. Although, as Sinno (2015) points out, this insider knowledge occasionally marks "local" things that are not funny, but rather shameful, like xenophobia and homophobia (133; 136).
17. The novel does not spare the Lebanese either, mocking Abeer's cousin for trying to attain impossible Western standards of beauty in order to look like Yana. See Sinno (2015).

18. Perhaps it is no coincidence that Launchbury *et al.* (2014) describe film and photography as the mode of representation most willing to engage with the visuality of war and its aftermath (459).
19. Andreas Pflitsch discusses this demand for one predominant representation of Arab culture in terms of the reception of Arabic literature in general in Europe in "The End of Illusions," 36.
20. This is not confined to Lebanon and Lebanese literary criticism. As Lauren Berlant argues in *Cruel Optimism* (2011), "trauma has become the primary genre of the last eighty years for describing the historical present as a site of exception" (9).
21. This is a point that Felix Lang brings up with respect to the Lebanese literary field as a whole in *The Lebanese Post-Civil War Novel* (2016).
22. This is one of the pseudonyms used by the main character in the Egyptian mini-series *Raʾfat al-Haggān*, based on the life of a former Egyptian spy who was embedded in Israel for many years. *32* contains many references to Egyptian and Lebanese pop culture, including the pseudonym used for one of the first-person protagonist's friends, Shwikar, the name of an Egyptian actress from the 1960s and 1970s.
23. The work of Veena Das springs to mind as a theoreticisation of this in a South Asian context; in a more Middle Eastern context, Lori Allen and Tobias Kelly have done fascinating work on the value of the ordinary in the Occupied Territories during the second *intifada.* See Allen, "Getting by the Occupation" (2008) and Kelly, "The Attractions of Accounting" (2008).
24. A good discussion of this can be found in Gardiner, *Critiques of Everyday Life* (2000), where he summarizes tactics as "dispersed, hidden and ephemeral, and improvised in response to the concrete demands of the situation at hand. They are also temporal in nature, and reliant on the art of collective memory, on a tradition of popular resistance and subversion passed on from generation to generation since time immemorial" (182). It is noteworthy that reading, for de Certeau, is inherently tactical by nature.
25. In her work on Syria, Lisa Wedeen (1999) argues that political humor can have value precisely because of the ways that it articulates mundane concerns – and transgressions (87–9).

Works Cited

Adnan, Etel (2011), *Sitt Marie Rose*, 8th ed., trans. Georgina Kleege, San Francisco CA: The Post-Apollo Press.

Aghacy, Samira (2015), *Writing Beirut: Mappings of the City in the Modern Arabic Novel*, Edinburgh: Edinburgh University Press.

Allen, Lori (2008), "Getting by the Occupation: How Violence Became Normal during the Second Palestinian Intifada," *Cultural Anthropology*, vol. 23, issue 3, 453–87 (DOI: 10.1525/can.2008.23.3.453).

Berlant, Lauren (2011), *Cruel Optimism*, Durham NC and London: Duke University Press.

Chouman, Hilal (2011), *Napolitana*, Beirut: Dar al-Adab.

—— (2013), *Līmbo Bayrūt*, Beirut, Cairo, Tunis: Dar al-Tanweer.

Chreiteh, Alexandra (2009), *Dāyman Coca-Cola*, Beirut: Dār al-ᶜArabiyya lil-ᶜUlūm.

—— (2012), *Always Coca-Cola*, trans. Michelle Hartman, Northampton MA: Interlink Books, e-book.

cooke, miriam (1996), *War's Other Voices: Women Writers on the Lebanese Civil War*, Cambridge: Cambridge University Press.

Fregonese, Sara (2009), "The urbicide of Beirut? Geopolitics and the built environment in the Lebanese civil war," *Political Geography* 28 (5), 309–18 (http://dx.doi.org/10.1016/j.polgeo.2009.07.005, accessed 5 July 2015).

Gardiner, Michael (2000), *Critiques of Everyday Life*, London and New York NY: Routledge.

Hanssen, Jens (2005), *Fin-de-Siècle Beirut: The Making of an Ottoman Provincial Capital*, Oxford: Clarendon Press.

Hayek, Ghenwa (2014), *Beirut, Imagining the City: Space and Place in Lebanese Fiction*, New York NY and London: I. B. Tauris.

Hutcheon, Linda (2000), *A Theory of Parody*, Urbana IL and Chicago IL: University of Illinois Press.

Kappert, Ines (2010), "Postmodernism: Facets of a Figure of Thought," in Angelika Neuwirth, Andreas Pflitsch and Barbara Winckler (eds), *Arabic Literature: Postmodern Perspectives*, London: Saqi.

Kassir, Samir (2011), *Beirut*, trans. M. B. DeBevoise, Berkeley CA: University of California Press.

Kelly, Tobias (2008), "The Attractions of Accountancy: Living an Ordinary Life during the Second Palestinian *Intifada*," *Ethnography*, vol. 9 (3), 351–76. (DOI: 10.1177/1466138108094975.)

Khoury, Elias (2002), *Yālo*, Beirut: Dar al-Ādāb.

—— (2012), "*Taʾammulāt fi-l-shaqāʾ al-Lubnānī*," *Bidāyāt* 1: Winter/Spring (29–31).

Lang, Felix (2016), *The Lebanese Post-Civil War Novel: Memory, Trauma and Capital*, New York NY and Basingstoke: Palgrave Macmillan.

Launchbury, Claire, Nayla Tamraz, Roger Célestin and Eliane DalMolin (2014), "War, Memory, Amnesia: Postwar Lebanon," *Contemporary French and Francophone Studies*, 18: 5, 457–61 (DOI: 10.1080/17409292.2014.276367).

Mandour, Sahar (2011), *32*, Beirut: Dar al-Adab.

Mubayi, Suneela (2012), Review of *Always Coca-Cola*, trans. Michelle Hartman, *Journal of Arabic Literature*, 43: 532–45 (http://www.nytimes.com/travel/guides/middle-east/lebanon/beirut/overview.html; DOI: 10.1163/1570064x-12341250, accessed 19 July 2015).

Pflitsch, Andreas (2010), "The End of Illusions," in Angelika Neuwirth *et al.* (eds), *Arabic Literature: Postmodern Perspectives*, London: Saqi.

Robinson, Jennifer (2006), *Ordinary Cities: Between Modernity and Development*, New York NY and London: Routledge.

Salem, Elise (2003), *Constructing Lebanon: A Century of Literary Narratives*, Gainesville FL: University Press of Florida.

Sawalha, Aseel (2012), *Reconstructing Lebanon*, Texas TX: University of Texas Press.

Schilling, Derek (2003), "Everyday Life and the Challenge to History in Postwar France: Braudel, Lefebvre, Certeau," *Diacritics*, vol. 33, no. 1 (Spring), 23–40.

Seigneurie, Ken (ed.), (2003), *Crisis and Memory: The Representation of Space in Modern Levantine Narrative*, Wiesbaden: Reichert Verlag.

—— (2011), *Standing by the Ruins: Elegiac Humanism in Wartime and Postwar Lebanon*, New York NY: Fordham University Press, 247.

Sinno, Nadine (2015), "Milk and Honey, *Tabbūleh* and Coke: Orientalist, Local and Global Discourses in Alexandra Chreiteh's *Dāyman Coca-Cola*," *Middle Eastern Literatures*, 18: 2, 122–43.

Stone, Christopher (2007), *Popular Culture and Nationalism in Lebanon: The Fairouz and Rahbani Nation*, New York NY and London: Routledge.

Traboulsi, Fawaz (2001), "De la Suisse d'Orient au Hanoi du monde arabe: Beyrouth, briève historique d'une representation," in Jad Thabet (ed.), *Beyrouth, La Brulûre des rêves*, Paris: Editions Autrement, Collection Monde, no. 127, 28–41.

Waugh, Patricia (1984), *Metafiction: The Theory and Practice of Self-Conscious Fiction*, New York NY and London: Routledge.

Wedeen, Lisa (1999), *Ambiguities of Domination: Politics, Rhetoric and Symbols in Contemporary Syria*, Chicago IL: University of Chicago Press.

Williams, Raymond (1977), *Marxism and Literature*, 2009 edition, New York NY and Oxford: Oxford University Press.

16

Translating Cairo's Hidden Lines: The City as Visual Text in Magdy El Shafee's *Metro*

Chip Rossetti

The graphic novel *Metro* (*Mitrū*), written and illustrated by Egyptian artist Magdy El Shafee, was first published in 2008 by the now-defunct Egyptian house Dar al-Malāmiḥ, which had a reputation for championing younger and politically outspoken authors.[1] Soon after *Metro*'s publication, the Egyptian government confiscated all printed copies of the book on the grounds of "offending public morals." The novel includes one panel showing partial nudity, but the underlying reason for the book's confiscation was likely its bleak view of late-Mubarak-era Egypt, in which bank-robbing is characterized as a justified response to a corrupt system stacked against the poor. Both El Shafee and his publisher were fined 5,000 Egyptian pounds for "infringing on public decency," which effectively banned the book in Arabic.[2] It was not until 2012 – a year after Mubarak's resignation – that the Arabic text, which had long been impossible to find, was republished in Egypt under the auspices of an artists' collective known as The Comic Shop. It was eventually translated into Italian, German, and English.

The government may also have found *Metro* objectionable because of the novel's grounding in the experience of city life in Cairo, and in particular the political, economic, and social frustration felt by its urban population. The city, in fact, plays a central visual and thematic role in the graphic novel. More specifically, *Metro* maps its narrative onto Cairo through its use of textual elements and through its spatial organization. The city is not merely the backdrop against which the narrative plays itself out, but rather forms the two-dimensional axis that structures the relationships between characters. This chapter will draw on Walter Benjamin's writings on cities, as well as on recent theoretical studies on comics and graphic novels, to examine how El Shafee renders Cairo both as space overwritten with text (covered in words that serve as visual as well as verbal background) and as space that embodies and reflects the novel's primary themes. *Metro*'s use of its visual elements, in other words, is central to its aesthetic aims.

This essay proceeds from Scott McCloud's much-debated definition of comics as "juxtaposed pictorial and other images, in deliberate sequence, intended to convey information and/or to produce an aesthetic response in the viewer," while acknowledging the limitations to that seemingly straightforward characterization.[3] *Metro* tells its story in the form of "juxtaposed images," but falls within the related genre of the graphic novel, a term coined in the 1960s, but which only gained currency a decade later through the work of writer–artists such as Will Eisner and Alan Moore.[4] Scholars have criticized the vagueness of the term, which has been applied to a broad array of comics, often for reasons of marketing: as Charles Hatfield has pointed out, labeling a book a "graphic novel" was a useful tool for getting "serious comics" onto the shelves of general-interest bookstores and into the hands of a larger readership.[5]

To begin with, *Metro* presents Cairo as a visual panorama awash with words, signs, and music lyrics, some of which serve more as aesthetic background than as language proper. The city becomes not only a spatial grid that structures the narrative, but a canvas for overlapping voices, signs, and demands for attention. The pictorial nature of the graphic novel thus blurs the distinction between words as signifiers and words as visual design, posing particular challenges about which elements "count" as text, and which ones the reader should treat as illustrations. Additionally, *Metro* employs a visual language of verticality to emphasize the disparities between the powerful and the powerless. The cinematic use of bird's-eye and worm's-eye perspectives within the panels visualizes the city's inequalities that are a recurring theme in the novel. Lastly, Cairo is visually woven into the text through El Shafee's use of the city's metro train system as the book's organizing metaphor, one that symbolizes the hidden lines that connect a city of vast socioeconomic differences. Like the metro itself, these hidden lines serve as the city's subterranean engine, a horizontal network of corrupt wealth and power that conspires to make Cairo "one big cage" to the rest of its inhabitants, as the protagonist puts it.[6]

The Author and the Work

The theme of political frustration and anger that undergirds *Metro* is informed by the political activism of its author. Magdy El Shafee was born in 1961 (making him somewhat older than many of his Egyptian comics-writing peers) and his commitment to democratic reform is central to his professional work.[7] After an early career in the pharmaceutical industry, he began publishing his comics in the weekly children's magazine *ᶜAlāʾ al-Dīn*,[8] and like a number of other Egyptian writers, he gravitated in the mid-2000s to the independent, reformist newspaper *al-Dustūr*, under the editorship of the charismatic journalist Ibrāhīm ᶜĪsā.[9] In 2006, El Shafee won a UNESCO award for his comics series highlighting issues of anti-migrant racism, and during the Tahrir Square demonstrations in early 2011, he used his artistic abilities to produce illustrated flyers and pamphlets that countered regime propaganda and called for Mubarak to step down (see Figure 16.1.) His activism continued after Mubarak's ousting, as he was arrested during a protest against the Morsi government in April, 2013, although he was released after four days.[10]

Metro appeared in 2008 as part of a wave of Arabic-language graphic novel writing that emerged in Cairo and Beirut in the first decade of the millennium. Several of the artists and writers from that wave, including El Shafee himself, have cited Marjane Satrapi's autobiographical graphic novel, *Persepolis*, as an inspiration for their own work,[11] as well as English-language writers of more serious "adult" comics, such as Daniel Clowes and Joe Sacco.[12] On his personal website, El Shafee credits American underground comics artist Robert Crumb and French satirical comics magazines *Hara-Kiri* and *Charlie Mensuel* as influences.[13] Egypt has its own history of comics and cartoons: political cartoons first appeared in the khedival period of the late nineteenth century,[14] and Arabic-language comics for children have long been popular, even if comics for adult readers are still a new phenomenon. More generally, comics in the Arab world have to date received only limited attention from scholars.[15] In the United States, by contrast, comics aimed specifically at adults began with the "underground comics" movement of the 1960s, and grew over the last several decades, particularly after the "watershed year" of 1986, to its current prominence.[16]

El Shafee employs a loose black-and-white style executed in pen-and-ink and watercolor washes. Two pages in the middle of *Metro* are given over to another artist, Muḥammad Sayyid Tawfiq, who illustrates a story-within-a-story in the

Figure 16.1 An example of the illustrated flyers and pamphlets El Shafee distributed during the Tahrir Square demonstrations in early 2011, countering regime propaganda and calling for Mubarak to step down.

form of a fable about a king that concludes with a moral about the nature of political oppression. The abrupt shift in style and tone brings to mind a similarly jarring visual switch in another recent Egyptian graphic novel: namely, Dunyā Māhir's *Fī Shaqqat Bāb al-Lūq*, which changes illustrators and narrative style midway through, replacing Aḥmad Nādī's pensive sketches of animals and inanimate objects with Ganzeer's more realistic, crime-story style.[17]

Metro tells the story of a disillusioned but principled young Cairo software programmer (and part-time hacker) named Shihāb who, after witnessing the murder of a businessman, finds himself uncovering a conspiracy of corrupt authorities in the process of clearing his name. Other characters include Shihāb's sidekick Muṣṭafā, who comes from a poor neighborhood; Dīnā, a journalist friend of Shihāb's; Wannas, a shoeshine who is losing his vision and who turns to begging when he can no longer afford to pay taxes; and Muṣṭafā's brother, Wāʾil, who works as a thug hired to assault and sexually harass anti-regime protestors. Shihāb sees his neighbor, a real estate contractor named Miṣbāḥ, being stabbed by his own chauffeur, and in a scuffle with the killer, Shihāb grabs the knife from the chauffeur, who flees the scene. Having heard Miṣbāḥ's cryptic dying words, Shihāb, with Dīnā's help, investigates to find out who ordered his murder; in doing so, he uncovers a corrupt real estate deal that involves high-level government authorities. Along the way, frustrated at the system that has brought him to bankruptcy, he bluffs his way into a bank and steals a bag of cash in the process of being handed over as a collateral-free loan to a corrupt official by obsequious bankers. The novel's climax occurs during a political protest in downtown Cairo that ends violently.

The Modern *Futuwwa*

The plot as described above is a somewhat disjointed whodunit, but Shihāb's actions throughout are motivated by his aspirations for professional and personal success, albeit tempered by his bleak sense of despair at a system that keeps people in poverty and is skewed towards the rich. In his refusal to acquiesce to the rule of unjust authorities, his willingness to physically fight with thugs, and his generous concern for the city's downtrodden (such as Wannas), Shihāb shares commonalities with a much older figure in the Egyptian popular imagination: namely, the *futuwwa*, a multivalent term referring both to the virtuous qualities attributed to young men, including chivalry, generosity, and courage, as well as to a class of men in medieval Baghdad and Cairo who embodied those qualities.

In the premodern context, the *futuwwa* were sometimes linked to Sufi orders or craft guilds, but by the twentieth century, the term had come to mean an urban thug or strongman, usually associated with crime. Shihāb is an educated software programmer rather than an illiterate gangster, but he shares the *futuwwa*'s resentment against the powers-that-be, and he is willing to break the law to defy an unjust system. Several times in the course of the novel, he demonstrates his ability to fight using single-stick fencing (*taḥṭīb*), a skill he learned as a child in Upper Egypt.[18] Oftentimes, Egyptian films and novels portrayed the *futuwwa* in a positive light as a champion of the underdog.[19] The *futuwwa* could also be seen as a Robin Hood-like figure who robs the rich to help the poor, and defends the urban masses from "atrocity, ruthlessness and tyrannical potentates."[20] Muhsin al-Musawi points to a number of Arabic novels that contain a *futuwwa*-like figure who dissents from an unjust or oppressive authority, often in anti-social ways.[21] Shihāb's character suggests two different aspects of the *futuwwa* figure: to his friends and colleagues, he represents an organic urban champion of justice, while to those in power he is a lawbreaker who threatens the social order.

The City as Verbal Assault

As the abundance of background signs, song lyrics, and advertisements in *Metro* makes clear, urban life is experienced as an assault of words printed, spoken, and sung, mingled with an array of visual stimuli. Take, for example, the series of large "wāw"s overlaying a train as it pulls into the station, which were rendered as "WHOOOOSH" in English (see Figure 16.2). Elsewhere, El Shafee carefully populates his panel backgrounds with advertisements, political slogans, and scattered words and sounds. Reflecting the prevalence of English in global commerce, many of the advertisements and business names are written in English ("Alfa Market," "Cilantro," "Misr Insurance," etc.). The commercial verbiage forms a kind of background noise to the narrative, as a visual embodiment of the surface distractions that the protagonists must tune out in order to locate the underlying truth, however unpleasant it may be. The clutter of conflicting visual stimuli on the page also compels the reader to piece together meaning and narrative: Charles Hatfield has argued that this more intensive, active form of reader interpretation is inherent in the comics format, which is "radically fragmented and unstable," and resistant to coherence.[22] It is perhaps unsurprising that the urban context figures so prominently in *Metro*, since, as scholars Jörn Ahrens and Arno Meteling have noted, "from an historical point of view … comics are inseparably tied to the notion of the

Figure 16.2 A series of large "wāw"s overlaying a train as it pulls into the station, rendered as "WHOOOOSH" in English

'city.'"[23] Comics in their modern form had their origins in urban mass culture in the nineteenth century, and in particular in the growth of print journalism in the United States. In examining the field of contemporary Lebanese comics, Ghenwa Hayek suggests that graphic novels are particularly suited to narratives with urban settings, and are "a new mode for defining, producing, and contesting the relationship between the individual and the city."[24]

In his introduction to the edited volume *Comics in Translation*, Federico Zanettin finds further connections between the visual narration of comics and the visual barrage of city life, stating that:

> As comics and the cityscape are very much alike in terms of their semiotics and their hybrid mixing of words and pictures, it is not only historically evident that each should be regarded as part of the other, but structurally and aesthetically evident as well.[25]

This assault of the verbal on the page dovetails with arguments made by Walter Benjamin in his essay "Einbahnstrasse," in which he laments the "dictatorial" nature of modern media over public life, stating that people in contemporary societies are exposed to "a blizzard of changing, colorful, conflicting letters" and "locust swarms of print."[26] Benjamin's aim is to decry reading's decline in status in modern societies: once reading was associated with the quiet contemplation of books, but it is now linked to a frenzy of billboards and popular media competing to capture our attention in contemporary urban life. At the same time, script that once was read horizontally is now routinely read vertically in newspaper columns and advertisements. As a medium that both grew out of the contemporary urban milieu and uses written language in ways akin to film and advertising, a graphic novel would seem to embody Benjamin's worst fears about the degradation of the written word. However, *Metro* manages to render effectively on the page the city's verbal assault, while also implicitly criticizing it as the surface distraction it is. Some of those background words, for example, comment ironically on the setting, such as an election banner touting Mubarak as a candidate "For A Better Tomorrow" that is stretched over a depressing back street in a lower-class neighborhood.

In other cases, the words seem to act more as images, or simply as "visual white noise" that clutters the background. In a graphic novel, pictures and words exist on a continuum of representation and meaning. R. Varnum and C. T. Gibbons argue that the genre of comics allows for the interchangeability of words and images, as a system of signification in which "words take on some of the properties of pictures, and conversely, pictures take on some of the properties of words."[27] Put another way, words can act as an extension of the aesthetic effect on the page, not solely as a signifier conveying dialogue or exposition in what is otherwise a wholly graphic medium.[28] The question of the semiotic status of some of the words in El Shafee's text had a direct impact on *Metro*'s translation into English. In some cases, the Arabic text was left untranslated where it seemed to act primarily as background visuals. In those cases, not all the text in a panel needed to be domesticated by being rendered into English. The office signs in Shihāb's building, for example, were left in Arabic. In other cases, the original already included text in English, which was left unchanged: Muṣṭafā, for example, always wears a T-shirt that plays off the commercial logo of the Nike shoe brand, slightly altered to read "Nile." And throughout the text, El Shafee introduces new chapters and scenes with maps of Cairo's metro stations in both English and Arabic.

The City as Vertical Hierarchy

The barrage of verbal images and written sounds reflects El Shafee's portrayal of Cairo as a city that is itself polysemiotic and dialogic. However, El Shafee also depicts the character of the city through the spatial organization of images. By its very nature, the medium of comics compels a narrative to play itself out spatially on the page, as the reader, through her "habituated strategy" of viewing images in right-to-left succession in Arabic (and left-to-right in English), encounters the text as a series of temporal moments, while supplying the inferences that link those moments into a cohesive whole. "In this way," as Elisabeth Potsch and Robert F. Williams argue, "comics substitute space for time."[29] Even more, comics require the reader to interpret the connections between space and time, and to internalize a visual sense that will let her translate the two-dimensional space of the page into a "four-dimensional narrative," that is, translate the panels into a sequence that expresses a narrative occurring in time.[30]

Within literary studies more broadly, the recent "spatial turn" has devoted more attention to the function and meaning of space, which had once been considered unproblematic and even neutral, in contrast to time – that is, history – which was seen as far more generative of meaning in texts.[31] If the uses and meanings of space are now being interrogated more fully for texts such as short stories and novels, they merit even more attention in any study of graphic novels or comics, which are ineluctably visual, and which necessarily organize space for the reader. This emphasis on space has been spurred in part by the insights of postcolonial studies, which have drawn attention to the colonial "overwriting" of space, the uses of geography and maps as imperial tools, and postcolonial spatial reimaginings.[32] Urban spaces, then, are not simply blank canvases, but are sites of meaning that themselves "prompt and start narratives."[33] This attention to the importance of space has also been taken up in studies of contemporary Arabic fiction. Sabry Hafez, for example, has pointed to the shift over the last decades in the relationship between fictional characters and the space they inhabit. At least since the 1960s, the tendency in Arabic novels has been that space in narrative is a site of tension, being "pregnant with fear and danger, defying the characters and constantly challenging them."[34] Similarly, Muhsin al-Musawi defines space as "the foremost referent" in postcolonial Arabic fiction, around which "emerge and emanate conflicts, desires, nostalgias, love and war."[35] For Shihāb and Muṣṭafā, the public and private spaces of Cairo are hostile to them. Much of their time in the city is spent on the run: even their office proves to be unsafe, and they routinely have to flee police officers they come across in the metro stations. With few exceptions – such as the house of Shihāb's aunt in Sayyida Zaynab, or the moulid that Shihāb visits almost by accident – the city is a series of dangerous places for the protagonists.

The impersonal, anti-human nature of space in Cairo is also reflected in El Shafee's use of vertical lines and perspective, both overhead views and worm's-eye views. The vertical positioning of the illustrations not only inscribes the dichotomies of wealth and poverty in the city, but serves to make visible the status of human characters as well. The morbidly obese government official who is receiving a corrupt bank loan, for example, is first viewed from below, from an angle looking up between his legs as he sits on a reclining chair. It is a deliberately grotesque perspective that places the reader at floor level.[36] Shihāb, on the other hand, is always drawn as a thin, vertical figure who is distinctly taller than the other characters. When we first see him on the first page, his head and shoulders appear beside the Bank Miṣr skyscraper and he has a set of speech balloons vertically stacked beside him.[37] The effect is to emphasize that he is rising above his circumstances (see Figure 16.3). Later, we also get to share Shihāb's bird's-eye view as he hides above the ceiling of a metro station while stashing away a briefcase of stolen goods.[38] But even though he towers above other characters, Shihāb is himself dwarfed by the power structures of the city. Perhaps the starkest example of this vertical hierarchy is the bird's-eye view of Shihāb and Muṣṭafā from the perspective of an equestrian statue, which appears to be modeled on the statue of Ibrāhīm Pasha, son of Muḥammad ᶜAlī Pasha, at Mīdān al-ᶜAtaba[39] (see Figure 16.4). The statue's arm seems to point down to Shihāb and Muṣṭafā on the street below, as if to emphasize their insignificance and powerlessness, even as they are discussing their financial desperation.[40]

At the same time, El Shafee uses vertical perspective to depict the frustration and quiet desperation of urban poverty, as Muṣṭafā, after a dangerous day of bank robbing and lying low, returns home to his neighborhood in ᶜIzbat al-Nakhl, near the northern end of the metro line.[41] Muṣṭafā's progress down his street is rendered as a series of nearly identical panels, each of which is ironically headed with the same cynical political banner mentioned earlier. The only difference in each panel is the quarrelsome, unpleasant language emerging from the windows of various apartments along the street, while Muṣṭafā himself seems to shrink and recede with each panel. The individual

Figure 16.3 Shihāb, drawn as a thin, vertical figure, distinctly taller than the other characters. On the first page, his head and shoulders appear beside the Bank Miṣr skyscraper and he has a set of speech balloons vertically stacked beside him.

Figure 16.4 A bird's-eye view of Shihāb and Muṣṭafā from the perspective of an equestrian statue modeled on the statue of Ibrāhīm Pasha at Midan ᶜAtaba.

is rendered as a powerless, minute figure, trapped in an environment of repetitive frustration and anger, under the banner of an unrealistic political slogan. Likewise, when the humble shoeshine Wannas is first introduced, he is seated cross-legged on the ground and hunched over with his face towards the ground. The impression is one of extreme powerlessness and despair felt by an uneducated worker on the verge of poverty.[42]

Both Muṣṭafā and Wannas confront an urban anomie that the novel characterizes as deliberately created by the media and those in power. At one point, Shihāb directly accuses the media of planting in the public a sense of hopelessness as a way to deflect attention from the regime that is the true source of popular frustration:

> I mean the papers and the TV. And everything else that keeps us so submissive. And feeling like there's no hope, that the corruption and injustice only lead to more of the same. And that people standing in lines for everything is totally normal. I can't be bothered with the crime [stories] in these rags, when they say nothing about the real criminal whose fault it all is.[43]

This same sense of the city as the source of despair and isolation occurs at the beginning of the "Maadi Station" chapter, in which a disembodied narrator (who turns out to be Shihāb) describes his fellow citizens as subway commuters who "hunker down" in the trains and try to make friends in order to "push away their loneliness," while buoyed by false hope.[44]

The City as a Horizontal Network

Cairo is a vertically-aligned city that renders the individual powerless and minute, but it is also visually represented as a network of hidden horizontal lines. The repeated images of metro lines and stations, where the characters make plans to meet each other, present Cairo as a networked map.[45] As Walter Benjamin has noted, city maps and individual street scenes represent two dichotomous ways of visualizing urban environments. In his essay "Paris im Spiegel" ("Paris in the Mirror"), Benjamin calls the photograph and the map the "ultraviolet and infrared knowledge of [the] city." The former can provide accurate knowledge of a specific space in detail, while the latter provides us with a view of the entire city at once, even if it is rendered abstractly or schematically.[46] The neat lines of the metro map contrast with the rest of the panels, which teem with chaotic street scenes and human figures. Just as the metro provides an abstracted network of lines that link up and make sense of the crowded metropolis, so Shihāb's investigations uncover the network of connections that link Wannas to Miṣbāḥ, Miṣbāḥ to government officials, and Shihāb's bullying moneylender to the ruling party.

But if these hidden lines offer a map of the true loci of power in Cairo, El Shafee makes it explicit that the map is incomplete, as the poor are excluded from it altogether. Wannas' house, for example, is located "on the other side of Maadi … at ʿIzbat al-Baṭṭ (which you won't find on a map)."[47] Wannas' home is, in a sense, the human reality that the metro's map leaves invisible. It is informal, ignored, and off the grid. Muṣṭafā, too, is keenly aware of his invisibility: at one point, he recounts to Shihāb how the authorities solved the problem of his family's unsightly slum neighborhood ("our wretched dump behind ʿIzbat al-Nakhl"), namely by building a wall around it to block out the sight of it.[48] Muṣṭafā reiterates his feeling of worthlessness at the end of the novel, when he betrays his friend Shihāb, describing himself as "one of many worthless people" ("*wāḥid min il-nās il-kitīr illī mālhāsh qīma*"[49]) who is now asserting his individuality. Muṣṭafā's betrayal is highlighted by the fact that he has called Shihāb using the same hackers' technique that the reader saw Shihāb use on Muṣṭafā at the beginning. Muṣṭafā, in other words, has turned the tables on his friend.

The City as Organic Community

There are some notable exceptions to the general portrayal of Cairo as a corrupt system that overshadows and erases human figures. In some instances, El Shafee conveys the vibrancy and power of its human life. When Shihāb brings the government official out of the bank, holding a gun at his back, he turns him over to a sullen-looking crowd, who are happy to beat him up, once Shihāb has pointed out to them that the official is to blame for their lives of poverty and misery. The crowd is rendered as a sea of floating heads, representing a broad palette of humanity, united in their anger at a system stacked against them.[50] Perhaps the most positive representation of an organic community in the book is the moulid of Sayyida Zaynab. There, too, individuals float in the background of the panel to convey the spectrum of people in attendance, as do the words of what seems to be a Sufi dhikr[51] (see Figure 16.5). In both instances, the floating figures seem untethered from the hierarchies of verticality that otherwise govern Cairo's social relations. Tellingly, the moulid scene includes no overhead or sidewalk-level perspectives, as the panels are presented from an eye-level view. While the

Figure 16.5 The moulid of Sayyida Zaynab, where individuals float in the background of the panel to convey the spectrum of people in attendance.

moulid section advances the narrative, since Shihāb meets with Wannas and learns key parts of the plot, it acts as an interlude before the violent climax, an alternative vision of Cairo buttressed by organic cultural practices (such as a fortune-teller and a dhikr) removed from the frustration and injustice the characters find elsewhere in the city.

Shihāb and the City

Finally, any examination of the horizontal and vertical axes of *Metro*'s illustrations must address the position of the protagonist, who is portrayed as trying to rise above the lowly position he occupies and struggling to break free of his metaphorical cage; at the same time, as a *de facto* investigator, he is dogged in tracing and exposing the hidden lines of power that conspire to keep him oppressed. His hacking skills allow him to circumvent restrictions and to make connections that the system is designed to stymie: among other things, he is able to make public payphones in metro stations accept calls, thus reversing a closed one-way communication. Early in the novel, he pulls off the trick of linking up his fellow citizens by making the cellphones of every commuter in the station start ringing at the same time. The result is a riot of ring-tones – snatches of pop songs, love songs, Umm Kulthum, and drumbeats – that turn the array of anonymous commuters into a chorus of individuals.[52]

One hidden connection escapes even the notice of Shihāb, although El Shafee offers the reader a privileged glimpse of it. At the end, the narrative lets readers in on the reason why the bank robbery was never reported in the newspapers, via a page that is printed upside down.[53] In flipping the book upside down to view the otherwise "hidden" panels and illegible words, the reader participates as both protagonist and author: like the protagonist, he finds a truth that exists below, one that must be brought to the surface to be understood – in this case, the corrupt means by which the bank will keep the loss of the stolen money off their books. The reader also becomes his own graphic novelist, as he manipulates the visual space of the page in order to construct the narrative.

Conclusion

Metro takes full advantage of the polysemiotic nature of graphic novels by using the spatial organization of the illustrations to further its themes of corruption and power. The novel's use of visual perspective emphasizes the dynamics of power and powerlessness that shape urban life, exemplified by Shihāb's efforts to escape the constrictions the system places on him. Among those constrictions is Cairo's torrent of words – commercial, political, and personal – that serve to distract people from uncovering the true sources of their frustrations. The solution is found by tracing the city's hidden patterns of power, exemplified by the network of Metro lines that link otherwise disparate locales. The metro map – Benjamin's "infrared knowledge of the city" – renders the city in abstract form, revealing connections while effacing those places (such as the neighborhoods of the poor) that, like Muṣṭafā, are considered "worthless." It is this array of visual motifs and complex use of space and language that has allowed *Metro* to expand the boundaries of graphic novel writing in Arabic, while providing a model for the merging of text and image on the page.

Notes

1. For convenience, I will refer to the book using the English-language title, *Metro*, and use the transliterated Arabic title *Mitrū* only when citing the published Arabic edition.
2. "Formerly Banned Graphic Novel 'Metro' Now Available in Cairo," *Arabic Literature (in English)* http://arablit.org/2013/01/28/formerly-banned-graphic-novel-metro-now-available-in-cairo/. Published 28 January 2013, accessed 25 October 2017.
3. McCloud (1993: 9). For more on McCloud's definition of comics, see John Holbo, "Redefining Comics," in Meskin and Cook (eds) (2012: 3–30). In their introduction to the same volume, Meskin and Cook also take McCloud to task for attributing ancient and medieval origins to modern comics, suggesting that he was "motivated by polemical goals" in the service of elevating comics' aesthetic pedigree (2012: xx).
4. Zanettin, "Comics in Translation: An Overview," in *Comics in Translation* (2008: 4, n4).
5. Hatfield (2005: 29–30).
6. El Shafee (2012 translation: 21).
7. ᶜAmr ᶜIzz al-Dīn, "Majdī al-Shāfiᶜī … al-ab al-rūḥī li-l-riwāya al-miṣriyya al-muṣawwara," *El Watan News*: http://www.elwatannews.com/news/details/168327. Published 20 April 2013 (accessed 25 October 2017).
8. http://www.magdycomics.com/page.php?pg=about (accessed 25 October 2017).
9. El Shafee (2012 translation: 94).
10. http://almogaz.com/news/crime/2013/04/20/866778. Published 20 April 2013, accessed 25 October 2017.

11. In the Lebanese context, Satrapi's influence is reflected in the prevalence of similarly autobiographical narratives by Lebanese comics artists, which Ghenwa Hayek refers to as "autographics" (2014: 178).
12. Ursula Lindsey, "Cairo Noir," *The National*: http://www.thenational.ae/arts-culture/books/cairo-noir#page1. Published 28 June 2008, accessed 25 October 2017. See also "Undiscovered Art: Comics and Graphic Novels Emerge in the Middle East," by Chip Rossetti. *Publishing Perspectives*, http://publishingperspectives.com/2010/07/undiscovered-art-comics-and-graphic-novels-emerge-in-the-middle-east/#.VoSNYY1dPIU. Published 7/13/2010.
13. http://www.magdycomics.com/page.php?pg=about (accessed 25 October 2017).
14. Marsot (1971: 2–15).
15. Even Robert S. Petersen's global history of graphic narratives and cartooning, which covers antecedents and predecessors to modern comics in a variety of countries outside the US and Europe, including India, China, Japan, and Indonesia, has nothing to say about graphic narrative in the Arab world. Petersen (2011: 113–32).
16. Meskin and Cook (2012: xxiv–xxv).
17. Māhir, Ganzīr, and Nādī (2013).
18. El Shafee (2012 translation: 15).
19. Irwin (2004: 167).
20. Al-Musawi (2003: 261, n. 16).
21. For al-Musawi, the first iteration of this character in contemporary Arabic fiction is Saᶜīd Mahrān, the desperate protagonist of Naguib Mahfouz' *The Thief and the Dogs*. Al-Musawi (2003: 277).
22. Hatfield *et al.* (2013: 36). See also Katalin Orbán's article on the graphic novel as a form of "hyperreading" across texts (Orbán, 2014).
23. Ahrens and Meteling, "Introduction," (2010: 4).
24. Hayek (2014: 168).
25. Zanettin (2008: 14).
26. Benjamin (1986: 78).
27. Varnum and Gibbons, "Introduction," (2001: xi).
28. Zanettin (2008: 13).
29. Potsch and Williams (2012: 14).
30. Dittmer (2010: 222).
31. Crang and Travlou (2001: 163).
32. Upstone (2009: 12).
33. Crang and Travlou (2001: 172).

34. Hafez (1994: 106).
35. Al-Musawi (2003: 281).
36. El Shafee (2012 translation: 30).
37. Ibid.: 1.
38. Ibid.: 38.
39. The statue in question was built in 1872 by French sculptor Charles Henri Joseph Cordier. Cordier's statue, however, depicts Ibrāhīm Pasha wearing a ṭarbūsh, not a turban. Lababidi (2008: 58–60).
40. El Shafee (2012 translation: 28).
41. Ibid.: 42.
42. Ibid.: 8.
43. Ibid.: 47.
44. Ibid.: 10.
45. In the very different context of American superhero comics, Scott Bukatman finds a similar relationship between comics protagonists and their city's horizontal layout. Specifically, the spatial grid of Manhattan's city streets represents an imposed rational system that the superhero is able to transcend. Bukatman (2013: 173).
46. Benjamin (1972: 357). (Translation mine.)
47. El Shafee (2012 translation: 18).
48. Ibid.: 21.
49. El Shafee (2011 original: 93).
50. El Shafee (2012 translation: 34.
51. Ibid.: 56–7.
52. Ibid.: 5.
53. El Shafee (2011 original: 96).

Works Cited

Books and Articles

Ahrens, Jörn and Arno Meteling (eds) (2010), *Comics and the City: Urban Space in Print, Picture and Sequence*, New York NY: Continuum.

Benjamin, Walter (1972), *Gesammelte Schriften,* vol. IV, Tillman Rexroth (ed.), Frankfurt am Main: Suhrkamp Verlag.

—— (1986), *Reflections: Essays, Aphorisms, Autobiographical Writings*, trans. Edmund Jephcott, New York NY: Schocken Books.

Bramlett, Frank (ed.) (2012), *Linguistics and the Study of Comics*, New York NY and Basingstoke: Palgrave Macmillan.

Bukatman, Scott (2013), "A Song of the Urban Superhero," in Hatfield *et al.*, *The Superhero Reader*, Jackson MS: University of Mississippi Press: 170–98.

Crang, Mike and Penny S. Travlou (2001), "The City and Topologies of Memory," *Environment and Planning D: Society and Space* 19: 161–77.

Dittmer, Jason (2010), "Comic Book Visualities: A Methodological Manifesto on Geography, Montage and Narration," *Transactions of the British Institute of Geographers* 35, no. 2: 222–36.

El Shafee, Magdy (2011), *Mitrū: riwāya muṣawwara*, 2nd ed., Cairo: The Comic Shop.

—— (2012), *Metro: A Story of Cairo*, trans. Chip Rossetti, New York NY: Metropolitan Books.

Hafez, Sabry (1994), "The Transformation of Reality and the Arabic Novel's Aesthetic Response," *Bulletin of the School of Oriental and African Studies,* vol. 57, no. 1 (February): 93–112.

Hatfield, Charles (2005), *Alternative Comics: An Emerging Literature*, Jackson MS: University of Mississippi Press.

Hatfield, Charles, Jeet Heer, and Kent Worcester (2013), *The Superhero Reader*, Jackson MS: University of Mississippi Press.

Hayek, Ghenwa (2014), *Beirut, Imagining the City: Space and Place in Lebanese Literature*, New York NY and London: I. B. Tauris.

Irwin, Robert (2004), "Futuwwa: Chivalry and Gangsterism in Medieval Cairo," *Muqarnas* 21: 161–70.

Lababidi, Lesley (2008), *Cairo's Street Stories: Exploring the City's Statues, Squares, Bridges, Gardens, and Sidewalk Cafes,* Cairo: American University in Cairo Press.

Māhir, Dunyā, Ganzīr, and Aḥmad Nādī (2013), *Fī Shaqqat Bāb al-Lūq*, Cairo: Dār Mīrīt.

Marsot, Afaf Lutfi al-Sayyid (1971), "The Cartoon in Egypt," *Comparative Studies in Society and History* 13, no. 1: 2–15.

McCloud, Scott (1993), *Understanding Comics: The Invisible Art*, New York: Harper-Collins.

Meskin, Aaron and Roy T. Cook (eds) (2012), *The Art of Comics: A Philosophical Approach*, Chichester: Wiley-Blackwell.

al-Musawi, Muhsin (2003), *The Postcolonial Arabic Novel: Debating Ambivalence*, Boston MA and Leiden: Brill.

Orbán, Katalin (2014), "A Language of Scratches and Stitches: The Graphic Novel between Hyperreading and Print," *Critical Inquiry* 40, no. 3: 169–81.

Petersen, Robert S. (2011), *Comics, Manga, and Graphic Novels: A History of Graphic Narratives*, Santa Barbara CA: Praeger.

Potsch, Elisabeth and Williams, Robert F. (2012), "Image Schemas and Conceptual Metaphor in Action Comics," in Frank Bramlett (ed.), *Linguistics and the Study of Comics*, Basingstoke and New York NY: Palgrave Macmillan: 13–36.

Rossetti, Chip (2010), "Undiscovered Art: Comics and Graphic Novels Emerge in the Middle East," *Publishing Perspectives*, 7 April. (http://publishingperspectives.com/2010/07/undiscovered-art-comics-and-graphic-novels-emerge-in-the-middle-east/#.VoSNYY1dPIU, accessed 25 October 2017).

Upstone, Sara (2009), *Spatial Politics in the Postcolonial Novel*, Burlington VT and Farnham: Ashgate.

Varnum, R. and C. T. Gibbons (eds) (2001), *The Language of Comics: Word and Image*, Jackson MS: University of Mississippi Press.

Zanettin, Federico (ed.) (2008), *Comics in Translation*, Kinderhook NY and Manchester: St. Jerome Publishing.

Websites

All accessed 25 October 2017

Almogaz http://www.almogaz.com/

Arabic Literature (in English) http://www.arablit.org/

El Watan News http://www.elwatannews.com/

Magdy El Shafee Comics http://www.magdycomics.com/index.html

The National http://www.thenational.ae/

Publishing Perspectives http://publishingperspectives.com/

About the Contributors

Valerie Anishchenkova is Associate Professor of Arabic Studies, Core Faculty in Film Studies, and Affiliate in Comparative Literature at the University of Maryland, College Park. She received her M.A. with Honors in Oriental and African Studies (Arabic Philology) from St Petersburg State University, Russia, and M.A. and Ph.D. in Near Eastern Studies from the University of Michigan, Ann Arbor. Her current research interests are in identity studies; popular culture, particularly cinema, television and digital media; and cultural discourses on war. Her book *Autobiographical Identities in Contemporary Arab Culture* was published in 2014 with Edinburgh University Press.

Sarah R. bin Tyeer is Assistant Professor of Arabic Literature at Columbia University. After finishing her Ph.D. at the School of Oriental and African Studies (SOAS), University of London, she was an Andrew W. Mellon Postdoctoral Fellow at the American University of Beirut in 2012. Her research interests span the Qurʾān, Arabic literature, and Comparative literature. She has lived, studied, and taught in Beirut, Cairo, and London and is the author of the monograph *The Qurʾan and the Aesthetics of Premodern Arabic Prose* (2016).

Anna C. Cruz holds a Ph.D. in Near Eastern Studies from the University of California, Berkeley and was a Mellon Sawyer Postdoctoral Fellow in Comparative Global Humanities, Tufts University in 2016–17. During her time at Tufts, Anna worked towards completing a manuscript entitled *In Memory of al-Andalus: The Poetics of Affect in Medieval and Modern Arab*

Literary and Material Culture. She is currently a member of the faculty of Arabic and Spanish Language and Literature at Choate Rosemary Hall and a visiting researcher at Yale University.

Huda Fakhreddine is Assistant Professor of Arabic literature at the University of Pennsylvania. Her work focuses on modernist movements or trends in Arabic poetry and their relationship to the Arabic literary tradition. She is the author of *Metapoesis in the Arabic Tradition* (2015), a study of the modernizing movement in Arabic poetry from the Abbasid age to the twentieth century. She holds an M.A. in English literature from the American University of Beirut and a Ph.D. in Near Eastern Languages and Civilizations from Indiana University, Bloomington.

Ghenwa Hayek is Assistant Professor of Modern Arabic Literature in the Department of Near Eastern Languages and Civilizations at the University of Chicago. She works on the entangled relationships between literary and cultural production, space and place, and identity formation in Arabic literature from the nineteenth century to the present. Her first book, *Beirut, Imagining the City* was published in 2014. Her current research project, tentatively titled *"Carrying Africa," Becoming Lebanese*, explores the transnational imaginings of Lebanese diaspora through the lens of the sexual, racial and national anxieties that emigration elicits within Lebanon.

Gretchen Head is Assistant Professor of Literature at Yale-NUS College in Singapore and book review editor for the *Journal of Arabic Literature*. She holds a Ph.D. in Arabic literature from the University of Pennsylvania and has been a Mellon Postdoctoral Fellow in the Department of Comparative Literature at the University of California, Berkeley. Her work has appeared in *Alif: Journal of Comparative Poetics*, *Portal 9: Stories and Critical Writing about the City*, and *The Global South*, among other journals. Her current research project addresses the intersection of space, identity, and genre in Moroccan literature in Arabic (fourteenth to twentieth centuries).

Nizar F. Hermes holds a Ph.D. in Comparative Literature from the University of Toronto and is currently an Associate Professor of Middle East and South Asian Studies at the University of Virginia. He is the author of *The [European] Other in Medieval Arabic Literature and Culture, Ninth–Twelfth Century* AD (2012) and has published numerous articles and book chapters. He is currently working on a monograph titled *Of Cities and the Poetic Imagination in the Premodern and Precolonial Maghrib.*

William Maynard Hutchins, translator of Mohammed Khudayyir's *Basrayatha: Portrait of a City*, was awarded the National Endowment for the Arts grants for literary translation for 2005–6 and 2011–12. He was co-winner of the 2013 Saif Ghobash/Banipal Prize for his translation of *A Land without Jasmine* by Wajdi al-Ahdal and won the American Literary Translators Association National Prose Translation award in 2015 for *New Waw* by Ibrahim al-Koni. His critical works include *Tawfiq al-Hakim: A Reader's Guide* (2003) and "Ibrahim al-Koni's Lost Oasis as Atlantis …" in *Ancient Greek Myth in World Fiction Since 1989*, edited by Justine McConnell and Edith Hall (2016).

Boutheina Khaldi is Associate Professor of Arabic and Comparative Literature at the American University of Sharjah. In English, she has published the monograph, *Egypt Awakening in the Early Twentieth Century* (2012), and in Arabic: *Al-Muḍmar fī al-Tarassul al-Niswī al-ᶜArabī* (2015) (The Implicit in Arab Women's Epistolary Writing), in addition to a number of peer-reviewed articles, and three co-edited textbooks (all 2010): *Al-Adab al-ᶜArabī al-Ḥadīth: Mukhtārāt, Al-Wāfī fī Turāth al-ᶜArab al-Thaqāfī*, and *Turāth al-ᶜArab al-Maᶜrifī.*

Harry Munt is Lecturer in Medieval History at the University of York and was previously a British Academy Postdoctoral Fellow in the Faculty of Oriental Studies and Wolfson College at the University of Oxford. His research and teaching focuses on the history of the Islamic world, *ca.* 600–1500. He is the author of *The Holy City of Medina* (2014).

Bilal Orfali is Associate Professor of Arabic Studies at the American University of Beirut and previously held the M. S. Sofia Chair in Arabic Studies at Ohio State University. He holds a Ph.D. from Yale University (2009) and specializes in Arabic literature, Sufism, and Qurᵓānic Studies. His recent publications include: *The Anthologist's Art* (2016), *The Book of Noble Character* (2015), *The Comfort of the Mystics* (2013), *Sufism, Black and White* (2012), and *In the Shadow of Arabic* (2011).

Yasmine Ramadan is Assistant Professor of Arabic and Co-Director of the Arabic Program at the University of Iowa. Yasmine holds a Ph.D. from the Department of Middle Eastern, South Asian, and African Studies at Columbia University and is currently working on a manuscript entitled *Space in Modern Egyptian Fiction*. She has contributed articles, chapters, and reviews to *Journal of Arabic Literature*, *Alif: Journal of Comparative Poetics*, *Arab Studies Journal*, and other publications.

Chip Rossetti has a Ph.D. in Arabic literature (specializing in modern Iraqi fiction) from the University of Pennsylvania and works as the Editorial Director for the Library of Arabic Literature translation series. His translations include Sonallah Ibrahim's *Beirut, Beirut* (2014); Magdy El Shafee's graphic novel *Metro* (2012); Ahmed Khaled Towfik's sci-fi novel *Utopia* (2011); and *Three Poems* by Syrian poet Liwaa Yazji (with Samantha Kostmayer Sulaiman, 2016). In 2010, he won a PEN America Translation Fund grant for his translation of Muhammad Makhzangi's short-story collection *Animals in our Days*.

Mohammad Salama is Associate Professor of Arabic Studies and the Director of the Arabic Program at San Francisco State University. He is the author of numerous articles on Arabic literature and film and the monograph, *Islam, Orientalism, and Intellectual History* (2011) and co-editor of *German Colonialism* (2011).

Hanadi Al-Samman is an Associate Professor of Arabic Language and Literature in the Department of Middle Eastern and South Asian Languages and Cultures at the University of Virginia. Her research focuses on contemporary Arabic literature, diaspora, and sexuality studies, as well as transnational and Islamic feminism(s). She has published several articles in *Journal of Arabic Literature*, *Women's Studies International Forum*, *Alif: Journal of Comparative Poetics*, and various edited collections. She is the co-editor of an *International Journal of Middle East Studies*' special issue, "Queer Affects" (2013), *The Beloved in Middle Eastern Literatures* (2017), and author of *Anxiety of Erasure* (2015).

Adam Talib teaches classical Arabic literature at Durham University and is an assistant editor of the *Journal of Arabic Literature*. His first book, *How do you Say "Epigram" in Arabic?*, was published in 2017. Adam also translates contemporary Arabic literature into English. His most recent translation, Raja Alem's *The Dove's Necklace* (co-translated with Katharine Halls) was published in 2016. From 2012 to 2017, he taught at the American University in Cairo.

Kelly Tuttle is Assistant Professor of Arabic at Earlham College in Indiana. She holds a Ph.D. in Arabic literature from the University of Pennsylvania. Her work has appeared in *Postmedieval: a Journal of Medieval Cultural Studies* and *Essays in Arabic Literary Biography II, 1350–1850*. Her research interests include premodern commentary, compilation, and other so-called secondary genres.

Index

Note: italic page numbers refer to illustrations